Pro SharePoint 2013
App Development

Steve Wright

Apress

Pro SharePoint 2013 App Development

ISBN-13 (pbk): 978-1-4302-5884-1

ISBN-13 (electronic): 978-1-4302-5885-8

President and Publisher: Paul Manning
Lead Editor: Jonathan Hassell
Technical Reviewer: Corey Erkes
Editorial Board: Steve Anglin, Mark Beckner, Ewan Buckingham, Gary Cornell, Louise Corrigan, Jonathan Gennick, Jonathan Hassell, Robert Hutchinson, Michelle Lowman, James Markham, Matthew Moodie, Jeff Olson, Jeffrey Pepper, Douglas Pundick, Ben Renow-Clarke, Dominic Shakeshaft, Gwenan Spearing, Matt Wade, Steve Weiss, Tom Welsh
Coordinating Editor: Mark Powers
Copy Editor: Vanessa Moore
Compositor: SPi Global
Indexer: SPi Global
Artist: SPi Global
Cover Designer: Anna Ishchenko

Distributed to the book trade worldwide by Springer Science+Business Media New York, 233 Spring Street, 6th Floor, New York, NY 10013. Phone 1-800-SPRINGER, fax (201) 348-4505, e-mail orders-ny@springer-sbm.com, or visit www.springeronline.com. Apress Media, LLC is a California LLC and the sole member (owner) is Springer Science + Business Media Finance Inc (SSBM Finance Inc). SSBM Finance Inc is a Delaware corporation.

For information on translations, please e-mail rights@apress.com, or visit www.apress.com.

Apress and friends of ED books may be purchased in bulk for academic, corporate, or promotional use. eBook versions and licenses are also available for most titles. For more information, reference our Special Bulk Sales–eBook Licensing web page at www.apress.com/bulk-sales.

Any source code or other supplementary material referenced by the author in this text is available to readers at www.apress.com/9781430258841. For detailed information about how to locate your book's source code, go to www.apress.com/source-code/.

To my wife, Janet. Thanks for 25 great years.

Contents at a Glance

Contents

About the Author

Steve Wright is a senior manager in business information management (BIM) for Sogeti USA, LLC in Omaha, Nebraska. Over the past 25+ years, Steve has worked on air traffic control, financial, insurance, and a multitude of other types of systems. He enjoys speaking at user group meetings and other technical events and holds 49 Microsoft certifications. Steve has authored and performed technical reviews for many previous titles covering Microsoft products, including Windows, SharePoint, SQL Server, and BizTalk. For the past several years, he has focused on building highly customized, SharePoint-based business intelligence solutions.

About the Technical Reviewer

Corey Erkes is a manager consultant in the business intelligence management (BIM) practice for Sogeti USA in Omaha, Nebraska. Corey has worked within a variety of verticals implementing SharePoint solutions. His work with SharePoint dates back nearly 8 years to the Microsoft SharePoint Portal Server 2003 product. He enjoys working with customers to help them understand the capabilities of the platform and how to align the functionality with business needs. In addition to his work as a consultant, Corey was also the co-author of Pro SharePoint 2010 Governance and is a co-founder and current co-leader of the Omaha SharePoint User Group.

Acknowledgments

This book came about because of a series of conversations between myself and David Petersen in the fall of 2012. David and I had previously co-authored *Pro SharePoint Designer 2010* (Apress, 2011) together for Apress. With the release of SharePoint 2013, we were considering an update to that book. In November 2012, we agreed to discuss it while we were both attending the SharePoint Conference 2012 in Las Vegas. By the time we managed to get together, we had both realized that SPD 2013 was not what we wanted to write about. The new Cloud App Model in SharePoint was way too interesting! We set out to create the book you have before you now. Unfortunately, David was not able to complete the journey with me, but I deeply appreciate his insight and encouragement.

I would also like to thank my editors at Apress, Jon Hassell and Mark Powers, for all their help in completing this, my first solo title. Thanks to Corey Erkes for acting as my technical editor on this book as well as my co-author on *Pro SharePoint 2010 Governance* (Apress, 2012). I also appreciate the help I got from Chris Fox at Microsoft to find the resources I needed to research the internals of the cloud app platform.

And last but not least, thank you to my wife, Janet, for putting up with all the time I spend in the basement when working on these projects. I love you.

Introduction

SharePoint 2013 Server and SharePoint Online provide an entirely new model for developing enterprise solutions called the Cloud App Model. This style of application is architected to run in a hosted environment without unduly impacting the host servers. This provides for levels of scalability and reliability that were difficult, or impossible, to achieve using SharePoint's previous models that included full-trust and sandboxed solutions.

Pro SharePoint 2013 App Development contains the techniques for delivering advanced solutions on the SharePoint 2013 platform. Using step-by-step tutorials, the reader creates and elaborates on a sample SharePoint app throughout the course of the book. Once complete, the developer will be ready to tackle even the most demanding SharePoint apps with confidence. In this book, we will cover the following points:

- We will introduce the Cloud App Model architecture for creating and hosting SharePoint apps.

- We will walk through the creation and deployment of a complete solution.

- We will examine the security features of the SharePoint app model.

- We will learn to leverage SharePoint data in our apps over the network, securely.

- We will learn to utilize search and other SharePoint services to create rich SharePoint solutions.

- We will explore how to use these techniques to deliver data on a multitude of web and mobile platforms.

This book is intended for developers and IT professionals responsible for delivering solutions on the SharePoint 2013 platform. These solutions may run on-site, in the cloud, or in a hybrid deployment across many locations. We will provide the background and step-by-step introduction needed to create massively scalable SharePoint applications using standard tools such as Visual Studio, and web standards such as HTML and JQuery. Once created, SharePoint apps can be deployed internally or sold through the Microsoft SharePoint Store across the Internet.

The objective is to empower organizations to create a new generation of web-based applications on the SharePoint platform. SharePoint enables both on-site and cloud-based deployments of mission-critical business applications, using all of the same tools and technologies, regardless of the environment. Using modern web standards for user interfaces, data access, and most important, security, SharePoint apps can safely break down the wall between internal data and external customers.

The book is designed to introduce each technique in the order necessary for each solution to build on the ones that have come before. In some cases, it may be necessary to use a technique before we have discussed it fully. In these cases, we will try to convey the necessary information and refer the reader to the later section.

Chapter 1: Introduction to SharePoint Apps

This chapter will introduce the new SharePoint app model. We will describe why the app model exists, how it differs from the previous development models for SharePoint, and where SharePoint apps fit into the Microsoft ecosystem, including Azure, Windows 8, and Windows Phone. This is the 30,000-foot view.

Chapter 2: Creating and Debugging Apps

This chapter will introduce the tools used to create SharePoint apps. We will create a basic app that will begin the book-wide sample project. This sample will be elaborated on in later chapters to demonstrate the techniques presented in each chapter.

Chapter 3: Managing the App Life Cycle

This chapter will introduce the concept of an application life cycle. This includes all of the steps used to create and maintain an app. We will look at each stage in the order they will be encountered by the typical app.

Chapter 4: Client-Side Logic with JavaScript

This chapter will provide the reader with an introduction to client-side programming using JavaScript and modern programming patterns. We will introduce JavaScript, JQuery, and Knockout for those readers that are not familiar with them. We will also introduce the Model-View-ViewModel (MVVM) design pattern that will be used throughout the book.

Chapter 5: Accessing the SharePoint Environment

This chapter will cover the means of accessing data that is stored in SharePoint using the SharePoint 2013 client-side object model (CSOM) libraries. This will include lists, libraries, and other SharePoint-specific content.

Chapter 6: SharePoint App Security

This chapter will cover the extensive security mechanisms that are inherent in deploying a mission-critical application to SharePoint. This will include SharePoint apps' means of performing both authentication and authorization. We will also cover the security infrastructure used in Microsoft Azure.

Chapter 7: Web Services with REST and OData

This chapter will cover accessing data from network sources via generic data transfer methods. Unlike accessing SharePoint with the CSOM, this style of data access uses the methods and data elements exposed through standard interfaces such as REST and OData.

Chapter 8: Business Connectivity Services

In this chapter, we will examine the use of BCS within an app. These techniques allow an organization to leverage internal data assets in the cloud, while retaining security and control of that data. We will discuss the best ways to query and update BCS-based data.

Chapter 9: App Logic Components

Much of the development effort for an app involves accessing data and rendering a user experience. This chapter will focus on the techniques for adding sophisticated logic within a SharePoint app. These techniques will allow us to respond to SharePoint events and manage workflows.

Chapter 10: Developing the User Experience

This chapter will deal with the details of creating a modern user experience in a SharePoint app. We will cover the different types of UIs that a SharePoint App can expose and the best tools to use for creating them. We will also learn to make our apps conform to the style of the site in which they reside.

Chapter 11: Accessing SharePoint Search

The user interface in SharePoint 2013 sites can be driven more by search results than by content stored locally within the SharePoint site. Microsoft calls this a "search-driven" site. In this chapter, we will discuss the techniques needed to access and display search results with a SharePoint App.

Chapter 12: Using SharePoint's Social Features

This chapter will describe the social features of the SharePoint 2013 platform as they relate to creating apps. We will cover the MySite and SkyDrive Pro features, as well as newsfeeds, posts, and activities.

Chapter 13: Enhancing Apps with SharePoint Services

The SharePoint 2013 platform contains many integrated services that apps can leverage. These services provide basic infrastructure such as logging and error reporting. They also provide specialized data for metadata, search, and navigation. In this chapter, we will look at how to use some of these services to make our apps more robust and functional.

Chapter 14: Using Other App Environments

This chapter will explore the Cloud App Model as it applies to platforms other than SharePoint and how apps can be used to integrate information across the enterprise. SharePoint apps are only one type of "app" in the Microsoft ecosystem. This chapter will delve into creating apps that cross between SharePoint, Windows 8 and RT, Microsoft Office, and Windows Phone.

Summary

In creating the Cloud App Model, Microsoft has attempted to create an architecture that places cloud development at the center. The focus was on creating rich Internet apps that are scalable, maintainable, and robust in a variety of hosting environments. As a result, SharePoint apps can seem overly complex at times. As you will see in the coming chapters, there are reasons for these design decisions. You are encouraged to absorb all of the concepts that you need to design the next great app. Try not to get buried in the details the first time around.

■ ■ ■

CHAPTER 1

Introduction to SharePoint Apps

This chapter will introduce the new SharePoint 2013 application model. We will describe why the app model exists, how it differs from the previous development models for SharePoint, and where SharePoint apps fit into the Microsoft ecosystem, including Azure, Windows 8, and Windows Phone. In this chapter, we will go over the following points:

- Why there is a new application model for SharePoint 2013.

- How full-trust and sandbox solutions fit into the new paradigm.

- How SharePoint apps relate to Microsoft's online offerings, including Office 365, Azure, and SQL Azure.

- When and why to use SharePoint solutions in on-premise, cloud, and hybrid deployments.

- The sample application that will be developed throughout this book.

Introduction to the Cloud App Model

In SharePoint 2013, Microsoft has introduced a new way to build solutions for SharePoint. This new method is called the Cloud App Model. This model is similar to the development model introduced for Windows 8, the Windows Runtime (WinRT), Office 2013, and Windows Phone 8.

A SharePoint app is a single package of functionality that can be deployed and activated on a site with very little overhead or footprint on the SharePoint server farm. An app package contains all of the SharePoint artifacts (lists, libraries, etc.) needed by the application along with any pages, scripts, styles, or other web files needed to complete the application. Apps are designed to be easy to provision on a site and to be removed cleanly when no longer needed.

The Cloud App Model for SharePoint was designed with (surprise!) the cloud in mind. When an app is deployed to a site, the configuration of the files and settings in SharePoint are handled automatically. The server farm is protected from defective installation packages and file updates because apps cannot be installed like traditional SharePoint solution packages. App package files are managed entirely by SharePoint itself.

When running in the cloud, it is imperative that no one application can produce an unmanageable load on the farm or corrupt memory and require restarting of processes in the farm. SharePoint apps are prevented from causing problems on the farm by eliminating use of the SharePoint Server-Side Object Model (SSOM) in app code. In fact, all server-side code execution is off limits to SharePoint apps. To a developer familiar with developing applications for previous versions of SharePoint, this would seem to make apps totally useless in a SharePoint context. As we will see later, the combination of client-side technologies, like HTML and JavaScript, and sophisticated web service call mechanisms, like REST and OData, make building scalable, reliable apps for SharePoint quite possible.

The rest of this chapter will introduce the concepts associated with the Cloud App Model as it applies to SharePoint. We will discuss the components that make up a SharePoint app and how they are managed. The remaining chapters of this book will discuss each of these in detail to enable you to create rich user applications in SharePoint 2013.

Developing Solutions in Previous Versions of SharePoint

Let's take a moment to revisit SharePoint 2010. Specifically, we will take a look at how custom applications were developed and deployed prior to SharePoint 2013.

When designing a custom application for SharePoint pre-2013, we first had to decide what type of application it would be: full-trust or sandboxed. We then had to consider things like what features that would go into the application. The developer would create the files that make up the application and create feature manifests to manage their installation. Finally, we would create a solution package file (.WSP) that could be deployed to SharePoint. Project templates for Visual Studio made this process easier in later versions, but there were still times when the developer had to work with raw XML or CAML files in order to accomplish even routine tasks.

For *full-trust solutions*, a farm administrator would need to deploy the solution package to each SharePoint server in the farm. This would have the effect of copying files into various folders throughout the server farm. Most of these files ended up in the "14 hive." The hive is a folder on the server's hard drive that contains many of SharePoint's own files, which might be overwritten or altered by some package installations. Finally, the farm administrator would need to activate the features of the solution in order to begin using them within the farm.

Creating full-trust applications in SharePoint can have several unwanted side effects on the server farm's stability and performance.

- All code in a full-trust application runs within SharePoint's own server processes. Any corruption caused by the application has the potential to crash the server or farm.

- Any slow or inefficient code in an application can consume CPU cycles, memory, or disk space on the farm's servers and hurt performance.

- If the application does not take appropriate security precautions, it can compromise information stored in the farm because a full-trust application can always elevate its privileges to perform virtually any action.

When deploying a solution file containing a full-trust application to a farm, extensive testing is required to ensure that the application will not cause damage to the farm. As a result, many organizations have adopted policies that drastically limit or completely rule out the use of full-trust applications.

In a hosted or cloud environment, the server farm may support multiple end-user organizations or *tenants*. In these scenarios, including using SharePoint Online, full-trust applications are simply not an option. No outside code can be allowed to run in full-trust without risking harm to other customers in the farm.

In SharePoint 2013, full-trust applications are still supported and are appropriate for certain types of applications. Any custom functionality that deals with managing the farm or accessing specialized hardware may require elevated privileges and should still be created as a full-trust application. These solution packages will continue to be supported as they have been, but they are only for use in locally hosted, on-premise farm deployments. They are not appropriate for any functionality being deployed to a hosted or cloud environment.

The other option, prior to the release of SharePoint 2013, was to create a *sandboxed* solution. These solutions are developed using the same techniques and file formats as full-trust solutions, but with certain limitations.

- Sandboxed applications do not run with full-trust and cannot elevate their privileges to acquire it.

- Sandboxed applications run in a separate isolated process to prevent them from corrupting the server farm's own processes.

- Applications that run in the sandbox are only allowed to access a subset of the SharePoint Server-Side Object Model (SSOM) through a proxy object that forwards the requests to the main SharePoint processes.

- Sandboxed applications are deployed and managed at the site collection level and can only access resources within the local site collection. They cannot access other resources within the farm or elsewhere on the network, even when using the Client-Side Object Model (CSOM).

The sandbox was introduced in SharePoint 2010 in an attempt to isolate custom applications from SharePoint and limit their potential for harming the overall farm. While this was accomplished, the restrictions placed on sandboxed applications have limited their usefulness. The sandbox model has also been found insufficient for hosting and cloud deployments.

- The code in a sandboxed application still runs on the servers in the SharePoint farm. Poorly written or managed applications can still cause performance problems or limit scalability.

- Sandboxed applications that corrupt their own memory or use too many resources may be automatically restarted periodically, further draining server resources.

- The limitations on what data can be accessed from a sandboxed application limits their usefulness in enterprise-style applications that require broader access to SharePoint and network resources.

- Limiting access to the Server-Side Object Model, and the limited implementation of the Client-Side Object Model in SharePoint 2010, made creating rich applications in the sandbox very difficult or impossible.

- Because sandboxed solutions are deployed at the site collection level, they are managed by site collection administrators. These users have to install, activate, configure, and remove these packages within each site collection they own. In many organizations, site collection administration is delegated to non-technical *power users* who typically find managing solution packages very confusing.

The sandbox was created to solve the application management problems created by full-trust applications, but it has created new problems and imposes severe limitations on the types of applications that can be developed. As a result, sandboxed solutions have been deprecated in SharePoint 2013. In this case, *deprecated* is Microsoft's way of saying "Oops, that didn't work!" In practical terms, deprecated means that while the sandbox still exists in SharePoint 2013 for backward compatibility, it may not be a part of future releases. No new development should be done in sandboxed solution packages.

With full-trust applications limited to living behind the organization's firewall and sandboxed solutions on the way out, how do we make the leap into the cloud? The answer, of course, is to create SharePoint apps using the Cloud App Model.

Developing Apps for SharePoint 2013

Using apps for SharePoint is very similar to using apps on mobile devices such as Android- or iOS-based phones.

When a cell phone's user wants to extend the functionality of their device, they go an *app store* of some sort. This could be the *Google Play Store* for Android or the *Apple Store* for iOS. They find the app they want to install and select it. The app is paid for, in some cases, and then automatically downloaded and installed on their device. Once the user is finished using the app, they can uninstall it from their device as if it had never been there. The key to this usability is the fact that no one but the end user ever needs to be involved.

In the case of SharePoint apps, an app is installed into a SharePoint site. As with mobile apps, a SharePoint app can be acquired from the SharePoint Store (`http://office.microsoft.com/en-us/store/apps-for-sharepoint-FX102804987.aspx`) managed by Microsoft, as shown in Figure 1-1. An app adds functionality to the site while it is installed. The app may add SharePoint artifacts, such as lists and web parts, to the site. It can also add menu options, pages, and other behaviors to the site.

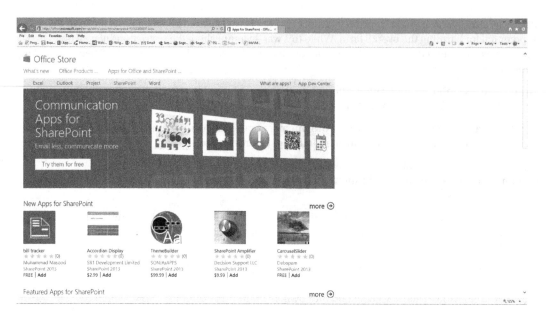

Figure 1-1. *The SharePoint Store*

The most important difference between a SharePoint app and a full-trust or sandboxed solution is in what is *not* installed in SharePoint. A SharePoint app cannot contain any server-side code at all. The data access, business logic, and user interface logic of the app is executed entirely outside of the SharePoint server farm. SharePoint may host the HTML, CSS, and JavaScript files for the app, but the logic executes either within the client browser, or other user agent, or on a remote web server outside of the farm. The end user is completely unaware of this, of course, but it makes all the difference in the world to maintaining the scalability and stability of the farm.

In the Cloud App Model, SharePoint is essentially acting as a portal for storing data and exposing applications, rather than directly hosting their logic. When creating a SharePoint app, the most important decisions to be made involve distributing the components of the application in the most effective manner available. In the next section, we will examine the concepts surrounding SharePoint app development and how these decisions are made.

Designing Cloud App Solutions

A typical application built using the Cloud App Model is composed of various components that communicate over a network. This is contrary to traditional development models that assume that most of the code will run on one platform (a server) or two platforms (a client and a server). In a cloud app, the assumption is that there is a client-side user agent, either a web browser or mobile device, and one or more servers.

In the context of a SharePoint app, one of the servers will always be a SharePoint server. This server will manage the user's access to the app and host any SharePoint data that is included in the solution. It will not execute server-side code. To perform custom logic, it will either hand off requests to other non-SharePoint web servers or it will serve client-side code files to be executed by the client browser.

When constructing a SharePoint app, there are two basic patterns. One pattern emphasizes the use of client-side code and the other uses server-side code executing outside of SharePoint.

Client-Side Code Pattern

The simplest pattern for experienced SharePoint developers to understand is the client-side pattern. In SharePoint 2010, Microsoft introduced the SharePoint Client-Side Object Model (CSOM). CSOM is a set of components that allow applications running outside of SharePoint to connect to a SharePoint site using web services. These applications become clients to the SharePoint site. These libraries have been greatly expanded in SharePoint 2013 and serve as the basis for much of the client-side functionality available to SharePoint apps.

Apps built using a client-side approach are not that different from traditional web applications in which all of the server-side logic has been refactored to the client side, as shown in Figure 1-2.

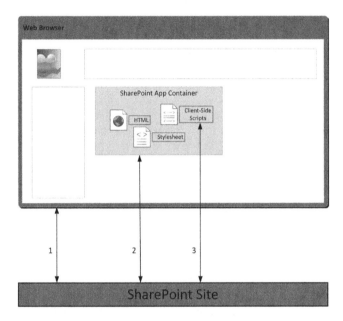

Figure 1-2. *The client-side code pattern*

The process begins when the user (1) requests a page from SharePoint that contains elements provided by an app. There are different types of elements possible in a SharePoint app, from individual menu entries up to entire web pages. In this example, the page contains an IFrame element whose content is supplied by the app. When the IFrame is rendered in the browser, another request (2) is made to return the contents of the frame. The SharePoint app returns all of the HTML, CSS, and JavaScript files needed to render the app's user interface. Note that this does not include rendering ASPX pages containing server-side code, since these are not permitted in an app. ASPX pages can be used in this context, but they can only contain server controls, not code blocks or code-behind files.

In most cases, the contents to be displayed will not be static, but will require additional data to be returned. To do this, the scripts rendered as part of the app will make client-side calls (3) to the SharePoint site to retrieve the data to be displayed. Using web service calls and other techniques that will be described later, client-side calls can also be used to access resources outside of SharePoint.

This pattern has the benefit of simplicity. All of the files needed by the app are stored in SharePoint and served without the use of server-side code. In some cases, however, it may be necessary to execute parts of the app's logic on a server. This will require using the server-side pattern.

Server-Side Code Pattern

The client-side pattern eliminated server-side code by moving all logic to the client browser. What if doing so is not possible, practical, or desirable? This is where the server-side pattern comes in, as shown in Figure 1-3.

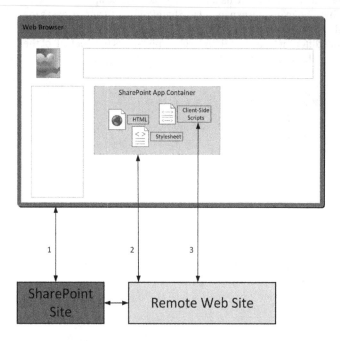

Figure 1-3. *The server-side code pattern*

Using this pattern, instead of moving the logic to the client web browser, we are moving it to another web site running outside of SharePoint. The remote web site can use server-side logic to render the HTML that is sent into the app's container. It can access data local to its host system or even access data within the app's SharePoint site using one of the client API libraries described later in this chapter.

This remote web site could be an ASP.NET site running under IIS, or a PHP site running under Apache. It could be running within your organization, in the Windows Azure cloud, or in some other vendor's cloud. Because the app's logic has been decoupled from the SharePoint server, it can run anywhere on the network.

In complex enterprise-level apps, you will find that neither the client-side model nor server-side model is appropriate for all of the interactions needed by the app. These apps will most likely depend on a combination of client-side and server-side techniques.

Deployment Options

To understand the deployment of apps to SharePoint 2013, it is important to start with the concept of a *tenant*. A tenant refers to a customer or organization which uses a SharePoint farm but may share that farm with other tenants. Starting in SharePoint 2010, SharePoint Server has supported a multi-tenant hosting model. This model is greatly improved in SharePoint 2013.

Assume for a moment that you work for a web-hosting company that is going to sell space on a SharePoint server farm to your customers. Your customers will be able to log on and use their SharePoint sites just as they would in an intranet scenario. The difference is that they will be doing this over the Internet and there will be other customers doing the same in different site collections on the same server farm. How would such an environment need to behave?

- Each tenant's data will need to be isolated from all others to ensure that it is only used for that tenant.

- You will need to track the usage of storage, network, and server resources so that you can bill your customers appropriately.

- You will need the ability to configure services, such as Search and Excel Services, relevant to each tenant without affecting the others.

- Any customizations (master pages, themes, etc.) deployed by one tenant should not affect any other tenant's sites.

- Each tenant will need to be able to assign their own URLs to their sites without regard for the structure of the SharePoint farm.

This type of environment is precisely what the multi-tenancy support in SharePoint Server is designed to allow. Once this infrastructure is in place, there are several ways it might be used.

- A commercial web-hosting company, as described above, could use multi-tenancy to host a large number of smaller customers on one or more farms.

- A large organization could use multi-tenancy to share a large centrally managed SharePoint farm to host separate intranets for the various divisions or subsidiaries of the company. With data isolation and usage analysis, a chargeback system could be used to bill the cost of the farm back to the business units that use it.

- A very large company, like Microsoft, could use these features to create a vast hosting infrastructure for SharePoint sites.

Of course, the last of these options isn't just a possibility—it's called *SharePoint Online* and is now part of *Office 365*.

When designing an app for SharePoint, it is useful to consider a multi-tenant environment even if the app isn't intended to be deployed in one. The reason is that this is the environment that the Cloud App Model was designed to support. In fact, one of the most compelling scenarios for SharePoint apps is when they are used to support multiple customers in multiple types of deployments. There are three main types of deployments: on-site (a.k.a. on-premise), cloud, and hybrid.

An *on-site deployment* is the way SharePoint has been traditionally rolled out. The product is installed on a set of servers behind an organization's firewalls to support only that organization's needs. This type of deployment has the advantages of being internally controlled, having access to all of the organization's network resources and support for full-trust custom applications. On-site deployments also avoid the need to expose internal data resources to the Internet, either by drilling holes in the firewall or moving the data into the cloud. The disadvantage is that all of the cost of deploying and maintaining the farm's infrastructure must be absorbed by the organization.

A *cloud deployment* shifts the burden of deploying and maintaining the infrastructure to a third party, such as Microsoft in the case of SharePoint Online. This frees up resources for developing the content and functionality of the site rather than maintaining the underlying servers. The disadvantage is a loss of control and a dependence on the hosting organization to keep the farm robust. Cloud deployments can also include non-SharePoint platforms such as Exchange Online, Windows Azure sites, and SQL Azure databases.

Right now, most organizations that use SharePoint do so in an on-site deployment. Over time, the cost savings of cloud deployments will likely entice many organizations to move at least some of their deployments into the cloud. This is where *hybrid deployments* come in (see Figure 1-4).

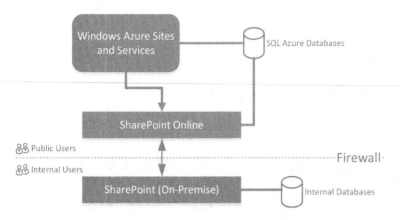

Figure 1-4. A hybrid SharePoint deployment

In a hybrid scenario, a SharePoint solution contains elements hosted on-site and in the cloud. In Chapter 6, we will look at the security mechanisms that allow such an environment to function smoothly. There may be some advanced or customized features of SharePoint, such as Business Intelligence or workflows, which organizations chose to keep on-site for security, performance, or cost-of-ownership reasons. Hybrid deployments have the advantage of maintaining control over the most vital and private parts of the solution, while offloading the maintenance of as much infrastructure as is feasible.

SharePoint apps also support deployment scenarios beyond the Windows platform. Because all of the components of a SharePoint app use standard web technologies to communicate and transfer control (HTML, JavaScript, URLs, web service calls, etc.), there is no reason that these components have to be limited to the Microsoft development stack or even to Windows-based servers.

- An app's non-SharePoint web content can be hosted on any type of web stack including one of the LAMP variants—Linux, Apache, MySQL, and PHP, for example.

- Non-Microsoft databases such as Oracle, DB2, and MySQL, and even non-relational databases, can be used to serve data for a SharePoint app.

- Media files can be served, streamed, queued, and delivered over Content Delivery Networks (CDNs).

- Web services hosted anywhere on the network, including behind firewalls, can be leveraged as well.

Of course, creating these alternate types of web resources may require tools other than those supplied by Microsoft. In this book, we will focus on the Microsoft toolset.

Distributing SharePoint Apps

After your app has been built and tested, it needs to be distributed. SharePoint and Office apps use the same type of distribution system as apps for Android or iOS devices. In this case, Microsoft has established the *Office Store* (http://office.microsoft.com/en-us/store/) for both Office and SharePoint apps.

The Office Store will sometimes be referred to as the *SharePoint Store* (http://office.microsoft.com/en-us/store/apps-for-sharepoint-FX102804987.aspx) when referring only to apps for SharePoint. Developers and organizations can publish apps to the Office Store and get paid for them. The store can also be used to distribute free apps. Online service providers, such as LinkedIn or Facebook, will often provide free apps in online app stores like the Office Store to provide easy integration with their services.

Not all apps belong in the SharePoint Store, however. What if your organization creates a line-of-business app that is proprietary to your business? Obviously, you wouldn't publish an app like that to a public app store. For these cases, SharePoint 2013 contains a new site collection template called the *App Catalog*. The App Catalog acts as a private app store that users of your sites can use to deploy custom apps from within your organization. In a multi-tenant scenario, each tenant can have their own App Catalog.

■ **Note**   Chapters 2 and 3 will describe the app publishing and distribution process in more detail.

Development Environment

In order to begin creating SharePoint apps, we need to set up a development environment. Just as when developing solutions for previous versions of SharePoint, we will need both a development client to write and compile code and a server environment in which to test the app.

In SharePoint 2010, it was possible to load SharePoint Server on a client operating system such as Windows 7. SharePoint 2013 no longer supports this type of installation. You will need to either set up a local server farm with SharePoint 2013 or use SharePoint Online.

When using a local server farm for app development, you will want to use the new *Developer Site Template*. This site collection template includes tips for getting started (see Figure 1-5) and, more importantly, allows for *side-loading* of applications. Side-loading is a new feature that allows apps to be deployed directly to a SharePoint site without first being published to an App Catalog. When deploying an app for debugging, your development tool can deploy the app directly to a site that uses this template and begin debugging immediately without going through the normal app acquisition and installation process.

Figure 1-5. *Developer Site Template*

SharePoint Online is an excellent choice for developing SharePoint apps, as opposed to full-trust or sandboxed solutions, because this is the intended environment for apps. Microsoft provides different options for Office 365 development depending on whether you own an MSDN subscription (http://msdn.microsoft.com) or just want to sign up for a limited developer site (http://msdn.microsoft.com/en-us/library/office/apps/fp179924%28v=office.15%29). When a developer site is created in Office 365, a new tenant is created in SharePoint Online and a new site collection using the Developer Site Template is deployed. This makes developing apps in the cloud almost indistinguishable from developing them on a local server farm. The options and costs associated with SharePoint Online change from time to time. See Microsoft's SharePoint Online page (http://sharepoint.com) for their current offerings.

Now that we have determined where we will deploy and test our apps, let's look at the options for developing them. Most of the components of a SharePoint app include standard files, such as HTML and CSS files, which can be created in many free and commercial tools. Packaging and testing apps is best done using one of Microsoft's own development tools: Visual Studio 2012 or the "Napa" Office 365 Development Tools.

Visual Studio 2012 is the latest edition of Microsoft's Integrated Development Environment (IDE). You will need the Professional, Premium, or Ultimate edition of Visual Studio to develop SharePoint apps. Visual Studio is a full-featured development tool that includes interactive debuggers and code analysis tools. By default, VS 2012 only comes with project templates for SharePoint 2010, not 2013. To get the templates for SharePoint 2013, you will need to use the Web Platform Installer application available from Microsoft at http://msdn.microsoft.com/en-US/office/apps/fp123627. Through this tool, you will install the *Microsoft Office Developer Tools for Visual Studio 2012*. This will add all of the project templates and object editors necessary to develop SharePoint 2013 apps and solutions.

A new option for developing Office and SharePoint apps is the *"Napa" Office 365 Development Tools*. Unlike Visual Studio, this is a free tool that does not need to be loaded onto a client computer. Napa is actually a SharePoint app itself! It is available in the SharePoint Store for free. You simply deploy Napa to the developer site you have created and begin creating apps right in the browser. To make finding Napa simple, the "Build an app" tile in Figure 1-5 is actually a link to install the Napa tools on the local site or to launch Napa if it is already installed.

For simple apps, Napa is an excellent, ready-to-use tool. For more complex apps, where various types of projects and rich debugging is needed, Visual Studio is still a better option. The good news is that apps created in Napa can be easily ported to Visual Studio for further enhancement. Napa uses all of the same file formats and technologies as Visual Studio for developing apps.

SharePoint App Components

In this section we will describe the components and concepts that go into building an app for SharePoint. We will start with an overview of the terms and organization of an app. Then, we will look at the data, business logic, and user interface components. This section will only present these concepts at a high level. More detail can be found in the later chapters of this book.

App Organization and Terminology

A SharePoint app is distributed using an *App Package* file with an .APP file name extension. An app file is similar to the solution package files (.WSP) used for full-trust and sandboxed solutions. Whereas WSP files are actually cabinet (.CAB) format files, APP files are actually compressed folders (.ZIP). To see the contents of an APP file, just rename it with a .ZIP extension and open it in Windows Explorer, as shown in Figure 1-6. The app file contains a manifest, features, and other content files needed to deploy the app to SharePoint.

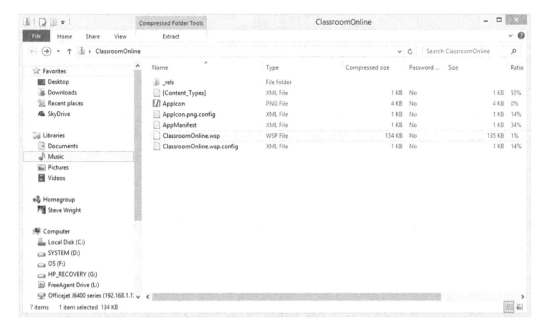

Figure 1-6. *Contents of a simple APP file*

The *AppManifest* file contains the basic configurations of the app including its title and unique identifier, as shown in Listing 1-1. The app manifest controls the start page and security settings for the app as well.

Listing 1-1. A Sample AppManifest File

```
<?xml version="1.0" encoding="utf-8" ?>
<!--Created:cb85b80c-f585-40ff-8bfc-12ff4d0e34a9-->
<App xmlns="http://schemas.microsoft.com/sharepoint/2012/app/manifest"
     Name="ClassroomOnline"
     ProductID="{7fca2693-a952-49f7-93a0-bec36e7041d1}"
     Version="1.0.0.0"
     SharePointMinVersion="15.0.0.0">
  <Properties>
    <Title>Classroom Online</Title>
    <StartPage>~appWebUrl/Pages/Default.aspx?{StandardTokens}</StartPage>
  </Properties>
  <AppPrincipal>
    <Internal />
  </AppPrincipal>
</App>
```

When an app is deployed to a SharePoint site, there are actually up to three types of sites involved: the host web, the app web, and a remote web (see Figure 1-7). Every app will have a host web, but the app and remote webs are optional.

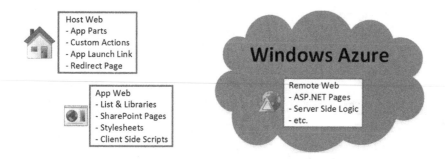

Figure 1-7. *Web types in a SharePoint app*

The *host web* refers to the SharePoint site into which the app was installed. The app will appear on the Site Contents page as though it were a list or library in the site, as shown in Figure 1-8. In this example, the Napa tools are deployed to this site and appear as an app on the Site Contents page.

Figure 1-8. *Site Contents page including the Napa app*

The host web can also show elements of the app using *client web parts* (a.k.a. *app parts*). App parts are similar to ordinary web parts except that all of their logic occurs in the client web browser or on a remote web site. When an app is deployed to a host web, any app parts exposed by the app become available for use in the host web. The same is true for any *custom actions* contained in the app. These actions are added to the ribbon and context menus of the host site.

When the user accesses a SharePoint app from the host web for the first time in a session or navigates back to it later, an App Redirect Page will handle directing the user's browser to the correct page in the app. It does this based on the configuration found in the app manifest.

■ **Tip** A remote web site is considered a "client" from SharePoint's point of view because it can retrieve information from SharePoint through the client-side APIs, described later in this chapter.

Most non-trivial SharePoint apps will also include an *app web*. The app web is a separate SharePoint site that is deployed to host the components of the app. For example, if the app includes lists or libraries, they would reside in the app web. The app web may also contain SharePoint pages but these pages may not contain server-side code blocks, only server controls. The app web is deployed to the SharePoint server farm but it is not in the same domain as the rest of the site. This is a security feature that will be described in more detail in Chapter 6.

The app web is deployed using a specialized site template called the *App Site Template*. This site template does not contain the usual infrastructure for a SharePoint site because it is only intended to host app components. Pages in the app web use the *app.master* master page by default.

The final type of site commonly found in a SharePoint app file is a *remote web*. A remote web is a normal ASP.NET web site, not a SharePoint site. It is designed to be deployed outside of SharePoint, often in the Windows Azure cloud. Server-side code is permitted in a remote web and the web can make secure calls back to the host web and app web as needed.

Remember, since the remote web is not running within SharePoint, it does not have access to the SharePoint Server-Side Object Model. It can, and often will, make use of SharePoint's client-side APIs. The CSOM for .NET can be used by server-side code in the remote web and the JavaScript CSOM is available to the pages served from a remote site.

Installation Scopes

The normal installation sequence for a SharePoint app is quite straightforward.

1. A tenant administrator adds the app to the App Catalog in use by the sites within a tenant.

2. A site administrator adds the app to the web site where it will be used.

In this case, the app is said to be installed with *web scope*. An app's *installation scope* only refers to how the app was installed. The app developer has no control over this scope. This is different from the feature scope in a solution package for SharePoint. Apps installed with web scope have certain properties.

- Each SharePoint site on which the app is installed will get a separate instance of the app web, if the app uses one. This isolates each site's processing for all other sites using the same app, since they run in separate IIS web sites.

- The app can add client web parts (app parts) to the site's app part catalog.

- The app can introduce new custom actions on the site's ribbon menu.

The other possibility for installing apps is to perform a *tenant scope* installation. The procedure for installing this type of app is somewhat different.

1. The tenant administrator adds the app to the App Catalog within the tenancy.

2. The tenant administrator installs the app to the App Catalog site. ***Note that this is the site containing the catalog, not one of the end-user sites contained in the tenant.***

3. The tenant administrator uses the App Catalog site to deploy the app immediately to one or more, or all, of the sites in the tenant.

4. SharePoint installs the app on each selected site in a background batch process.

The site administrators never get the chance to install the app at a web scope because the tenant administrator has already installed it in their site. Note that an app can only be installed once on a particular site.

■ **Tip** It is easy to confuse *app installation scopes* with other concepts because they share similar terminology, such as *web* and *tenant*. Installation scopes are not feature scopes or security levels. They are not properties of the app. The installation scope only affects a single installation of the app.

The key difference between a web scope and a tenant scope app installation is that there is only one app web for a tenant installation (see Figure 1-9). Each site gets a separate app web when using web scope. Consider the impact of using web scope installations when thousands of sites are involved. This would cause the configuration of thousands of new SharePoint web sites that may not be needed.

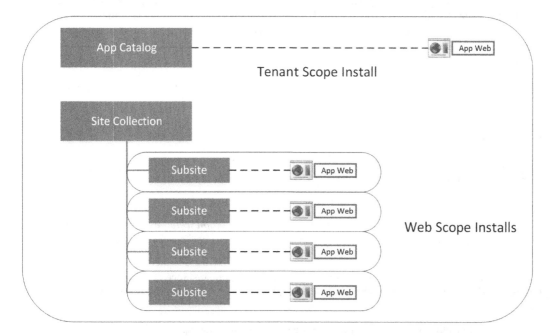

Figure 1-9. App installation scopes

Consider using tenant installation scopes when the following situations apply:

- There will be a large number of sites using the app. Web scope installs create additional copies of the app web.

- The sites need to share their data. The SharePoint data stored by the app, including SharePoint lists and libraries, is stored in the app web. If this data should be common to all sites in the tenant, use tenant scope.

- The app does not store any data in the app web. In this case, there may be no reason to create the extra app webs for a web scope install.

- The app does not expose any app parts or ribbon menu custom actions. Note that custom actions that surface in the Edit Control Block (ECB) can be used within tenant installed apps.

Client API Libraries

Most SharePoint apps store or retrieve data from somewhere on the network. This could include data from SharePoint lists, search, user profiles, or social networking information. Any data stored in SharePoint can be accessed using one of the client APIs described next. This data may also be retrieved from sources outside of SharePoint, such as relational databases using Business Connectivity Services (BCS), or other web sites through web services. Accessing data securely and efficiently is a key design feature of any SharePoint app.

Because apps are limited to executing their logic outside of SharePoint, a set of client APIs is needed. This section will briefly introduce the client-side APIs supported by SharePoint 2013. Although some of these libraries existed in SharePoint 2010, they have been greatly enhanced in 2013. Any operation that an app might want to perform should be possible using one or more calls from these APIs. Any action not available in the client APIs is probably best performed by a full-trust solution instead of an app.

The SharePoint Client-Side Object Model (CSOM) for JavaScript is a set of scripts that can be included in an app to provide client-side access from the browser back into SharePoint. These scripts manage calls to SharePoint in batches, providing better performance than a simple call-and-response pattern. This is the most generally applicable CSOM API because JavaScript is supported on all modern browsers and devices.

The CSOM for .NET Framework is a set of managed code that allows .NET code to make calls into a SharePoint site. The .NET Framework code using this library could be running in any environment that supports .NET, including in a desktop application on Windows. The most common use of this API in apps is in a remote ASP.NET web site to support server-side code. This library will be covered in Chapter 5.

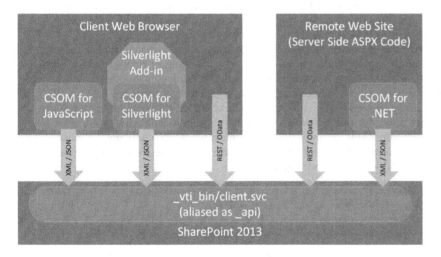

Figure 1-10. *Client API libraries*

The CSOM for Silverlight allows a Silverlight application to access a SharePoint site. The CSOM libraries need to be packaged with the Silverlight application. The CSOM for Silverlight is primarily intended to support stand-alone Silverlight applications or those hosted directly in the SharePoint Silverlight web part. The application could be exposed through an app part in a SharePoint app but, in most cases, a simple web application using the JavaScript API is preferable to support all modern browsers. In this book, we will not be covering Silverlight development.

■ **Note** At this point in time, Microsoft's commitment to the future development of Silverlight is unclear. Given that the tools provided for developing apps for SharePoint are clearly geared toward HTML and JavaScript, it seems like a good idea to favor these over Silverlight for developing SharePoint apps.

The SharePoint Mobility Object Model is a client-side model used by applications running on the Windows Phone platform. SharePoint apps have no need to use this library. We will discuss developing Windows Phone apps that use SharePoint data, and therefore the Mobility Object Model, in Chapter 14.

A new addition to SharePoint 2013 that does not require a custom CSOM library is the inclusion of a set of Representational State Transfer (REST) endpoints. REST uses a simple URL encoding system to request data from SharePoint and transfer the responses using either the ATOM or JavaScript Object Notation (JSON) formats. For example, a list item stored in SharePoint can be retrieved by simply issuing a GET web request to a URL, as in the following:

```
http://mydomain.com/mysite/_api/web/lists/getbytitle("MyList")/items
```

The Atom Publishing Protocol is appropriate for feeds such as blogs. JSON is easier to work with in JavaScript when traversing complex data structures.

▪ **Note**   Chapters 5, 6, and 7 will cover each of these APIs in much greater detail.

Connecting Tiers of the App

In our discussion of deployment options, we discussed the host, app, and remote webs that can contain the various parts of an application. In addition to designing the distribution of these components, we also have to be able to communicate between them. Communicating between tiers presents two major hurdles.

First is the fact that each of these webs is located in a separate Internet domain, even when hosted on the same servers. This is intentional in order to ensure isolation. The challenge this presents is that, normally, client-side scripts running in a browser are not allowed to make calls into other domains. Since all of our logic is running in the client or a remote web site, this makes directly accessing these web resources impossible from within the browser.

Second, we must ensure that we maintain secure, encrypted connections between the server(s) and the client. We need to be able to perform authentication and authorization functions as appropriate to each location in the app.

SharePoint 2013 contains multiple components to enable this communication. Which component is most appropriate depends on the situation. As shown in Figure 1-11, there are different ways to communicate between SharePoint and a remote site and between a remote site and SharePoint.

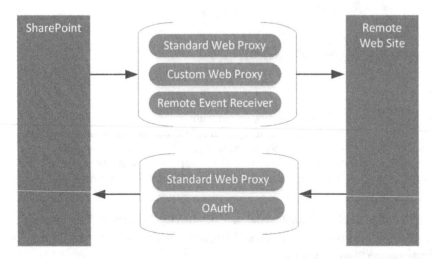

Figure 1-11. Communication options

Figure 1-11 includes two different web proxy options. A *web proxy* refers to a system whereby a client script can make a call to a domain other than its own by using a component that is loaded into a hidden IFrame element on the page. The creation of the IFrame and the retrieval of the information from the remote domain are managed by a client-side script library called the *cross-domain library*. This library is delivered as a JavaScript file in SharePoint and can be referenced by any page associated with the app.

SharePoint 2013 contains a standard web proxy page called `AppWebProxy.aspx`. This page accepts a specially formatted request from the browser and returns the requested data. That data is loaded into the hidden IFrame element managed by the cross-domain library. The web proxy can be used to access resources within SharePoint or to initiate calls to other web services on the Internet. Because these calls originate on the server, they are not limited to the local domain.

The other web proxy option allows the developer to create their own web proxy. When making a request to a remote site, where the `AppWebProxy.aspx` file does not exist, a custom web proxy page can be created to perform the same function. This eliminates the need to go back to the SharePoint server farm before accessing remote data. There are limitations when creating custom web proxies. The developer of the proxy is responsible for most aspects of the security of the call. An alternative to the cross-domain library is the *OAuth* protocol. This protocol handles server-to-server security using an open standard. This protocol will be described briefly later in the chapter and in more detail in Chapter 6.

Another useful mechanism that can be used to communicate directly from SharePoint to a remote web site are *remote event receivers*. An event receiver in SharePoint is a piece of code that is triggered when a particular type of event happens on the server farm. For example, creating a new site or updating a list item could both generate events. In full-trust solutions, an event receiver would be coded as a .NET component that would be called when the event occurs. Because SharePoint apps cannot use server-side code, another option is needed. A remote event receiver essentially provides SharePoint with a web URL to call when the event happens. This URL can trigger server-side code in a remote web that handles the event.

▪ **Note** Remote event handlers are covered in depth in Chapter 9.

User Interface Components

Apps for SharePoint use standard web technologies to render their user interface. The components that make up an app combine to render a rich user experience that hides the fact that many of these components may be served from different locations, as described in the previous section *"Deployment Options."*

The user experience presented by a SharePoint app consists of one or more components that fall into three categories: immersive web pages, client web parts , and custom actions.

Immersive web pages are complete web pages that replace the entire page in the web browser. These pages can either be SharePoint pages served from the application's app web or external pages served from a remote web site. For example, when a user launches an app, the redirect page may send the user to a start page that fills the browser window. Using client-side scripts and libraries provided by SharePoint 2013, immersive pages can be made to take on the appearance of the host web by inheriting the host web's menus and style sheet.

Client web parts, also known as app parts, allow the app to expose part of its user interface within the host web's pages using a control similar to a traditional SharePoint web part. In reality, an app part's user interface is created by rendering an IFrame element on the host web's page. The IFrame launches a *Client Web Part Page* from either the app web or a remote web, as shown in Figure 1-12.

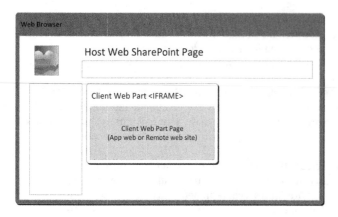

Figure 1-12. An app part on a host web page

Like ordinary server web parts in SharePoint, client web parts can declare parameters that are passed into the web part. Instead of being passed as values on a .NET web part control, these parameters are passed on the query string of the URL launched by the IFrame. The client web part page can then use those values to customize the output of the app part.

The third type of user interface component available to app developers are custom actions. As the name implies, these allow the developer to declare actions on the host web that trigger a response from the app. These are useful in two specific areas: the ribbon menu and the Edit Control Block (ECB). See Figure 1-13.

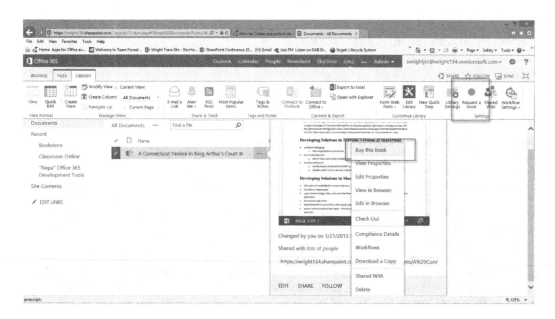

Figure 1-13. Custom actions

The *ribbon menu* is familiar to anyone that has used SharePoint sites or Microsoft Office. A custom app action can add elements to this menu that can be selected by the user. Custom actions can be placed on any tab or command group and include a custom icon, as shown in Figure 1-13. In this figure, the "Request a book" action is a custom action in the ribbon menu.

The *Edit Control Block (ECB)* is the context menu associated with a list item or document. Using a custom action, the app developer can create new actions to be taken with respect to a given item. The list and item IDs are passed to the app's URL for use in executing the action. In Figure 1-13, the "Buy this book" action is a custom action in the ECB.

A serious problem with SharePoint development has always been the tendency to have everything look the same. Users often complain that their sites are too "SharePoint-looking." The challenge has always been to use master pages, themes, and styles to customize the look of SharePoint without leaving it unusable. As a result, most customizations are limited to changing colors, fonts, and the like. SharePoint 2013 has introduced a new page rendering system that is designed to help with this problem. These new branding elements are managed with the Design Manager. Site branding in SharePoint 2013 is beyond the scope of this book. Just remember that, using Design Manager, the layout of the host web may look very different from the out-of-the-box user experience included in SharePoint 2013.

Apps for SharePoint introduce a new dimension to this problem. Now that many elements are being served from outside of SharePoint, how can the app present a UI that is consistent with the rest of the site? Consider an app that is purchased from the SharePoint Store. Such an app may be deployed into a variety of sites with very different layouts, languages, colors, etc. The app needs to adapt to the branding of the host web or its components will stick out like a sore thumb. There are three primary components that help to alleviate this problem: the app master page, the chrome control, and the site style sheet retrieval link (`defaultcss.ashx`).

As described previously, the app master page is the master page used by immersive pages in a SharePoint app. This master page includes the menus and headers associated with the host web. It also links the host web's style sheet into the page so that any HTML markup generated by the app will automatically be styled consistently. However, the app master page is only available for app pages that run within the app web. Pages running in a remote web do not have the option to use it.

The *chrome control* is designed to bring the elements provided by the app master page to pages hosted in remote webs. The chrome control is a client-side component that uses calls back to the host web to retrieve the information necessary to render the menus and styles from the host site. This control can be configured to create additional menus and options to tailor the chrome to the needs of the app page.

What if the app page is being used in a client web part that is displayed inside an IFrame on a host web page? Replicating the menus and header of the site is not appropriate, but we still need to make the styles available to our HTML markup. This can be accomplished using the `defaultcss.ashx` request handler in the layouts directory in SharePoint. This handler is a piece of server-side logic that SharePoint provides to retrieve the default style sheet for the local web site. In order to style your app page, just add a style sheet link to `<HostWebUrl>/_layouts/15/defaultcss.ashx`. The correct style sheet will be returned and your markup will conform to the host web's styles.

Security

In this section, we will briefly examine the key concepts around security in apps for SharePoint. A far more complete description of these topics is presented in Chapter 6.

In any application, there are two primary security tasks to be performed. The first is *authentication* which deals with establishing the user's identity. The second is authorization. *Authorization* deals with calculating the permissions associated with the user and the potential actions the user is allowed to take within the application.

Put simply, authentication answers the question "Who are you?" whereas authorization answers the question "What are you allowed to do?"

Authentication

SharePoint 2013 uses *claims-based authentication*. This means that users are identified by presenting SharePoint with a token, or claim, that represents their identity as ensured by a trusted identity service.

The most common identity service used in on-premise SharePoint installations is Microsoft Active Directory (AD). This is a directory service that verifies a user's identity by validating a set of credentials, usually a user name and password.

When using SharePoint Online, you will use the Microsoft Online Directory Service (MSODS) as the identity service. This is the same service that is used for Microsoft Online IDs (formerly known as Microsoft Live IDs). SharePoint Online accepts claims from MSODS to allow users to log in.

What if your organization has an internal SharePoint farm but also wants to leverage SharePoint Online? You could log on to your internal farm using your Active Directory account and then switch to a Microsoft Online ID when you go into the cloud, but that would be very awkward and annoying. More importantly, it would prevent your SharePoint apps from interacting across these platforms without asking for credentials over and over again.

To solve this problem, MSODS is designed as a *federated identity service*. This means that it has the ability to synchronize and exchange user identities with other services, like Active Directory. Using a tool provided by Microsoft, an organization can automatically synchronize their internal Active Directory information with MSODS. This allows users, and their apps, to move back and forth between SharePoint Online and SharePoint on-premise seamlessly. The server handshakes, trusts, and encryption going on under the covers is quite complex but, fortunately, SharePoint app developers need not be concerned with that. Once everything is configured and the proper tokens are passed, it just works.

User identities are only one type of authentication used in SharePoint apps. An app can also have its own *app identity*. This identity token identifies the app to SharePoint and allows the app to act on behalf of its users.

App and user identities together control what access an app has while acting for a user. When certain calls are made between the components of an app, either the app identity, the user identity or both may be required. When calls are made within the SharePoint environment, or from the client browser into SharePoint, these identities are resolved and appropriate checks are made automatically. When calls cross into SharePoint from another service, OAuth tokens are passed to provide this information. OAuth will be introduced in the next section and detailed in Chapter 6.

Introduction to OAuth 2.0

OAuth is an open standard protocol for enabling authorization between servers and applications across a network. The goal of OAuth is to allow one service to request actions and resources from another service without being required to share the user's credentials. Tokens are passed between applications that represent the user's identity and permissions.

OAuth's development began in 2006 as part of the Twitter OpenID effort. The protocol was first published in 2010. OAuth version 2.0 was published in late 2012 and is the version used by SharePoint 2013.

How SharePoint Apps Use OAuth

OAuth is used when calls are made between components of a SharePoint app that do not originate within SharePoint or within the client browser's session. SharePoint provides the information necessary for remote web sites within the application to use OAuth tokens to access SharePoint resources securely, as shown in Figure 1-14.

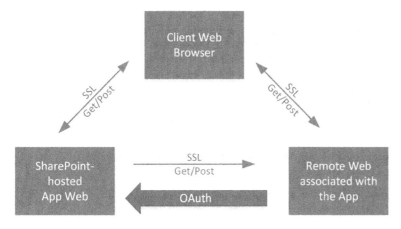

Figure 1-14. *OAuth in apps for SharePoint*

By default, when a call is made within an app that does not require OAuth, that request is made using the identity of the app and the current authenticated user. When making a call using OAuth, care must be taken to pass the necessary tokens so that the app and user can be identified and authorized as needed. When using one of the client libraries supplied by SharePoint 2013, these details are handled automatically for the developer.

OAuth uses SSL encryption to protect the tokens as they are transmitted across the network, so SSL is required on connections that use OAuth by default. It is possible to disable the requirement for an SSL connection but it is not recommended for any application that is passing or accessing data over the Internet.

The Security Token Service

OAuth depends on tokens to provide access to resources. The issuing of these tokens is therefore critical. In OAuth, a network service that acts as a source of these tokens is referred to as the *Security Token Service (STS)*. The STS must be trusted by both applications involved in the conversation in order to allow access.

When an application wants to access a remote resource, it retrieves an OAuth access token and passes it to the resource owner with the request. The resource owner validates the contents of the token and checks whether the requesting user or app has the right to read the resource in question. If so, the request is processed and the resource is accessed.

SharePoint Online uses the Windows Azure Access Control Service (ACS) as its OAuth security token service. In deployments outside of SharePoint Online, other STS services can be configured to be trusted by SharePoint. In addition to providing authorization tokens, ACS is the source of all app identity tokens used within SharePoint.

Authorization in SharePoint Apps

We have discussed how users are authenticated and how authorization information is passed between components in an app for SharePoint. Now we need to consider what SharePoint will do with that information in making decisions.

When a remote request is made into SharePoint by an app component, one of three policies is used to determine what access that request will have.

The first policy is the *user-only policy*. In this case, authorization decisions are made based only on the identity of the authenticated user. Essentially, this is the same security that existed in previous versions of SharePoint and when using SharePoint 2013 outside of the context of an app. The permissions within SharePoint's sites, lists, and libraries are compared to the user's identity, including any security groups they are a member of, to determine the access to be granted.

The most common policy used by SharePoint apps is the *user+app policy*. This policy takes into account both the user's identity and the app's identity. The permissions granted to an app are different from those granted to a user. Whereas a user might be given read access to a certain document or list, the app would need to have the more generic right to read data from lists before it would be allowed to complete the operation. The user+app policy is the policy normally used when an app component makes a request back into SharePoint.

The final authorization policy is the *app-only policy*. This type of policy is used when only the permissions of the app are relevant. Because the user's permissions are not being checked, this should be considered a form of elevated permissions. As a result, only certain users can install an app that requires the use of the app-only policy and, even then, it should be used with care. The intent of this policy is to allow the following types of requests:

- Some requests are made without user interaction, such as some workflow actions and remove event handler calls. Since there is no interactive user, there is no user identity to pass.

- An app that needs to perform an action on behalf of the application owner instead of the current user would use this policy as a form of elevated privilege to perform these tasks.

The app-only policy must be enabled explicitly by the site administrator when installing the app. Otherwise, the app will not be allowed to make such calls since they could be used to circumvent SharePoint's permissions.

App Permissions and Scopes

As mentioned previously, the permissions granted to an app are somewhat different from those granted to users. Most importantly, an app must request all of the permissions it needs in its app manifest file.

The user installing the app is presented with a listing of these permissions during installation and must approve their use by the app. Without this explicit granting of app permissions, the app cannot be installed. Of course, users cannot install an app that requires permissions they do not have themselves, since they would be unable to grant those permissions to the app.

A permission request within the app manifest consists of three parts: a scope, a right, and one or more properties. As shown in Listing 1-2, the app manifest entry contains the scope and right as attributes, and the properties as a list within the request tag.

Listing 1-2. App Permission Request XML

```
<AppPermissionRequest Scope="http://sharepoint/content/sitecollection/web/list" Right="Write">
    <Property Name="BaseTemplateId" Value="101"/>
</AppPermissionRequest>
```

The *permission request scope* defines what part of the host environment the app is to be granted rights to as represented by the URI in the scope attribute. In this example, the app is requesting access to list data within the site.

The *permission request right* is the type of permission being requested. Depending on the scope, different types of rights are available. In the Listing 1-2, the app is requesting to have write access to the list data. (Note that the attribute is spelled "Right" but the value is "Write". The authors feel that they should both be spelled "Wright" but that doesn't seem to work.)

The last piece of information to be provided is optional. The properties of a permission request can be used to further limit the scope of the request. The types of properties available depend on what scope is being used. The property shown in Listing 1-2 specifies that the request applies only to lists based on template number 101, which is any document library. Table 1-1 contains some of the most commonly used permission scopes.

Table 1-1. *Common Permission Request Scopes*

Scope URI	Includes Access To...
`http://sharepoint/content/tenant`	The entire tenant (or farm) containing the host web
`http://sharepoint/content/sitecollection`	The entire site collection containing the host web
`http://sharepoint/content/sitecollection/web`	The host web and all descendant sites
`http://sharepoint/content/sitecollection/web/list`	The lists within the host web
`http://sharepoint/search`	Controls access to the search service

All of the scopes listed in Table 1-1 use rights of READ, WRITE, MANAGE, and FULL CONTROL, except for search. The search scope only has one option (QueryAsUserIgnoreAppPrincipal) that permits the app to perform searches. Additional scopes apply to specific services within SharePoint 2013, such as BCS, taxonomy, and social features.

High-Trust Apps

A *high-trust app* in SharePoint 2013 is a specific type of deployment where both the SharePoint farm and a remote site exist behind the same firewall. This is an entirely on-premise scenario. In a high-trust app, the remote web application is responsible for creating the access tokens used to access SharePoint resources. This means that the remote site has the ability to emulate any valid user when connecting to SharePoint. That is why these apps are referred to as being high-trust.

A high-trust app requires special configurations to function within a farm. In general, the steps to set up a high-trust app are as follows:

1. Both the server farm and the remote site must be deployed internally, not in the cloud.

2. An application certificate is created to identify the app.

3. The certificate is configured in SharePoint so that SharePoint will trust the app to issue user identities.

4. A local OAuth Security Token Service (STS) is configured to support authorization. This is necessary because the Windows Azure Access Control Service (ACS) serves only cloud-based applications.

A high-trust app is not the same as a full-trust solution in SharePoint. A full-trust application can perform any action within the SharePoint farm simply by calling an API to elevate its own privileges. A high-trust app can only take on the permissions already assigned to a given user by supplying that user's identity. The remote app is responsible for determining the correct user to emulate. This may be as simple as returning the same logged in user name provided by SharePoint in the original request.

While the setup and security considerations of a high-trust app may seem daunting, many of these configurations only have to be performed once for each SharePoint farm. A high-trust app can be thought of as any provider-hosted app where both the SharePoint app web and the remote web reside inside the organization's firewall.

Tokens

Throughout this discussion, we have mentioned several types of tokens that are issued and passed between the components of an app and SharePoint. Let's take a closer look at the types of tokens and how they are used.

At its most fundamental level, a token is just a piece of data that has been encrypted using a token issuer's certificate. The contents of the token depend on the purpose of the token. The tokens used by SharePoint use the Security Assertion Markup Language (SAML) to represent the claims being made by the token. SAML defines XML documents that are encrypted and passed as tokens. An application receiving the token uses the token issuer's public certificate to decrypt the information in the token and use it to perform the necessary actions.

Tokens are only useful when the party receiving the token *trusts* the token issuer. The mechanism for establishing trust between an application and the issuer varies, but two applications that trust the same issuer can exchange tokens from that issuer and trust that the information contained in them is valid.

Identity (or User) Tokens

A user token (a.k.a. identity token) identifies the authenticated user and any groups or roles they belong to as verified by the issuer. The issuer is responsible for accepting and verifying the user's credentials. Therefore, the application receiving the token does not need to have access to the user's credentials, but only needs to trust an identity provider that does. In Figure 1-15, both the requesting application and the resource owner trust a common identity provider, thus allowing access.

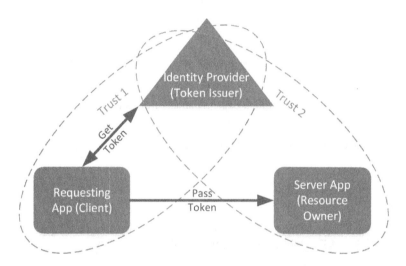

Figure 1-15. *User tokens*

In an on-premise deployment, user authentication can be done using Windows Active Directory or some other provider. The resulting identity information is then converted into an identity token for use by SharePoint. In the Azure and Office 365 cloud, the Microsoft Online Directory Service (MSODS) acts as the identity provider. By creating trusts between an on-premise Active Directory domain and MSODS, you can create hybrid scenarios where claims can be passed between environments enabling apps to pass control seamlessly between environments.

Server-to-Server Tokens (SharePoint)

A server-to-server token allows a remote web site to access resources within a SharePoint server farm. As discussed in the previous section, "*High-Trust Apps*," SharePoint can be configured to issue these tokens by installing a shared certificate and configuring a trusted high-trust app (see Figure 1-16).

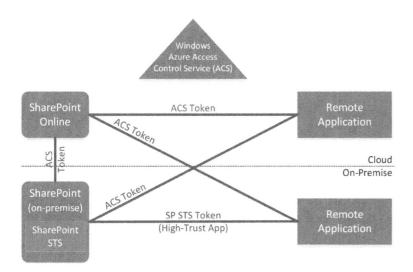

Figure 1-16. *Server-to-server (S2S) tokens*

Server-to-Server Tokens (ACS)

When accessing SharePoint resources from any other server, where either SharePoint or the remote application are in the cloud, an OAuth server-to-server token is required. Therefore, the Windows Azure Access Control Service (ACS) is used to make these connections possible, as shown in Figure 1-16.

The token issued contains information about the server making the request and the user on whose behalf the request is being made. The SharePoint server performs all of the usual permission checks before granting access. While the token contains user information, this is not a user token. In the Azure cloud, only MSODS issues identity tokens, not ACS.

Context Tokens

A *context token* contains information about the context of a request from a client browser to a remote component of an app. This information includes the user's identity token and the SharePoint web being accessed.

When SharePoint renders a page and discovers that part of the page, like a client web part, is going to be served by an app and the connection is using the Windows Azure Access Control Service (ACS), SharePoint makes a call into ACS to create a context token. The context token is then passed to the remote app page in the request.

■ **TIP**   If the request does not use ACS, then no context token is provided. This is the case in a high-trust app. The remote web site is responsible for constructing its own context token in this case.

The remote web can then extract the user and location information from the token and use the context token to construct access tokens (see the following section, "Access Tokens"). The context token is generated when the app is first launched. It can be cached for later use but it will expire after 12 hours and must be regenerated at that time.

Cache Key Value

The context token contains a valuable piece of data that should be understood. This is the *cache key value.* The cache key value is an encoded string that can be used to uniquely identify the user's session for an application. It is composed of the following:

- The user's login name

- The identity provider's ID that issued the identity

- The app's unique ID

- The realm

■ **Note**   Realm is a concept that is equivalent to a web application in a traditional SharePoint deployment or a tenant in a hosted deployment.

The combination of these keys provides a unique value that can be used to cache information for an app's users. This cache could be in memory, in a database, or elsewhere. Note that the cache key is unique to a user, an app, and a realm. If the same user uses the same app deployed to two different SharePoint sites in the same realm, they will share the same cache key. If the data must be cached separately by site, consider including the site ID in the key used to cache the information.

Refresh Tokens

A *refresh token* is a token contained in the context token. This token can be used to access resources on the SharePoint site. The refresh token is good for six months, which means it can be stored in a cookie or database to allow later resource requests back to SharePoint.

Access Tokens

When a remote web needs to make a request back into the SharePoint server farm, it creates an *access token.*

To create the token, the app extracts the refresh token from the context token it received from SharePoint. It adds the app's client ID and client secret value to the request, which is then sent to ACS. ACS creates the access token and returns it to the app, as shown in Figure 1-17. Remember, high-trust apps don't use ACS and must create their own tokens.

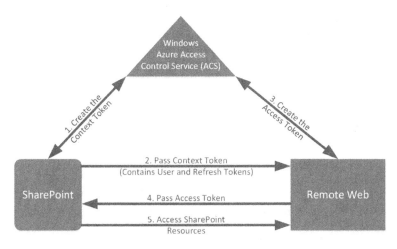

Figure 1-17. *Tokens passed to access resources with ACS*

___

■ **Note**   The client ID is assigned when the app is registered in the SharePoint Store. In the case of an app that will not be published to the store, a client ID can be generated locally by SharePoint.

___

An access token is good for a few hours. It is passed to SharePoint along with the web service or CSOM requests made by the app. The access token ensures SharePoint that the request came from the actual app component and not a hostile server on the Internet.

The access token can be cached but must be stored securely since anyone possessing a valid access token can access resources on the SharePoint server. An alternative is to cache only the context or refresh token and obtain a new access token with each new request or session.

Benefits of the Cloud App Model

Now that we have examined the components of a cloud app, let's consider how these apps benefit developers and users as compared to full-trust and sandboxed solutions.

One of the biggest complaints that many developers had about previous versions of SharePoint was the lack of sophisticated development tools. These tools include things like graphical designers for components such as web parts, features, and manifests. Over time, partial solutions to these issues have been rolled into SharePoint Designer and Visual Studio, but developing applications for the SharePoint platform has remained very different from developing non-SharePoint solutions on the Microsoft stack. With the Cloud App Model, developing solutions for SharePoint is now very similar to building Office apps, Windows Runtime apps or Windows Phone apps. Using Internet standards such as HTML and JavaScript along with web services has provided a common programming model throughout the platform.

The use of client-side code and the distribution of apps across the network has provided a boost to the scalability and reliability of SharePoint apps that has been very difficult to attain in previous versions of SharePoint. Using open standards like OAuth and REST to access SharePoint resources allows apps to be designed for performance and security without sacrificing a common development pattern or limiting functionality. The ability to mix and match app deployment and hosting strategies has enabled app designers a greater flexibility to use the technologies best suited to each part of their application. Instead of trying to find a means of fitting their solution into SharePoint's architecture, developers can now adopt the architecture that makes the most sense for their application.

The Cloud App Model's cloud-centric approach enables developers to leverage the infrastructure investments of Microsoft and other cloud vendors without reinventing their applications for each platform. Using the same model when developing Office apps also reduces the overhead and integration efforts for rich enterprise app development. Building apps for SharePoint allows developers to reuse standard components across complex sets of applications in a consistent manner.

Classroom Online Sample App

Throughout this book, we will build a sample SharePoint app that will demonstrate the concepts and techniques introduced in each chapter. The application will be called *Classroom Online*. This app will allow a SharePoint site to be used to host college classes that are taught online for students anywhere in the world. Our sample will be used by a fictional private college named *Underhill University*.

The students of Underhill ("The Fighting Hobbits") will be assigned to courses that will each be given a SharePoint site. This site will support discussion groups, assignment turn-in, grading, and any other activities needed for the class. Over the course of the book, we will add components to the application that demonstrate various techniques.

■ **Note**   The code for each of these exercises, as well as complete source code for the finished project, is available from the Source Code/Download area of the Apress web site (http://www.apress.com/source-code).

When writing a sample application for a book like this there is always a trade-off between demonstrating all of the various techniques and creating a complete, functional program using best practices. Creating a real commercial-ready app would require a lot more than 400 pages of explanation and probably wouldn't cover everything we need to cover. As a result, we ask your indulgence if, from time to time, we seem to go off on a tangent that leads to a dead end or do things in a way that doesn't seem optimal. We will also tend to avoid a lot of extensive exception handling, as that type of code tends to obscure the core techniques being presented. Each chapter is intended to describe certain topics, but in order to create a functional sample at each step, we will sometimes have to use techniques we have not described in depth yet. We will try to reference other chapters and describe what we are doing well enough for the current exercise to make sense. Just remember that the primary purpose of the sample app is to teach.

The Classroom Online app will be designed for deployment as an autohosted app. It will have local SharePoint host and app webs and a remotely deployed ASP.NET web site. Figure 1-18 depicts the major components that we will build throughout this book.

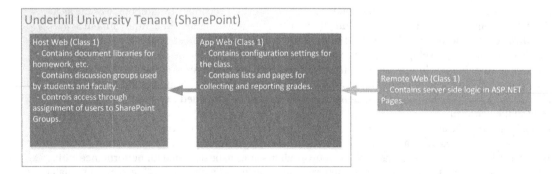

Figure 1-18. Classroom Online high-level design

The scenario used will be a college that has purchased the Classroom Online app from the SharePoint Store. They will deploy it to SharePoint Online although it could also be used on-premise, if desired.

Each classroom will have a host site in SharePoint. This will be used by the teacher, other staff members, and the students in the class. It will contain document libraries and discussion groups for carrying on the work of the course.

To create a classroom site, a tenant administrator will take the following steps:

1. Create a new web site within the Underhill University tenant in SharePoint Online.

2. Create one SharePoint group for the faculty and staff, and another for the students taking the class.

3. Install the Classroom Online app to the site.

4. Configure settings for the class such as the title, course number, and so on.

The students will then be given the URL for the site and instructed how to log in. The host web will expose menus and instructions to help the students understand what is required for the course. This may include menus, custom actions, web parts, or other user interface components.

The app web for the site will contain the course configuration and gradebook. The remote web application will contain other pages used to maintain the site.

Summary

In this chapter, we have explored the new SharePoint application model at a high level. We have reviewed the differences between the new model and the full-trust and sandbox solutions available in previous versions of SharePoint. We have discussed the use of the SharePoint app model in the cloud and in hybrid scenarios. Finally, we have laid out the plan for creating our sample classroom application throughout the remainder of this book.

Now, we will start building our first SharePoint apps. We will start by creating a set of projects and simple components to begin building out our sample app. Then we will learn to deploy and debug an app in SharePoint 2013.

CHAPTER 2

■ ■ ■

Creating and Debugging Apps

In this chapter, we will introduce the development experience for creating SharePoint apps. In traditional SharePoint development, all of the components are created in assemblies and solution packages that are deployed on the SharePoint server farm. In SharePoint apps, the components are distributed more like components in a client-server or service-oriented architecture. This makes developing and debugging these types of components significantly different from SharePoint programming in the past. In this chapter, we will go over the following points:

- The options available for creating a SharePoint app development environment.

- How to use the Napa Office 365 Development Tools to create a simple SharePoint app.

- How to create the same app using Visual Studio 2012.

- How to create some basic components in the app and deploy it to SharePoint.

- The basics of debugging app components in Visual Studio 2012.

Setting Up Your Development Environment

The first step in developing any software application is choosing the tools to use. In the case of SharePoint apps, there are multiple layers of tools to be considered, which we will go over in the following sections.

Choosing a Set of APIs

Before beginning to write code for our app, we need to make a few technical decisions. These decisions will drive our choice of tools and techniques.

First, we need to decide on the overall architecture of our app. In Chapter 1, we described these at a high-level, and in later chapters we will discuss them in more detail. For now, just remember the following considerations:

- ***SharePoint-Hosted***—All components in this type of app reside within a SharePoint web site. No server-side code of any kind is permitted. All logic must reside in the client layer.

- ***Auto-Hosted***—This type of app has both a SharePoint app web containing items, such as lists and libraries, and a remote web site containing ASP.NET pages that can contain server-side code. As a result, both client and server technologies are available. The deployment of the remote web site is automated by SharePoint using the Azure cloud. Each instance of the app will have its own app and remote webs.

- ***Provider-Hosted***—This type of app has both app and remote webs just as an auto-hosted app does. In this case, the remote web is centrally hosted by the app's vendor. The location of this site is hard-coded into the app when it is distributed and it is shared by all users of the app.

Second, we must choose our client-side libraries. Most SharePoint apps, even those that rely on a remote ASP.NET web site, will have some browser-based logic. Technologies like HTML, JavaScript, and Cascading Style Sheets are a given, but there are additional libraries to be considered. The SharePoint 2013 app templates come with the JQuery library already included. In this book, we have also chosen to use the Knockout library for data-binding as well. These will be described in more detail in Chapter 4.

To access the SharePoint server farm's resources, we will use either one of the Client-Side Object Model (CSOM) libraries or the Representational State Transfer (REST) protocol. These will be discussed in Chapters 5 and 7, respectively.

Finally, when creating more sophisticated apps that require some server-side logic, we will need to choose an ASP.NET programming language. Unlike in the browser where JavaScript is the only real choice, creating remote web sites that will form part of our app structure provides many options. If desired, we can even use non-Microsoft platforms for these since their integration with SharePoint is built on published standards. If we stick with the Microsoft stack, our best language choices are VB.NET and C# since these are the languages in which the SharePoint 2013 project templates are available. For our examples, we will use C#.

Now that we have identified the basic architecture components we will need to use, we can begin constructing an environment in which to code, package, and debug our app.

Choosing a Development Tool

Writing a SharePoint app involves creating several different types of artifacts and packaging these components into a deployable format. The tools that support creating these items typically run on a client computer (a desktop or a laptop) and connect to a SharePoint environment (one or more servers) for deployment and testing. Microsoft provides two development tools for this purpose: Visual Studio and Napa.

Visual Studio 2012 is the current version of Microsoft's flagship Integrated Development Environment (IDE). Visual Studio (VS) is the Swiss-army knife of development suites for the Microsoft platform. VS is a full-featured code editor, compiler, and debugger. *The Microsoft Office Developer Tools for Visual Studio 2012* are a set of project templates and object design components that are loaded as an add-on to Visual Studio. With these tools installed, most of the artifacts to be created for SharePoint can be designed easily without resorting to hand-coding of XML configuration files as has been necessary in the past. Visual Studio is available in several editions with varying capabilities. To create apps for SharePoint, you will need to be using either the Professional, Premium, or Ultimate edition.

■ **Tip** The Microsoft Office Developer Tools for Visual Studio 2012 are available as a free download from Microsoft at http://aka.ms/OfficeDevToolsForVS2012.

The Napa Office 365 Development Tools are a recent addition to the Microsoft platform. Napa allows the developer to work directly inside the browser without installing any client tools on their desktop. Napa is actually a provider-hosted SharePoint App that is installed into a SharePoint web site to support development. In addition to SharePoint apps, Napa can be used to create apps for other Office applications, such as Excel.

Table 2-1 contains a comparison of these tools. For applications that only require SharePoint artifacts, such as pages, lists, and libraries along with client-side code, Napa is a simple web-based tool that is available for free from the SharePoint Store. For developers that need integrated debugging or the ability to create server-side code for provider or auto-hosted apps, Visual Studio is the better choice.

Table 2-1. *Comparison of Visual Studio 2012 and Napa Office Development Tools*

	Visual Studio	Napa
Create SharePoint apps	Yes	Yes
Create Office apps	Yes	Yes
Create SharePoint-hosted apps	Yes	Yes
Create provider-hosted apps	Yes	No
Create auto-hosted apps	Yes	No
Interactive debugger	Yes	No
Web-based interface	No	Yes
FREE!	No	Yes

As a final consideration, remember that any app written in Napa can be instantly converted to a Visual Studio project by selecting the "Open in Visual Studio" icon within the Napa user interface. Also, because SharePoint apps are based on generally accepted web standards, such as HTML, JavaScript, Cascading Style Sheets, and web services, there are many additional tools, from Microsoft and other vendors, which can be used to create the components that go into an app.

Later in this chapter, we will introduce creating an app in Napa and then convert it into a Visual Studio project. This will be the beginning of the Classroom Online application that we will extend throughout the rest of this book.

Choosing a Target SharePoint Environment

In order to test our apps, we will need a SharePoint farm in which to deploy and debug them. The choices, with some variations, are either an on-premise or an online farm.

An on-premise farm is a traditional SharePoint Server deployment where all of the SharePoint components are installed and configured by hand. The servers in the farm can be physical computer systems or virtual systems running under Hyper-V or another virtualization system like VMWare. Do not forget to consider the deployment of one or more SQL Server database servers as well in this scenario.

Another option is to create a set of virtual servers in an *Infrastructure-as-a-Service (IaaS)* cloud, like Microsoft's Windows Azure, and deploy SharePoint Server there. SharePoint servers are now fully supported within Azure and can be quickly deployed using the Quick Start gallery of server images. Despite residing in the cloud, SharePoint servers deployed using IaaS in Windows Azure are still "on-premise" since they reside outside of SharePoint Online. An on-premise deployment provides great flexibility in the configuration of the farm at the expense of requiring support from an organization's IT staff.

■ **Caution**   SharePoint 2010 supports a development environment where both Visual Studio and SharePoint Server can run on a client operating system such as Windows 7 or 8. SharePoint 2013 does not support this type of configuration. To do SharePoint 2013 development on a single system, that system must run a server OS such as Windows Server 2008 Release 2 or Windows Server 2012.

An online farm provides a more limited environment in which to deploy and debug apps. SharePoint Online, which is part of Office 365, provides the basis for online deployments. These environments can be shared or dedicated. In a shared environment, each organization is a tenant on a shared server farm. In a dedicated environment, a large organization can rent an entire farm for its own use, but that farm is still managed by the cloud. Dedicated deployments are more flexible than shared deployments because more types of solutions can be supported without endangering other tenants. Shared environments are more cost-effective for small and medium organizations.

The good news is that as long as you are only building SharePoint apps, there is no pressing reason to pick one type of deployment over the other. This is because the Cloud App Model was designed for the cloud. The only need for an on-premise, or dedicated online, deployment would be if there is a need to create full-trust or sandboxed solutions. Another reason to use an on-premise deployment would be to use features of SharePoint 2013 Server that are not available in SharePoint Online, such as PerformancePoint Services. The examples in this book were created using a developer account in SharePoint Online, but they will work equally well using a local deployment of SharePoint.

Deploying the Developer Site Template

Whether we are creating our app with Napa or Visual Studio, we will need a SharePoint site to host it. SharePoint 2013 includes a new site collection template specifically for developing apps. In either SharePoint 2013 or SharePoint Online, create a new site collection and select the Developer Site Template, as shown in Figure 2-1.

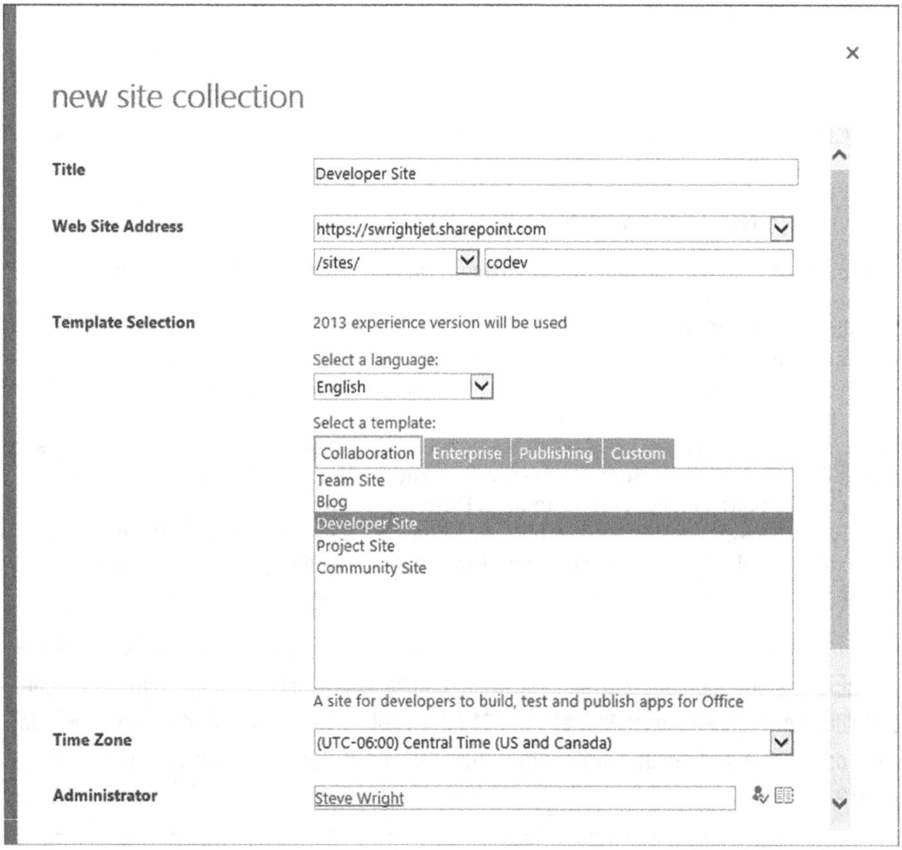

Figure 2-1. *Creating a developer site*

The site created with this template will support side-loading of apps with either Napa or Visual Studio. This feature enables the direct deployment of apps without going through an App Catalog. Even in SharePoint Online, this site collection template allows for full debugging in Visual Studio.

Creating Apps with Napa

The first tool we will explore is the Napa Office 365 Development Tools.

EXERCISE 2-1

In this exercise, we will deploy Napa to our development site and create a simple app that will be the starting point for our Classroom Online app. To illustrate the Napa development environment, we will create the app project and customize the app's default page.

We will deploy the Napa tools to the site, and will create the app using the SharePoint-Hosted template. We will also update the default page with images and links.

1. Open your Developer Site in a web browser.

2. Click on the link titled "Build an app" (see Figure 2-2).

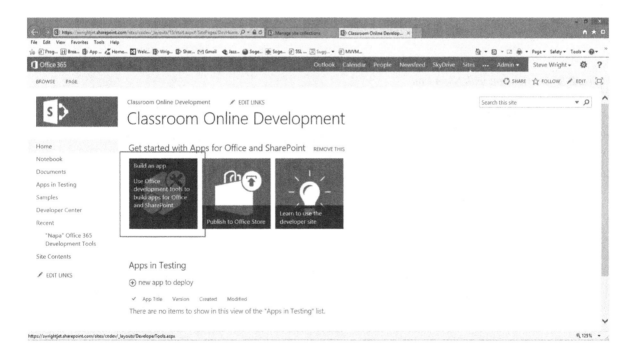

Figure 2-2. *Install Napa tools*

3. Your browser will be redirected to the SharePoint Store page for Napa. It is free, so just click Add It.

4. Click Trust It on the next dialog.

5. On the Site Contents page, you will see the Napa icon. It may take a few minutes to completely install (see Figure 2-3). When it is finished, click the icon.

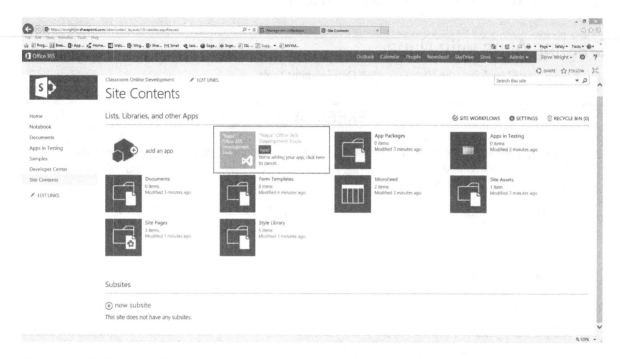

Figure 2-3. *Site Contents with Napa icon*

6. Click on the Add New Project tile.

7. Select App for SharePoint and set the project name to `ClassroomOnline`, as in Figure 2-4.

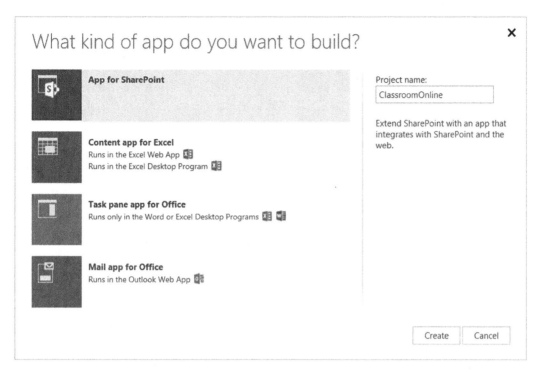

Figure 2-4. *Add New Project dialog in Napa*

8.   Click the Create button.

The new project created contains five items:

- **App.css**—This file is an empty style sheet for the project.

- **AppIcon.png**—This is a default icon for the app.

- **ClientWebPart.aspx**—This is a page that can be displayed inside a web part on a page in the developer site.

- **Default.aspx**—This file is the default page for the app.

- **App.js**—This JavaScript file contains some sample client-side code (see Figure 2-5).

Figure 2-5. *The default app created by Napa*

If you were to run this app right now, it would display a page with the message "Hello" followed by the name of the current user.

9. Select `Default.aspx` under `Pages` in the left-hand menu.

This is the ASPX markup for the default page. Note that there are no server-side code blocks. They are not allowed on this page. Only server controls are present. Specifically, there are three content controls.

- **PlaceHolderAdditionalPageHead**—Anything put in this placeholder will be placed in the `<head>` of the page. This is where JavaScript and CSS files are included in the page.

- **PlaceHolderPageTitleInTitleArea**—The contents of this control appear in the page's title area.

- **PlaceHolderMain**—This is the main content area where the user interface for the app will reside.

We will start by customizing the `Default.aspx` page with some branding elements for our app.

10. Replace "Page Title" with "Classroom Online" in the `PlaceHolderPageTitleInTitleArea` content area.

11. Replace the `<div>` tag in the `PlaceHolderMain` content area with the following markup:

```
<div id="menu">
  <ul>
    <li><a href="../Lists/Configuration Values">Site Configuration</a></li>
    <li><a href="../Lists/Site Assets">Site Assets</a></li>
  </ul>
</div>
```

12. Select the Images folder in the menu.

13. Select the menu icon to open the menu.

14. Click Upload.

15. Select the AppLogo.png file that is included in the files that can be downloaded from this book, available from the Source Code/Download area of the Apress web site (www.apress.com).

16. Open the App.js file under Scripts in the menu.

17. Replace the contents of the file with the following:

```
$(document).ready(function () {
    $('.ms-siteicon-img').attr('src','../Images/AppLogo.png');
});
```

This will replace the SharePoint logo on the page with the Classroom Online logo.

18. Click on the triangle in the menu to the lower-left side of the page.

This will compile, package, and run the app. It should look like Figure 2-6.

Figure 2-6. *The Classroom Online default page*

At this point, we have created a simple app in Napa and customized its user interface.

Creating Apps in Visual Studio 2012

In the next exercise, we will move our app into Visual Studio 2012 where we can use additional designers to create more sophisticated components for our app. You need to have Visual Studio 2012 Professional, Premium, or Ultimate installed on your local computer. You will also need to have installed the Office Developer Tools for Visual Studio 2012. These can be downloaded from http://msdn.microsoft.com/en-us/office/apps/fp123627.

EXERCISE 2-2

In this exercise, we will move the app we created in Napa into Visual Studio. Then we will continue adding components to Classroom Online.

First we will open the Napa app created in Exercise 2-1 in Visual Studio 2012. We will then add the Site Asset and Configuration Value lists, and add JavaScript code to the home page to load the organization's name and logo from the configuration list. We will also configure the site to include the organization's name and logo image.

1. If not already open, open the app from Exercise 2-1 in Napa.

2. Click on the Open in Visual Studio link in the lower-left Napa menu. This is the fourth item from the bottom of the page and includes the Visual Studio logo.

3. If your browser asks, allow it to run the `ProjectLauncher` executable from the site. This will trigger Visual Studio.

■ **Tip**   If you have User Account Control enabled on your desktop, a warning message will pop up at this point asking if you want to allow this program to open. This happens because Visual Studio is being opened *"as an Administrator."* This is necessary when developing SharePoint apps because of the need to deploy apps to the SharePoint environment.

---

4. When Visual Studio launches, you will see that the files from your project are available, plus several others that were not visible in Napa.

5. Since we will not be using the client web part that was created with the project, right-click on the `ClientWebPart` item in the Solution Explorer and select Delete.

6. Do the same to delete the `ClientWebPart1.aspx` page under the `Pages` folder.

7. Right-click on the `ClassroomOnline` project item and select Add ➤ New Item....

8. Select the List item and set the name to `SiteAssets`. (see Figure 2-7).

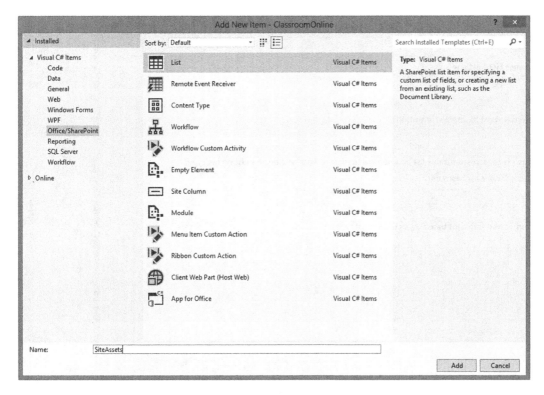

Figure 2-7. *Add New Item dialog*

9. Click the Add button.

10. Set the display name to `Site Assets`.

11. Select the second option (Create a non-customizable list based on an existing list type of:) and set the selection to Asset Library (see Figure 2-8).

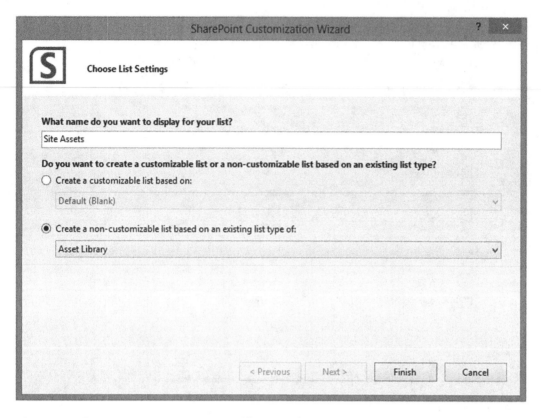

Figure 2-8. SharePoint Customization Wizard (Site Assets)

12.   Click the Finish button.

13.   In the resulting designer form, set the description to "This library stores images and other files for use within the site."

14.   Save and close the `Site Assets` list designer.

15.   Right-click on `ClassroomOnline` project item and select Add ➤ New Item....

16.   Select the List item and set the name to `ConfigurationValues`.

17.   Click Add.

18.   Set the display name to `Configuration Values`.

19.   Leave the other default settings and click Finish.

20.   In the resulting designer form, add a second column to the list called `Value`. Leave the type as Single Line of Text, and the required flag unchecked.

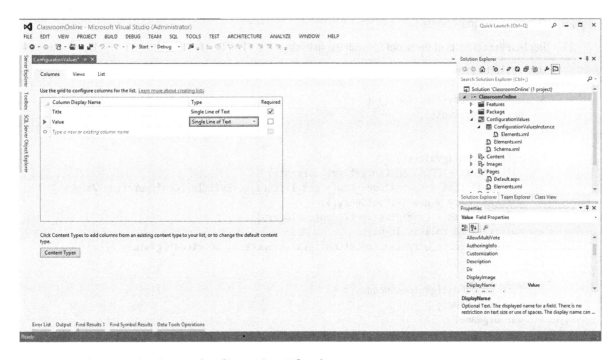

Figure 2-9. *SharePoint list designer (Configuration Values)*

21. Save and close the Configuration Values list designer.

The Configuration Values list will contain values that will enable the owner of the application to configure it for their own environment. For the purposes of this exercise, we will add two items into the list as it is created.

22. Expand the ConfigurationValues list in the Solution Explorer.

23. Expand the ConfigurationValuesInstance item.

24. Double-click the Elements.xml file to open it in the code editor.

25. Insert the following code immediately after the <ListInstance> opening tag, but before the </ListInstance> closing tag:

```
<Data>
  <Rows>
    <Row>
      <Field Name="Title">OrganizationName</Field>
      <Field Name="Value"></Field>
    </Row>
    <Row>
      <Field Name="Title">OrganizationLogoUrl</Field>
      <Field Name="Value"></Field>
    </Row>
  </Rows>
</Data>
```

Classroom Online uses the entries in the ConfigurationValues list to customize the app. We need to add some code to the App.js file to take advantage of these values.

26. Open `App.js` under `Scripts`.

27. Replace the contents of the script file with the following:

```
var collListItems;

$(document).ready(function () {
    getConfigValues();
});

function getConfigValues() {
    var context = SP.ClientContext.get_current();
    var configList = context.get_web().get_lists().getByTitle('Configuration Values');
    var camlQuery = new SP.CamlQuery();
    collListItems = configList.getItems(camlQuery);
    context.load(collListItems);
    context.executeQueryAsync(onGetConfigValuesSuccess, onGetConfigValuesFail);
}

function onGetConfigValuesSuccess() {
    var OrgLogoUrl;
    var OrgName;
    var listItemEnumerator = collListItems.getEnumerator();

    while (listItemEnumerator.moveNext()) {
        var oListItem = listItemEnumerator.get_current();
        var current = oListItem.get_item('Title');
        switch (current) {
            case 'OrganizationName':
                OrgName = oListItem.get_item('Value');
                break;
            case 'OrganizationLogoUrl':
                OrgLogoUrl = oListItem.get_item('Value');
                break;
        };
    }

    if (OrgName && OrgName.length > 0) {
        $('#DeltaPlaceHolderPageTitleInTitleArea').html(OrgName);
        $('.ms-siteicon-img').attr('title', OrgName);
    }

    if (OrgLogoUrl && OrgLogoUrl.length > 0)
        $('.ms-siteicon-img').attr('src', OrgLogoUrl);
    else
        $('.ms-siteicon-img').attr('src', '../Images/AppLogo.png');
}

function onGetConfigValuesFail(sender, args) {
    alert('Failed to get the Configuration Values. Error:' + args.get_message());
}
```

The getConfigValues() function loads all items from the Configuration Values list and passes the results to onGetConfigValuesSuccess() function. This function iterates through the collection of list items and updates the user interface accordingly. The calls being made to retrieve the items will be described in Chapter 5.

28.   Press F5 to run your application in debug mode. Visual Studio will package your application and deploy it to your development environment (see Figure 2-10).

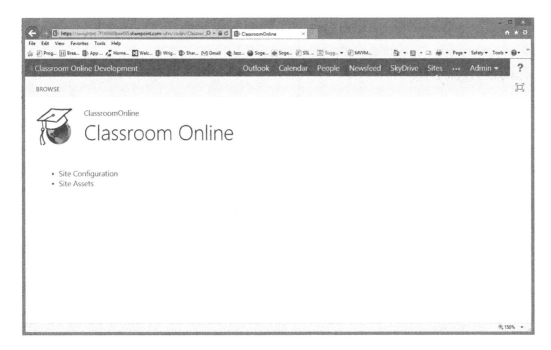

Figure 2-10. *Classroom Online*

The university name and logo are not showing up because the configuration values are empty. We need to set the configuration of the site so that it knows the name and logo of the organization.

29.   With the application running, click on the Site Assets link.

30.   Click on New Item.

31.   When the upload dialog appears, browse to the UULogo.png file on your computer. This is one of the files available for download from the Source Code/Download area of the Apress web site (www.apress.com).

32.   Press OK.

33.   When the logo file is finished uploading, you can set a title and click Save.

34.   You will see a listing of the files in the library. Hover over the UULogo.png file and click on the ellipsis (…) icon.

35.   The item's Edit Control Block (ECB) will open and the file's URL will be displayed. Copy the URL to your clipboard and close the dialog box.

36. Go back to the home page by clicking on the SharePoint App Site Icon at the top of the page.

37. Click on the Site Configuration link.

38. Find the `OrganizationLogoUrl` item and select Edit Item from the context menu.

39. When the edit form opens, paste the URL you copied into the `Value` field.

40. Click Save.

41. Find the `OrganizationName` item and select Edit Item from the context menu.

42. When the edit form opens, type "Underhill University" into the `Value` field.

43. Click Save (see Figure 2-11).

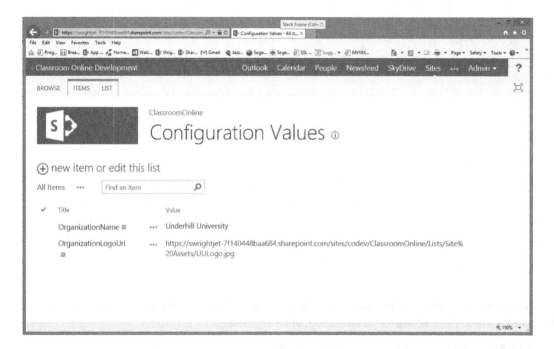

Figure 2-11. *Site configuration list*

44. Go back to the app's home page and you will see that the UI has been updated (see Figure 2-12).

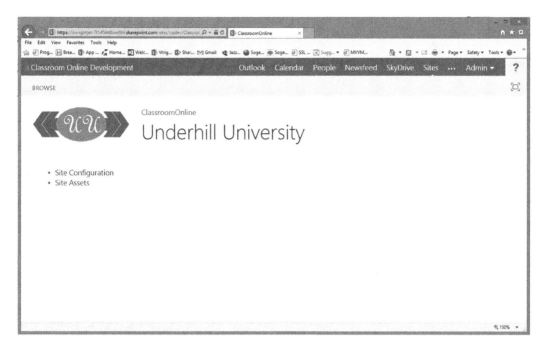

Figure 2-12. *Configured site home page*

Try working with the debugger while the app is running. Open the App.js file in Visual Studio and set a breakpoint somewhere in the JavaScript. When you refresh the web page and the code runs, you will see Visual Studio break in the code at that point.

Consider that what you are debugging is client-side code running in your web browser. You can also debug server-side code in a remote web site when that site is running in Visual Studio as well. This makes debugging SharePoint apps much easier than debugging SharePoint full-trust solutions has ever been.

We have now created a simple app that allows us to store information and customize the user interface to some extent. One thing you will notice is that when you shut down the application and run it again, the configuration information you entered in the previous exercise is gone. This is because the Site Asset library and Configuration Values list both reside in the Classroom Online app web. The app web is destroyed when the app is uninstalled, as is the case whenever you stop debugging. If we had intended the data in these lists to survive, we would have to have created them in the host web where the app was installed. This is certainly possible, but it requires additional permissions and coding techniques that we will cover in Chapters 5 and 6, respectively.

Summary

Microsoft has created a very flexible platform to develop web applications for SharePoint. It allows web developers to leverage their existing development skills, such as HTML and JavaScript, to create solutions for SharePoint. In this chapter, you learned how to set up a development environment in Visual Studio 2012 or the Napa Office 365 Development Tools. We also walked through debugging an app in Visual Studio.

In the next chapter, we will learn how to manage the app life cycle. The life cycle of an app, or any software, includes creation, deployment, installation, updating, and removal. We will examine how these stages apply to SharePoint apps and how we, as developers, can make our apps fit seamlessly into SharePoint.

CHAPTER 3

■ ■ ■

Managing the App Life Cycle

Now that you have created the next killer app, what next? You need to distribute the app to potential users and customers. Microsoft provides a framework for deploying, updating, and removing your apps from a central App Catalog or from the SharePoint Online Store. In this chapter, we will discuss the different options you have as an app developer for managing the life cycle of your app. Our exercises will guide you through the initial deployment and an update of our Online Classroom app. In this chapter, we will go over the following points:

- The stages in the app life cycle that must be planned for and implemented.
- How SharePoint apps are packaged for distribution.
- How to distribute your apps to users within your organization or in the cloud.
- The controls available to manage the installation and removal of the app from a SharePoint web site.
- How updates to an app can be handled smoothly across the Internet without losing the user's data.

Life Cycle Overview

When creating any software product, there are a set of phases that the product must go through to be successful. The same holds true for a SharePoint app. In full-trust or sandboxed solutions, these phases are managed by a farm or site collection administrator, respectively. The Cloud App Model was designed to allow individual site owners to manage the installation and removal of apps without intervention from a user with administrative privileges.

Figure 3-1 illustrates the phases of an app's life cycle. These phases will be described briefly here and in more detail throughout the rest of this chapter.

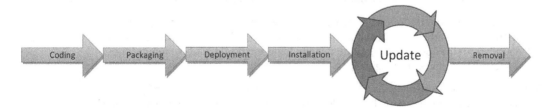

Figure 3-1. App life cycle phases

- *Coding*—As we saw in Chapter 2, SharePoint apps are coded using a development tool such as Visual Studio. Most professionally produced apps will be done using Visual Studio. Some internally developed apps within an organization may use Napa, but managing the full app life cycle is best done using the full Visual Studio toolset.

- *Packaging*—Packaging, also known as *publishing*, an app refers to the process of compiling the app's components into a structured deployment file that has an app manifest and an .APP file name extension.

- *Deployment*—Deployment is the process of copying the app package file to a distribution point. This is will be either the SharePoint Store or a private App Catalog.

- *Installation*—Installation occurs when a user goes to the SharePoint Store or App Catalog and requests that the app be installed in a particular SharePoint web site.

- *Update*—Like any software product, apps need to be updated from time to time. The update process is designed to allow the components of an app to be updated without adversely impacting the data stored in sites where the app is already installed. The update process is depicted as a circle in Figure 3-1 because it includes its own coding, packaging, deployment, and installation phases, and may occur multiple times over the lifetime of an app.

- *Removal*—Also called *uninstallation*, this process happens when a user requests that the app be removed from a web site. This has the effect of removing any artifacts that the app installed in the SharePoint host web along with the entire app web and, optionally, any auto-hosted remote web site associated with the app.

There is an additional term that should be understood with regard to the life cycle of an app. *Acquisition* refers to the process of taking possession of an app from the SharePoint Store. Acquiring an app may be as simple as adding it to a web site, as we did with the Napa tools in the Chapter 2. In reality, this involves two processes. The first makes the app available in the organization's App Catalog and the second installs the app on the web site. In a situation where the organization has placed controls on the deployment of new apps, there may be an approval process involved. The organization may have to deal with allocating funds or licenses for new apps that are requested. This workflow is managed by the App Catalog site collection template.

App Packaging

Once you have developed your app, and before you deploy it to the Office Store or an App Catalog, you need to package your app for deployment. You create the package using Visual Studio 2012 and the SharePoint Development Tools for Visual Studio 2012 add-in.

At a high level, the packaging process is as follows:

1. Using Visual Studio, you will use the **publishing** wizard to create your app package file.

2. For provider-hosted apps only, the wizard will request the information necessary to publish the app properly. This will include the URL of the provider-hosted remote web site and identifiers for the app to allow communication between the app and the remote site. This is referred to as the *publishing profile*.

3. Visual Studio generates all of the files necessary to publish your app. You can find your deployment package in the `app.publish` folder under your project's output folder (usually called bin). For example: `%UserProfile%\Documents\Visual Studio 2012\Projects\ClassroomOnline\bin\Debug\app.publish\1.0.0.0\ClassroomOnline.app`

4. In addition to the `.app` file for the app itself, this folder will contain deployment files for the remote web site for an auto-hosted or provider-hosted app.

EXERCISE 3.1

In this exercise, you will create a package to deploy the Classroom Online app to the Office Store or an App Catalog.

1. Open your project in Visual Studio 2012.

2. In the Solution Explorer, right-click on the project and select **Publish** (see Figure 3-2).

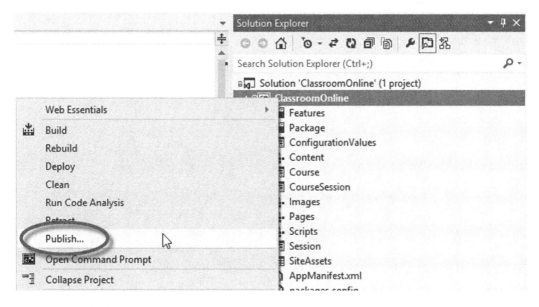

Figure 3-2. Publish menu

3. When the **publishing wizard** (see Figure 3-3) opens, you will only see one page because this is a SharePoint-hosted app.

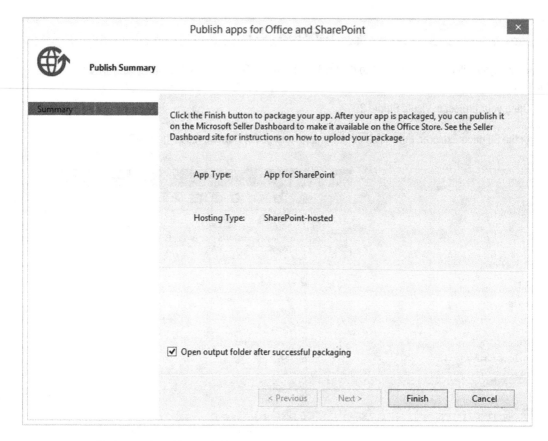

Figure 3-3. *Publish apps for Office and SharePoint wizard*

4.   Click the Finish button.

When the output folder opens, you will see the `ClassroomOnline.app` package. This is the file that you will upload to the Office Store or App Catalog.

Distribution

To enable users to acquire your app, it needs to be deployed to a central location. SharePoint 2013 provides two different locations to deploy your app:

- **Private App Catalog**—You can publish your apps to an internal instance of the SharePoint App Catalog site collection template to make them available only to users within your organization.

- **Office Store**—The Office Store, sometimes called the SharePoint Store, is a publically available app store for SharePoint. Once apps are deployed to the store, they can be acquired by users of any SharePoint deployment across the Internet.

Publishing to a Private App Catalog

An App Catalog is a special site collection within a web application or tenant in SharePoint 2013. Because a farm can contain more than one tenant, it can also have more than one App Catalog.

When you create an App Catalog you get two predefined libraries: *Apps for SharePoint* and *Apps for Office*. As their names imply, one is for managing SharePoint apps and the other is for Office apps. The App Catalog also contains the workflow for managing user requests for new apps and a link for accessing the SharePoint Store.

In an on-premise SharePoint installation, you create the App Catalog from SharePoint Central Administration. A farm administrator must first enable app management within the SharePoint farm. Then, selecting the Manage App Catalog link in Central Administration will trigger a wizard for creating a new App Catalog. For SharePoint Online, the App Catalog is created from the Office 365 Admin Site in a similar manner. While we will use an Office 365 tenant in our example, the process is essentially the same in an on-premise SharePoint deployment.

EXERCISE 3.2

In this exercise, we will use the Admin Site of our Office 365 Developer site to create a private App Catalog and then upload our Classroom Online app to it.

1. Sign in to your Office 365 Developer Site.

2. Select **Admin ➤ SharePoint** in the Office 365 menu (see Figure 3-4).

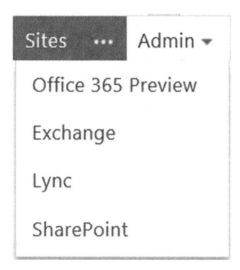

Figure 3-4. *Office 365 Admin menu*

3. When the SharePoint admin center opens (see Figure 3-5), click on **apps in the left-hand menu**. On the right-hand side, click on the **App Catalog** link to start the **New App Catalog** wizard.

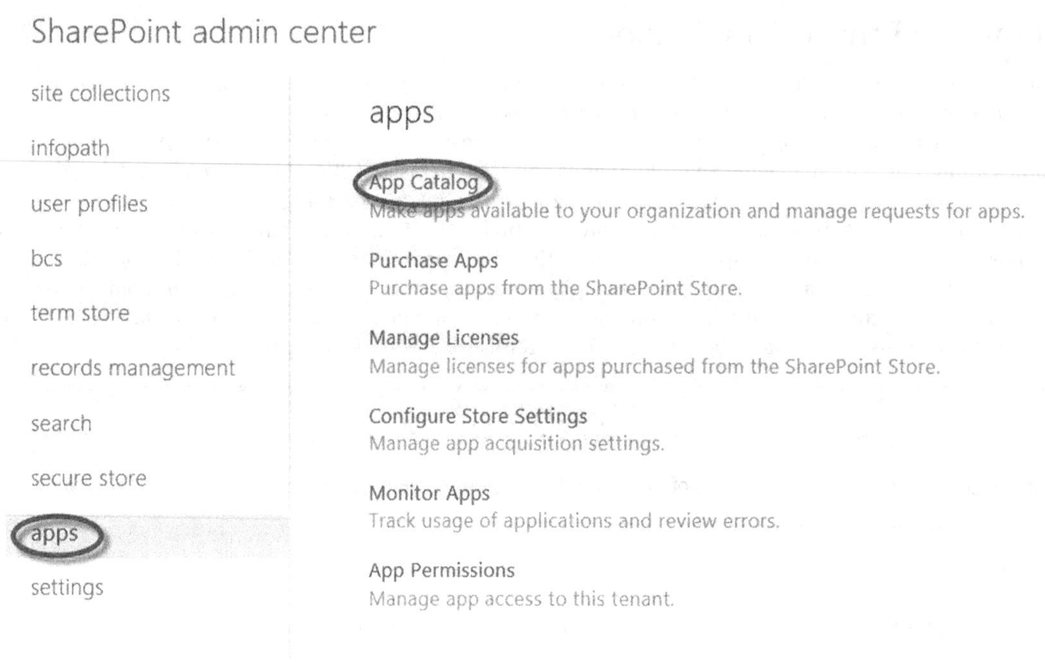

SharePoint admin center

site collections	**apps**
infopath	
user profiles	**App Catalog**
	Make apps available to your organization and manage requests for apps.
bcs	**Purchase Apps**
	Purchase apps from the SharePoint Store.
term store	
	Manage Licenses
records management	Manage licenses for apps purchased from the SharePoint Store.
search	**Configure Store Settings**
	Manage app acquisition settings.
secure store	
	Monitor Apps
apps	Track usage of applications and review errors.
settings	**App Permissions**
	Manage app access to this tenant.

Figure 3-5. App Catalog link in SharePoint admin center

4.   When the App Catalog Site dialog box opens, select **Create a new App Catalog site** (see Figure 3-6) and click the OK button.

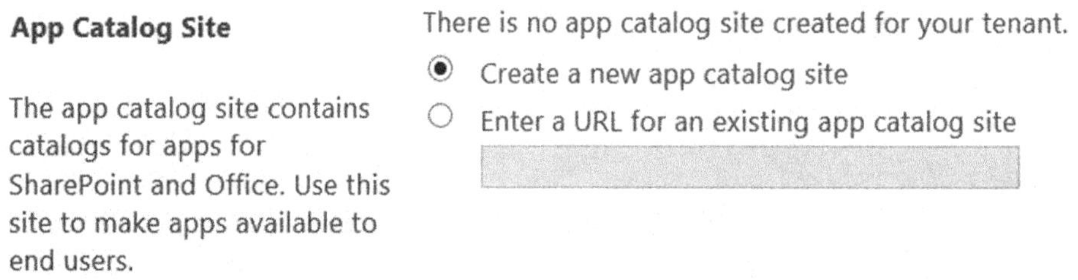

App Catalog Site

The app catalog site contains catalogs for apps for SharePoint and Office. Use this site to make apps available to end users.

There is no app catalog site created for your tenant.

◉   Create a new app catalog site

○   Enter a URL for an existing app catalog site

Figure 3-6. New App Catalog Site dialog

5.   On the **Create App Catalog Site Collection** screen, complete the form (see Figure 3-7).

Create App Catalog Site Collection

Title	App Catalog for SharePoint Online Developer Site
Web Site Address	http://www.prosharepointdeveloper.com ∨
	/sites/ ∨ appcatalog
Language Selection	Select a language: English ∨
Time Zone	(UTC-06:00) Central Time (US and Canada) ∨
Administrator	Administrator
Storage Quota	2000 MB of 15450 MB available
Server Resource Quota	300 resources of 800 resources available

OK   Cancel

Figure 3-7. *Create App Catalog Site Collection screen*

6. Click OK.

7. When the site collection is created, click on the App Catalog site collection link.

Look around your new App Catalog. As illustrated in Figure 3-8, there are three tiles that allow you to perform the basic functions of the App Catalog.

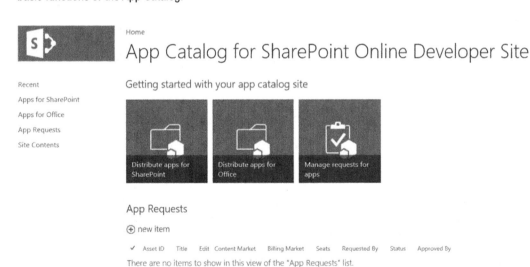

Figure 3-8. *App Catalog home page*

- *Distribute apps for SharePoint*—This link takes you to a library used to manage the SharePoint app packages in the catalog.

- *Distribute apps for Office*—This link takes you to a library used to manage the Office app packages in the catalog.

- *Manage requests for apps*—This link allows a tenant administrator to approve or reject end-user requests for new apps.

After your App Catalog is created, you can add your app for distribution.

8. Click on the **Distribute apps for SharePoint tile.**

9. In Windows Explorer, open the output folder from your app project in Visual Studio and locate the ClassroomOnline.app file.

10. There are two ways to upload your app to the library. You can click on +new app and manually upload the app file to the library, or you can drop the app file onto the library where it says "drag files here" (see Figure 3-9).

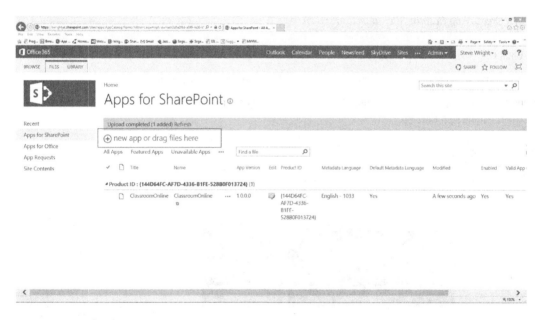

Figure 3-9. *Upload your app*

The app is now ready to be installed by your users.

11. Navigate back to your development site in the web browser.

12. Select Site Contents from the left-hand side menu.

13. Click on the add an app tile (see Figure 3-10).

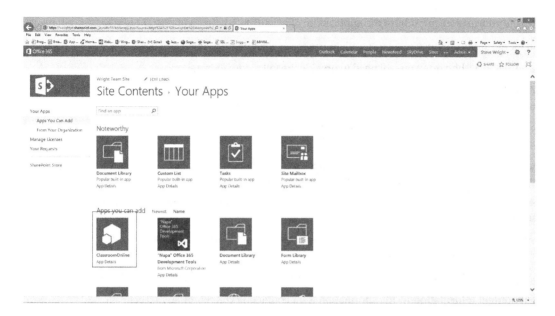

Figure 3-10. *Add an app*

14. Click on the ClassroomOnline tile. This tile appears because Classroom Online is present in the App Catalog for the site.

15. In the dialog that appears, click Trust It.

16. After the app has finished loading, click on the app's tile and the default page will appear.

After you have uploaded the app to the App Catalog, your users will be given the opportunity to install the app on their sites. However, since the App Catalog is private to your organization, users of other SharePoint environments will not see it.

Publishing to the Office Store

There are two phases to the process of publishing apps to the Office Store. First, you must establish a relationship with the store by creating a Seller Dashboard. Then, you must upload and configure the app to be distributed. There are separate approval processes that must be completed in each phase.

Creating a Seller Dashboard

To publish your app to the Office Store you must first sign up for a Microsoft seller account. This provides a Microsoft Seller Dashboard, which is the main location for app developers to submit apps for Office and SharePoint. A *seller* can be either an individual developer or a company.

The registration process and information required are somewhat different between the two types of accounts. At a high level, the process is as follows:

1. Collect the required information for the type of account you wish to create.

2. Visit the Seller Dashboard Registration page at
   `https://sellerdashboard.microsoft.com/Registration`.

3. Enter the information and submit the application.

4. Wait for the approval process to be completed and your dashboard to become active.

For *individual* Seller Dashboards, you will need to provide the following information:

- **Microsoft Online Account**—Your MS Online account will be used to log on to the Seller Dashboard.

- **Display Name**—The name to be shown to customers when they view your apps in the Office Store.

- **Logo** —A 96 × 96 pixel image file containing your logo in PNG, JPG, JPEG, or GIF format. The size must be exactly 96 × 96 pixels and the file can be no larger than 250 KB.

- **Web Site URL**—A web site URL associated with your business where customers and potential customers can find information about you.

- **Contact Information**—This information includes the e-mail address, street address, and phone number where your customers can reach you for support.

For a *company* Seller Dashboard, you will need to provide all of the preceding information plus the following items:

- **Legal Contact Information**—This information is for contacting your company's legal representative.

- **Company Reference**—A third party that can verify that you represent the company named and that the company is real and currently active.

After you submit an application for a seller account the application goes through an approval process. The application will be reviewed by representatives of the Office Store. If any problems are found with your application, you will receive an e-mail describing the problem and you will be instructed how to correct and resubmit the application. Some common problems that might result in your application being rejected include the following:

- The individual or company name entered is already in use.

- Microsoft was unable to verify the existence of the company or your authority to act on behalf of your company.

- The size or file format of the logo image submitted was incorrect.

- The web site URL provided is not owned by you or is, for some reason, not appropriate.

- The general quality of the submission is considered poor. This could be because of spelling, grammar, punctuation, or formatting issues.

Submitting Apps to the Office Store

The process for submitting an app to the Office Store is similar to that for creating the Seller Dashboard in the first place.

1. Collect the required information for the app (see the following bulleted list).

2. Log on to the Seller Dashboard web site at `https://sellerdashboard.microsoft.com`.

3. Upload the .APP file to the Seller Dashboard.

4. Enter the app's information.

5. Wait for the approval process to be completed.

The basic information needed to publish an app is as follows:

- App title

- App version and release date

- App client ID and client secret, if applicable

- Pricing information, unless the app will be free

- App logo file

  - Size: Exactly 96 × 96 pixels (< 250 KB)

  - Format: PNG, JPG, JPEG, or GIF

- The .APP package file produced by Visual Studio

- Trial and licensing information

- Screen shots

  - Between one and five are required

  - Size: Exactly 512 × 384 pixels (< 300 KB)

  - Format: PNG, JPG, JPEG or GIF

- Support, privacy, and end-user license agreement (EULA) information

After your application has been saved to your Seller Dashboard, you can submit your app for approval. Note that you will not be able to submit your first app until after your account has been approved. Your app will be evaluated by the Office Store and its personnel. Some of the reasons your app might be rejected include the following:

- The app file was not formatted correctly or included options that are not allowed in Office Store apps, such as the app-only permission policy or features that go beyond the web scope.

- The app is a duplicate, unfinished, or provides no value to the customer.

- Your app includes advertising or add-on features that do not comply with Microsoft's standards.

- Your app may be buggy or incomplete. This may include incompatibilities with certain OS's or devices. Your app must also be usable on touch-only devices.

- Your app cannot include pornography, excessive profanity, or other objectionable content.

There are many other reasons that an app might be rejected. You will need to work with the Office Store through the Seller Dashboard to remediate any problems as they arise. After your app is approved, customers will be able to download it from the store and install it in SharePoint.

Installation

Now that we have deployed our app to an App Catalog, users can request to install it on a SharePoint web site.

When installing, the user will choose whether to install the app with web scope or tenant scope, as described in Chapter 1. Remember that a tenant installation allows the tenant administrator to push the app to a large number of sites, but that all of those sites will share a single app web. In that case, any data stored in the app web would be shared across the tenant sites.

The installation of the app will cause several possible changes to be made in SharePoint. The app will be registered and installed in the host web. The app web will be created in a domain under the host web. Any lists, libraries, content types, or other SharePoint items will be created in the app web. If the app contains an auto-hosted remote web site, that site will be deployed and configured in Windows Azure.

As a final step, SharePoint can optionally invoke a web service in the remote web that can perform any additional updates that are needed. This might include creating a list in the host web, setting permissions, or generating initial configuration data. This web service call is what is known as a *remote event receiver* in SharePoint 2013. In this case, because they are directly associated with the app life cycle, these are known as *app event receivers*. These event receivers provide the opportunity for the developer to inject their own logic into the installation sequence of the app without introducing any server-side code within SharePoint.

EXERCISE 3.3

In this exercise, we update the Classroom Online app to create an installation log. This log will record the installation event in the configuration values list.

First, we will enable app events to create the `AppEventReceiver` web service endpoint. Next, we will add code to the installation event to record the scope of the installation that was performed. Finally, we will walk through deploying and installing the app.

1. Open the Classroom Online solution in Visual Studio.

2. Click on the Classroom Online project in the Solution Explorer.

3. If the Properties pane is not visible, press F4.

4. In Properties, switch the Handle App Installed property from false to true (see Figure 3-11).

Figure 3-11. Enable app events

At this point, a message box will appear saying that Visual Studio needs to create a new web project. This will be an auto-hosted ASP.NET web called `ClassroomOnlineWeb`. The project will include an empty `AppEventReceiver` web service, as shown in Figure 3-12.

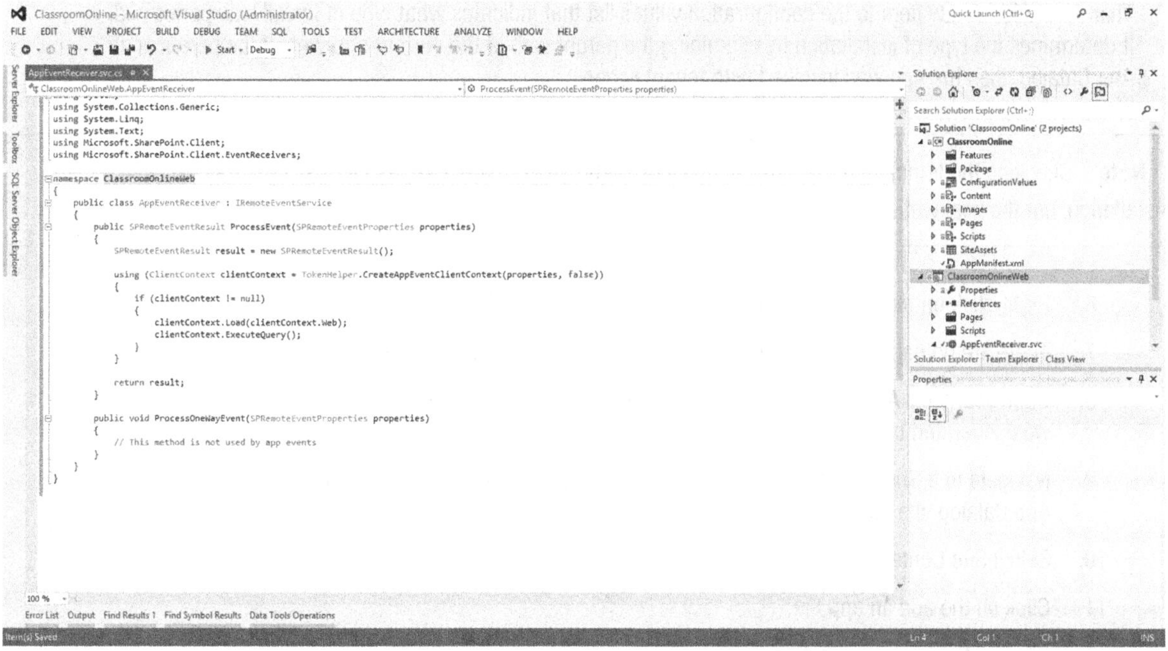

Figure 3-12. *App event receiver template code*

5. Replace the code in ProcessEvent() with the following:

```
SPRemoteEventResult result = new SPRemoteEventResult();

using (ClientContext clientContext
        = TokenHelper.CreateAppEventClientContext(properties, true))
{
    if (clientContext != null)
    {
        WebInformation parentWeb = clientContext.Web.ParentWeb;
        clientContext.Load(parentWeb);
        clientContext.ExecuteQuery();

        List lst = clientContext.Web.Lists.GetByTitle("Configuration Values");
        ListItem item = lst.AddItem(new ListItemCreationInformation());
        item["Title"] = "AppInstalled";
        item["Value"] = (parentWeb.WebTemplate == "APPCATALOG")
                            ? "Tenant Installation" : "Web Installation";
        item.Update();
        clientContext.ExecuteQuery();
    }
}

return result;
```

This code adds a new item to the configuration values list that indicates what type of install was performed. It determines the type of installation by examining the parent web of the current app web. If the parent is an App Catalog, then the app was installed with tenant scope.

■ **Note**   Checking the template of the host web would not be appropriate here, as the app web is shared in a tenant installation, but the host web is not.

---

6. Right-click on the Classroom Online project and select Publish....

7. There are no parameters to set when publishing this type of app, so click Finish.

8. Open your local App Catalog in a web browser and upload the ClassroomOnline.app file that was generated by Visual Studio.

9. Navigate to a SharePoint site within the tenancy associated with the App Catalog, but not the App Catalog site itself.

10. Select Site Contents.

11. Click on the add an app tile.

12. Click on the ClassroomOnline tile.

13. Click the Trust It button.

14. Wait for the app to complete installation.

15. Click on the ClassroomOnline tile in Site Contents.

16. Click on the Site Configuration link.

When the app was installed and after the auto-hosted site was deployed, our remote event receiver was called. As a result, the installation was noted in our configuration list (see Figure 3-13).

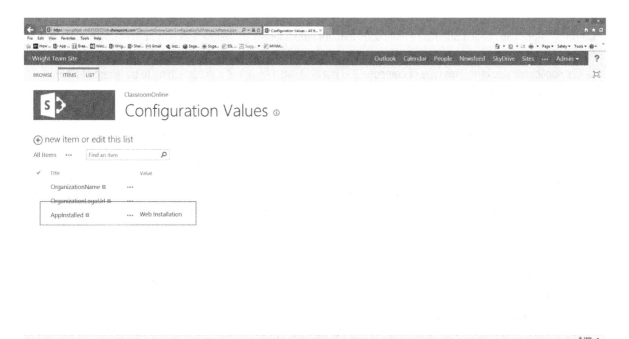

Figure 3-13. *Result of the* AppInstalled *event*

Distributing Updates

Now that our app is in the wild, we need to be able to update it. SharePoint apps are not updated through a service such as Windows Update. There are no hot fixes, patches, or service packs.

To update your app, you need to create a new version of the app and distribute it to the App Catalog or Office Store where it was originally distributed. Within the new app package will be the logic to upgrade any existing artifacts associated with your app. SharePoint can handle many of these tasks itself, such as updating list definitions in the app web or pages in an auto-hosted remote web. Other types of updates may require hand-coded logic.

As was the case with app installation, you can add a remote event receiver to handle custom upgrade logic. That logic can perform specific upgrade tasks, depending on the version of the app that was previously installed. This allows users to skip a few updates without getting locked out of the upgrade path.

There are two pieces of information in the app manifest that control the installation and upgrade process. The *product ID* was generated when your project was created. This is a GUID that can be viewed in the XML of the app manifest. Do not change this value. If you do, SharePoint will not recognize the new version of your app as an upgrade for the previous versions of the app.

The other item is the *version number* for the app. The version number is in standard .NET format: `MajorVersion.MinorVersion.Build.Revision`. By default, the version number is set to 1.0.0.0. When a new version of the app is created, one of these numbers needs to be incremented. This tells SharePoint that the new package is a later version than the old one.

Caution Apps can contain SQL Azure databases that are automatically provisioned as part of the remote web site in an auto-hosted app. In this case, it may be necessary to create additional data manipulation logic as part of a *data-tier application package*. This type of component is not discussed here, but it is something to be aware of when creating a new version of an existing application.

An important consideration when planning for an update is the fact that the *user decides* when to perform an update, not the developer and not SharePoint. Updates are "pulled," not "pushed." In some cases, a tenant administrator can push updates to host webs in a tenant-scoped installation, but the developer has no control over this either. This means that any components that may be accessible by more than one installation, such as a provider-hosted web site, need to be prepared to be accessed by multiple versions of the app at one time. For a large commercial app with thousands of users, this means that you need to maintain backward compatibility as long as any part of the user base has not upgraded.

EXERCISE 3.4

In this exercise, we will update the Classroom Online app that we installed in the previous exercise. Our update will add the ability to record app version upgrades to the installation log in addition to the `AppInstalled` event.

1. Open Visual Studio 2012 and the Classroom Online solution.

2. Click on the Classroom Online project in the Solution Explorer.

3. If the Properties pane is not visible, press F4.

4. In Properties, switch the Handle App Upgraded property from false to true.

5. Open the `AppManifest.xml` file and change the revision version to 1 (see Figure 3-14).

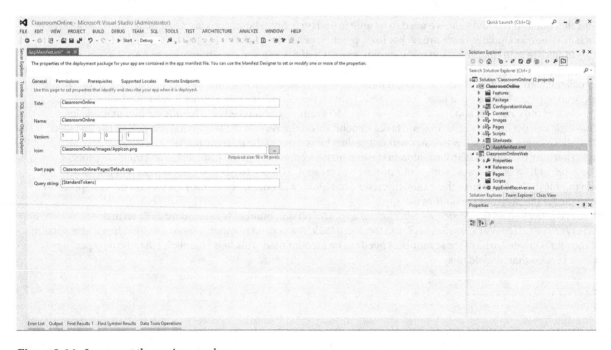

Figure 3-14. Increment the version number

6. Save changes and close the app manifest file.

7. Replace the `ProcessEvent()` method with the following code in the
   `AppEventReceiver.svc.cs`:

```
public SPRemoteEventResult ProcessEvent(SPRemoteEventProperties properties)
{
    switch (properties.EventType)
    {
        case SPRemoteEventType.AppInstalled:
            return ProcessInstallation(properties);
        case SPRemoteEventType.AppUpgraded:
            return ProcessUpgraded(properties);
    }

    return new SPRemoteEventResult();
}

public SPRemoteEventResult ProcessInstallation(SPRemoteEventProperties properties)
{
    SPRemoteEventResult result = new SPRemoteEventResult();

    using (ClientContext clientContext
                = TokenHelper.CreateAppEventClientContext(properties, true))
    {
        if (clientContext != null)
        {
            WebInformation parentWeb = clientContext.Web.ParentWeb;
            clientContext.Load(parentWeb);
            clientContext.ExecuteQuery();

            List lst = clientContext.Web.Lists.GetByTitle("Configuration Values");
            ListItem item = lst.AddItem(new ListItemCreationInformation());
            item["Title"] = "AppInstalled";
            item["Value"] = (parentWeb.WebTemplate == "APPCATALOG")
                                ? "Tenant Installation" : "Web Installation";
            item.Update();
            clientContext.ExecuteQuery();
        }
    }

    return result;
}

private SPRemoteEventResult ProcessUpgraded(SPRemoteEventProperties properties)
{
    SPRemoteEventResult result = new SPRemoteEventResult();
```

```
            using (ClientContext clientContext
                        = TokenHelper.CreateAppEventClientContext(properties, true))
        {
            if (clientContext != null)
            {
                List lst = clientContext.Web.Lists.GetByTitle("Configuration Values");
                ListItem item = lst.AddItem(new ListItemCreationInformation());
                item["Title"] = "AppUpgraded";
                item["Value"] = "Upgraded "
                            + properties.AppEventProperties.PreviousVersion.ToString()
                            + " to " + properties.AppEventProperties.Version.ToString();
                item.Update();
                clientContext.ExecuteQuery();
            }
        }

        return result;
    }
```

This code has been restructured to handle both the AppInstalled and AppUpgraded events. In the case of an upgrade, the app will record the version numbers before and after the upgrade.

8. Right-click on the Classroom Online project and select Publish....

9. Click Finish.

10. Open your App Catalog in a web browser and upload the ClassroomOnline.app file that is generated by Visual Studio. *Be sure to get the file from the version 1.0.0.1 folder, not the 1.0.0.0 folder.*

11. Navigate to the same SharePoint site where version 1.0.0.0 of Classroom Online is already installed.

12. Select Site Contents.

13. Open the Edit Control Block for the Classroom Online app and select About.

14. You should see the message "There is a new version of this app. Get it now."

15. Click the GET IT button.

16. You will be asked to trust the app again. Click Trust It to begin the upgrade.

17. Wait for the app to complete the upgrade.

18. Click on the ClassroomOnline tile in Site Contents.

19. Click on the Site Configuration link (see Figure 3-15).

When the user chooses to install the upgrade for the app, the upgrade event will be triggered in the event receiver.

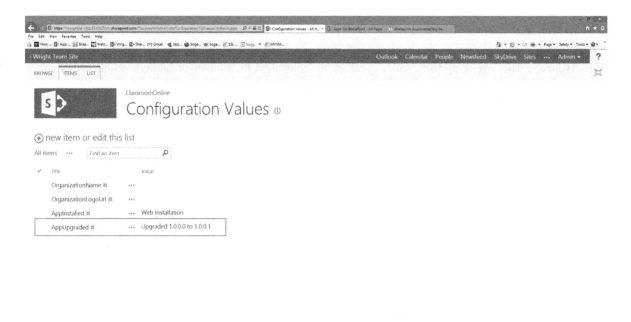

Figure 3-15. *Upgrade completed*

Uninstallation

Site owners can choose to uninstall an instance of an app for SharePoint. Uninstallation of the app occurs cleanly. Everything that is installed by the app is removed through the uninstall process. This includes the app web and all its contents, any client web parts deployed by the app, and the remote web site in the case of an auto-hosted app. Any data stored in the host web is left intact.

The technique for injecting code into the uninstall sequence is the same as for installation and updates. Just turn on the Handle App Uninstalling property for the app and add logic to the AppEventReceiver web service to perform any actions needed.

■ **Note**   There is one important difference between uninstallation and the previous two types of events. AppInstalled and AppUpgraded are both performed *after* the corresponding action. AppUninstalling occurs *before* the app is removed. This makes sense if you consider that calling this event receiver after the remote web site has been deleted would be impossible.

Summary

Writing an app is just the beginning. As you have seen, Microsoft provides a framework for managing the entire life cycle of your app. The developer can control the packaging, deployment, installation, updating, and uninstallation of the app. For internally developed and distributed apps, the App Catalog template provides all the tools needed to manage your organization's apps. When moving to the cloud and selling your apps online, the Microsoft Office Store (SharePoint Store) provides a secure, managed means to distribute your apps without investing in expensive marketing and e-commerce applications.

In the next chapter, we will take a look at how we can use client-side technologies, such as JavaScript and JQuery, to create application logic that presents a rich user experience while interacting with the host SharePoint server.

CHAPTER 4

■ ■ ■

Client-Side Logic with JavaScript

Now that we know how to create and deploy simple apps, we need to start building more sophisticated user experiences. In this chapter, we will explore the technologies that are going to help us create rich web apps that run without depending on server-side logic for routine user interface tasks. This code will run in the user's web browser and will be written in JavaScript. In this chapter, we will go over the following points:

- How JavaScript supports object-oriented programming without being strongly typed.

- How to use the JQuery library to create simpler, more efficient JavaScript code while manipulating the HTML DOM.

- Why the Model-View-ViewModel (MVVM) pattern is a good choice for developing user interface code for SharePoint apps.

- How to use the Knockout library to create web UXs that leverage data binding and the MVVM pattern.

Welcome to the Client Side

Creating SharePoint apps requires learning some new techniques that might be unfamiliar. If you have been creating SharePoint Server solutions for previous releases, then you are probably comfortable writing code that runs in ASP. NET web controls. These could be in ASCX files (a.k.a. custom controls or visual web parts) with code-behind files, or they could be C# or VB.NET classes that derive directly from the control classes in the .NET Framework. Neither of these techniques is appropriate for creating apps for SharePoint 2013 because they rely on server-side code to load, validate, and save their data.

Most web developers have used JavaScript at some point. For many, it may have been to avoid round-trips to the server or to prevent page refreshes. Client-side code has always had the advantage of speed over doing the same thing on the server. If your experience with JavaScript is limited, you may not have really dived into the details of JavaScript or some of its supporting libraries.

Over the past few years, several JavaScript libraries have been introduced as open source projects that encapsulate common functionality used in web-based applications. These libraries have simplified the use of JavaScript significantly. In this chapter, we will introduce two such libraries, which will be used throughout the rest of this book. These are jQuery and Knockout. jQuery is included in the SharePoint 2013 templates provided by Microsoft for Visual Studio 2012. Knockout is a library that handles data binding in JavaScript. While we will use these extensively throughout this book, it is important to remember that they are not required for building SharePoint apps. You may use whatever libraries you are comfortable with, or none at all.

If you built solutions for SharePoint Server 2010, then you may be familiar with the Client-Side Object Model (CSOM) libraries that were introduced with that product. The JavaScript version of this library allows developers to access SharePoint resources from inside a web browser. CSOM is designed to provide efficient batching of requests to reduce the load on SharePoint and latency for the client browser. The SharePoint 2013 version of the CSOM has been expanded quite a bit to allow a client-side code to perform any action that would be appropriate for an app to perform. There are some APIs that are still only available in the server-side model, but these are functions that would only be needed by SharePoint solutions running in full-trust mode.

This chapter assumes that the developer has a working understanding of JavaScript language syntax and the HTML Document Object Model (DOM). If this is not the case, it is strongly recommended that you familiarize yourself with these before continuing on through this book. These are the keys to client-side programming and you cannot build non-trivial SharePoint apps without them.

We will start by looking at some of the more advanced aspects of JavaScript. Specifically, we will explore how JavaScript supports object-oriented programming. Then, we will describe the jQuery library that is the basis of most of the code samples in this book. We will then describe the Model-View-ViewModel (MVVM) pattern and how to implement effective data-oriented HTML pages using MVVM and the Knockout library.

Using Advanced JavaScript Concepts

Anyone who has done any web development has probably done some simple JavaScript tasks, such as setting properties on DOM objects or responding to events. For example, the HTML page shown in Listing 4-1 simply displays some text on a page and then uses JavaScript to change some of that text.

Listing 4-1. A Simple HTML Page Containing Script

```
<!DOCTYPE html PUBLIC "-//W3C//DTD XHTML 1.0 Strict//EN"
"http://www.w3.org/TR/xhtml1/DTD/xhtml1-strict.dtd">
<html>
<body>
    <div>
        <h1>The Joy of JavaScript!!!</h1>
        <p>Lorem ipsum dolor sit amet, consectetur adipiscing elit.</p>
        <ol>
            <li>Pellentesque quis justo a orci euismod accumsan. </li>
            <li>Mauris eu purus ligula, ac pellentesque augue.</li>
            <li>Fusce non metus eu libero feugiat luctus. </li>
            <li>Maecenas volutpat varius nunc, et sagittis neque euismod quis.</li>
        </ol>
    </div>

<script type="text/javascript">

    // Set some text in a DOM element.
    document.getElementsByTagName('li')[1].innerText = "This is my text.";

</script>

</body>
</html>
```

If you copy this HTML into a text file and view it in a browser, it looks like Figure 4-1. The second bullet in the list has been changed by the script using the DOM.

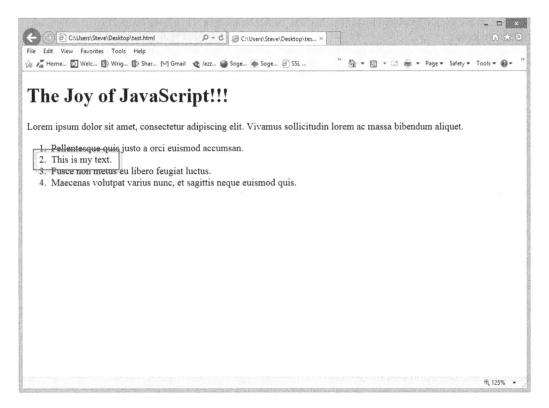

Figure 4-1. *A simple page in the browser*

We will use a simple text file like this one to demonstrate all of the JavaScript in this chapter. You will notice that we do not need to use Visual Studio or SharePoint in order to explore JavaScript coding because it is all built into the browser.

■ **Note** JavaScript, as used in web browsers, is actually a standard language called ECMAScript. Various browser implementations support their own variations from the standard. We will try to stick to the ECMAScript standard as much as possible since this will allow our code to run in any modern browser. jQuery and Knockout will also help to shield us from non-standard implementations of JavaScript.

Creating JavaScript Objects

JavaScript's support for object-oriented programming is somewhat different than that found in strongly typed, compiled languages like C# or VB.NET. Specifically, JavaScript does not define "classes" as are used in most object environments. JavaScript uses "prototypes" instead. We will discuss some of the intricacies of prototypes in the next section. For now, we will look at some generic objects without using prototypes explicitly.

Objects in JavaScript are similar to object instances in class-based languages. They have properties to store data and methods to perform logic.

EXERCISE 4-1

In this exercise, we will add some JavaScript to the simple HTML page we looked at before. Since it can be difficult to understand the structure of objects in JavaScript, we will use the Internet Explorer debugger to examine the objects as we create them.

■ **Note** The complete code for each of the examples in this chapter is available from the Source Code/Download area of the Apress web site (http://www.apress.com/source-code).

---

1. Download or type in the code from Listing 4-1.

2. Add the following code to the script block.

   ```
   // Create identical empty objects.
   var o1 = new Object();
   var o2 = {};
   ```

3. Save the file and load it into Internet Explorer.

4. Press F12 to open the debugger.

■ **Note** If you are using a browser other than Internet Explorer, you may need to download an add-on, such as FireBug for Firefox, before you can follow these steps.

The debugger opens and displays the DOM tree by default (see Figure 4-2).

Figure 4-2. *The Internet Explorer debugger window*

We need to see the values of local JavaScript variables, so we need to switch views.

5.   Click on the Script tab on the debugger window.

6.   Select Locals from the options over the right panel.

7.   Find the script line containing var o1 = new Object(); in the panel on the left.

8.   Right-click on that line and select Insert Breakpoint.

9.   Click the Start debugging button over the left panel.

10.   At this point, you will be placed into the debugger at that line. Notice that it is highlighted in yellow. You may need to refresh the page to trigger the breakpoint.

11.   Press F10 to execute the selected line.

In the right-hand panel of the debugger, you will see the variable o1 with its value no longer undefined. The variable now contains an empty object with no custom properties or methods, as shown in Figure 4-3.

Figure 4-3. *IE Debugger Locals window*

12. Click Stop debugging in the debugger window to break out of the code.

Next we will look at some more examples of using objects in JavaScript. You can always use the same technique to view the results in the debugger.

As we just saw, there are two styles of notation that can be used to create objects in JavaScript. You can call new Object() or you can use {}.

The first approach uses a *constructor*. A constructor is simply a JavaScript function that is used to initialize an object. If you have used constructors in class-based languages like C#, then this concept should be familiar to you. The Object() constructor initializes an instance of the base JavaScript object. You can also declare your own constructors to initialize custom objects, as in Listing 4-2. The constructor takes parameters that are used to set properties on the object.

Listing 4-2. A Constructor

```
// Create a template for creating objects. This is a 'Constructor'.
function Person(firstName,lastName,heightInches,weight)
{
    var self = this;
    self.firstName = firstName;
    self.lastName = lastName;
    self.heightInches = heightInches;
    self.weight = weight;
}

// Construct a person object.
var personObj = new Person("Steve", "Wright", 72, "None of your business!");
```

Notice that the properties on the Person object are being set without being declared. This is normal in JavaScript. Properties are created as they are used. The keyword this is used to refer to the object being created by the constructor. Using a local variable (self) is common to avoid confusion about what this refers to. Doing so is not required. Once the call is complete, the personObj variable contains a Person object with the given values (see Figure 4-4).

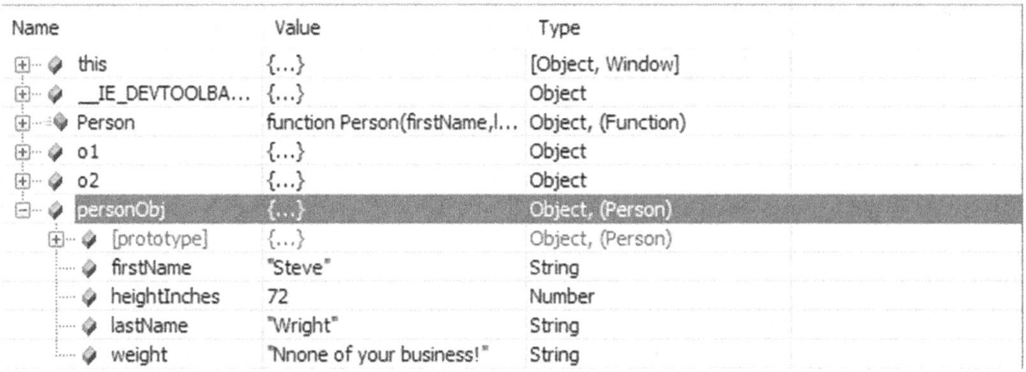

Name	Value	Type
⊞ ◈ this	{...}	[Object, Window]
⊞ ◈ __IE_DEVTOOLBA...	{...}	Object
⊞ ◈ Person	function Person(firstName,l...	Object, (Function)
⊞ ◈ o1	{...}	Object
⊞ ◈ o2	{...}	Object
⊟ ◈ personObj	{...}	Object, (Person)
⊞ ◈ [prototype]	{...}	Object, (Person)
◈ firstName	"Steve"	String
◈ heightInches	72	Number
◈ lastName	"Wright"	String
◈ weight	"Nnone of your business!"	String

Figure 4-4. *Constructed object*

The other way to initialize an object is to use object notation. {} is the simplest form of this notation and represents an empty object. You can also include properties and values, as shown in Listing 4-3.

Listing 4-3. Creating an Object with Object Notation

```
var personObj = {firstName:"David", lastName:"Petersen", heightInches:73.5,
                 weight:"He was a Marine. Don\'t Ask!" };
```

This creates an object, as shown in Figure 4-5.

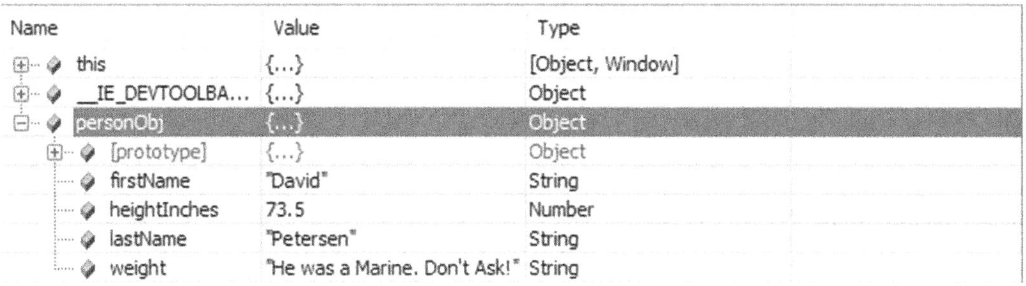

Name	Value	Type
⊞ ◈ this	{...}	[Object, Window]
⊞ ◈ __IE_DEVTOOLBA...	{...}	Object
⊟ ◈ personObj	{...}	Object
⊞ ◈ [prototype]	{...}	Object
◈ firstName	"David"	String
◈ heightInches	73.5	Number
◈ lastName	"Petersen"	String
◈ weight	"He was a Marine. Don't Ask!"	String

Figure 4-5. *Object created with object notation*

We can also declare methods on JavaScript objects that can be called using the data included in the object, as in Listing 4-4. The stretch method updates the heightInches property with a new value, resulting in the object shown in Figure 4-6.

Listing 4-4. Creating a Method on an Object

```
// Create a template for creating objects. This is a 'Constructor'.
function Person(firstName,lastName,heightInches,weight)
{
    var self = this;
    self.firstName = firstName;
    self.lastName = lastName;
    self.heightInches = heightInches;
    self.weight = weight;

    // Declare a method on the constructed objects.
    self.stretch = function(factor) { this.heightInches = this.heightInches * factor; }
}

// Construct a person object and call the method.
var personObj = new Person("Steve", "Wright", 72, "None of your business!");
personObj.stretch(1.3);
```

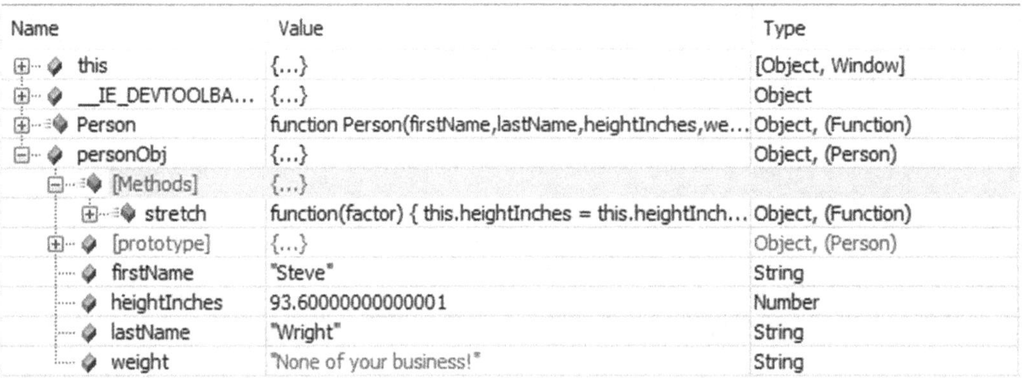

Name	Value	Type
⊞ ◆ this	{...}	[Object, Window]
⊞ ◆ __IE_DEVTOOLBA...	{...}	Object
⊞ ⋮◆ Person	function Person(firstName,lastName,heightInches,we...	Object, (Function)
⊟ ◆ personObj	{...}	Object, (Person)
⊟ ⋮◆ [Methods]	{...}	
⊞ ◆ stretch	function(factor) { this.heightInches = this.heightInch...	Object, (Function)
⊞ ◆ [prototype]	{...}	Object, (Person)
◆ firstName	"Steve"	String
◆ heightInches	93.60000000000001	Number
◆ lastName	"Wright"	String
◆ weight	"None of your business!"	String

Figure 4-6. *Property updated by the* stretch *method*

Prototypes

If you look closely, you will see an important difference between Figure 4-4 and Figure 4-5. The object in the first case has a type of Object, (Person). In the second, it is just Object. The difference is the presence of a *prototype*. A prototype acts as a template for a set of objects in JavaScript. The prototype for an object is determined by the name of the constructor used to create it. If no constructor is used, the object uses the default Object prototype.

Prototypes allow JavaScript to inherit behaviors across a set of related objects, like classes in C#. Prototypes can also be chained to create multiple levels of inheritance, like class hierarchies.

Looking at the code in Listing 4-5, we begin by declaring the Person function as we did before (lines 1–12) and then we create two objects using this constructor (lines 15–16). On line 22, we add another method but we use the prototype property of the Person constructor instead of a specific instance of the object. The prototype property contains a reference to the object's constructor. The person objects, person1 and person2, contain the properties and methods declared directly on them; however, as you can see in Figure 4-7, the Person prototype contains the new method diet.

Listing 4-5. Creating a Prototype

```
1: // Create a template for creating objects. This is a 'Constructor'.
2: function Person(firstName,lastName,heightInches,weight)
3: {
4:     var self = this;
5:     self.firstName = firstName;
6:     self.lastName = lastName;
7:     self.heightInches = heightInches;
8:     self.weight = weight;
9:
10:    // Declare a method on the constructed objects.
11:    self.stretch = function(factor) { this.heightInches = this.heightInches * factor; }
12: }
13:
14: // Construct a person object and call the method.
15: var person1 = new Person("Steve", "Wright", 72, 180);
16: var person2 = new Person("David", "Petersen", 73.5, 175);
17:
18: // This calls a method on the OBJECT, not on the PROTOTYPE.
19: person1.stretch(1.3);
20:
21: // Add a method to the person prototype.
22: Person.prototype.diet = function(factor) { this.weight = this.weight * factor; }
23:
24: // The method is automatically usable from any object using that prototype.
25: person1.diet(0.8);
26: person2.diet(0.8);
27:
28: // true because Person is the contructor we used.
29: alert(person1 instanceof Person);
30:
31: // true because everything is an Object.
32: alert(person1 instanceof Object);
33:
34: // false because String does not exist anywhere in the objects chain.
35: alert(person1 instanceof String);
```

Figure 4-7. *Object inheritance with prototypes*

The stretch method appears directly on the object, not the prototype, because it was added directly to the object in the constructor. The diet method is part of the prototype because it was added to the prototype that originally constructed the object. Prototypes in JavaScripts are objects themselves. The prototype property is really no different from any other. For person1 and person2 it contains a reference to the Person prototype. Since both person1 and person2 refer to the same prototype, when it is updated by adding a method, both objects see the change.

It can be confusing to understand the difference between a constructor and a prototype. In effect, they are the same object that plays two different roles. The Person() function is the constructor for the Person prototype. The Person object is a reference to the Person prototype. Note that Person appears in the debugger as a local variable in Figure 4-7. The best way to understand these concepts is to experiment by writing scripts and examining the objects that result.

JavaScript implements inheritance using the concept of a *prototype chain*. When you call a method on an object, JavaScript has to determine which function to actually call. It does this by walking the object's prototype chain. First, the method is sought on the object itself. If it is found, that version is used. You can always override a prototype's methods by declaring them directly on the object. If the method is not found on the object, the object's prototype object is examined for a method with the same name. If the method is still not found, the prototype's prototype is examined. This process continues until either the method is found or the Object prototype is reached. Object will always be the last prototype in any chain (see Figure 4-8).

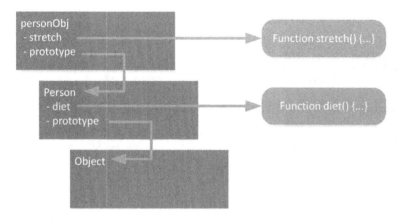

Figure 4-8. *Prototype chains*

The last few lines of Listing 4-5 demonstrate a useful method of examining an object's prototype chain. The instanceof operator is used to scan an object's chain for another object. In our example, the person1 variable refers to an object instance that has a prototype of Person, which has a prototype of Object. Therefore, instanceof returns true when used with parent1 and either Person or Object. It returns false for any other prototype object because it is not in its chain.

Prototypes will be important as we examine the coding pattern that will be used to implement our client-side JavaScript. The Model-View-ViewModel (MVVM) pattern uses objects to provide behavior from one part of the pattern to another, so understanding JavaScript's use of objects is vital.

JavaScript Object Notation (JSON)

The last advanced JavaScript topic we are going to look at involves the object notation we saw in Listing 4-3. JavaScript Object Notation (JSON) is capable of rendering complex object graphs in a simple string format. Because of this simplicity, JSON is one of two major data formats used to pass information on the Internet. The other is the Extensible Markup Language (XML).

XML was created to allow strongly typed data to be passed in an application-independent format. XML is easily parsed by machines and understood by humans, making it a good choice for a data format on the web. Using XML Schema Definition (XSD) or Data Type Definition (DTD) files, XML documents can be validated against a strict set of rules to ensure that they are properly constructed. In fact, the HTML pages rendered by SharePoint use the XHTML notation, which is an HTML document in XML form.

XML does have drawbacks however. Most importantly, XML documents tend to be quite large compared to the data they carry. This is because of the start and end tags and attribute names that have to be repeated over and over again to format the document. Second, while XML can be used in JavaScript, JSON is much easier to work with. Using the JavaScript eval() function, a JSON string received from a web service or other data source can be quickly converted into a set of JavaScript objects in the browser. For these reasons, JSON has become an alternative to XML in many scenarios when communicating across the Internet.

The examples we looked at previously used {} to create an empty object or name-value pairs to create an object with a set of properties. There are more sophisticated structures that can be created as well.

Listing 4-6 is the JSON for an object that has multiple levels and types of structures. The outer object contains three properties: name, numberOfPets and favoriteValues. The last of these is an array as depicted using brackets [ ]. This array contains four elements. The first element is a string. Note that the escape character (\) is needed in order to use a double quote inside a string. The last item is a new object that has two properties of its own: hobby and motorcycle. By nesting objects and arrays, it is possible to create very complex object graphs in JSON.

Listing 4-6. JavaScript Object Notation (JSON)

```
{ "name" : "Steve Wright",
  "numberOfPets" : 2,
  "favoriteValues" :
        [ "Janet says \"Hi\"."
          , 47
          , true
          , { "hobby" : "Woodworking",
              "motorcycle" : "Honda"
            }
        ]
}
```

Look at the differences between Listing 4-3 and Listing 4-6. Notice that the latter example has double quotes around the property names, but the first does not. The reason for this is because the object literal notation used in JavaScript and the JSON standard format are not exactly the same thing. When JavaScript was originally invented, the quotes were not there. As the notation became popular, it was standardized outside of the language as a separate data format. At that time it was named JSON and the quotes were added. They are *valid* in JavaScript, but *not required*. When data is passed into or out of JavaScript using JSON, *the quotes are required*. If you are not sure how the data will be used, or just have a heartfelt love of consistency, you can always use the quotes and never think about it again.

Introducing jQuery

jQuery is an open source library of JavaScript routines that provide a much easier alternative to navigating the HTML DOM. In SharePoint apps, this will allow us to find, alter, and manipulate the user interface using client-side code more effectively than using standard JavaScript alone. Using jQuery is not necessary for creating SharePoint apps, but Microsoft has adopted it for use in the project templates for SharePoint 2013. We will use jQuery throughout this book to simplify the ClassroomOnline app's client code.

The version of jQuery used in the SharePoint 2013 templates is version 1.7.1. You can always use a different version by replacing the library files with a different version. By default, Visual Studio deploys three jQuery files to a new SharePoint app project.

- `jquery-1.7.1.intellisense.js`—This file contains method signature information for Visual Studio's Intellisense feature.

- `jquery-1.7.1.js`—This is the main jQuery library that should be linked to your rendered pages.

- `jquery-1.7.1.min.js`—This is the minimized version of the library. Use this version when releasing your code to production to save download time for your apps. This file is 92 KB as opposed to the non-minimized library's 252 KB.

■ **Tip** You can also link directly to a content distribution network (CDN) that hosts the jQuery files. In this chapter, we will link to `http://code.jQuery.com/jQuery-1.7.1.min.js` since we will not be working with Visual Studio.

---

jQuery is useful for any type of client-side coding, including DOM manipulation, event handing, and web service calls. In SharePoint apps, we will be using SharePoint's libraries for Ajax-style web service calls, and we will use jQuery mostly for DOM and event handling.

In the next section, we will explore the jQuery library to gain a working knowledge of the types of operations we can perform. A complete jQuery tutorial is beyond the scope of this chapter. For complete information, see the jQuery community web site at `http://jquery.com`.

Basic Concepts

jQuery is designed to be incredibly flexible, while also being very simple to use. As a result, you will find that there are a large number of ways to carry out almost any operation. All uses of jQuery follow a similar pattern.

1. Select a set of DOM elements in the current HTML document.

2. Refine the selection.

3. Perform operations on the selected elements.

4. Chain together operations for maximum efficiency.

The first step is to create a *wrapper* or *wrapped set* of elements. Think of this as an object containing an array of references to DOM elements. The wrapper object also defines a wide variety of methods for manipulating the wrapped set. This object is the core of the jQuery system. For example, you could select all of the <P> tags on a page using `var s = jQuery("p");`. The `jQuery()` method searches for all elements in the document that match the selector passed in the parameter string and creates a wrapper object for the results. The jQuery function, and its alias `$()`, are the primary entry points into jQuery.

After selecting an initial set of elements, you will often want to filter within that set or find other tags related to those elements. This refinement updates the list of elements in the wrapper. jQuery also contains many operations for setting the attributes, styles, and contents of HTML DOM elements. These operations allow you to update the content and implement event handlers that create a rich user experience.

■ **Note** The complete API documentation for jQuery can be found at `http://api.jquery.com`.

Searching through the entire DOM object hierarchy can be expensive on a large page. This is the reason for one of jQuery's most valuable coding patterns: *method chaining*. Each method in the jQuery library, with a few exceptions, is designed to be used in a chain with other jQuery methods. To accomplish this, each method returns a wrapped set. In many cases, this is simply the set that was used to execute the method in the first place. For example, the `css()` method is used to set a cascading style sheet property on all of the elements in the wrapped set. Once complete, instead of just returning nothing, it returns the wrapped set so that other methods can be chained to it, as shown in Listing 4-7. In this example, a set of elements is selected, their background is set, and text is added. At each step, the wrapped set is passed down the chain for the next method to use.

Listing 4-7. Chaining jQuery Methods

```
$("p")
    .css("background-color","gray");
    .prepend("This text is added at the beginning of the paragraph. ")
```

Chaining is more than just a way to simplify jQuery code. By maintaining a copy of the wrapper object to be reused, we can avoid performing additional searches of the DOM hierarchy. We can also use methods in our chain that will alter and restore the set of elements selected in the wrapper, allowing nested sequences of operations.

EXERCISE 4-2

In this exercise, we will create an HTML page that includes some simple jQuery operations.

1. Add the following markup to a new HTML file.

■ **Note** You can download the code for this exercise, and all exercises in this book, from the Source Code/Download area of the Apress web site (`http://www.apress.com/source-code`).

```
<!DOCTYPE html PUBLIC "-//W3C//DTD XHTML 1.0 Strict//EN"
"http://www.w3.org/TR/xhtml1/DTD/xhtml1-strict.dtd">
<html>
<head>
    <script type="text/javascript"
            src="http://code.jquery.com/jquery-1.7.1.min.js"></script>
</head>
<body>
    <script type="text/javascript">

    $(document).ready(startProcessing1);
    // Could also be written as:  $(startProcessing1);

    function startProcessing1()
    {
        // Change the background on all <LI> tags to pink.
        jQuery("li").css("background-color","pink");
```

```
        // Get the text in ALL of the the <P> tags and bold them using a chain.
        alert($("p").css("font-weight","bold").text().length);
    }

    </script>

    <h1>The Joy of JavaScript!!!</h1>

    <div>
        <p>Lorem ipsum dolor sit amet, consectetur adipiscing elit. Vivamus sollicitudin
lorem ac massa bibendum aliquet.</p>
        <ol>
            <li>Pellentesque quis justo a orci euismod accumsan. </li>
            <li>Mauris eu purus ligula, ac pellentesque augue.
                <div myattr='findthediv'>
                    <ol>
                        <li>Pellentesque quis justo a orci euismod accumsan. </li>
                        <li class='byclass'>Mauris eu purus ligula, ac pellentesque augue.</li>
                        <li>Fusce non metus eu libero feugiat luctus. </li>
                        <li>Maecenas volutpat varius nunc, et sagittis neque euismod quis.</li>
                    </ol>
                </div>
            </li>
            <li>Fusce non metus eu libero feugiat luctus. </li>
            <li id='byid'>Maecenas volutpat varius nunc, et sagittis neque euismod quis.</li>
        </ol>
    </div>

    <p class='byclass'>Justo a orci euismod accumsan. Mauris eu purus ligula, ac pellentesque
augue.</p>
</body>
</html>
```

At the top of the script block, there is a call to the `ready()` method. This method records a function reference that will be executed when the DOM is finished loading and ready to be processed by jQuery. There is a shortcut for this method that can be used by simply passing a function reference into the `jQuery()` method directly.

2.   View the page.

In the function launched after the document is ready are two statements. The first sets the background color on all of the `<LI>` tags in the document to pink (so pretty). The other emboldens the text in all of the `<P>` tags and then counts the characters in them.

Remember, each method in the chain is applied to *each of the elements* in the wrapped set. The `text()` method returns the text from within the elements as a single concatenated string. The length reported in the alert box is the total number of characters in both paragraphs, as shown in Figure 4-9.

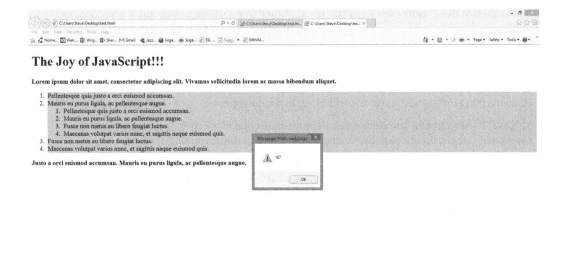

Figure 4-9. *A simple use of jQuery*

Understanding Selectors

Selectors are the strings passed to the jQuery function. They describe which elements are to be selected. Note that it is always DOM elements that are selected, not attributes or any other HTML DOM objects. Selectors can take many forms, as shown in Table 4-1.

Table 4-1. *Forms of jQuery Selectors*

Selector	Search Type	Description
$("*")	All	Selects all of the elements in the document.
$("a")	Tag Name	Selects all of the <A> elements.
$(".hdrtxt")	Class Name	Selects all elements containing the hdrtxt class.
$("#main-menu")	ID	Selects the element with ID="main-menu".
$(document)	DOM Object	Creates a wrapped set containing the HTML DOM object(s) passed in the parameter.
$(selector, context)	Context	Searches using the selector within the context of the results of another selector.
$(":first")	Filter	Filters the results by matching elements against the condition. Returns all of the elements that are first among their sibling elements.
$("*[myattr=value1]")	Attribute	Searches for all elements that have a myattr attribute with a value of value1.

83

In addition to each of these forms, selectors can be combined in many ways to produce sets based on multiple conditions.

- $("a,li,p")—Combines the results of searching for multiple selectors. This example returns all <A>, <LI>, and <P> elements in the document.

- $("li a")—Searches for one element within the subtree of another. This returns all of the <A> elements that exist anywhere within an <LI> tag in the document.

- $("li>a")—Searches for one element as an immediate child of another. This returns all of the <A> elements that exist immediately beneath an <LI> tag in the document.

- $("li.myclass:last[attr1=value1]")—Conditions can be chained together to select more and more specific sets of elements. This example returns all of the <LI> elements that have a class of myclass, an attr1 attribute value of value1 and are the last sibling in their group.

Add the function in Listing 4-8 to the HTML file from Exercise 4-2, and switch the ready() function to use startProcessing2.

Listing 4-8. Selector Samples

```
function startProcessing2()
{
    // Set the first paragraph to normal weight.
    $("p:first").css("font-weight","normal");

    // Set the element with ID=byid.
    $("#byid").text('This is the text set by ID.');

    // Select elements by class.
    $(".byclass").text('This is the text set by class.');
    $("p.byclass").text($("p.byclass").text() + ' And this is on the paragraph!');

    // Use multiple selectors to return ALL matching elements.
    $("#byid,.byclass").css("background-color","yellow");

    // Search for elements based on the document structure.
    $("li ol").css("background-color","red");
    $("ol","li").css("background-color","green");
    $("li>ol").css("background-color","blue");

    // Search for attributes.
    $("*[myattr]")
        .prepend("This text is prepended to the DIV.")
        .css("background-color","gray");
}
```

Running this page results in Figure 4-10.

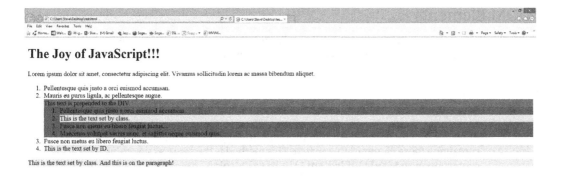

Figure 4-10. *Selector sample page*

The rules being applied by these selectors are as follows:

- `$("#byid").text('This is the text set by ID.');`
  - Finds the list item with `id="byid"`.
- `$(".byclass").text('This is the text set by class.');`
  - Finds both elements with `class="byclass"`.
  - One is a list item and the other is a paragraph.
- `$("p.byclass").text($("p.byclass").text() + ' And this is on the paragraph!');`
  - Finds only the paragraph with `class="byclass"`.
- `$("#byid,.byclass").css("background-color","yellow");`
  - Finds all three elements with `id="byid"` *or* `class="byclass"`.
- `$("li ol").css("background-color","red");`
  - Finds the inner `<OL>` element because it is a descendant of an `<LI>` element.
- `$("ol","li").css("background-color","green");`
  - Finds the same set of elements as the previous line.
- `$("li>ol").css("background-color","blue");`
  - Finds nothing because there are no `<OL>` elements that are direct children of `<LI>` elements.
- `$("*[myattr]").prepend("...").css("background-color","gray");`
  - Finds any tag that has a `myattr` attribute.
  - The value of the attribute does not matter. The attribute just needs to be present.

Querying DOM Elements

The jQuery() method is always the first method in a chain, but other methods can be used to refine the set of elements in the current set. Table 4-2 contains a description of the most common such methods.

Table 4-2. *Common jQuery Query Methods*

Method	Description
.find(sel)	Applies a selector to the descendants of the current wrapped set and returns a new set containing those elements that match. This method is the same as searching with a context because $(sel1).find(sel2) = $(sel2,sel1).
.filter(sel) .filter(func)	Applies a selector, or a function, to each element in the set and returns those that match. Filter() is different from the find() method because filter() only applies to the elements in the set, not to their descendants.
.eq(index)	Returns the element at the index given. Remember, array indexes are 0-based. The first element's index is 0, the second's is 1, and so on.
.slice(start,end)	Returns a subset of the elements in the wrapper based on their indexes. The elements from index start to end (inclusive) are returned.
.end()	Reverses the effect of the last filtering operation. See the following discussion.
.andSelf()	Merges the current wrapped set with the previous set on the result stack. See the following discussion. (This method is being renamed addBack as of jQuery 1.8.)

The end() method deserves further explanation. Whenever a method changes the elements in the wrapped set, it pushes the previous set onto a stack of results associated with the chain (see Figure 4-11). The end() method is used to restore the set to its previous value.

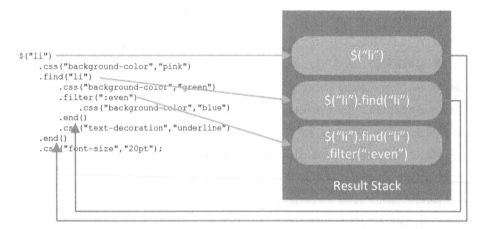

Figure 4-11. *The jQuery result stack*

The use of filters and the end() method allow you to write long chains of method calls that act on varying sets of elements. While this may seem confusing at first, it becomes clearer when you consider that HTML documents and DOM objects are inherently hierarchical in nature. This nested approach allows you to perform hierarchical operations that correspond to the structure of the page.

The addSelf() method is used to merge the top two wrapped sets on the stack. For example, if you wanted to perform an operation against an <OL> element *and* each of the <LI> elements beneath it, you would use $("ol#mylist").filter("li").addSelf() to select that set.

Add the function in Listing 4-9 to the HTML file from Exercise 4-2, and switch the ready() function to use startProcessing3.

Listing 4-9. Filtering Samples

```
function startProcessing3()
{
    // Chain calls and nest filters
    $("li")
        .css("background-color","pink")
        .find("li")
            .css("background-color","green")
            .filter(":even")
                .css("background-color","blue")
            .end()
            .css("text-decoration","underline")
        .end()
        .css("font-size","20pt")
        ;
}
```

Running this page results in Figure 4-12.

The Joy of JavaScript!!!

Lorem ipsum dolor sit amet, consectetur adipiscing elit. Vivamus sollicitudin lorem ac massa bibendum aliquet.

1. Pellentesque quis justo a orci euismod accumsan.
2. Mauris eu purus ligula, ac pellentesque augue.
   1. Pellentesque quis justo a orci euismod accumsan.
   2. Mauris eu purus ligula, ac pellentesque augue.
   3. Fusce non metus eu libero feugiat luctus.
   4. Maecenas volutpat varius nunc, et sagittis neque euismod quis.
3. Fusce non metus eu libero feugiat luctus.
4. Maecenas volutpat varius nunc, et sagittis neque euismod quis.

Justo a orci euismod accumsan. Mauris eu purus ligula, ac pellentesque augue.

Figure 4-12. *jQuery query sample page*

The rules being applied by these queries are as follows:

- $("li").css("background-color","pink")
  - Finds all <LI> tags and colors them pink.

87

- `.find("li").css("background-color","green")`
  - Finds *only* the second level of <LI> tags and colors them green.
- `.filter(":even").css("background-color","blue")`
  - Finds the even numbered (by index, not position) <LI> tags and colors them blue.
  - This includes the first (index=0) and third (index=2) elements in the list.
- `.end().css("text-decoration","underline")`
  - Restores the set containing all of the second level of <LI> tags.
  - The underline is applied to all of the blue and green <LI> tags.
- `.end().css("font-size","20pt")`
  - Restores the set containing all <LI> tags and sets their font size to 20 points.

Traversing the Document

Once a set of elements is selected, it is often necessary to move around the DOM hierarchy to perform operations on different parts of it. jQuery contains many methods designed to make traversing the DOM easier. These make your code more efficient because they provide alternatives to creating new selections that require searching the entire document.

Table 4-3. *Common jQuery DOM Traversal Methods*

Method	Description
`.parent()`	Selects the parent of each element.
`.children()`	Selects all children of each element.
`.siblings()`	Selects all siblings of each element.
`.next()`	Selects the sibling immediately after each element.
`.nextAll()`	Selects *all* siblings after each element.
`.prev()`	Selects the sibling immediately before each element.
`.prevAll()`	Selects *all* siblings before each element.

These methods are fairly self-explanatory. Be sure to remember that the navigation logic for each method is applied to *every member* of the wrapped set. The result is a collection containing all of the resulting elements. See Listing 4-10 for an example.

Listing 4-10. Traversal Samples

```
function startProcessing4()
{
    $("body")
        .children()
        .eq(2)
        .prev()
        .nextAll()
        .eq(0)
        .find("ol ol")
        .parent()
        .css("background-color","black");
}
```

Add the function in Listing 4-10 to the HTML file from Exercise 4-2, and switch the ready() function to use startProcessing4.

Running this page results in Figure 4-13.

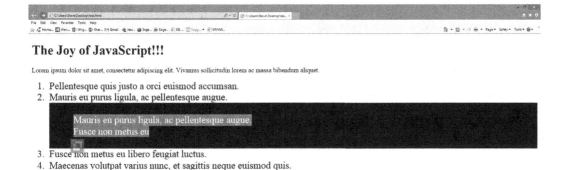

Figure 4-13. *Traversal sample page*

The rules being applied by these filters are as follows:

- $("body")
  - Finds the document's <BODY> tag.
- .children()
  - Finds all immediate children of the <BODY> tag.
  - The set includes: [<SCRIPT>, <H1>, <DIV>, <P>].
- .eq(2)
  - Finds the <DIV> tag at index=2.
- .prev()
  - Finds the <H1> element immediately before the <DIV>.
- .nextAll()
  - Selects the <DIV> and <P> elements.
- .eq(0)
  - Finds the <DIV> tag at index=0.

89

- `.find("ol ol")`
  - Finds the second-level <OL> element within the <DIV>.
- `.parent()`
  - Finds the <DIV> that encloses the <OL>.
  - Note: This is the <DIV> with `myattr='findthediv'`.
- `.css("background-color","black");`
  - Color the entire <OL> element with a `black` background.

Obviously, this is a contrived example. No one would write code to wonder aimlessly through the DOM just to redact an entire list like that. It is easy to go overboard when traversing the DOM with these methods. When possible, try to use a simple selector to reach your destination but, when necessary, these methods can allow you to perform some pretty intricate gyrations through the DOM.

Updating DOM Objects

Selecting, filtering, and traversing the DOM would be fairly pointless if we could not do anything once we got where we were going. jQuery contains methods that allow the programmer to make minor, or major, changes to the page from within JavaScript. We have seen some of these methods in action already. Table 4-4 contains a description of these and some other very useful update methods.

Table 4-4. *jQuery DOM Update Methods*

Method	Description
`.text([value])`	Gets, or sets if `value` is present, the text within an element. Any HTML reserved characters are escaped to make them render as text.
`.val([value])`	Gets or sets the value of an <INPUT> form field.
`.html([value])`	Gets or sets the HTML markup within an element. The markup is converted into DOM objects, as needed.
`.attr([value])`	Gets or sets the value of an attribute.
`.css(prop[, value])`	Gets or sets a CSS style property of the element.
`.hide()`	Makes the selected elements invisible on the page.
`.show()`	Makes the selected elements visible on the page.
`$(htmlstring)`	The jQuery method can be used to parse HTML into a DOM fragment that can then be added to the page.
`.append(domobjs)`	This is a class of methods that adds DOM objects into the structure of a page based on the position of other elements.
	Similar methods include `appendTo()`, `prepend()`, `prependTo()`, `after()`, `before()`, `insertAfter()`, `insertBefore()`, `replaceWith()`, and `replaceAll()`.
`.remove(sel)`	Removes the selected elements, and any descendants, from the DOM hierarchy.
`.clone()`	Creates a deep copy of a DOM hierarchy and returns it. Options include whether to include data values and event handlers in the new copy.

Looping in jQuery

Looping in jQuery is not usually necessary. It is possible to use a normal JavaScript for-loop to cycle through each element in a wrapped set, but there is always a better way. Usually, it is a matter of creating the correct filter or wrapped set before applying an operation. In rare cases, it may be necessary to apply logic to each selected member of a set. In these cases, we can use the each() method.

The each() method takes a function as a parameter. That function is executed for each member of the set. The index and element associated with each call are passed into the function. The function can perform whatever operations are needed on that single element. This is basically like using a JavaScript for statement to loop through the elements in the set. For example, see Listing 4-11.

Listing 4-11. jQuery Looping Sample

```
$("li").each(
    function(index) {
        if (index % 3 == 0)
            $(this).css("background-color","red");
    }
);
```

This code selects all of the <LI> elements in the page and loops through them. For each element, the index is checked to see whether it is divisible by 3. If so, the background is set to red. Within the function, this refers to the current element in the loop. Alternatively, you can include a second variable in the function's declaration and the element will be passed in. Note that this is a DOM element reference so, if you want to use jQuery methods on it, you will need to use $(this) to create a wrapper set for it.

Event Handling

The last area of jQuery we are going to look at is event handling. Event handling will allow us to capture the events that occur in our pages, such as mouse clicks and key presses. Most of the event handlers we will use when building SharePoint apps will be for data validation routines or animation effects. JQuery contains methods for easily connecting to the DOM's event system. Table 4-5 contains a description of these methods.

Table 4-5. jQuery Event Methods

Method	Description
.bind('event'[,data],handler)	Binds an event handler function to an event. Optionally, a data object can be added to the event that is passed into the handler when it fires.
.unbind('event',handler)	Removes an existing event handler.
.trigger('event',data)	Programatically fires the event handlers for a given event type, optionally passing a data item to each.
.click([data,]handler)	This is a class of shorthand methods for simplifying binding event handlers to specific types of events. Optionally, a data object can be added to the event that is passed into the handler when it fires.
	Similar methods include blur(), change(), dblclick(), focus(), focusin(), focusout(), hover(), keydown(), keypress(), keyup(), mousedown(), mouseenter(), mouseleave(), mousemove(), mouseout(), mouseover(), mouseup(), resize(), and scroll().

An event handler function always has the same signature. The function takes a parameter containing the event object. The jQuery event object, unlike the native browser's event object, is always passed and always contains the same structure regardless of the browser being used. Here are some of the important properties of the event object.

- event.type—Identifies the type of event such as click.

- event.target—The DOM element that originally fired the event.

- event.currentTarget—The element currently handling the event in the DOM's event propagation sequence.

- event.data—The data item, if any, that is associated with the event.

- event.result—The most recent result value, assigned by an event handler, for this event.

EXERCISE 4-3

In this exercise, we will create an HTML form and perform some basic data manipulation with it. The form allows the user to modify some UI settings such as font size and background color. As the changes are made, the new values are applied to a sample area. When the user is satisfied, they can apply the settings to the entire page.

1. Add the following markup to a new HTML page.

```
<!DOCTYPE html PUBLIC "-//W3C//DTD XHTML 1.0 Strict//EN"
"http://www.w3.org/TR/xhtml1/DTD/xhtml1-strict.dtd">
<html>
<head>
    <script type="text/javascript"
            src="http://code.jquery.com/jquery-1.7.1.min.js"></script>
</head>
<body>
    <script type="text/javascript">

    $(document).ready(startProcessing);

    function startProcessing()
    {
        $("#btn").bind("click", btnClick);

        $("#txtSample").change(onChange);
        $("#chkBold").change("This is the data I passed.", onChange);
        $("#selBgcolor").change(onChange);
        $("#selFontFamily").change(onChange);
        $("#selFontSize").change(onChange).trigger("change");
    }

    function btnClick(event)
    {
        applyStyles("*");
    }
```

```javascript
    function onChange(event)
    {
        $("#log").append("<span>" + event.target.id + "." + event.type + ": " +
event.target.value + "</span><br />");

        if (event.data)
            $("#log").append("<span>Data Received: " + event.data + "</span><br />");

        applyStyles("#sample");
    }

    function applyStyles(selector)
    {
        $(selector)
          .css("font-family",$("#selFontFamily").val())
          .css("font-size",$("#selFontSize").val())
          .css("background-color",$("#selBgcolor").val())
          .css("font-weight", ($("#chkBold").is(":checked")) ? "bold" : "normal")
          .each(function(index)
              {
                  if (this.id == "sample")
                      $(this).text($("#txtSample").val());
              });
    }

    </script>

    <h1>Data Entry Validation with JQuery</h1>

    <table>
        <tr>
            <td>Sample Text:</td>
            <td><input type="text" id="txtSample" value="Sample Text" /></td>
        </tr>
        <tr>
            <td>Bold?</td>
            <td><input type="checkbox" id="chkBold" /></td>
        </tr>
        <tr>
            <td>Font Family:</td>
            <td>
                <select id="selFontFamily">
                    <option>Verdana</option>
                    <option>Helvatica</option>
                    <option>Garamond</option>
                </select>
            </td>
        </tr>
        <tr>
            <td>Font Size:</td>
            <td>
                <select id="selFontSize">
                    <option>10pt</option>
```

```
                        <option>20pt</option>
                        <option>30pt</option>
                    </select>
                </td>
            </tr>
            <tr>
                <td>Background:</td>
                <td>
                    <select id="selBgcolor">
                        <option>White</option>
                        <option>Red</option>
                        <option>Blue</option>
                        <option>Green</option>
                    </select>
                </td>
            </tr>
        </table>

        <div id="sample" style="width:200px;height:100px;border-style:solid;margin:15px">
        </div>
        <div id="log" style="width:600px;border-style:solid;margin:15px">
        </div>

        <input type="button" id="btn" value="Set on Page" />
</body>
</html>
```

2. View the page in a web browser (see Figure 4-14).

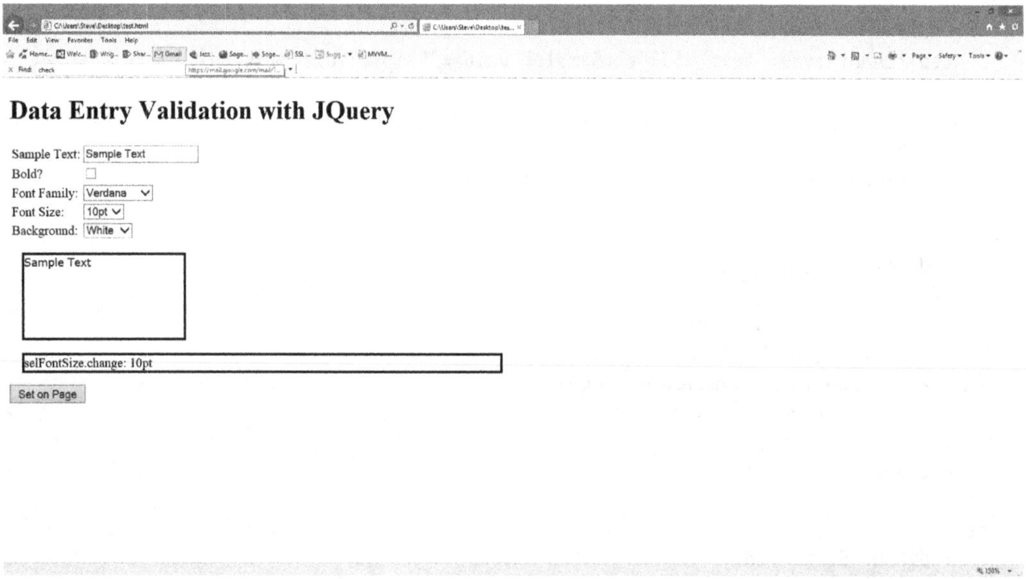

Figure 4-14. *Data entry page*

3. Select Red from the background select list.

4. Check the bold check box (see Figure 4-15).

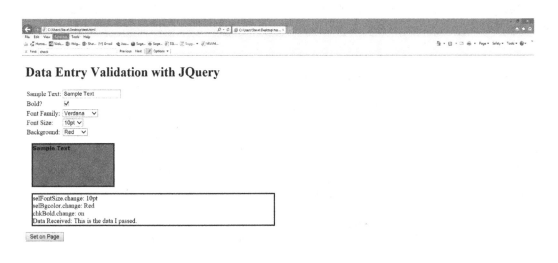

Figure 4-15. *Data entry page after selections*

5. Click the Set on Page button (see Figure 4-16).

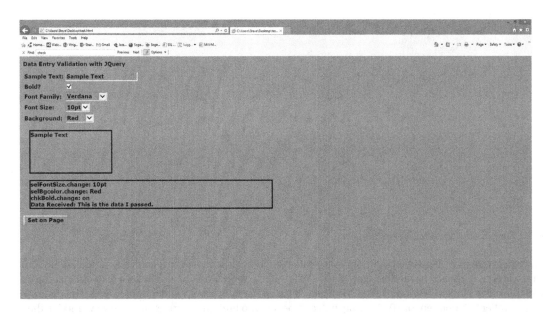

Figure 4-16. *Data entry page after applying to the page*

The startProcessing() function sets up event handlers on all of the input elements. The last line includes a trigger() call to fire the change event and apply the formatting to the sample <DIV> area. Note that the onChange() method writes each event to a log <DIV> area so we can see each event as it happens. The applyStyles() function is used to apply the selected styles either to the sample area or to the entire page when the button is clicked.

Using the Knockout Library with the MVVM Pattern

The final area of advanced client-side development we will be looking at involves bringing our SharePoint data together with the visual elements used to display it. Traditional JavaScript coding would involve reading the data into JavaScript variables, getting a reference to each visual DOM element, and copying the value of the data into the element. This can result in a great deal of hard-to-maintain client-side code. Instead, we will be using another open source JavaScript library called *Knockout*.

The Knockout library (http://www.knockoutjs.com) was designed to provide client-side data binding. This means that the developer only needs to map their data to the visual elements and the actual moving of data will be handled by the library. Anyone familiar with coding Windows Forms or Web Forms using the .NET Framework has probably used a data-binding system of some sort. Knockout is not dependent on any other libraries, such as jQuery, but only on JavaScript. However, it works very well with jQuery and that is how we will be using it throughout this book.

The Model-View-ViewModel (MVVM) Pattern

Design patterns have been used in strongly typed server-side languages such as C# and VB.NET for many years. In JavaScript, however, patterns need to be adapted to the JavaScript style of coding with objects. Knockout was designed with one specific design pattern in mind: the Model-View-ViewModel pattern (see Figure 4-17).

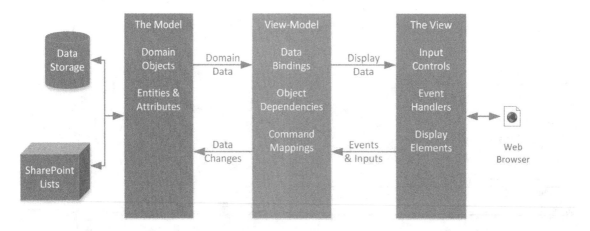

Figure 4-17. *The Model-View-ViewModel pattern*

Programmers that have developed solutions using Microsoft's Silverlight or Windows Presentation Foundation (WPF) frameworks may already be familiar with the MVVM design pattern. MVVM also bears a resemblance, and a history, with the older Model-View-Controller (MVC) model used in many development frameworks. The difference is that the "controller" component of MVC has been decomposed into multiple components: the view-model, the controller, and the binder. In most MVVM implementations, the controller and binder are standard parts of the framework. Only the view-model is custom coded for the solution.

As shown in Figure 4-17, the *Model* in MVVM represents the data being manipulated. Implementations vary but most are either based on a domain model that represents the conceptual objects in the system or on a data access layer (DAL) that acts as a wrapper or façade for a back-end data store such as a relational database. The purpose of the model object is to handle retrieving and storing the data for the system. In our case, SharePoint will be used as the back-end storage system and data will be represented either using JSON or SharePoint CSOM objects.

The *View*, just as in MVC, represents the visual interface of the program or web page. This includes display and input controls, as well as the events they generate. These can be lists, tables, text boxes, combo boxes, or buttons. The view is concerned with how the data is presented and managing interactions with the user.

The *View-Model* (a.k.a. "the model of the view") is concerned with mediating the interaction between the model and the view. The view-model plays multiple roles. From the model's point-of-view, it acts as the view. From the view's point-of-view, it acts as the model. Another way to think of the view-model is as a policeman directing traffic between the model and the view.

In our apps, we will implement the MVVM pattern using JavaScript and HTML. The view will be defined using standard HTML tags and CSS styles. Knockout implements a template system that allows us to define an HTML pattern that can be replicated over and over again, as needed, to build the view. The model will be composed of JavaScript objects that represent SharePoint data items. Many of these objects will be provided by the SharePoint client-side object model (CSOM) but some will be created using JSON data passed over the network. Our view-models will be created using JavaScript objects running in the browser. Using Knockout with MVVM will greatly simplify the coding of data-intensive pages using only client-side code.

Introducing Knockout

To effectively use Knockout, you need to understand the way the library implements communication between the view-model and the view. The three primary concepts are declarative data bindings, observable objects, and templates.

Declarative data binding refers to the manner in which data is routed to elements in the view. The view is composed of HTML markup. A new attribute will be introduced into our markup called `data-bind`. The `data-bind` attribute will identify what data is to go into each visual element.

For delivering static values to HTML elements, data binding is sufficient, but in order to create a two-way connection we need to be able to track the events and dependencies between our data and view elements. This is where *observable objects*, or just *observables*, come in. An observable is an object wrapper that can be placed around a data element to allow Knockout to track changes and dependencies for the data. Using observable objects and arrays, we can handle events that occur in the view and properly apply them to the underlying data. Observables are declared within the view-model and are the key to keeping the user interface synchronized.

Templates allow us to generate additional HTML markup, as needed, to display our data. For example, if we need to display a table of information, we could hand code an HTML table to display it. But the data could have any number of rows. How many `<TR>` tags do we need to put in the table? There is no way to know. Templates in Knockout allow us to declare what the HTML markup should look like for each item in the list. Knockout then replicates this template as many times as needed to render the data found at runtime.

The version of Knockout we will use is version 2.2.1. Complete documentation and tutorials can be found at `http://knockoutjs.com`. You can download the library and embed it in your SharePoint app project or you can reference a copy from Microsoft's content delivery network at `http://ajax.aspnetcdn.com/ajax/knockout/knockout-2.2.1.js`. We will use the CDN.

Connecting Data with Declarative Bindings

Data binding is the key technique in Knockout. The `data-bind` attribute provides a simple way to connect the data in the view-model to the view elements. For example, if a `<SPAN>` element should display a person's name, the HTML markup might be `<span data-bind="text: name"></span>`. This tells Knockout that the `text` value of the `<SPAN>` element should be associated with the data element called `name` in the view-model. The `data-bind` attribute can also specify other properties of the binding, such as event handlers, looping, and display properties.

EXERCISE 4-4

In this exercise, we will create an HTML page that binds data to entries in a table. First, we will define our view. This is a simple HTML page containing a table.

1. Create a new HTML file and add this markup to it.

```
<!DOCTYPE html PUBLIC "-//W3C//DTD XHTML 1.0 Strict//EN"
"http://www.w3.org/TR/xhtml1/DTD/xhtml1-strict.dtd">
<html>
<head>
    <script type="text/javascript"
            src="http://code.jquery.com/jquery-1.7.1.min.js" ></script>
    <script type="text/javascript"
            src="http://ajax.aspnetcdn.com/ajax/knockout/knockout-2.2.1.js" ></script>
</head>
<body>
  <h1>Data Binding with Knockout</h1>

  <div style='position: absolute; top: 100px; left: 0px'>
    <h2>Read/Only</h2>
    <table>
     <tr>
        <td>Student Name:</td>
        <td><span data-bind="text: student"></span></td>
     </tr>
     <tr>
        <td>Course Name:</td>
        <td><span data-bind="text: course"></span></td>
     </tr>
     <tr>
        <td>Academic Term:</td>
        <td><span data-bind="text: term"></span></td>
     </tr>
     <tr>
        <td>Credit Hours:</td>
        <td><span data-bind="text: hours"></span></td>
     </tr>
     <tr>
        <td>Grade:</td>
        <td><span data-bind="text: grade"></span></td>
     </tr>
     <tr>
        <td>GPA Points Earned: </td>
        <td><span data-bind="text: gpaPoints"></span></td>
     </tr>
    </table>
  </div>
</body>
</html>
```

Notice the `data-bind` attributes in the table. These declarations will act as signposts for Knockout to deliver data to the elements. If we view this page as is, we will see the view, but no data. This is because we have not attached a view-model to it yet.

2. Add the following `script` tag to the page.

```
<script type="text/javascript">

$(document).ready(startProcessing);

function startProcessing()
{
    ko.applyBindings(new GradeViewModel());
}

function GradeViewModel() {
    this.student = 'Steve Wright';
    this.course = 'Creative Writing';
    this.term = 'Spring 2013';
    this.hours = 4;
    this.grade = 'B-';
    this.gpaPoints = 3.0;
};
</script>
```

3. View the page in a web browser. The result should resemble Figure 4-18.

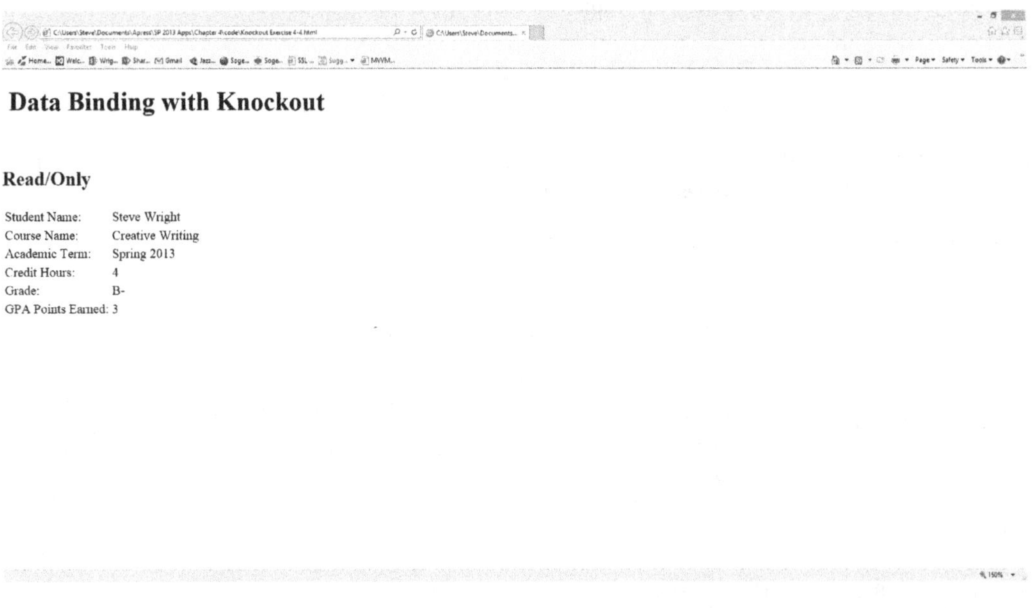

Data Binding with Knockout

Read/Only

Student Name:	Steve Wright
Course Name:	Creative Writing
Academic Term:	Spring 2013
Credit Hours:	4
Grade:	B-
GPA Points Earned:	3

Figure 4-18. *Data binding in Knockout*

The `GradeViewModel()` object defines the view-model for the page. It exposes the data elements referred to in the `data-bind` attributes in the view. In a real system, these values would not be constants, but would be read from an underlying model.

The `ko.applyBindings()` method takes an instance of the view-model as a parameter. This model is used to satisfy the references in the view. The root HTML element of the view could be passed in as an optional parameter. In this case, our view is the entire document, which is the default, so passing it is not necessary.

Dependency Tracking with Observable Objects

Observable objects are used wrap the data elements provided by the view-model. This allows changes in the view to be handled as events. When the value contained in an observable object is altered, the object interacts with the Knockout runtime to pass those updates to other observable objects that are dependent on it.

There are three types of observable objects to understand.

1. `ko.observable()`—This wraps a single data item and identifies it to the Knockout runtime. Data written through the object will trigger dependent actions in other observable objects.

2. `ko.observableArray()`—An observable array is a wrapper for an array of data elements. The purpose of such an array is to track changes to the membership in the array, not the values of each element. In many cases, you will want to make the individual elements observable as well. To do this, you would wrap each element using `ko.observable()` prior to adding them to the array.

3. `ko.computed()`—A computed observable uses a function to define the relationship between observable objects to produce a computed value. The computed value can be used like any other observable except that it cannot be updated. It is automatically recalculated whenever one of the observable values it depends on is updated.

EXERCISE 4-5

In this exercise, we will add a set of input fields to the page from Exercise 4-4. The page will do some validation on the inputs and supply the updated values to other controls on the page.

1. Create a new HTML file and add this markup to it.

```
<!DOCTYPE html PUBLIC "-//W3C//DTD XHTML 1.0 Strict//EN"
        "http://www.w3.org/TR/xhtml1/DTD/xhtml1-strict.dtd">
<html>
<head>
    <script type="text/javascript"
            src="http://code.jquery.com/jquery-1.7.1.min.js" ></script>
    <script type="text/javascript"
            src="http://ajax.aspnetcdn.com/ajax/knockout/knockout-2.2.1.js" ></script>
</head>
<body>
  <h1>Data Binding with Knockout</h1>
  <div style='position: absolute; top: 100px; left: 0px'>
    <h2>Read/Only</h2>
    <table>
```

```
        <tr>
            <td>Student Name:</td>
            <td><span data-bind="text: student"></span></td>
        </tr>
        <tr>
            <td>Course Name:</td>
            <td><span data-bind="text: course"></span></td>
        </tr>
        <tr>
            <td>Academic Term:</td>
            <td><span data-bind="text: term"></span></td>
        </tr>
        <tr>
            <td>Credit Hours:</td>
            <td><span data-bind="text: hours"></span></td>
        </tr>
        <tr>
            <td>Grade:</td>
            <td><span data-bind="text: grade"></span></td>
        </tr>
        <tr>
            <td>GPA Points Earned:</td>
            <td><span data-bind="text: gpaPoints"></span></td>
        </tr>
        <tr>
            <td>Class Name:</td>
            <td><span data-bind="text: className"></span></td>
        </tr>
    </table>
</div>
<div style='position: absolute; top: 100px; left: 400px'>
    <h2>Editable</h2>
    <table>
        <tr>
            <td>Student Name:</td>
            <td><input data-bind="value: student" /></td>
        </tr>
        <tr>
            <td>Course Name:</td>
            <td><input data-bind="value: course" /></td>
        </tr>
        <tr>
            <td>Academic Term:</td>
            <td><input data-bind="value: term" /></td>
        </tr>
        <tr>
            <td>Credit Hours:</td>
            <td><input data-bind="value: hours" /></td>
        </tr>
    </table>
```

```
            <tr>
                <td>Grade:</td>
                <td><input data-bind="value: grade" /></td>
            </tr>
            <tr>
                <td>GPA Points Earned:</td>
                <td><input data-bind="value: gpaPoints" /></td>
            </tr>
        </table>
      </div>
    </body>
  </html>
```

The `data-bind` attributes in the second table are on generic `<INPUT>` tags. These have no type, id, or value attributes. Knockout will supply these values. Notice that we are using the `value` binding instead of the `text` binding as we did in the first table. This tells Knockout that these are input fields that use the value attribute instead of setting their text.

2. Add the following `script` tag to the page to define an initial view-model object.

```
<script type="text/javascript">

$(document).ready(startProcessing);

function startProcessing()
{
    ko.applyBindings(new GradeViewModel());
}

function GradeViewModel() {
    this.student = ko.observable('Steve Wright');
    this.course = ko.observable('Creative Writing');
    this.term = ko.observable('Spring 2013');
    this.hours = ko.observable(4);
    this.grade = ko.observable('B-');
    this.gpaPoints = ko.observable(3.0);

    this.className =
        ko.computed(
            function() { return this.course() + " (" + this.term() + ")"; }
            , this);
};
</script>
```

3. View the page in a web browser.

4. Edit the Course Name field. The result should resemble Figure 4-19.

Data Binding with Knockout

Read/Only

Student Name:	Steve Wright
Course Name:	Creative Writing II
Academic Term:	Spring 2013
Credit Hours:	4
Grade:	B-
GPA Points Earned: 3	
Class Name:	Creative Writing II (Spring 2013)

Editable

Student Name:	Steve Wright
Course Name:	Creative Writing II
Academic Term:	Spring 2013
Credit Hours:	4
Grade:	B-
GPA Points Earned: 3	

Figure 4-19. *Data binding with observables*

By wrapping values in ko.observable(), we have made them active parts of the view-model. When we make changes in the value of the input fields, those changes are forwarded to all of the elements that depend on that observable object. In this case, that causes the read-only version of the table to be updated.

The ko.computed() method is used to create a new data element called className. When we update the Course Name, the className is updated as well because the observable object wrapping that value is used in the calculation. This tells Knockout that the computed value should be recalculated.

Now let's look at how Knockout handles events and data validation.

5. Add these functions to the GradeViewModel function.

```
this.validateData = function() {
    if (this.student().length == 0) alert("Student name is blank.");
    if (this.course().length == 0) alert("Course name is blank.");
    if (this.term().length == 0) alert("Academic term is blank.");
    if (this.grade().length == 0) alert("Grade is blank.");

    if ((isNaN(this.hours())) || (parseInt(this.hours()) <= 0))
        alert("Credit hours is not a positive number.");

    if ((isNaN(this.gpaPoints())) || (parseInt(this.gpaPoints()) <= 0))
        alert("GPA points is not a positive number.");
}

this.requireNumeric = function(mv,event) {
    if (isNaN($(event.target).val()))
    {
        alert("This field must be a number");
        $(event.target)
```

```
                .val(0)              // Set the value to "0"
                .trigger("change"); // First the CHANGE event to update Knockout.
        }
    }
```

6. Add this HTML button just before the first <DIV>.

    ```
    <button data-bind="click: validateData">Validate Data</button>
    ```

7. Add event: { change: requireNumeric } to the data-bind attribute for credit hours and
    GPA points.

    ```
    <td><input data-bind="value: hours, event: { change: requireNumeric }" /></td>

    <td><input data-bind="value: gpaPoints, event: { change: requireNumeric }" /></td>
    ```

The validataData() function is the click event handler for the button that has been added. The
requireNumeric() function is the event handler for the change event on the two fields that must be numbers.
Notice that the event handler is only referenced by name in the view. The implementation is in the view-model.
This is normal for the MVVM pattern.

Notice that when we read data from the view-model fields, we are using a function call instead of just reading the
value. For example, this.term() instead of this.term. This is because these values have been wrapped in an
observable object wrapper that is a JavaScript function. The observable object can also be used to set the data
value. To do this, we would pass the new value into the function, as in this.term('Summer 2013').

In the requireNumeric() function, we are setting the value of the input field, not the observable object, using
jQuery's val() function. As a result, Knockout does not know it has been updated. To take care of that, we just
need to call the .trigger() method to fire the change event. Knockout will then carry out all of the updates
necessary in the view-model.

Generating Complex Views with Templates

The last major design concept in Knockout is the use of templates. A *template* is a set of HTML markup with
embedded data binding that can be replicated and bound multiple times to adapt the view to the size and structure of
the data.

Knockout actually supports multiple templating systems. *Native templates* in Knockout use special types of
bindings to specify how the template should be applied. External templating systems, also known as *string-based
templates*, allow Knockout to use templates developed using techniques and libraries other than Knockout. For
simplicity's sake, we will only use native Knockout templates in this book.

Rendering Repeating Templates with FOREACH

The foreach binding type allows the view to specify a segment of HTML markup that should be replicated for each
data element in an array. This is usually an observable array, as it allows the user interface to support adding and
removing data elements. Knockout also contains binding types of if, ifnot, and with to allow more flexibility and
decision-making within a template area.

```
┌────────────────────────────────────────────────────────────────┐
│                         EXERCISE 4-6                            │
└────────────────────────────────────────────────────────────────┘
```

In this exercise, we will create a data entry page that supports adding and removing records and nesting multiple layers of objects in a user interface.

1. Create a new HTML file and add this markup to it.

```
<!DOCTYPE html PUBLIC "-//W3C//DTD XHTML 1.0 Strict//EN"
"http://www.w3.org/TR/xhtml1/DTD/xhtml1-strict.dtd">
<html>
<head>
    <script type="text/javascript"
            src="http://code.jquery.com/jquery-1.7.1.min.js" ></script>
    <script type="text/javascript"
            src="http://ajax.aspnetcdn.com/ajax/knockout/knockout-2.2.1.js" ></script>
</head>
<body>

<script type="text/javascript">

$(document).ready(startProcessing);

function startProcessing()
{
    ko.applyBindings(new GradeViewModel());
}

// Represents a student's grade in a course.
function StudentGrade(student, grade) {
    var self = this;

    self.student = ko.observable(student);
    self.assignedGrade = ko.observable(grade);

    self.gpaPoints = ko.computed(function() {
        return self.assignedGrade().points.toFixed(2);
    });
}

// View-Model for this screen, along with initial state
function GradeViewModel() {
    var self = this;

    self.possibleGrades = [
        {gradeLabel:"A",points:4},{gradeLabel:"A-",points:3.75},
        {gradeLabel:"B+",points:3.25},{gradeLabel:"B",points:3},
        {gradeLabel:"B-",points:2.75},{gradeLabel:"C+",points:2.25},
        {gradeLabel:"C",points:2},{gradeLabel:"C-",points:1.75},
        {gradeLabel:"D+",points:1.25},{gradeLabel:"D",points:1},
        {gradeLabel:"D-",points:0.75},{gradeLabel:"F",points:0}
        ];
```

```
        // This would be read from SharePoint or a database.
        self.grades = ko.observableArray([
            new StudentGrade("Steve Wright", this.possibleGrades[7]),
            new StudentGrade("David Petersen", this.possibleGrades[3]),
            new StudentGrade("Mark Twain", this.possibleGrades[0])
        ]);

        self.averageGrade = ko.computed(function() {
            if (self.grades().length == 0) return "";

            var totalPoints = 0;
            for (var i = 0; i < self.grades().length; i++)
                totalPoints += parseFloat(self.grades()[i].gpaPoints());
            return (totalPoints / self.grades().length).toFixed(2);
        });

        // Operations
        self.addStudent =
            function() { self.grades.push(new StudentGrade("", self.possibleGrades[0])); }
        self.delStudent =
            function(studentGrade) { self.grades.remove(studentGrade) }
    }
</script>

<h2>Enter Grades: <button data-bind="click: addStudent">Add a Grade</button></h2>

<table border="1" cellspacing="0" cellpadding="10">
    <thead style='background-color:gray;color:white'><tr>
        <th>Student Name</th>
        <th>Grade</th>
        <th>GPA Points</th>
        <th></th>
    </tr></thead>
    <tbody data-bind="foreach: grades">
        <tr>
            <td><input data-bind="value: student" /></td>
            <td><select data-bind="options: $root.possibleGrades, value: assignedGrade,
optionsText: 'gradeLabel'"></select></td>
            <td data-bind="text: gpaPoints" align="right"></td>
            <td><a href="#" data-bind="click: $root.delStudent">Remove</a></td>
        </tr>
    </tbody>
    <tfoot style='background-color:lightgray'>
        <tr>
            <td colspan="2">Average GPA Points Awarded: </td>
            <td data-bind="text: averageGrade()" align="right"></td>
            <td></td>
        </tr>
    </tfoot>
</table>

</body>
</html>
```

2. View the page in a web browser (see Figure 4-20).

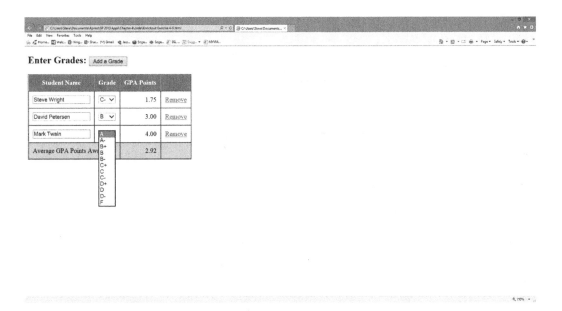

Figure 4-20. *Using foreach templates in Knockout*

The view-model for this page consists of two layers because the page contains a list of individual items. The outer view-model, GradeViewModel, encapsulates the behavior of the list as a whole. The inner view-model, StudentGrade, encapsulates a single item in the list.

In GradeViewModel, instead of using this throughout the class, we have switched to using a locally defined variable, self. This prevents confusion when creating functions such as averageGrade where this would refer to the browser's window object instead of the GradeViewModel object.

```
var self = this;
```

We are creating two arrays within GradeViewModel. The grades array is created by passing a standard JavaScript array object to the observableArray() method, converting it to an observable array. This enables Knockout to add and remove elements from the array in response to user interactions and update all related observable objects correctly. The possibleGrades array is left as a standard JavaScript array because it is only used to populate the select list and will not be updated.

```
self.possibleGrades = [
        {gradeLabel:"A",points:4},{gradeLabel:"A-",points:3.75},
        {gradeLabel:"B+",points:3.25},{gradeLabel:"B",points:3},
        {gradeLabel:"B-",points:2.75},
        {gradeLabel:"C+",points:2.25},{gradeLabel:"C",points:2},
        {gradeLabel:"C-",points:1.75},
        {gradeLabel:"D+",points:1.25},{gradeLabel:"D",points:1},
```

```
                {gradeLabel:"D-",points:0.75},
                {gradeLabel:"F",points:0}
    ];

    self.grades = ko.observableArray([
                new StudentGrade("Steve Wright", this.possibleGrades[7]),
                new StudentGrade("David Petersen", this.possibleGrades[3]),
                new StudentGrade("Mark Twain", this.possibleGrades[0])
    ]);
```

The `foreach` data binding is used in the `<TBODY>` element to instruct Knockout to replicate its contents for each item in the `grades` collection.

```
<tbody data-bind="foreach: grades">
    <tr>
        <td><input data-bind="value: student" /></td>
        <td><select data-bind="options: $root.possibleGrades, value: assignedGrade,
optionsText: 'gradeLabel'"></select></td>
        <td data-bind="text: gpaPoints" align="right"></td>
        <td><a href="#" data-bind="click: $root.delStudent">Remove</a></td>
    </tr>
</tbody>
```

- `$root` is used to obtain a reference to the outer view-model. This is only needed when the binding context has moved to a lower level, `StudentGrade`, as in this case.

- `options: $root.possibleGrades` instructs Knockout to use the `possibleGrades` list as the source of the options in the select list.

- `optionsText: 'gradeLabel'` tells Knockout the name of the property to use for displaying the option. Note that when the user selects an option, it is the underlying object that is assigned, not the text value.

- `<a href="#" data-bind="click: $root.delStudent">Remove</a>` renders a link that calls a method in the view-model when it is clicked. The function receives the data element associated with the row as a parameter.

As the user makes changes to the data and adds or removes rows from the table, the underlying view-model receives each change as well. In a real application, the view-model would be responsible for invoking actions on a model object to reflect those data changes in the permanent data store.

Rendering with Named Templates

Using `foreach` to render repetitive HTML segments is a natural way to handle simple lists and grids. These templates are generally small HTML segments and repeated based on data elements in an array of some sort. There are cases where this type of template becomes cumbersome or inappropriate. In these situations, we need to be able to separate the template from the flow of the HTML document and refer to it wherever it is needed. It might be applied multiple times in different parts of the document, or it may just be too large to be understandable unless it is on its own.

Named templates were created for these situations. Named templates are scripts that are written in HTML instead of JavaScript. They are placed into separate `<SCRIPT>` tags and referred by name in a special data-bind option called template. The template binding triggers the replication of the HTML markup in the script block based on the data specified in the data-bind attribute.

EXERCISE 4-7

In this exercise, we will rework the page from the last exercise to use named templates.

1. Create a new HTML file and add this markup to it.

```
<!DOCTYPE html PUBLIC "-//W3C//DTD XHTML 1.0 Strict//EN"
"http://www.w3.org/TR/xhtml1/DTD/xhtml1-strict.dtd">
<html>
<head>
    <script type="text/javascript"
            src="http://code.jquery.com/jquery-1.7.1.min.js" ></script>
    <script type="text/javascript"
            src="http://ajax.aspnetcdn.com/ajax/knockout/knockout-2.2.1.js" ></script>
</head>
<body>

<script type="text/javascript">

$(document).ready(startProcessing);

function startProcessing()
{
    ko.applyBindings(new GradeViewModel());
}

// Represents a student's grade in a course.
function StudentGrade(student, grade) {
    var self = this;

    self.student = ko.observable(student);
    self.assignedGrade = ko.observable(grade);

    self.gpaPoints = ko.computed(function() {
        return self.assignedGrade().points.toFixed(2);
    });
}

// View-Model for this screen, along with initial state
function GradeViewModel() {
    var self = this;

    self.possibleGrades = [
        {gradeLabel:"A",points:4},{gradeLabel:"A-",points:3.75},
        {gradeLabel:"B+",points:3.25},{gradeLabel:"B",points:3},
        {gradeLabel:"B-",points:2.75},
        {gradeLabel:"C+",points:2.25},{gradeLabel:"C",points:2},
        {gradeLabel:"C-",points:1.75},
```

```
            {gradeLabel:"D+",points:1.25},{gradeLabel:"D",points:1},
            {gradeLabel:"D-",points:0.75},
            {gradeLabel:"F",points:0}
            ];

    // This would be read from SharePoint or a database.
    self.grades = ko.observableArray([
        new StudentGrade("Steve Wright", this.possibleGrades[7]),
        new StudentGrade("David Petersen", this.possibleGrades[3]),
        new StudentGrade("Mark Twain", this.possibleGrades[0])
    ]);

    self.professor = {name:"Professor Moriarty",office:"Olvidy Basement"};
    self.assistant = {name:"Raj Bashir, TA",office:"Greenwich 243"};

    self.averageGrade = ko.computed(function() {
        if (self.grades().length == 0) return "";

        var totalPoints = 0;
        for (var i = 0; i < self.grades().length; i++)
            totalPoints += parseFloat(self.grades()[i].gpaPoints());
        return (totalPoints / self.grades().length).toFixed(2);
    });

    // Operations
    self.addStudent = function() { self.grades.push(new StudentGrade("",
self.possibleGrades[0])); }
    self.delStudent = function(studentGrade) { self.grades.remove(studentGrade) }
}
</script>

<script type="text/html" id="faculty-template">
    <span data-bind="text: name"></span>
    - (<span data-bind="text: office"></span>)
</script>

<script type="text/html" id="grade-line-template">
    <tr>
        <td><input data-bind="value: student" /></td>
        <td><select data-bind="options: $root.possibleGrades, value: assignedGrade,
optionsText: 'gradeLabel'"></select></td>
        <td data-bind="text: gpaPoints" align="right"></td>
        <td><a href="#" data-bind="click: $root.delStudent">Remove</a></td>
    </tr>
</script>

<h2>Enter Grades: <button data-bind="click: addStudent">Add a Grade</button></h2>
<div data-bind="template: { name: 'faculty-template', data: professor }"></div>
<div data-bind="template: { name: 'faculty-template', data: assistant }"></div>
```

```
<table border="1" cellspacing="0" cellpadding="10">
    <thead style='background-color:gray;color:white'><tr>
        <th>Student Name</th>
        <th>Grade</th>
        <th>GPA Points</th>
        <th></th>
    </tr></thead>
    <tbody data-bind="template: { name: 'grade-line-template', foreach: grades }">
    </tbody>
    <tfoot style='background-color:lightgray'>
        <tr>
            <td colspan="2">Average GPA Points Awarded: </td>
            <td data-bind="text: averageGrade()" align="right"></td>
            <td></td>
        </tr>
    </tfoot>
</table>

</body>
</html>
```

2. View the page in a web browser (see Figure 4-21).

Figure 4-21. *Using named templates in Knockout*

The view-models for this page are structured the same as in the previous exercise. We have added additional data items for the course's professor and assistant. Note that these are standard JavaScript objects, not arrays or observables.

111

```
self.professor = {name:"Professor Moriarty",office:"Olvidy Basement"};
self.assistant = {name:"Raj Bashir, TA",office:"Greenwich 243"};
```

A script called `faculty-template` has been added to define how these data elements should be rendered.

```
<script type="text/html" id="faculty-template">
    <span data-bind="text: name"></span>
    - (<span data-bind="text: office"></span>)
</script>
```

`<DIV>` tags have been added to invoke this template twice—once for the professor and once for the assistant. Note that we could not use a `foreach` template in this case, because they are not in an array.

```
<div data-bind="template: { name: 'faculty-template', data: professor }"></div>
<div data-bind="template: { name: 'faculty-template', data: assistant }"></div>
```

We have also converted the `foreach`-style template from Exercise 4-6 into a named template called `grade-line-template`.

```
<script type="text/html" id="grade-line-template">
    <tr>
        <td><input data-bind="value: student" /></td>
        <td><select data-bind="options: $root.possibleGrades, value: assignedGrade,
optionsText: 'gradeLabel'"></select></td>
        <td data-bind="text: gpaPoints" align="right"></td>
        <td><a href="#" data-bind="click: $root.delStudent">Remove</a></td>
    </tr>
</script>
```

To complete the use of the named template, we replaced the `<TBODY>` element with a `template` data binding.

```
<tbody data-bind="template: { name: 'grade-line-template', foreach: grades }">
</tbody>
```

The markup in the `template` is no different from the markup that used to reside in the `<TBODY>` element. It has just been pulled out of the flow of the document and placed into a named template. It can now be reused in different areas of the page with different data items as needed.

Summary

In this chapter, we worked on developing the skills needed to write sophisticated user interfaces within SharePoint apps. The key to good interactive pages is client-side scripts in JavaScript. We have introduced using advanced object structures in JavaScript, and the JQuery and Knockout libraries that use them.

Next, we will start building the infrastructure for our application by implementing security around our data. We will learn to enable the various components of the app to pass data. We will look at how authentication and authorization are handled in the SharePoint 2013 app model.

■ ■ ■

CHAPTER 5

Accessing the SharePoint Environment

In the last chapter, we learned how to code application logic that runs in the user's web browser. This is important because SharePoint apps are not allowed to use server-side code running within SharePoint. Now that we have these tools, we will apply them to the core task associated with most SharePoint apps. That is interacting with objects in the SharePoint environment, including sites, lists, and documents. In this chapter, we will go over the following points:

- The types of APIs that are available in SharePoint 2013.

- How these APIs apply to creating SharePoint apps.

- How to create efficient client-side code using request batching.

- The structure of the most common objects available to client-side code.

- How to use JavaScript to create rich web pages that leverage SharePoint site data.

The SharePoint 2013 APIs

SharePoint 2013 includes several types of interfaces for writing applications that access data on the server. These can be divided into server-side and client-side APIs. The client-side APIs can be further separated by the type of remote access provided.

The Server-Side Object Model

The SharePoint 2013 Server-Side Object Model (SSOM) is a set of .NET Framework assemblies that directly access SharePoint 2013 server's data structures. These assemblies contain code for accessing sites, lists, documents, and more. They also contain classes for creating and configuring the SharePoint environment. Application code using this interface has the ability to elevate its permissions and run in full-trust.

Prior to SharePoint 2010, SSOM was the only practical interface for writing sophisticated SharePoint applications. Developers can use SSOM to create custom web parts, timer jobs, and event handlers that run within the SharePoint server processes. Unfortunately, because of the power of the server-side object model, poorly written applications can cause performance and security problems that SharePoint is unable to limit or avoid.

In SharePoint 2010, Microsoft introduced a new model for developing SharePoint applications called the "sandbox." A sandboxed application was given access to a limited subset of the SSOM library and it was limited to operating only within a single site collection. Sandboxed applications run in a separate process outside of SharePoint but on the same physical server. The idea of the sandbox is to give developers access to some of the power of SharePoint programming without jeopardizing the stability and performance of the server farm. Applications running under the old SSOM programming model are referred to as "full-trust" applications because they can elevate their own privileges to gain access to data that the user is not allowed to access.

Because of the limitations of the sandbox's security constraints, most developers have been forced to abandon it for all but the most trivial applications. Since sandboxed applications still run on the SharePoint server, there is also the potential for these applications to hurt farm performance. Because of these issues, the sandbox is considered deprecated in SharePoint 2013. Applications developed using this technique will still function, but they will probably not be supported in future versions.

Since the Cloud App Model requires that all application logic execute outside of the SharePoint server farm, the SSOM is not available for SharePoint app development. The server-side object model still has value for developing full-trust applications for on-premise SharePoint 2013 deployments, but they cannot be deployed to SharePoint Online.

The Client-Side Object Model

With SharePoint 2010, a new API was added to SharePoint. The client-side object model (CSOM) is actually a family of APIs that share a common design and structure. The CSOM libraries in SharePoint 2010 were somewhat limited because, like sandboxed applications, they were limited to a single network domain and SharePoint site collection. They also contained only a small subset of the server-side APIs functionality. In SharePoint 2013, these libraries have been greatly expanded to allow client-side application code to perform any operation that does not require full-trust, including support for cross-domain calls.

One of the main design goals of the CSOM is to promote efficient use of the network interface. It uses various strategies to accomplish this, including the following:

- Batching requests into fewer web requests and responses.

- Creating more compact data structures on the wire.

- Retrieving only the information explicitly requested by the application.

We will discuss request batching later in this chapter. The data structures used on CSOM are based on the JavaScript Object Notation (JSON) standard rather than XML. This allows objects to be represented using less markup than is possible with XML. When making requests through the CSOM, the application can specify that only certain fields actually be included. This is possible because the object model is designed to allow most of an object's properties to remain uninitialized until they are explicitly requested and retrieved from the server.

As mentioned before, CSOM is not a single library but a set of libraries each targeted to a different type of application. In SharePoint 2013, the following client-side object models are available:

- **.NET Framework CSOM**—Allows programs written in any .NET language (C#, VB.NET, etc.) to interact with SharePoint.

- **Silverlight CSOM**—Allows Silverlight client applications to use SharePoint.

- **JavaScript CSOM**—For use in web browsers or browser-enabled devices.

- **Windows Phone CSOM**—This library is part of the *Windows Phone SharePoint SDK* and allows for the creation of mobile applications that interact with SharePoint.

In the context of SharePoint apps, we are interested in two of these environments: .NET and JavaScript. We will use the JavaScript CSOM to create browser-based logic for our apps. The .NET Framework library will be used in server-side code that runs in a remote ASP.NET web site associated with our app.

Web Service Endpoints

The last and perhaps most flexible API supported by SharePoint 2013 is based on standard web service calls. Starting in the 2007 version, SharePoint contained some limited web service APIs. SharePoint 2010 expanded on these along with the introduction of the client-side object models described previously. SharePoint 2013 has created a standard implementation for web services based on the REST pattern using OData.

Representational State Transfer (REST) refers to a design pattern where requests are encoded in the URL and HTML web request data sent to a web service. A REST API provides a very uniform method for accessing and updating data. The data elements returned by a REST service are typically objects formatted using XML markup. However, by itself, a REST web service may or may not be secure.

OData is an open standard protocol that uses the REST design pattern to implement a standard data exchange protocol. The choices made for the OData protocol include using HTTP verbs (GET, POST, etc.) in certain ways and using alternative data formats such as ATOM and JSON. SharePoint ensures security by requiring these calls to be encapsulated in an OAuth connection between the client and the SharePoint server. The OAuth protocol will be discussed in Chapter 6.

SharePoint implements both the OData web service API and the client-side object models using the same server-side component as shown in Figure 5-1. Every site within SharePoint exposes the client.svc web service. The CSOM libraries use this endpoint to process batched requests. The OData interface is exposed using the URIs passed into the service.

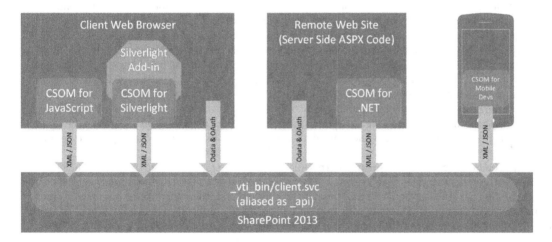

Figure 5-1. *SharePoint 2013 client-side APIs*

The advantage of the CSOM libraries is that they encapsulate and manage the relationships between objects on the client side. When using OData, the developer is responsible for managing these relationships. The advantage of the OData interface is that no special client-side library is required. All calls are made using the standard OData protocol.

■ **Note** There are many utility libraries available that make using OData easier. SharePoint 2013 includes one called the RequestExecutor. If you choose to use another library, ensure that it also supports OAuth encapsulation, as this is necessary when accessing SharePoint server.

Using the OData web service interface to write client-side logic will be covered in Chapter 7. The rest of this chapter will focus on writing code using the CSOM libraries.

Request Batching in Client-Side Code

For developers familiar with SharePoint server-side programming, writing client-side code using CSOM can seem awkward. While the objects are similar (sites, webs, lists, etc.), the way they are used is not. For example, when using a list, there may be a need to perform the following actions:

- Load a list item.

- Read and update various fields on the list item.

- Update the list item in SharePoint.

When writing server-side code, these steps can simply be performed in order. In client-side script, the order and grouping of these actions requires more planning. When using the client object model, a *client context* object records the requests made against the client-side objects but it does not immediately execute them. It only sends those requests to the server when explicitly instructed to do so using the ExecuteQuery() or ExecuteQueryAsnyc() methods. At that time, it packages the requests into an XML document, establishes a connection to the server, and transfers the data. The server then transmits the response data back to the proxy layer as JSON objects. Each group of requests and the response generated are referred to as a *request batch*.

Request batching improves performance and scalability of the solution because the overhead associated with the call (connecting, error correcting, etc.) is fairly consistent for all calls made, no matter how big or small. To maximize the efficiency of the interaction between the client and server, we need to reduce the number of calls by planning the request batches that will be sent to the proxy layer in the client context object. Each batch should contain as many requests as possible. In some cases, the results of one operation are needed as inputs to the next one. Those operations will have to be in separate batches, but the client object model was designed to minimize this type of dependency. For example, it is possible to open a web, find a list, and create list items, all before sending anything to the server.

When you retrieve an object using the server-side SharePoint API, you generally expect the object to be populated with all of the properties for the object. In the client object models, you can specify which properties you are interested in so that only those properties are retrieved in the batch. The size of the response sent from the server to the client can be greatly reduced by carefully selecting only those properties that you are actually going to use once the object is loaded.

Updates to SharePoint objects follow a similar pattern. Unless you need to read properties from an item, it is not necessary to load the object before updating it. This may seem counterintuitive at first. The client objects in CSOM are designed to track the changes made to them and pass them in a request batch without loading the original data into the object first. For example, to update a list item with an ID of 200, you need only create a reference to an object with that ID and update it, as shown in Listing 5.1. Of course, if item ID 200 does not exist, or the user does not have the right to update it, this request will fail when the batch is submitted to SharePoint.

Listing 5.1. Update a List Item

```
var clientContext = SP.ClientContext.get_current();
var list = clientContext.get_web().get_lists().getByTitle('My List');

var item = list.getItemById(200);   // create a client-side object using ID=200
item.set_item('Title', 'New Item Title!');
item.update();                       // add a request for the update to the next batch

clientContext.executeQueryAsync(...); // Now the batch is sent!
```

You should also limit the number of items being returned. Running queries against the properties of objects is an operation that is much better done on the server side. Imagine looking for a particular document in a library of a million items by pulling the entire list into the client web browser and then looping through it. The CAML query object is ideal for retrieving only those items and fields that are actually needed as part of the batch response using the Collaborative Application Markup Language (CAML). A CAML query is used in the same way as a SQL query is used to retrieve records from a database. The best practice is to filter the data on the server and return only that which is needed.

When designing batches in CSOM code, remember that your goal is to minimize the number of request batches and to make each response message as small as possible. To do this, carefully organize the operations being performed to minimize the dependencies between them. Do as much as possible with each batch while returning only the objects and properties absolutely required to accomplish your needs. This will improve the responsiveness of the user interface, reduce network traffic and improve the scalability of the entire solution.

Introduction to CSOM Objects

In this section, we will introduce the most commonly used objects in the client-side object model. This is not intended to be an exhaustive list. These are the general purpose objects that support the most common scenarios. CSOM also contains objects to support Business Connectivity Services (BCS), which we be covered in Chapter 8, as well as other service application-specific APIs that are not included in this section.

■ **Tip** Full documentation for the JavaScript model can be found at
http://msdn.microsoft.com/en-us/library/jj193034.aspx. For the .NET CSOM assemblies,
the documentation is at http://msdn.microsoft.com/en-us/library/jj193041.aspx.

With a few exceptions, all of these objects can be found in the SP JavaScript namespace and are contained in the default CSOM library, sp.js. For the .NET Framework CSOM, these objects are in the Microsoft.SharePoint.Client namespace in the Microsoft.SharePoint.Client.dll assembly. These are referred to as the *core* CSOM libraries.

Context and Infrastructure

Table 5-1 lists the objects used to connect to SharePoint and manage the request batching and response sequence. These objects will be used by all client side applications either directly or indirectly.

Table 5-1. *CSOM Context and Infrastructure Objects*

Object Name	Description
ClientContext	The ClientContext object is the main proxy object for interacting with SharePoint. The context batches requests and handles response messages. Most CSOM objects are associated with a ClientContext object in some way.
ClientObject	The ClientObject is the base class for all client-side objects. It tracks the object's relationship to the client context object and what properties are loaded.
ClientValueObject	The ClientValueObject is the base class for all client side property values. These values may or may not be populated, depending on the state of the object.
AppContextSite	The AppContextSite object is used to access SharePoint data in one of the app's context webs. Since the ClientContext object already provides access to the app's app web, this object is most often used to access information in the app's host web.
CamlQuery	A CamlQuery is used to query the content in a SharePoint site. The query can define which type of items should be returned, which properties to retrieve, and what conditions are to be met for an object to be included in the result set.
RequestExecutor	The RequestExecutor provides a simple interface for calling remote web services using the cross-domain library. This allows a client application to make web service calls using a proxy on the SharePoint server that it could not make directly because of the cross-site scripting limitations in modern browsers. This object handles the inclusion of OAuth headers to enable these calls to be made securely (see Chapter 7).

Content Objects

The most common use of the client-side object models is to read and write content items within the SharePoint environment. Table 5-2 lists the objects used to read and manipulate content in SharePoint sites.

Table 5-2. *CSOM Content Access Objects*

Object Name	Description
Site	This object represents a site collection in SharePoint.
Web	This object represents an individual site.
List	This object represents a list or document library.
ListItem	This object represents a list item or document in SharePoint.
Field	This is an attribute in a list or document library.
ContentType	This represents a SharePoint content type.
File	This can be any file in a SharePoint content database. This includes web content files and documents in document libraries.
Folder	This is a folder within SharePoint that can contain files. These folders may or may not be within a document library or list.

Security

Table 5-3 lists some of the objects used to query permissions within a SharePoint site. There are additional classes that permit client applications to assign permissions, create SharePoint groups, and assign roles.

Table 5-3. CSOM Security Objects

Object Name	Description
PermissionKind	This is an enumeration that lists the base SharePoint permissions for use with the BasePermissions object. Examples of these permissions include AddListItems, DeleteVersions, and ManageLists.
BasePermissions	This class represents a set of base SharePoint permissions such as viewing pages and adding list items. This class can be used to query permissions on an objects.
SecurableObject	SecurableObject is the base class for any SharePoint object that can have permissions assigned to it. These objects include webs, lists, and list items.
Principal	Principal is the base class for a SharePoint object that can be given permissions on a securable object. This includes users and groups.
User	A User is a type of principal object that represents either an individual user account or a security group account defined by the site's identity provider (for example, Active Directory or MS-ODS).
Group	A Group is a principal that represents a SharePoint Group.

Managing the App

The objects listed in Table 5-4 allow a client application to access information about the app and its installation environment, and control certain aspects of its presentation.

Table 5-4. CSOM App Management Objects

Object Name	Description
Navigation	This object is used to query and modify the site navigation menus, such as the quick launch and top menu, of a SharePoint site.
App	This represents an app package that is available in the SharePoint site's App Catalog. The app may or may not be installed on the current web site. This object identifies the app and contains other metadata such as the app's version.
AppInstance	This represents an app that has already been installed on a SharePoint web site. This object is specific to one app installed on one SharePoint web. It contains references to the app's context webs and permission information. This object is used to control the app instance's life cycle, such as installation, upgrades, and removal.
AppLicense	For apps that manage user licenses, this represents a user's license for an installed app instance.

Social

Social computing is pervasive throughout SharePoint 2013. Table 5-5 contains the primary objects associated with querying social activities and preferences within SharePoint.

Table 5-5. *CSOM Social Computing Objects*

Object Name	Description
PeopleManager	The PeopleManager object is the main controller object for SharePoint's social computing features. This object is used to retrieve, query, and manipulate user profiles, tags, and follows.
UserProfile	A UserProfile contains all of the user's metadata, including name, address, department, etc. The profile can also contain custom properties defined by the organization.
SocialFeed	A SocialFeed object represents a feed in SharePoint. A feed contains a series of posts and threads from the user, or items and users that the user has followed.
SocialActor	A SocialActor object represents any object that may create or trigger feed activity. These objects include users, documents, sites, and tags.
SocialPost	A SocialPost object represents a single item in a social feed. This could be an initial posting or a reply to a posting.
SocialThread	A SocialThread object represents a related set of posts and replies in a feed.

These objects are contained in separate libraries outside the core CSOM libraries. In JavaScript, the social objects are contained in the SP.UserProfiles and SP.Social namespaces in the sp.userprofiles.js file. For .NET, these objects are in the Microsoft.SharePoint.Client.UserProfiles and Microsoft.SharePoint.Client.Social namespaces in the Microsoft.SharePoint.Client.UserProfiles.dll assembly.

User profiles will be discussed in Chapter 6. SharePoint's social features will be explored in Chapter 12.

.NET Framework CSOM

Accessing SharePoint from server-side code in a remote web site requires that certain security conditions be met. In general, .NET Framework CSOM code is simpler to write than JavaScript CSOM because request batches can be executed synchronously. Therefore, we will move on to writing CSOM logic in JavaScript.

■ **Tip** For an example of using the CSOM in .NET, see Chapter 6.

JavaScript Object Model (JSOM)

The client-side object model for JavaScript (JSOM) is used to create rich client applications that run in the web browser. In Chapter 4, we explored how to create advanced web pages using logic coded in JavaScript with JQuery and Knockout. In this chapter, we will apply these techniques to accessing data and objects in the SharePoint environment using a series of exercises.

In our first exercise, we will look at how to embed the JSOM library in a web page and carry out basic operations such as opening a connection to SharePoint, reading information, and displaying that information on a web page. In our second example, we will return to the Classroom Online application and look at how to create a fully functional app configuration page using the Model-View-ViewModel (MVVM) pattern. This will allow us to experiment with the basic reading and updating of list items in SharePoint. Next, we will create a document library for submitting homework and create a page listing the most recent submissions using a CAML query. The last exercise will demonstrate the extra consideration to be taken when accessing SharePoint data outside of the local site associated with the current app.

EXERCISE 5.1

In this exercise, we will create a simple SharePoint app that renders a web page. That web page will read some information from the app web and display it on the page. We will not be using the Classroom Online project for this exercise.

1. Open Visual Studio 2012.

2. Select New Project… from the Start Page or File menu.

3. Create an App for SharePoint 2013 project and name it JSOMTest.

4. On the new app dialog, select SharePoint-hosted for the hosting option.

The default project template already has some of the code we will use in it, but it does not use Knockout or the MVVM pattern.

5. Open the `Default.aspx` file in the `Pages` folder.

6. Add the following script link for Knockout to the page with the other links:

```
<script type="text/javascript"
        src="https://ajax.aspnetcdn.com/ajax/knockout/knockout-2.2.1.js" ></script>
```

7. Replace the `<DIV>` tag in the page with this markup:

```
<div>
    <p data-bind="text: message()">
    </p>
</div>
```

8. Open the `App.js` file in the `Scripts` folder.

9. Replace the contents of this file with the following JavaScript:

```
$(function () {
    ko.applyBindings(new defaultViewModel());
});

function defaultViewModel() {
    var self = this;
    self.message = ko.observable();

    self.startLoad = function () {
        self.context = SP.ClientContext.get_current();

        self.web = self.context.get_web();
        self.context.load(self.web);  // adds a "load" request to the next batch
```

```
                    self.user = self.web.get_currentUser();
                    self.context.load(self.user); // adds a "load" request to the next batch

                    // send the request batch to the server
                    self.context.executeQueryAsync(
                        Function.createDelegate(self, self.onGetUserNameSuccess),
                        Function.createDelegate(self, self.onGetUserNameFail)
                        );
                }

            self.onGetUserNameSuccess = function () {
                    self.message('Hello ' + self.user.get_title() + ' from ' + self.web.get_title());
                }

            self.onGetUserNameFail = function (sender, args) {
                    self.message('Failed to get user name. Error:' + args.get_message());
                }

            self.startLoad();
        }
```

This JavaScript contains the view-model for our page. The paragraph tag on the page is bound to the `message` value in the model. We begin by retrieving a copy of the current context object.

```
self.context = SP.ClientContext.get_current();
```

This context object is already configured to allow us to communicate with our application's app web in SharePoint. All of the security headers have been prepared for us.

Next, we retrieve references to the current web and the current user. We call `Load()` on the context to indicate that SharePoint should populate these objects on the client side during the next request batch.

```
self.web = self.context.get_web();
self.context.load(self.web);

self.user = self.web.get_currentUser();
self.context.load(self.user);
```

Since this is all we wish to do in this batch, we begin the execution of the batch.

```
self.context.executeQueryAsync(...);
```

When the batch is finished processing, our callback routine is invoked.

```
self.onGetUserNameSuccess = function () {
    self.message('Hello ' + self.user.get_title() + ' from ' + self.web.get_title());
}
```

Because `self.user` and `self.web` have now been populated, we can access their properties. In this case, we are accessing their title properties using the standard JavaScript getter function `get_title()`. For a web, this is the site name. For a user, it is the user's full name.

10. Run the app to display the web page (see Figure 5-2).

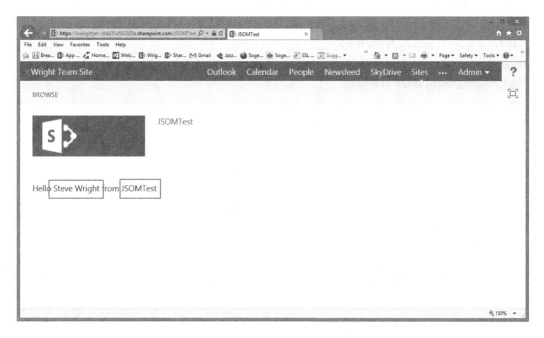

Figure 5-2. *Page containing web site title and user name*

This very simple sample demonstrates how to create apps that access data about their environment within SharePoint. Take a moment to examine the other properties that are available on the `SP.Web` and `SP.User` objects we have created. An easy way to do this is to set a breakpoint in the JavaScript code in the `onGetUserNameSuccess` function.

EXERCISE 5.2

In this exercise, we will begin using the JSOM objects to query list data in our SharePoint site and make updates to it. We will demonstrate this by re-implementing the configuration page for Classroom Online that we created in Chapter 2 using CSOM, Knockout, and MVVM.

In this exercise we will add an MVVM model object that represents the site's configuration settings. We will also add code to read and save the settings from an app web list. We will create a view-model object for the configuration page. In addition, we will update the configuration page to use the view-model object, and update the app's home page to use the site configuration model.

Add a Site Configuration Model Object

1. Open Visual Studio 2012.

2. Open the Classroom Online solution from the end of Chapter 2 or download it from the book's web site (see the Source Code/Download area of the Apress web site at www.apress.com).

3. Open the Elements.xml file under the ConfigurationValues/ ConfigurationValuesInstance folder.

4. Replace the <Data> tag in the file with the following markup. This will define default values for the configuration values in the list.

```
<Data>
  <Rows>
    <Row>
      <Field Name="Title">OrganizationName</Field>
      <Field Name="Value">Underhill University</Field>
    </Row>
    <Row>
      <Field Name="Title">OrganizationLogoUrl</Field>
      <Field Name="Value">../images/Sample.jpg</Field>
    </Row>
    <Row>
      <Field Name="Title">CourseName</Field>
      <Field Name="Value">Introduction to Computer Science</Field>
    </Row>
    <Row>
      <Field Name="Title">CourseNumber</Field>
      <Field Name="Value">CS 110</Field>
    </Row>
    <Row>
      <Field Name="Title">Schedule</Field>
      <Field Name="Value">MWF 10:30-11:30</Field>
    </Row>
    <Row>
      <Field Name="Title">Location</Field>
      <Field Name="Value">Comp Sci 318</Field>
    </Row>
  </Rows>
</Data>
```

5. Create a new folder under Scripts and name it Models.

6. Create a new JavaScript file in the Scripts/Models folder called siteconfigs.js and add this script to it:

```
var CO = CO || {};

$(function() {
    CO.Configs = new CO_Configs();
})
```

```
        // model object for the app's configuration
        CO_Configs = function () {
            var self = this;
            self._loadComplete = 0;
            self._callbacks = []; // holds a list of callbacks during page load

            self.ensureConfigs = function (callback) {
                if (self._loadComplete)
                    callback();
                else
                    self._callbacks.push(callback);
            }
        }

        // utility routine
        function getQueryStringParameter(paramToRetrieve) {
            var params =
                document.URL.split("?")[1].split("&");
            var strParams = "";
            for (var i = 0; i < params.length; i = i + 1) {
                var singleParam = params[i].split("=");
                if (singleParam[0] == paramToRetrieve)
                    return singleParam[1];
            }
        }
```

This first piece of script contains code for controlling the loading of the model object. Because this object represents the site's configuration, it will automatically start loading its data whenever the script file is included in a page.

```
var CO = CO || {};

$(function() {
    CO.Configs = new CO_Configs();
})
```

The CO object will be used to hold Classroom Online objects that are to be accessed globally. The CO.Configs object will contain the configuration values, once they are loaded.

The constructor for the object contains code that will help control the sequence of loading for the object. Consider what would happen if a page included this model object's script file and immediately began using the values before the object was fully loaded. We need a way to inform other objects that the load has completed. We will do this using a callback mechanism similar to the one JQuery uses in the $().ready() function.

```
self._loadComplete = 0;
self._callbacks = [];          // holds a list of callbacks during page load

self.ensureConfigs = function (callback) {
    if (self._loadComplete)
        callback();
```

```
    else
        self._callbacks.push(callback);
}
```

The `ensureConfigs()` function accepts a callback function as a parameter. If the configuration is already loaded, it immediately calls the callback. If not, the callback is pushed into an array of callbacks for later use. This allows a user of this model object to wait for the loading to complete using a call like this:

```
$(function () {
    CO.Configs.ensureConfigs(startProcessingNow);
})
```

First JQuery finishes loading, then the configuration load is allowed to complete. Only then is the callback function called.

7. Add these declarations inside the model's constructor:

```
        self._pendingItems;    // holds a collection of client-side object references
        self._loadConfigs = function () {
            var clientContext = SP.ClientContext.get_current();

            var list =
                clientContext.get_web().get_lists().getByTitle('Configuration Values');
            self._pendingItems = list.getItems(new SP.CamlQuery.createAllItemsQuery());
            clientContext.load(self._pendingItems);

            clientContext.executeQueryAsync(
                Function.createDelegate(self, self._onConfigLoadSucceeded),
                Function.createDelegate(self, self._onConfigLoadFailed)
                );
        }

        // start loading the configuration
        self._loadConfigs();
```

This code creates a batch to retrieve all items from the configuration list.

■ **Caution**   The call to the `self._loadConfigs()` function must remain at the bottom of the constructor so that all of the other declarations occur before it runs.

---

8. Now add the event callback functions to the model object. (Remember, these go BEFORE the load function.)

```
        self._onConfigLoadSucceeded = function (sender, args) {
            // load configuration values from the list
            var listEnumerator = self._pendingItems.getEnumerator();
            while (listEnumerator.moveNext()) {
```

```
                var item = listEnumerator.get_current();
                eval("self." + item.get_item("Title")
                        + " = '" + item.get_item("Value") + "'");
        }

        // replace the site logo with the school logo
        $(".ms-siteicon-img").attr("src", self.OrganizationLogoUrl).show();

        // get tokens from the URL
        self.SPAppWebUrl = decodeURIComponent(getQueryStringParameter("SPAppWebUrl"));
        self.SPLanguage = decodeURIComponent(getQueryStringParameter("SPLanguage"));
        self.SPClientTag = decodeURIComponent(getQueryStringParameter("SPClientTag"));
        self.SPProductNumber =
                decodeURIComponent(getQueryStringParameter("SPProductNumber"));
        self.SPHostUrl = decodeURIComponent(getQueryStringParameter("SPHostUrl"));
        self.scriptBase = self.SPHostUrl + "/_layouts/15/";
        self.StandardTokens = document.URL.split("?")[1];

        self._loadComplete = 1;
        while (self._callbacks.length > 0)
            self._callbacks.pop()();
        }

        self._onConfigLoadFailed = function (sender, args) {
            alert('Unable to load app configuration: '
                    + args.get_message() + '\n' + args.get_stackTrace());
        }
```

There are several interesting things happening in this function. First, we need to retrieve the configuration values from the list that was loaded during the batch.

```
var listEnumerator = self._pendingItems.getEnumerator();
while (listEnumerator.moveNext()) {
    var item = listEnumerator.get_current();
    eval("self." + item.get_item("Title")
            + " = '" + item.get_item("Value") + "'");
}
```

This is an example of a common pattern found in JSOM coding. In our batch, we queried for list items that were returned in a SP.ListItemCollection object. We use an enumerator to loop through the items in the list. The get_current() function of the enumerator returns the SP.ListItem object for each item in the list. Since the title of each object is the name of the configuration setting, we can use JavaScript's eval() function to add those properties directly to the current model object as *expando properties*.

The rest of this function decodes and stores several of the properties passed to the app by SharePoint in the query string, such as the app and host web URLs. Having these values in our configuration object makes them easier to use later.

The last lines of the event handler pop the callbacks off of the array and call each of them in turn. In most cases, there will only be one callback on this list, but this mechanism supports an arbitrary number of callbacks:

```
while (self._callbacks.length > 0)
    self._callbacks.pop()();
```

Add Support for Saving Changes

9. Add the following script inside the model object, but prior to the _loadConfigs() function call.

```
self.saveConfigs = function(callback) {
    if (callback) self._callbacks.push(callback);

    var clientContext = SP.ClientContext.get_current();
    var list = clientContext.get_web()
                    .get_lists().getByTitle('Configuration Values');

    var item;
    item = list.getItemById(1);
    item.set_item('Title', 'OrganizationName');
    item.set_item('Value', self.OrganizationName);
    item.update();

    item = list.getItemById(2);
    item.set_item('Title', 'OrganizationLogoUrl');
    item.set_item('Value', self.OrganizationLogoUrl);
    item.update();

    item = list.getItemById(3);
    item.set_item('Title', 'CourseName');
    item.set_item('Value', self.CourseName);
    item.update();

    item = list.getItemById(4);
    item.set_item('Title', 'CourseNumber');
    item.set_item('Value', self.CourseNumber);
    item.update();

    item = list.getItemById(5);
    item.set_item('Title', 'Schedule');
    item.set_item('Value', self.Schedule);
    item.update();

    item = list.getItemById(6);
    item.set_item('Title', 'Location');
    item.set_item('Value', self.Location);
    item.update();
```

```
clientContext.executeQueryAsync(
    Function.createDelegate(self, self._onConfigSaveSucceeded),
    Function.createDelegate(self, self._onConfigSaveFailed)
    );
}

self._onConfigSaveSucceeded = function(sender, args) {
    // replace the site logo with the school logo
    $(".ms-siteicon-img").attr("src", self.OrganizationLogoUrl).show();

    while (self._callbacks.length > 0)
        self._callbacks.pop()();
}

self._onConfigSaveFailed = function(sender, args) {
    alert('Save failed. ' + args.get_message() + '\n' + args.get_stackTrace());
}
```

The assumption is that the configuration object has already been updated prior to calling this function. These values are used to update the list items. This function uses the same type of callback mechanism as the load function.

Notice that we did not have to load the configuration list items before updating them. We simply created in-memory references to them by ID number, updated their properties, and then called update(). This creates a batch of update requests for these list items that is passed to SharePoint.

Add a View-Model Object for the Page

Next, we will update the configuration page's script file to contain a view-model object for the page.

10. Open the config.js file from the Scripts/ViewModels folder.

11. Replace the script in this file with the following:

```
$(function () {
    CO.Configs.ensureConfigs(
        function () {
            ko.applyBindings(new ConfigViewModel());
        });
})

function ConfigViewModel() {
    var self = this;
    self.OrganizationName = ko.observable(CO.Configs.OrganizationName);
    self.OrganizationLogoUrl = ko.observable(CO.Configs.OrganizationLogoUrl);
    self.CourseName = ko.observable(CO.Configs.CourseName);
    self.CourseNumber = ko.observable(CO.Configs.CourseNumber);
    self.Schedule = ko.observable(CO.Configs.Schedule);
    self.Location = ko.observable(CO.Configs.Location);
```

```
        self.updateConfigs = function () {
            CO.Configs.OrganizationName = self.OrganizationName();
            CO.Configs.OrganizationLogoUrl = self.OrganizationLogoUrl();
            CO.Configs.CourseName = self.CourseName();
            CO.Configs.CourseNumber = self.CourseNumber();
            CO.Configs.Schedule = self.Schedule();
            CO.Configs.Location = self.Location();

            CO.Configs.saveConfigs(
                function () {
                    location.href = "Default.aspx?" + CO.Configs.StandardTokens;
                });
        }
    }
```

The view model uses the model object to load the configuration values and binds them to the view in the ASPX page. When the view indicates that the values should be saved, by calling the updateConfigs() function, the view-model copies the values into the model and invokes the model's saveConfig() function. The delegate function passed to the save method redirects the user back to the app's home page once the save operation is complete.

Update the Configuration Page Markup

Now we will update the configuration page itself. This is the view in the MVVM pattern.

12. Open the Config.aspx file from the Pages folder.

13. Replace *both* content placeholder controls with the following markup:

```
<asp:Content ID="Content1" runat="server"
        ContentPlaceHolderId="PlaceHolderAdditionalPageHead">
    <script type="text/javascript" src="../Scripts/jquery-1.7.1.min.js"></script>
    <script type="text/javascript" src="../Scripts/knockout-2.2.1.js"></script>
    <script type="text/javascript" src="/_layouts/15/sp.runtime.debug.js"></script>
    <script type="text/javascript" src="/_layouts/15/sp.debug.js"></script>

    <script type="text/javascript" src="../Scripts/Models/siteconfigs.js"></script>
    <script type="text/javascript" src="../Scripts/ViewModels/config.js"></script>
</asp:Content>

<asp:Content ContentPlaceHolderId="PlaceHolderPageTitleInTitleArea" runat="server">
    Settings
</asp:Content>

<asp:Content ID="Content2" ContentPlaceHolderId="PlaceHolderMain" runat="server">
    <div id="configvaluescontainer">
        <table>
            <tbody>
                <tr>
                    <td>School Name</td>
                    <td><input data-bind="value: OrganizationName" size="30"/></td>
                </tr>
```

```
        <tr>
            <td>URL of School Logo</td>
            <td><input data-bind="value: OrganizationLogoUrl" size="30"/></td>
        </tr>
        <tr>
            <td>Course Name</td>
            <td><input data-bind="value: CourseName" size="30"/></td>
        </tr>
        <tr>
            <td>Course Number</td>
            <td><input data-bind="value: CourseNumber" size="15"/></td>
        </tr>
        <tr>
            <td>Schedule</td>
            <td><input data-bind="value: Schedule" size="15"/></td>
        </tr>
        <tr>
            <td>Location</td>
            <td><input data-bind="value: Location" size="15"/></td>
        </tr>
    </tbody>
</table>
<a href="#" data-bind="click: updateConfigs">Update Configurations</a>
</div>
</asp:Content>
```

This markup lays out controls for configuring the app using Knockout for data binding. Note that the anchor's `click` event has been bound to the view-model's `updateConfigs()` function.

Update the App Home Page

14. Open the `Default.aspx` file from the `Pages` folder.

15. Replace the content placeholder control named `PlaceHolderMain` with the following markup:

```
<asp:Content ID="Content1" runat="server"
            ContentPlaceHolderId="PlaceHolderPageTitleInTitleArea">
    Classroom Online Home Page
</asp:Content>

<asp:Content ContentPlaceHolderID="PlaceHolderMain" runat="server">
    <table width="100%">
        <tr>
            <td width="600">
                <div class="orglogo"><span id="schoolName"></span></div>
                <div id="mainmenu">
                    <ul>
                        <li><a href="config.aspx?{StandardTokens}" title="Configure
                        Application">Configure Classroom Online</a></li>
                        <li><a href="../Lists/SiteAssets" title="Site Assets">Site
                        Assets</a></li>
```

```
                                <li><a href="../Lists/Homework" title="Homework">Homework
                                Library</a></li>
                                <li><a href="hwlist.aspx?{StandardTokens}" title="List HW
                                Assignments">List Homeworks Submitted this week</a></li>
                            </ul>
                        </div>
                    </td>
                    <td class="applogo">
                        <div><img src="../Images/AppLogo.png" /></div>
                        <span>Classroom Online</span>
                    </td>
                </tr>
            </table>
        </asp:Content>
```

The menu will now contain items for (1) the configuration page, (2) the site assets library, (3) the homework library that we will add in the next exercise, and (4) a page to display the most recent homework submissions.

Now we will create a view-model object for the default page.

16. Update the script link to include a file named ../Scripts/ViewModels/default.js instead of the current App.js file.

17. Create a new JavaScript file named default.js in the Scripts/ViewModels folder.

18. Add this script to the file:

```
$(function () {
    CO.Configs.ensureConfigs(onConfigLoaded);
})

function onConfigLoaded() {
    $("#schoolLogo").attr("src", CO.Configs.OrganizationLogoUrl);
    $("#schoolName").text(CO.Configs.OrganizationName);

    // replace the standard token placeholder in any links that require tokens
    updateLinkTokens("StandardTokens", CO.Configs.StandardTokens);
}

// This function looks for a token surrounded by braces {} and
// replaces it with the string value provided.
function updateLinkTokens(token, value) {
    $("a[href *= '{" + token + "}']")
        .each(
            function (ind, a) {
                $(a).attr("href",
                        $(a).attr("href").replace("{" + token + "}",
                                                    value));
            });
}
```

The code in this view-model uses the site configuration model object to load the configuration and update the UI elements with information from the configuration.

■ **Tip** The `updateLinkTokens()` function handles forwarding the query string from the current page to any pages linked from this page. By embedding `{StandardTokens}` in our HTML anchors, this function can update the links to include these tokens no matter how many links there are on the page.

---

19. Execute the project. After trusting the app, you will see the home page, as shown in Figure 5-3.

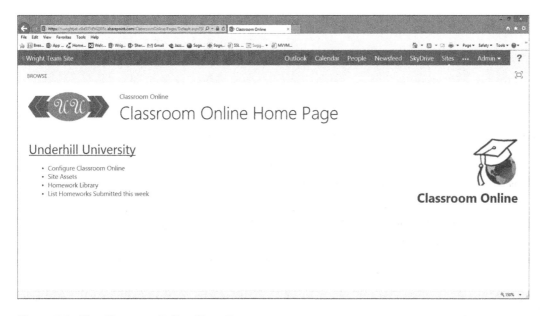

Figure 5-3. *New Classroom Online Home Page*

20. Click on the Configure Classroom Online link (see Figure 5-4).

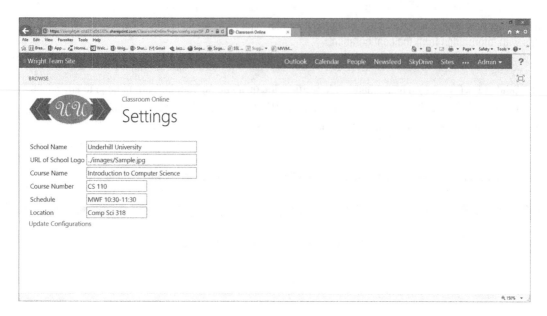

Figure 5-4. *New Classroom Online Settings configuration page*

21. Update any of these values and click on the Update Configurations link. If the save completes successfully, you will be redirected back to the home page.

As an optional step: Because the need for a configuration page is so common when writing apps, SharePoint 2013 has a standard way of presenting them. The markup in the app manifest has an option to set a SettingsPage for the app. This option is not available in the manifest designer window. To add a settings page you need to open the AppManifest.xml file in an XML editor, *not the designer.* Then, you can add the settings page to the configuration of the app, as shown here:

```
<Properties>
  <Title>Classroom Online</Title>
  <StartPage>~appWebUrl/Pages/Default.aspx?{StandardTokens}</StartPage>
  <SettingsPage>~appWebUrl/Pages/Config.aspx?{StandardTokens}</SettingsPage>
</Properties>
```

This adds a Settings option to the app's launch icon, as shown in Figure 5-5.

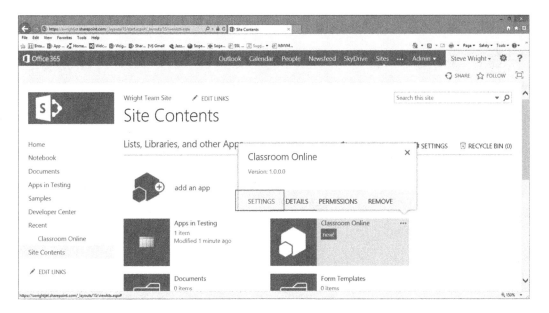

Figure 5-5. *Settings link for the configuration page*

EXERCISE 5.3

In this exercise, we will explore how to work with documents and document libraries using CSOM code. We will create a library for submitting homework assignments and a page for displaying a list of recently submitted assignments.

First we will create a new Homework library in the app web. Then we will create a page to display a list of homework assignments. Finally, we will create a view-model object to query the SharePoint app web for homework assignments to display.

Create the Homework Document Library

1. Open Visual Studio 2012 and the Classroom Online solution.

2. Right-click the Classroom Online project and select Add ➤ NewItem… from the context menu.

3. Select the List template and name the new item Homework.

4. Select Document Library from the Create a customizable list based on drop-down list (see Figure 5-6).

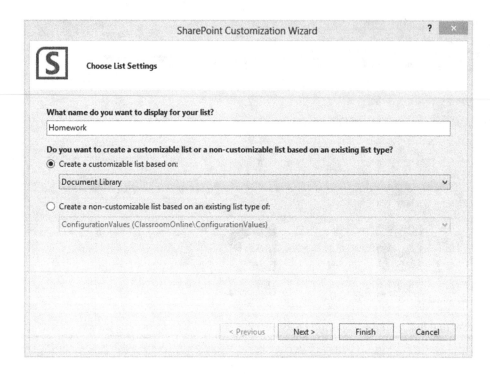

***Figure 5-6.** Create the homework list*

5. Press the Finish button to create the library.

6. Leave the default values for the library in the designer and close the window.

Create the Homework Listing Page

7. Create a new page in the Pages folder called `hwlist.aspx`.

8. Replace the content placeholder controls with this markup:

```
<asp:Content ID="Content1" runat="server"
            ContentPlaceHolderId="PlaceHolderAdditionalPageHead" >
    <script type="text/javascript" src="../Scripts/jquery-1.7.1.min.js"></script>
    <script type="text/javascript" src="../Scripts/knockout-2.2.1.js"></script>
    <script type="text/javascript" src="/_layouts/15/sp.runtime.debug.js"></script>
    <script type="text/javascript" src="/_layouts/15/sp.debug.js"></script>

    <script type="text/javascript" src="../Scripts/Models/siteconfigs.js"></script>
    <script type="text/javascript" src="../Scripts/ViewModels/hwlist.js"></script>
</asp:Content>

<asp:Content ContentPlaceHolderId="PlaceHolderPageTitleInTitleArea" runat="server">
    Homework File List
</asp:Content>
```

```
<asp:Content ID="Content2" ContentPlaceHolderId="PlaceHolderMain" runat="server">
    <div>
        <h2>…Working…</h2>
        <table border="1" cellspacing="0" cellpadding="10" style="display:none">
            <thead style='background-color:gray;color:white'>
                <tr>
                    <td>Date Submitted</td>
                    <td>Student</td>
                    <td>Title</td>
                    <td>Size</td>
                </tr>
            </thead>
            <tbody data-bind="foreach: assignments">
                <tr>
                    <td data-bind="text: dateSubmitted"></td>
                    <td data-bind="text: studentName"></td>
                    <td>
                        <a href="#"
    data-bind="attr: { href: url, title: title }, text: title ? title : url"></a>
                    </td>
                    <td data-bind="text: size"></td>
                </tr>
            </tbody>
        </table>
    </div>
</asp:Content>
```

This ASPX markup will display "…Working…" until the list is ready to be displayed:

```
<h2>…Working…</h2>
<table border="1" cellspacing="0" cellpadding="10" style="display:none">
```

The <h2> header will be displayed until it is hidden by a call to the JQuery hide() function and the <table> is made visible using show().

The file list will be rendered using Knockout's foreach binding. The anchor for the file will be customized using the following binding:

```
<a href="#" data-bind="attr: { href: url, title: title }, text: title ? title : url"></a>
```

The attr binding is used to bind the anchor's title and URL. The text for the anchor is calculated using either the file's title, if present, or the URL.

Create a View-Model for the Page

9. Create a new JavaScript file in the `Scripts/ViewModels` folder named `hwlist.js`.

10. Add this script to the file:

```javascript
$(function () {
    CO.Configs.ensureConfigs(
        function () {
            ko.applyBindings(new HomeworkListViewModel());
        });
})

function HomeworkListViewModel() {
    var self = this;
    self.assignments = ko.observableArray();

    self._loadList = function () {
        var clientContext = SP.ClientContext.get_current();

        var list = clientContext.get_web().get_lists().getByTitle('Homework');

        var query = new SP.CamlQuery();
        query.set_viewXml("<View>"
                        + "  <Query>"
                        + "  <OrderBy>"
                        + "    <FieldRef Name='Modified' Ascending='False' />"
                        + "    <FieldRef Name='Title' Ascending='True' />"
                        + "  </OrderBy>"
                        + "  <Where>"
                        + "    <Geq>"
                        + "      <FieldRef Name='Modified' />"
                        + "      <Value Type='DateTime'>"
                        + "        <Today OffsetDays='-7' />"
                        + "      </Value>"
                        + "    </Geq>"
                        + "  </Where>"
                        + "  </Query>"
                        + "  <ViewFields>"
                        + "    <FieldRef Name='Title' />"
                        + "    <FieldRef Name='Modified' />"
                        + "    <FieldRef Name='Editor' />"
                        + "    <FieldRef Name='FileRef' />"
                        + "    <FieldRef Name='FileLeafRef' />"
                        + "    <FieldRef Name='File_x0020_Size' />"
                        + "  </ViewFields>"
                        + "  <RowLimit>100</RowLimit>"
                        + "</View>");

        self._pendingItems = list.getItems(query);
        clientContext.load(self._pendingItems);
```

```
            clientContext.executeQueryAsync(
                Function.createDelegate(self, self._onLoadListSucceeded),
                Function.createDelegate(self, self._onLoadListFailed)
                );
        }

        self._onLoadListSucceeded = function (sender, args) {
            var listEnumerator = self._pendingItems.getEnumerator();
            while (listEnumerator.moveNext()) {
                var item = listEnumerator.get_current().get_fieldValues();

                self.assignments.push(
                    {
                        title: item.Title,
                        url: item.FileRef,
                        dateSubmitted: item.Modified.toString(),
                        studentName: item.Editor.get_lookupValue(),
                        size: item.File_x0020_Size
                    });
            }

            $('h2').hide();
            $('table').show();
        }

        self._onLoadListFailed = function (sender, args) {
            alert('Unable to load file list: ' + args.get_message() + '\n' + args.get_stackTrace());
        }

        self._loadList();
    }
```

This view-model object follows the same pattern we have used before. The only property exposed is an observable array that initially contains no items.

The _loadList() function creates a reference to the Homework document library and then queries the list for a certain set of items using a CamlQuery Object.

```
var query = new SP.CamlQuery();
query.set_viewXml("<View>"
                ...
                + "</View>");
```

This object is used to represent the conditions to be met to retrieve a subset of items from the list. Setting the ViewXml property allows us to specify the query directly in Collaborative Application Markup Language (CAML), which is a dialect of XML.

The <Query> tag defines which items should be returned. The elements within this tag bear some resemblance to a SELECT statement in SQL. The <OrderBy> tag is used to specify the order the items should be returned in.

```
<OrderBy>
    <FieldRef Name='Modified' Ascending='False' />
    <FieldRef Name='Title' Ascending='True' />
</OrderBy>
```

In this case, we will sort by the date when the file was last modified (most recent first) and the title of the document.

The next part of the query determines which items are to be selected. The `<Where>` tag is like the WHERE clause in a SQL statement. It can contain many nested tags to define very complex conditions.

```
<Where>
    <Geq>
        <FieldRef Name='Modified' />
        <Value Type='DateTime'>
            <Today OffsetDays='-7' />
        </Value>
    </Geq>
</Where>
```

This condition compares the modification date of the document to a date/time value equal to today's date minus 7 days. This retrieves only those files posted within the last week.

The `<ViewFields>` tag defines which properties of the items should be returned. This limits the bandwidth used to retrieve items and ensures that all of the fields needed are returned.

```
<ViewFields>
    <FieldRef Name='Title' />
    <FieldRef Name='Modified' />
    <FieldRef Name='Editor' />
    <FieldRef Name='FileRef' />
    <FieldRef Name='FileLeafRef' />
    <FieldRef Name='File_x0020_Size' />
</ViewFields>
```

You will notice that the field names listed are not all visible when you list the files in the library. All fields in SharePoint have an internal name used by SharePoint and a display name that appears in the user interface. For example, "Title" is a field associated with every list in SharePoint but it often has a different display name, such as "Full Name" or "Subject." The field names used in CAML are the internal names, not the display names. There are several online resources that map internal to display names. A good one is available at http://sharepointmalarkey.wordpress.com/2008/08/21/sharepoint-internal-field-names/.

The last line in the CAML query limits the number of items returned to 100. There are also CAML query options that allow for easy paging through a set of items when needed. In this case, we will assume that we are only interested in the first 100 items.

```
<RowLimit>100</RowLimit>
```

■ **Note**   Additional documentation and examples for using CAML in queries are available at
http://msdn.microsoft.com/en-us/library/dd623934(v=office.15).aspx.

A useful function to become familiar with is get_fieldValues(). This function exists on many CSOM objects.

```
var item = listEnumerator.get_current().get_fieldValues();
```

This function makes working with CSOM objects much easier by converting their properties to JavaScript expando properties. This means that instead of accessing the item's properties using functions such as get_title() or get_item('FileRef') you can simply use item.Title or item.FileRef, respectively. These properties are read-only, however. Updates made to them cannot be written back to SharePoint by calling update().

11. Execute the project and trust the app.

12. On the app's home page, click the Homework Library link.

13. Upload two or three files to this library. Be sure to set some of the files' titles.

14. Return to the app's home page and click the List Homeworks Submitted this week link (see Figure 5-7).

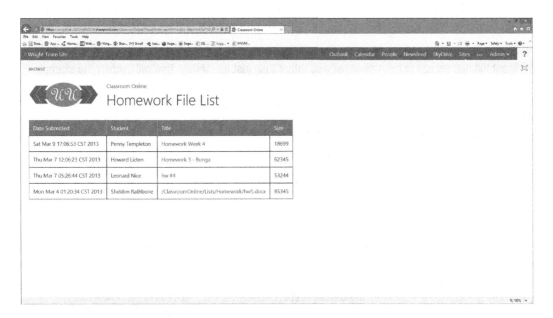

Figure 5-7. *List of recent homework submissions*

If you run this app in the debugger multiple times you may notice something disturbing. Each time the app is run in the debugger, it is retracted (i.e., deleted) from the host site and redeployed. Since the homework library resides in the app web, any files uploaded to this library vanish when the app is retracted. When the app is redeployed, a new, empty library is created.

This is one limitation of creating lists and libraries within the app web. They only exist as long as the app is installed. In some cases, where the data should be retained even if the app is no longer in use, it is preferable to create the list or library in the host web. In the next exercise, we will work with this type of scenario.

EXERCISE 5.4

This exercise will demonstrate how to access SharePoint content that resides outside of the app's app web. We will rewrite the homework page we created in Exercise 5.3 to use a homework library in the host site instead of the app site. Accessing lists in the app's host web is different in two important ways from accessing them in the app web.

First, a list in the host web cannot be created by adding elements to the app in Visual Studio. Those items are created in the app web. The app either has to assume that the list already exists or create the list after the app is installed. The list can also be created using an app event handler. App event handlers will be covered in Chapter 9.

Second, because an app only has access to its own app web by default, the app must be explicitly given access to the host web content that it will need to access. The security surrounding apps will be discussed in detail in Chapter 6.

For this exercise, we will assume that a library named Homework exists in the host web. We will add a permission request to grant the app access to the entire host web rather than just this library. This will simplify the example.

We will create a Homework document library in the host site. We will also update the view-model object for the homework list page to access the list in the host site rather than the app web.

1. Open the SharePoint site where you are testing your apps.

2. Create a new document library called Homework in that site.

3. Add files to the library, as you did in the previous exercise.

4. Open Visual Studio 2012 and the Classroom Online solution. The solution should contain the code added in Exercise 5.3.

5. Open the hwlist.js file in the Scripts/ViewModels folder.

6. Replace the line beginning var list = with these lines:

```
var hostWebContext = new SP.AppContextSite(clientContext, CO.Configs.SPHostUrl);
var list = hostWebContext.get_web().get_lists().getByTitle('Homework');
```

The first line creates a new object called an AppContextSite. This object acts as a context wrapper for handling calls to SharePoint webs that are associated with the app. In this case, we pass in the URL of the host site. This associates the AppContextSite object with the host site. We then use this object to access content in the host site the same way we would using the ClientContext object.

There is an important difference between the `ClientContext` and `AppContextSite` objects. The `ClientContext` object manages all requests between the client and SharePoint including those created using `AppContextSite` objects. `AppContextSite` uses the context object supplied in its constructor to carry out its operations. That is why none of the other uses of the `ClientContext` in this function, such as loading objects or executing batches, were updated. These are functions of the `ClientContext` object, not the `AppContextSite` object.

If you execute this project right now, you will find that it appears to work but no files are listed. This is because we have not granted permission for the app to read from the Homework library in the host web.

7. In Visual Studio, open the designer for the `AppManifest.xml` file.

8. Switch to the Permissions tab.

9. Add a permission request for the Web scope using the Read permission, as shown in Figure 5-8.

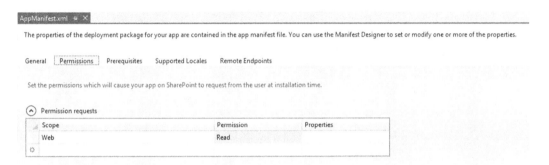

Figure 5-8. *Request read permission on the host web*

10. Execute the project.

11. Click the List Homeworks Submitted this week link on the home page.

The file list from the host web document library is displayed. If you remove and redeploy the app, you will see that the files remain in the library. This is because the library is owned by the host web, not the app itself. We will discuss the permissions required for apps to access data in the Chapter 6.

Summary

In this chapter, we have explored the basics for creating apps that access and update data within a SharePoint site. The Client-Side Object Models (CSOM) for SharePoint 2013 provide the primary entry point for apps to access the SharePoint environment. In Chapter 7, we will look at another strategy for accessing SharePoint data using REST and OData.

Before we begin building our apps, we need to understand the security restrictions that surround apps and users. In the next chapter, we will discuss app and user security. We will create apps that request access to resources and adapt to the permissions the user has been granted.

■ ■ ■

SharePoint App Security

Now we begin to put the pieces of our app together. We will begin by making sure that we cannot only present our data but protect it as well. In this chapter, we will go over the following points:

- How the Cloud App Model supports authentication of both users and applications.

- What types of access an app can be granted to the SharePoint environment.

- What controls SharePoint has for managing authorization of users and apps to read, write, and manage information stored in the site.

- How the concepts of authentication and authorization can be extended into the cloud using Windows Azure and the services it supplies.

- How to connect remote resources to our SharePoint apps while maintaining security and flexibility.

Declaring App Permissions and Scopes

When a user adds an app to a SharePoint host site, it becomes a part of the site. If the app contains hostile code, such as a virus or a Trojan horse, it could cause severe problems for the user. To prevent this, SharePoint 2013 implements a layer of protection for apps above and beyond the traditional permissions assigned to users within SharePoint. Every SharePoint app must declare what actions it intends to take before being installed. SharePoint then ensures that only those actions are allowed.

An app must request permissions from the user before it is allowed to perform any action. These requests are contained in the app's manifest file. During installation of the application, the installing user is presented with a page that asks for explicit permission to install the app, as shown in Figure 6-1. The permissions requested by the app, and granted by the user, are recorded in SharePoint during installation. If the app attempts to access any resources other than those listed, SharePoint will deny the access.

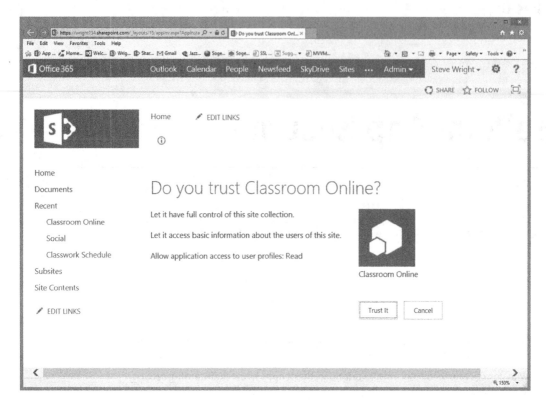

Figure 6-1. *App permissions granted during installation*

To request permissions, the app developer includes XML in the app manifest file, like that shown in Listing 6-1. Visual Studio 2012 contains an app manifest designer to simplify creating these permissions. The manifest designer is shown in Figure 6-2. You can launch the designer by double-clicking on the AppManifest.xml file in Visual Studio. There are three parts to each request: a scope, a right, and optional properties.

Listing 6-1. App Permission Request XML

```
<AppPermissionRequest Scope="http://sharepoint/content/sitecollection/web/list" Right="Write">
    <Property Name="BaseTemplateId" Value="101"/>
</AppPermissionRequest>
```

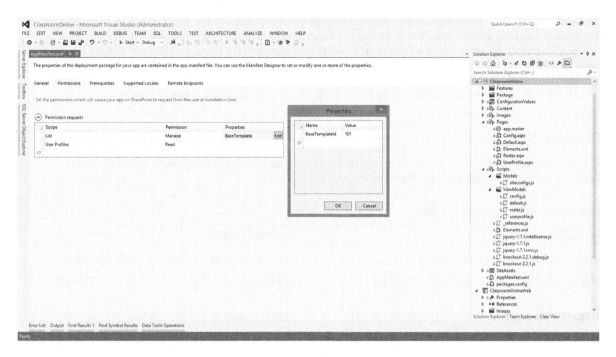

Figure 6-2. *App manifest designer (app permissions) in Visual Studio 2012*

The *scope* identifies how wide an area within the SharePoint environment the permission request applies or what SharePoint service the app needs permission to use. The scope can provide access to a list, a web (site), a site collection, a tenant, or a SharePoint service application. A scope sets the boundary within which the app must operate. Any action taken outside the allowed scopes for an app will be prevented by SharePoint.

Granting a permission scope to an app does not imply that any user interacting with the app will be able to use all of the rights granted. App permissions are only one aspect of app security. User permissions, such as read or write permission on a list, are also checked when an app takes an action. SharePoint provides access to resources only if both the app and the user permissions allow it. This is called the *app+user authentication policy*.

■ **Tip** Besides app+user, there are two other authentication policies available in SharePoint 2013. The *user-only policy* is the normal way users are granted access to resources in SharePoint when they are not using an app. The *app-only policy* is used only for high-trust on-premise apps that are granted the ability to impersonate users by providing a user identity other than the logged on user. High-trust apps will be discussed later in this chapter.

The *right* parameter on the permission request specifies the level of access to be granted. Different scopes have different possible values for this parameter. The most common rights are Read, Write, Manage, and Full Control. Each scope has rights that are appropriate to the actions enabled by that scope.

The final part of a permission request is a set of optional *properties* that control the behavior of the scope. The only out-of-the-box use of this feature was demonstrated back in Listing 6-1. The list scope allows a `BaseTemplateId` property to be provided, which filters the lists in the host web based on the list template used to create them. The installing user can only pick from lists that derive from the base template provided when this parameter is present. A list of SharePoint's list template IDs can be found at `http://msdn.microsoft.com/en-us/library/ms415091.aspx` under the Type property.

Additional scopes can be defined by creating an *app permission provider* assembly. This is a software component that must be installed in SharePoint before any app can use the permissions provided. The provider cannot be packaged as part of the app because it must be installed at the farm level. For example, Microsoft Project Server declares a set of app permissions that can be used to write custom apps for project server. A custom permission provider determines the hierarchy, the available rights, and the properties associated with its own permission scopes.

The next sections describe the standard permission scopes and break them down by category.

Content Scopes

The most common permission scopes relate directly to the site structure within SharePoint. These are shown in Table 6-1. This table lists these scopes from largest to smallest.

***Table 6-1.** Content Permission Scopes*

Scope URI	Includes Access To...
`http://sharepoint/content/tenant`	The entire tenant (or farm) containing the host web
`http://sharepoint/content/sitecollection`	All items within the site collection containing the host web
`http://sharepoint/content/sitecollection/web`	The host web and all descendant sites and lists
`http://sharepoint/content/sitecollection/web/list`	One list within the host web

The scopes listed in Table 6-1 all use the same set of rights: Read, Write, Manage, and Full Control. When a permission is granted to an app for a given location, that same permission is applied to all of the subsites and lists associated within that scope.

Service Scopes

SharePoint also supports permission scopes beyond those that control the site hierarchy. These scopes can provide an app with permission to use SharePoint services. These are listed in Table 6-2.

***Table 6-2.** Service Permission Scopes*

Scope URI	Available Rights
`http://sharepoint/bcs/connection`	Read
`http://sharepoint/search`	QueryAsUserIgnoreAppPrincipal
`http://sharepoint/social/core`	Read, Write, Manage, Full Control
`http://sharepoint/social/microfeed`	Read, Write, Manage, Full Control
`http://sharepoint/social/tenant`	Read, Write, Manage, Full Control
`http://sharepoint/taxonomy`	Read, Write

The most commonly used scope in Table 6-2 is `http://sharepoint/social/tenant`. This oddly named scope provides access to the User Profile Service. The other scopes listed provide access to service applications hosted within SharePoint, such as BCS, Search, or Taxonomy.

Scope Rules

There are certain rules to understand about permission scopes. These rules reflect how app permissions are intended to be used. They can be confusing and counterintuitive in some situations.

- ***Scopes only provide rights to the app, not to the user***—While an app may have the right to access a certain list or item, the user may not. In this case, the more restrictive permission is enforced by SharePoint and access is denied.

- ***Scopes are always stated relative to the host web***—An app automatically has full rights within its own app web, so no additional permission requests are needed. Instead, permission scopes are associated with the host web for the application. The "web" scope refers to everything in the *host* web site. The "list" scope refers to one list within the *host* web site.

- ***Scopes are hierarchical***—This means that any permission granted at a higher level in the site structure will automatically roll down to the lower levels. For example, requesting permission at the "web" level will automatically grant the same rights to the lists within the host site and any subsites under the host site. Granting different types of rights can cause permissions to interact with one another. For example, if the app requests read access at the "web" level and write access at the "list" level, it will be able to read anything in the host web but write only to the selected list.

- ***A scope can only be used once in an app manifest file***—Each scope URI can only appear in a single `AppPermissionRequest` tag in an app manifest. The designer will enforce this restriction. If you hand code multiple requests for the same scope into the XML for the app manifest, only the first request is acted on. All additional requests for the same scope, even if they use different rights or properties, will be ignored. For example, it makes no sense to request both read and manage permission at the same scope since the manage permission already allows reading. This rule can become a problem when lists are involved. Imagine a case where your app needs access to two different lists in the host web. There is no way to request access to two different lists because the list scope can only be activated once. The only option in this case is to request access to the entire host web.

EXERCISE 6.1

In this exercise, we will create a page for testing the permissions granted to our app. This will be a simple page with two buttons. One button will read from the Documents list in the host site. The other will attempt to write to the same list.

This exercise will not add any features to the Classroom Online app, so we will use a new project. Make sure that the host site you are using contains a document library named Documents and that it contains at least one document.

1. Open Visual Studio 2012.

2. Create a new C# SharePoint 2013 app called `PermissionTest`.

3. Switch the hosting option to SharePoint-hosted and click Finish (see Figure 6-3).

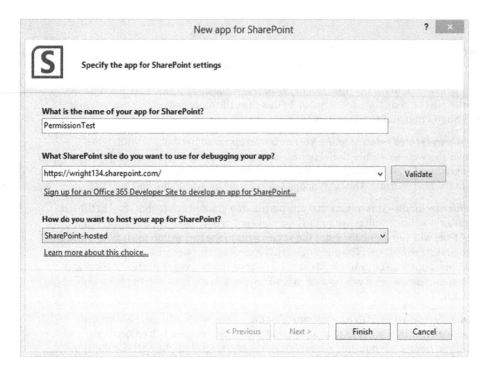

Figure 6-3. *Create a new SharePoint-hosted app*

4. Replace the contents of Default.aspx with the following markup:

```
<%@ Page
    Inherits="Microsoft.SharePoint.WebPartPages.WebPartPage, Microsoft.SharePoint,
Version=15.0.0.0, Culture=neutral, PublicKeyToken=71e9bce111e9429c"
    MasterPageFile="~masterurl/default.master" Language="C#" %>

<%@ Register TagPrefix="Utilities" Namespace="Microsoft.SharePoint.Utilities"
    Assembly="Microsoft.SharePoint, Version=15.0.0.0, Culture=neutral,
PublicKeyToken=71e9bce111e9429c" %>
<%@ Register TagPrefix="WebPartPages" Namespace="Microsoft.SharePoint.WebPartPages"
    Assembly="Microsoft.SharePoint, Version=15.0.0.0, Culture=neutral,
PublicKeyToken=71e9bce111e9429c" %>
<%@ Register TagPrefix="SharePoint" Namespace="Microsoft.SharePoint.WebControls"
    Assembly="Microsoft.SharePoint, Version=15.0.0.0, Culture=neutral,
PublicKeyToken=71e9bce111e9429c" %>

<asp:Content ID="Content1" ContentPlaceHolderID="PlaceHolderAdditionalPageHead"
runat="server">
    <script type="text/javascript" src="../Scripts/jquery-1.7.1.min.js"></script>
    <script type="text/javascript" src="https://ajax.aspnetcdn.com/ajax/knockout/
knockout-2.2.1.js" ></script>
    <script type="text/javascript" src="/_layouts/15/sp.runtime.debug.js"></script>
    <script type="text/javascript" src="/_layouts/15/sp.debug.js"></script>
```

```
    <script type="text/javascript" src="../Scripts//App.js"></script>
</asp:Content>

<asp:Content ID="Content2" ContentPlaceHolderId="PlaceHolderPageTitleInTitleArea"
runat="server">
    App Permission Test
</asp:Content>

<asp:Content ID="Content3" ContentPlaceHolderID="PlaceHolderMain" runat="server">
    <button data-bind="click: readList">Press here to read from Documents.</button>
    <br />
    <button data-bind="click: writeList">Press here to write to Documents.</button>
</asp:Content>
```

5. Open App.js and replace the contents with the following JavaScript:

```javascript
$(function () {
    ko.applyBindings(new testPermissionsViewModel());
});

function testPermissionsViewModel() {
    var self = this;
    self.result = null;

    self.readList = function () {
        var context = new SP.ClientContext.get_current();
        var hostWebContext =
            new SP.AppContextSite(
                context, decodeURIComponent(getQueryStringParameter("SPHostUrl")));

        self.result =
            hostWebContext.get_web().get_lists().getByTitle("Documents")
                .getItems(new SP.CamlQuery.createAllItemsQuery());
        context.load(self.result);

        context.executeQueryAsync(
            Function.createDelegate(self, self.onSuccess),
            Function.createDelegate(self, self.onFail)
            );
    }

    self.writeList = function () {
        var context = new SP.ClientContext.get_current();
        var hostWebContext =
            new SP.AppContextSite(
                context, decodeURIComponent(getQueryStringParameter("SPHostUrl")));

        self.result =
            hostWebContext.get_web().get_lists().getByTitle("Documents")
                .getItemById(1);
        self.result.set_item("Title", "My Updated Book Title");
        self.result.update();
```

```
            context.executeQueryAsync(
                Function.createDelegate(self, self.onSuccess),
                Function.createDelegate(self, self.onFail)
                );
        }

    self.onSuccess = function () {
        if (self.result instanceof SP.ListItemCollection) {
            if (!self.result.get_item(0))
                alert("Success, but nothing returned!");
            else
                alert("Success! First Title = "
                            + self.result.get_item(0).get_item("Title"));
        }
        else
            alert("Success!");
    }

    self.onFail = function(sender, args) {
        alert("Failed: " + args.get_message());
    }
}

function getQueryStringParameter(paramToRetrieve) {
    var params =
        document.URL.split("?")[1].split("&");
    var strParams = "";
    for (var i = 0; i < params.length; i = i + 1) {
        var singleParam = params[i].split("=");
        if (singleParam[0] == paramToRetrieve)
            return singleParam[1];
    }
}
```

6. Open the AppManifest.xml designer.

7. Select the Permissions tab.

8. Create a permission request with a scope of List and a permission of Read (see Figure 6-4).

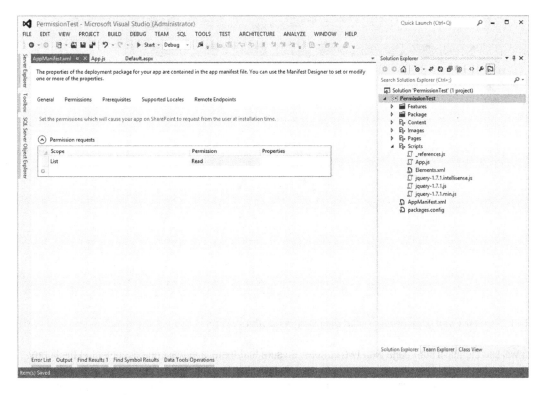

Figure 6-4. *Request the List app permission*

9. Save your changes.

10. Click Start in the Visual Studio menu (or press F5) to run the app.

11. Once the app loads, you will need to grant it permission to the Documents library (see Figure 6-5).

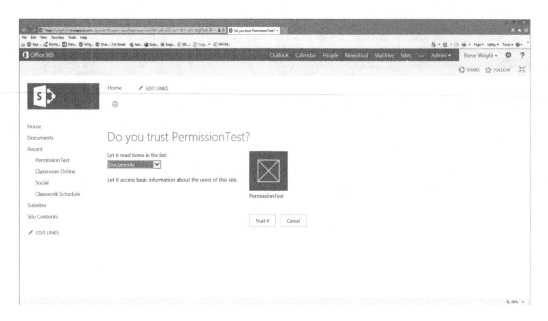

Figure 6-5. *Grant the app permission to read the Documents library*

Now you will see the app's start page with two buttons. Be sure that there is at least one document in the library. If you press the top button, the page will attempt to read from the list. You should see "Success!" along with the title of the first document in that library. When you press the other button, you will get an access denied message.

12. Stop the debugger.

13. Switch the `List` permission request to `Write` in the `AppManifest.xml` file.

14. Save and run the app again.

Now the second button should work correctly. You should be able to see that the title changed on the first document in the library.

Let's examine a few key lines in the code.

```
var context = new SP.ClientContext.get_current();
var hostWebContext =
    new SP.AppContextSite(
        context, decodeURIComponent(getQueryStringParameter("SPHostUrl")));

self.result =
    hostWebContext.get_web().get_lists().getByTitle("Documents")
        .getItemById(1);
self.result.set_item("Title", "My Updated Book Title");
self.result.update();

context.executeQueryAsync(
    Function.createDelegate(self, self.onSuccess),
    Function.createDelegate(self, self.onFail)
    );
```

The first line creates the default client context object. This object is connected to the app web, not the host web. If we attempt to read from this context, we will be looking at the wrong SharePoint site. The `SP.AppContextSite` is an object designed to access sites associated with the app other than the app web. In this case, we create the context site object using the URL of the host web, which was passed in as a query string parameter. Then we use this context to update the title property of the item with an ID of 1.

■ **Tip** For more details on client-side objects like `SP.AppContextSite`, refer to Chapter 5.

Using this simple test project, try experimenting with different permission settings to see their effects.

Set the `List` permission to `Write` but select a list other than `Documents`. You will find that the read button works, but no list items are found. The write button fails.

Set the permission to web or site collection scope. Try altering the code to see which areas of the site collection or tenant you can access with each scope.

Controlling Authentication and Identities

SharePoint 2013 uses *claims-based authentication*. This means that users are identified by presenting SharePoint with claims that represent their identity and their groups as ensured by a trusted identity service. After we have established the identity of a user, we generally need to retrieve additional information about the user. There are two sources of this information, depending on the level of detail needed. These are the user information list and the user profile service.

First, we will look at how SharePoint exposes the user's identity to our code. Then, we will experiment with retrieving user information for use in our app.

Principals

The end-user of the app is only one of the identities that we need in order to communicate securely. These identities are referred to as *principals*. Different types of principals include user, app, and resource principals.

A *user principal* identifies the user that is using the app and the identity service that has verified their credentials. The user principal can take one of two forms when rendered as a text string.

- Microsoft Online ID—`i:0#.f|membership|myuser@mydomain.com`

- Windows Active Directory (NTLM)—`i:0#.w|mydomain\myuser`

The tools provided by SharePoint, such as TokenHelper and the User Information List, generally make it unnecessary to parse these string manually. Both of these tools will be described later in this chapter.

An *app principal* identifies the app when it attempts to access a resource outside of its own domain. For example, in a provider-hosted or auto-hosted app, the app's remote web site resides in a separate domain. Therefore, it must identify itself to SharePoint before accessing any SharePoint resources.

The app principal is used to create access tokens by contacting a trusted security token service (STS). The fact that both the app and the SharePoint instance being accessed trust the same STS is what allows the access to take place.

The format of an app principal looks like this:

7a6b7a6f-b2da-454b-a19b-703f8009eb74@720c6f2b-c6f9-48b5-b622-47b92700ad33

The GUID before the at sign (@) identifies the app. This is known as the app's *client ID* and can be found in the remote site's web.config file. The GUID after the at sign identifies the realm in which the app resides. An app will have the same client ID in any realm where it is installed. The combination of the ID and realm is necessary to uniquely identify the installation instance of the app.

A *resource (a.k.a. target) principal* identifies the owner of a resource that is to be accessed. This string looks similar to the app principal described before except that it has an extra element. The principal string consists of three parts, like this:

00000003-0000-0ff1-ce00-000000000000/wright134.sharepoint.com@720c6f2b-c6f9-48b5-b622-47b92700ad33

The GUID before the slash (/) identifies the application that will be receiving the request. The value shown in this example (00000003-0000-0ff1-ce00-000000000000) is the identifier for SharePoint 2013. This value will always be the same when accessing SharePoint.

The value between the slash and the at sign is the authority part of the target URL. This is the fully qualified server name. The value after the at sign is the realm of the target system.

Depending on how a principal is used, it will need to be formatted appropriately. The TokenHelper file provided by Microsoft has this formatting logic built in. We will discuss TokenHelper utility later in this chapter.

Retrieving User Information

The *user information list* in SharePoint contains a listing of all users in the site collection. The app can retrieve a limited set of properties from this list, including the user's name, e-mail address, and account name. A SharePoint app always gets access to the information in this list since it is necessary to identify the current user. During installation, the user grants access to this list when they see the message *"Let it access basic information about the users of this site."* This appears for any app, as it is always required. No app permission request is needed in the app manifest. The information stored in the user information list is retrieved using the SP.User object through functions such as get_currentUser().

SharePoint 2013 has the ability to store much more information about users than is available in the user information list. This is where the *user profile service* comes into play. A user's profile contains all of the information SharePoint holds about the user. This includes first and last name, contact information, department and manager information, and social computing preferences. The user's profile can also contain custom information beyond that which is defined by SharePoint. Accessing data from the user profile service allows us to tailor the presentation of our app for the user.

EXERCISE 6.2

In this exercise, we will retrieve user information from both the user information list and the user profile service. This will allow us to compare the fields available in both.

We will create a new app specifically for this exercise, rather than adding it to Classroom Online. We will start by displaying the fields available in the SP.User object. Then, we will add information available only in the user's profile.

1. Open Visual Studio 2012.

2. Create a new C# SharePoint 2013 app called UserProfileTest.

3. Switch the hosting option to SharePoint-hosted and click Finish.

4. Replace the contents of `Default.aspx` with the following markup:

```
<%@ Page
    Inherits="Microsoft.SharePoint.WebPartPages.WebPartPage, Microsoft.SharePoint,
Version=15.0.0.0, Culture=neutral, PublicKeyToken=71e9bce111e9429c"
    MasterPageFile="~masterurl/default.master" Language="C#" %>

<%@ Register TagPrefix="Utilities" Namespace="Microsoft.SharePoint.Utilities"
    Assembly="Microsoft.SharePoint, Version=15.0.0.0, Culture=neutral,
PublicKeyToken=71e9bce111e9429c" %>
<%@ Register TagPrefix="WebPartPages" Namespace="Microsoft.SharePoint.WebPartPages"
    Assembly="Microsoft.SharePoint, Version=15.0.0.0, Culture=neutral,
PublicKeyToken=71e9bce111e9429c" %>
<%@ Register TagPrefix="SharePoint" Namespace="Microsoft.SharePoint.WebControls"
    Assembly="Microsoft.SharePoint, Version=15.0.0.0, Culture=neutral,
PublicKeyToken=71e9bce111e9429c" %>

<asp:Content ID="Content1" ContentPlaceHolderID="PlaceHolderAdditionalPageHead"
runat="server">
    <script type="text/javascript" src="../Scripts/jquery-1.7.1.min.js"></script>
    <script type="text/javascript" src="https://ajax.aspnetcdn.com/ajax/knockout/
knockout-2.2.1.js" ></script>
    <script type="text/javascript" src="/_layouts/15/sp.runtime.debug.js"></script>
    <script type="text/javascript" src="/_layouts/15/sp.debug.js"></script>
    <script type="text/javascript"
src="/_layouts/15/sp.userprofiles.debug.js"></script>

    <script type="text/javascript" src="../Scripts//App.js"></script>
</asp:Content>

<asp:Content ID="Content2" ContentPlaceHolderId="PlaceHolderPageTitleInTitleArea"
runat="server">
    User Information
</asp:Content>

<asp:Content ID="Content3" ContentPlaceHolderID="PlaceHolderMain" runat="server">
    <h2>Current User Properties</h2>
    <table data-bind="with:currentUser">
        <tr><td>title</td><td data-bind="text: get_title()"></td></tr>
        <tr><td>Id</td><td data-bind="text: get_id()"></td></tr>
        <tr><td>loginName</td><td data-bind="text: get_loginName()"></td></tr>
        <tr><td>email</td><td data-bind="text: get_email()"></td></tr>
        <tr><td>isSiteAdmin</td><td data-bind="text: get_isSiteAdmin()"></td></tr>
    </table>
</asp:Content>
```

Notice that this markup links an additional SharePoint JavaScript library (`sp.userprofiles.debug.js`). This file contains the user profile objects that we will use to read the user's information.

5. Open `App.js` and replace the contents with the following JavaScript:

```javascript
$(function () {
    ko.applyBindings(new userProfileProps());
});

function userProfileProps() {
    var self = this;
    self._currentUser = null;
    self.currentUser = ko.observable();

    self.load = function () {
        var context = new SP.ClientContext.get_current();
        self._currentUser = context.get_web().get_currentUser();
        context.load(self._currentUser);

        context.executeQueryAsync(
            Function.createDelegate(self, self.onSuccess),
            Function.createDelegate(self, self.onFail)
            );
    }

    self.onSuccess = function () {
        // bind the CSOM object to the View-Model
        self.currentUser(self._currentUser);
    }

    self.onFail = function (sender, args) {
        alert("Unable to access information: " + args.get_message());
    }

    self.load();
}
```

6. Click Start in the Visual Studio menu (or press F5) to run the app.

7. The page displayed will be similar to Figure 6-6.

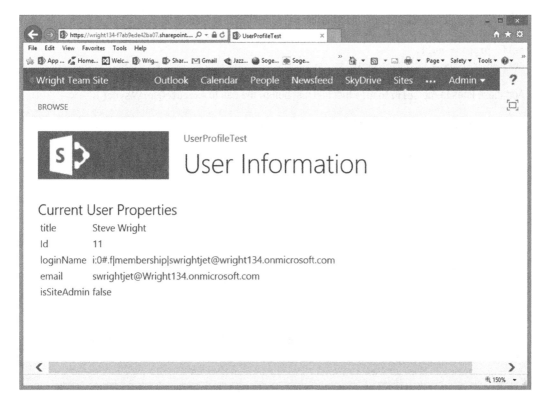

Figure 6-6. *Display user information list data*

For basic security checking, this information is sufficient. To implement personalization, we will need the user's profile.

8. Stop the debugger.

9. Open `Default.aspx` and add this markup just before the last `</asp:Content>` tag:

```
<br />
<h2>User Profile Properties</h2>
<table data-bind="with:userProps">
    <tr><td>AccountName</td><td data-bind="text: AccountName"></td></tr>
    <tr><td>UserName</td><td data-bind="text: UserName"></td></tr>
    <tr><td>FirstName</td><td data-bind="text: FirstName"></td></tr>
    <tr><td>LastName</td><td data-bind="text: LastName"></td></tr>
    <tr><td>PreferredName</td><td data-bind="text: PreferredName"></td></tr>
    <tr><td>WorkEmail</td><td data-bind="text: WorkEmail"></td></tr>
    <tr><td>WorkPhone</td><td data-bind="text: WorkPhone"></td></tr>
    <tr>
        <td>PictureURL</td>
        <td><img src="#" data-bind="attr: {src: PictureURL}" /></td>
    </tr>
</table>
```

10. Open `App.js` and add these lines just after the `var self=this;` declaration:

```
self._props = null;
self.userProps = ko.observable();
```

11. Add these lines to the `self.load()` function just before the call to `executeQueryAsync()`:

```
var pm = new SP.UserProfiles.PeopleManager(context);
self._props = pm.getMyProperties();
context.load(self._props);
```

12. Add this line to the `self.onSuccess()` function:

```
self.userProps(self._props.get_userProfileProperties());
```

13. Open the designer for the `AppManifest.xml` file.

14. Select the Permissions tab.

15. Create a permission request for scope = User Profiles and permission = Read.

16. Click Start in the Visual Studio menu (or press F5) to run the app.

17. You will be prompted to grant the app permissions. Click Trust It. The page displayed will be similar to that shown in Figure 6-7.

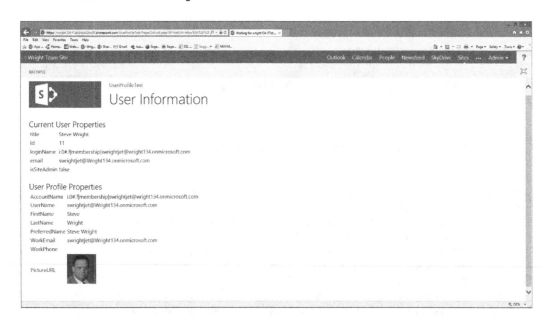

Figure 6-7. *Display user profile data*

There are many properties available in the user profile service. You can also create custom user profile properties. The call to `self._props.get_userProfileProperties()` creates an object that has all of the profile properties assigned to it. This makes it easy to browse the profile in the debugger or bind its values to HTML elements.

SharePoint Groups, Roles, and Permissions

In addition to granting rights to the app, the user must also have permission to access any resources the app needs to use. These permissions are managed by SharePoint 2013 in the same way as in previous versions. The difference between app permissions and user permissions from the app developer's perspective is that we can assume our app had been granted the required app permissions. If not, the app would not be installed and running. User permissions must be checked by the app to avoid receiving "access denied" messages or other app errors.

Figure 6-8 illustrates the key concepts in assigning permissions in SharePoint. Table 6-3 describes each of these and how they are accessed in the client-side object model.

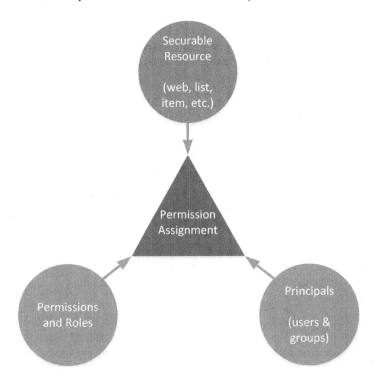

Figure 6-8. *Assigning permissions in SharePoint*

Table 6-3. *SharePoint Permission Objects*

Concept	Description	CSOM Object(s)
Securable Object	Any object in SharePoint that can have permissions assigned to it.	`SP.SecurableObject` (base object) `SP.Site`, `SP.Web`, `SP.List`, `SP.ListItem`, etc.
Permission	A discrete type of action that a user may be granted the right to perform. Examples include reading list items, creating subsites, managing lists, etc.	`SP.BasePermissions`
Role	A named collection of permissions used to create user roles such as Contribute, Design, or Full Control. Roles are called "Permission Levels" in the SharePoint user interface.	`SP.RoleDefinition` `SP.RoleDefinitionBinding`

(continued)

Figure 6-8. (*continued*)

Concept	Description	CSOM Object(s)
Principal	A user, security group or SharePoint group used to identify one or more users to be granted a permission.	SP.Principal (base object) SP.User—user or security group SP.Group—SharePoint group
Role Assignment	An assignment joins the principal, securable object, and permissions together to grant a permission.	SP.RoleAssignment

A role assignment contains a reference to a principal and a list of roles and permissions. The assignment is added to the securable object's assignment collection. When determining the permissions available on an object, the role assignment list can be scanned to determine which principals have which permissions.

EXERCISE 6.3

In this exercise, we will begin setting up the security for our Classroom Online app. In our app, we have two roles: students and faculty. We could implement these roles using either SharePoint groups or permission levels.

Permission levels would be preferable if we had different sets of base permissions that apply to each set of users. We would create a new role definition when our app was installed and users would be granted that role in the host web to identify them as having that role.

In our case, we will use SharePoint groups. Creating permission levels for students and faculty does not provide us any utility because both faculty and students will have the same base permissions equivalent to the Contribute role. The site administrator will be responsible for assigning students and faculty to the site and groups are generally easier for users to understand than permission levels.

Our app will allow the site owner to configure a group for students and a group for faculty. By default, the site's "member" group will be used for students and the "owner" group will be used for faculty, but these defaults can be changed. The faculty group for a Classroom Online site should have Full Control rights; whereas the student group only needs Contribute rights.

In this exercise, we will update the app configuration page to include configuring of the student and faculty groups for the site. We will add logic to the configuration page to prevent its use by anyone that is not a site administrator. We will also create a roster page that lists all of the faculty and student users, and add a link to the home page for the roster.

Before starting this exercise, create groups in the host web called "Faculty" and "Students." We will assume that these are the names of these groups throughout the exercise.

First, we will update the app settings page to include the two new configuration settings.

1. Open Visual Studio 2012 and load the Classroom Online solution. The files created in previous chapters can be downloaded from the book's web site, available from the Source Code/Download area of the Apress web site (www.apress.com).

2. Open the Elements.xml file under the ConfigurationValues/ConfigurationValuesInstance node in the solution explorer.

3. Add this markup to the `<Rows>` collection:

```
<Row>
  <Field Name="Title">facultyGroupID</Field>
  <Field Name="Value"></Field>
</Row>
<Row>
  <Field Name="Title">studentGroupID</Field>
  <Field Name="Value"></Field>
</Row>
```

4. Save and close `Elements.xml`.

5. Create a new directory under `Scripts` in the project called `Models`.

6. Create a new JavaScript file named `siteconfigs.js` in the `Scripts/Models` project directory.

7. Add this JavaScript to the file:

```
var CO = CO || {};

$(function() {
    CO.Configs = new CO_Configs();
})

// data model object for the app's configuration
CO_Configs = function () {
    var self = this;
    self._loadComplete = 0;
    self._callbacks = [];
    self._pendingItems;

    self.faculty = [];
    self.students = [];

    self.facultyGroupID = null;
    self.studentGroupID = null;
    self.isCurrentUserFaculty = 0;
    self.isCurrentUserStudent = 0;
    self.isCurrentUserSiteAdmin = 0;

    self.ensureConfigs = function (callback) {
        if (self._loadComplete)
            callback();
        else
            self._callbacks.push(callback);
    }

    self._loadConfigs = function () {
        var clientContext = SP.ClientContext.get_current();
```

```
        var list = clientContext.get_web().get_lists()
                    .getByTitle('Configuration Values');
        self._pendingItems = list.getItems(new SP.CamlQuery.createAllItemsQuery());
        clientContext.load(self._pendingItems);

        self._currentWeb = clientContext.get_web();
        clientContext.load(self._currentWeb);

        self.siteGroups = self._currentWeb.get_siteGroups();
        clientContext.load(self.siteGroups, 'Include(Title,Id)');

        self._currentUser = self._currentWeb.get_currentUser();
        clientContext.load(self._currentUser);

        self._currentUserGroups = self._currentWeb.get_currentUser().get_groups();
        clientContext.load(self._currentUserGroups);

        self._ownerGroup = self._currentWeb.get_associatedOwnerGroup();
        clientContext.load(self._ownerGroup);

        self._memberGroup = self._currentWeb.get_associatedMemberGroup();
        clientContext.load(self._memberGroup);

        clientContext.executeQueryAsync(
            Function.createDelegate(self, self._onConfigLoadSucceeded),
            Function.createDelegate(self, self._onConfigLoadFailed)
            );
    }

    self._onConfigLoadSucceeded = function (sender, args) {
        var clientContext = SP.ClientContext.get_current();

        // load configuration values from the list
        var listEnumerator = self._pendingItems.getEnumerator();
        while (listEnumerator.moveNext()) {
            var item = listEnumerator.get_current();
            eval("self." + item.get_item("Title")
                    + " = '" + item.get_item("Value") + "'");
        }

        // replace the site logo with the school logo
        $(".ms-siteicon-img").attr("src", self.OrganizationLogoUrl).show();

        // get tokens from the URL
        self.SPAppWebUrl = decodeURIComponent(getQueryStringParameter("SPAppWebUrl"));
        self.SPLanguage = decodeURIComponent(getQueryStringParameter("SPLanguage"));
        self.SPClientTag = decodeURIComponent(getQueryStringParameter("SPClientTag"));
        self.SPProductNumber =
                decodeURIComponent(getQueryStringParameter("SPProductNumber"));
        self.SPHostUrl = decodeURIComponent(getQueryStringParameter("SPHostUrl"));
        self.scriptBase = self.SPHostUrl + "/_layouts/15/";
        self.StandardTokens = document.URL.split("?")[1];
```

```
        // determine group and user permissions
        if (self.facultyGroupID == "null")
            self.facultyGroupID = self._ownerGroup.get_id();
        if (self.studentGroupID == "null")
            self.studentGroupID = self._memberGroup.get_id();

        self.facultyGroup = self.siteGroups.getById(self.facultyGroupID);
        self._facultyUsers = self.facultyGroup.get_users();
        clientContext.load(self.facultyGroup);
        clientContext.load(self._facultyUsers);

        self.studentGroup = self.siteGroups.getById(self.studentGroupID);
        self._studentUsers = self.studentGroup.get_users();
        clientContext.load(self.studentGroup);
        clientContext.load(self._studentUsers);

        var p = new SP.BasePermissions();
        p.set(SP.PermissionKind.manageWeb);
        self._perms = clientContext.get_web().doesUserHavePermissions(p);

        clientContext.executeQueryAsync(
            Function.createDelegate(self, self._onGroupLoadSucceeded),
            Function.createDelegate(self, self._onConfigLoadFailed)
        );
    }

    self._onGroupLoadSucceeded = function () {
        self.currentUser =
            {
                name: self._currentUser.get_title(),
                email: self._currentUser.get_email(),
                loginName: self._currentUser.get_loginName(),
                userId: self._currentUser.get_userId(),
                isSiteAdmin: self._perms.get_value()
            };
        self.isCurrentUserSiteAdmin = self.currentUser.isSiteAdmin;
        var uid = self.currentUser.loginName;

        // load faculty members
        var listEnumerator = self._facultyUsers.getEnumerator();
        while (listEnumerator.moveNext()) {
            var member = listEnumerator.get_current();
            self.faculty.push({
                name: member.get_title(),
                email: member.get_email(),
                loginName: member.get_loginName(),
                userId: member.get_userId(),
                isSiteAdmin: member.get_isSiteAdmin()
            });
            if (member.get_loginName() == uid)
                self.isCurrentUserFaculty = 1;
        }
```

```
        // load students
        listEnumerator = self._studentUsers.getEnumerator();
        while (listEnumerator.moveNext()) {
            var member = listEnumerator.get_current();
            self.students.push({
                name: member.get_title(),
                email: member.get_email(),
                loginName: member.get_loginName(),
                userId: member.get_userId(),
                isSiteAdmin: member.get_isSiteAdmin()
            });
            if (member.get_loginName() == uid)
                self.isCurrentUserStudent = 1;
        }

        // mark the load complete and call the callbacks
        self._loadComplete = 1;
        while (self._callbacks.length > 0)
            self._callbacks.pop()();
    }

    self._onConfigLoadFailed = function (sender, args) {
        alert('Unable to load app configuration: '
                + args.get_message() + '\n' + args.get_stackTrace());
    }

    self.saveConfigs = function(callback) {
        if (callback) self._callbacks.push(callback);

        var clientContext = SP.ClientContext.get_current();
        var list = clientContext.get_web().get_lists()
                        .getByTitle('Configuration Values');

        var item;
        item = list.getItemById(1);
        item.set_item('Title', 'OrganizationName');
        item.set_item('Value', self.OrganizationName);
        item.update();

        item = list.getItemById(2);
        item.set_item('Title', 'OrganizationLogoUrl');
        item.set_item('Value', self.OrganizationLogoUrl);
        item.update();

        item = list.getItemById(3);
        item.set_item('Title', 'CourseName');
        item.set_item('Value', self.CourseName);
        item.update();
```

```
        item = list.getItemById(4);
        item.set_item('Title', 'CourseNumber');
        item.set_item('Value', self.CourseNumber);
        item.update();

        item = list.getItemById(5);
        item.set_item('Title', 'Schedule');
        item.set_item('Value', self.Schedule);
        item.update();

        item = list.getItemById(6);
        item.set_item('Title', 'Location');
        item.set_item('Value', self.Location);
        item.update();

        item = list.getItemById(7);
        item.set_item('Title', 'facultyGroupID');
        item.set_item('Value', self.facultyGroupID);
        item.update();

        item = list.getItemById(8);
        item.set_item('Title', 'studentGroupID');
        item.set_item('Value', self.studentGroupID);
        item.update();

        clientContext.executeQueryAsync(
            Function.createDelegate(self, self._onConfigSaveSucceeded),
            Function.createDelegate(self, self._onConfigSaveFailed)
            );
    }

    self._onConfigSaveSucceeded = function(sender, args) {
        // replace the site logo with the school logo
        $(".ms-siteicon-img").attr("src", self.OrganizationLogoUrl).show();

        while (self._callbacks.length > 0)
            self._callbacks.pop()();
    }

    self._onConfigSaveFailed = function(sender, args) {
        alert('Save failed. ' + args.get_message() + '\n' + args.get_stackTrace());
    }

    // start loading the configuration
    self._loadConfigs();
}

// utility routine
function getQueryStringParameter(paramToRetrieve) {
    var params =
        document.URL.split("?")[1].split("&");
```

```
            var strParams = "";
            for (var i = 0; i < params.length; i = i + 1) {
                var singleParam = params[i].split("=");
                if (singleParam[0] == paramToRetrieve)
                    return singleParam[1];
            }
        }
```

This code implements a model object for the site's configuration settings in the Model-View-ViewModel pattern. The following lines record whether the user has Manage Web rights on the site. This is the permission we will use to identify a site administrator.

```
var p = new SP.BasePermissions();
p.set(SP.PermissionKind.manageWeb);
self._perms = clientContext.get_web().doesUserHavePermissions(p);
...
// process the request asynchronously
...
self.currentUser =
    {
        name: self._currentUser.get_title(),
        email: self._currentUser.get_email(),
        loginName: self._currentUser.get_loginName(),
        userId: self._currentUser.get_userId(),
        isSiteAdmin: self._perms.get_value()
    };
```

Once the request is executed, the variable will contain either `true` or `false`. Each permission within SharePoint is essentially a flag. This request asks SharePoint "Does the current user have all of the permissions for which I have set the flags?" If so, the call returns `true`. Otherwise, if any of the permissions are missing, it returns `false`.

```
listEnumerator = self._studentUsers.getEnumerator();
while (listEnumerator.moveNext()) {
    var member = listEnumerator.get_current();
    self.students.push({
        name: member.get_title(),
        email: member.get_email(),
        loginName: member.get_loginName(),
        userId: member.get_userId(),
        isSiteAdmin: member.get_isSiteAdmin()
    });
    if (member.get_loginName() == uid)
        self.isCurrentUserStudent = 1;
}
```

This code loops through the members of the student group and creates a JavaScript array containing the students. Client-side collections are usually traversed using an enumerator object rather than a simple `for` loop.

8. Create a view model file for the configuration page named `config.js` in the `Scripts/ViewModel` directory.

9. Add the following code to this file:

```
$(function () {
    CO.Configs.ensureConfigs(
        function () {
            if (!CO.Configs.isCurrentUserSiteAdmin) {
                alert("Access Denied!");
                window.history.back();
            }
            else
                ko.applyBindings(new ConfigViewModel());
        });
})

function ConfigViewModel() {
    var self = this;
    self.OrganizationName = ko.observable(CO.Configs.OrganizationName);
    self.OrganizationLogoUrl = ko.observable(CO.Configs.OrganizationLogoUrl);
    self.CourseName = ko.observable(CO.Configs.CourseName);
    self.CourseNumber = ko.observable(CO.Configs.CourseNumber);
    self.Schedule = ko.observable(CO.Configs.Schedule);
    self.Location = ko.observable(CO.Configs.Location);

    self.siteGroups = [];
    var listEnumerator = CO.Configs.siteGroups.getEnumerator();
    while (listEnumerator.moveNext()) {
        var grp = listEnumerator.get_current();
        var grpItem = { groupID: grp.get_id(), groupName: grp.get_title() }
        self.siteGroups.push(grpItem);

        if (grp.get_id() == CO.Configs.facultyGroupID)
            self.facultyGroup = ko.observable(grpItem);
        if (grp.get_id() == CO.Configs.studentGroupID)
            self.studentGroup = ko.observable(grpItem);
    }

    self.updateConfigs = function () {
        CO.Configs.OrganizationName = self.OrganizationName();
        CO.Configs.OrganizationLogoUrl = self.OrganizationLogoUrl();
        CO.Configs.CourseName = self.CourseName();
        CO.Configs.CourseNumber = self.CourseNumber();
        CO.Configs.Schedule = self.Schedule();
        CO.Configs.Location = self.Location();
        CO.Configs.facultyGroupID = self.facultyGroup().groupID;
        CO.Configs.studentGroupID = self.studentGroup().groupID;

        CO.Configs.saveConfigs(
            function () {
                location.href = "Default.aspx?" + CO.Configs.StandardTokens;
            });
    }
}
```

The first lines of this file load the current configuration values. Then, a check is made to ensure that the user is an administrator before showing the page.

```
$(function () {
    CO.Configs.ensureConfigs(
        function () {
            if (!CO.Configs.isCurrentUserSiteAdmin) {
                alert("Access Denied!");
                window.history.back();
            }
            else
                ko.applyBindings(new ConfigViewModel());
        });
})
```

Remember that the check we are doing here does not prevent the user from updating the list if they should not be allowed to. The permissions on the list do that. This check just allows us to control the user experience so that we do not present the user with options they do not really have.

■ **Note** Instead of checking the Manage Web permission on the web, we could have checked for write access to the Configuration Values list. In this case, the result is the same.

---

10. Update the contents of the `Config.aspx` file, in the `Pages` directory of the `ClassroomOnline` project, to contain the following markup.

```
<%@ Page language="C#" MasterPageFile="app.master"
    Inherits="Microsoft.SharePoint.WebPartPages.WebPartPage, Microsoft.SharePoint,
    Version=15.0.0.0, Culture=neutral, PublicKeyToken=71e9bce111e9429c" %>
<%@ Register Tagprefix="SharePoint"
    Namespace="Microsoft.SharePoint.WebControls"
    Assembly="Microsoft.SharePoint, Version=15.0.0.0, Culture=neutral,
    PublicKeyToken=71e9bce111e9429c" %>
<%@ Register Tagprefix="Utilities"
    Namespace="Microsoft.SharePoint.Utilities" Assembly="Microsoft.SharePoint,
    Version=15.0.0.0, Culture=neutral, PublicKeyToken=71e9bce111e9429c" %>
<%@ Register Tagprefix="WebPartPages" Namespace="Microsoft.SharePoint.WebPartPages"
    Assembly="Microsoft.SharePoint, Version=15.0.0.0, Culture=neutral,
    PublicKeyToken=71e9bce111e9429c" %>

<asp:Content ID="Content1" ContentPlaceHolderId="PlaceHolderAdditionalPageHead"
runat="server">
    <script type="text/javascript" src="../Scripts/jquery-1.7.1.min.js"></script>
    <script type="text/javascript" src="../Scripts/knockout-2.2.1.js"></script>
    <script type="text/javascript" src="/_layouts/15/sp.runtime.debug.js"></script>
    <script type="text/javascript" src="/_layouts/15/sp.debug.js"></script>

    <script type="text/javascript" src="../Scripts/Models/siteconfigs.js"></script>
    <script type="text/javascript" src="../Scripts/ViewModels/config.js"></script>
</asp:Content>
```

```
<asp:Content ContentPlaceHolderId="PlaceHolderPageTitleInTitleArea" runat="server">
    Settings
</asp:Content>

<asp:Content ID="Content2" ContentPlaceHolderId="PlaceHolderMain" runat="server">
    <div id="configvaluescontainer">
        <table>
            <tbody>
                <tr>
                    <td>School Name</td>
                    <td><input data-bind="value: OrganizationName" size="30"/></td>
                </tr>
                <tr>
                    <td>URL of School Logo</td>
                    <td><input data-bind="value: OrganizationLogoUrl" size="30"/></td>
                </tr>
                <tr>
                    <td>Course Name</td>
                    <td><input data-bind="value: CourseName" size="30"/></td>
                </tr>
                <tr>
                    <td>Course Number</td>
                    <td><input data-bind="value: CourseNumber" size="15"/></td>
                </tr>
                <tr>
                    <td>Schedule</td>
                    <td><input data-bind="value: Schedule" size="15"/></td>
                </tr>
                <tr>
                    <td>Location</td>
                    <td><input data-bind="value: Location" size="15"/></td>
                </tr>
                <tr>
                    <td>Faculty Group</td>
                    <td><select data-bind="options: siteGroups, value: facultyGroup,
optionsText: 'groupName'"></select></td>
                </tr>
                <tr>
                    <td>Student Group</td>
                    <td><select data-bind="options: siteGroups, value: studentGroup,
optionsText: 'groupName'"></select></td>
                </tr>
            </tbody>
        </table>
        <a href="#" data-bind="click: updateConfigs">Update Configurations</a>
    </div>
</asp:Content>
```

Note the data-bind attributes used to connect the view model to the drop-down lists using Knockout. The value in the view model will be updated automatically when the user changes the value in the control. Running the app and configuring the app displays a page, as shown in Figure 6-9.

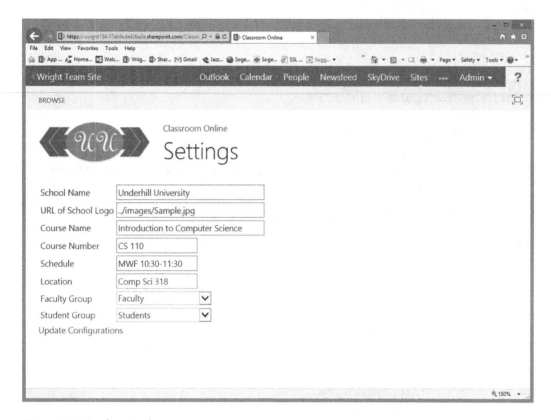

Figure 6-9. *Configuring the app*

Now we will build the roster page. This page will be accessible to anyone. It will present lists of the faculty members and students associated with the class. This page will only have a view model because it will use the model object associated with the site configuration settings.

11. Create a file named `roster.js` in the `Scripts/ViewModel` folder and add this JavaScript to it:

```
$(function () {
    CO.Configs.ensureConfigs(
        function () {
            ko.applyBindings(new RosterViewModel());
        })
})

function RosterViewModel() {
    var self = this;

    // Note: none of these properties are observables because this page is read-only.
    self.faculty = CO.Configs.faculty;
    self.students = CO.Configs.students;
    self.isSiteAdmin = CO.Configs.isCurrentUserSiteAdmin;
    self.isFaculty = CO.Configs.isCurrentUserFaculty;
    self.isStudent = CO.Configs.isCurrentUserStudent;
```

```
        self.courseName = CO.Configs.CourseName;
        self.courseNumber = CO.Configs.CourseNumber;
}
```

Because this is a read-only page, the view model only needs to provide the model data to the view. There is no need to use Knockout's observable objects, as they will not be updated.

■ **Note**   You may have noticed that our view models are getting simpler as our components build upon one another. This is typical of the MVVM pattern and is one of its strengths.

---

12.   Add a new page named `Roster.aspx` to the project in the `Page` folder.

13.   Add this markup to the new page:

```
<%@ Page Inherits="Microsoft.SharePoint.WebPartPages.WebPartPage,
Microsoft.SharePoint,
    Version=15.0.0.0, Culture=neutral, PublicKeyToken=71e9bce111e9429c"
    MasterPageFile="app.master" Language="C#" %>
<%@ Register TagPrefix="Utilities" Namespace="Microsoft.SharePoint.Utilities"
    Assembly="Microsoft.SharePoint, Version=15.0.0.0, Culture=neutral,
    PublicKeyToken=71e9bce111e9429c" %>
<%@ Register TagPrefix="WebPartPages" Namespace="Microsoft.SharePoint.WebPartPages"
    Assembly="Microsoft.SharePoint, Version=15.0.0.0, Culture=neutral,
    PublicKeyToken=71e9bce111e9429c" %>
<%@ Register TagPrefix="SharePoint" Namespace="Microsoft.SharePoint.WebControls"
    Assembly="Microsoft.SharePoint, Version=15.0.0.0, Culture=neutral,
    PublicKeyToken=71e9bce111e9429c" %>

<asp:Content ContentPlaceHolderID="PlaceHolderAdditionalPageHead" runat="server">
    <script type="text/javascript" src="../Scripts/jquery-1.7.1.min.js"></script>
    <script type="text/javascript" src="../Scripts/knockout-2.2.1.js"></script>
    <script type="text/javascript" src="/_layouts/15/sp.runtime.debug.js"></script>
    <script type="text/javascript" src="/_layouts/15/sp.debug.js"></script>

    <script type="text/javascript" src="../Scripts/Models/siteconfigs.js"></script>
    <script type="text/javascript" src="../Scripts/ViewModels/roster.js"></script>
</asp:Content>

<asp:Content ID="Content1" ContentPlaceHolderId="PlaceHolderPageTitleInTitleArea"
runat="server">
    Class Roster for <span data-bind="text: courseNumber"></span> -
<span data-bind="text: courseName"></span>
</asp:Content>

<asp:Content ContentPlaceHolderID="PlaceHolderMain" runat="server">
    <p data-bind="visible: isFaculty" style="display:none">You are a member of the
faculty for this course.</p>
```

```
    <p data-bind="visible: isStudent" style="display:none">You are a registered student
in this course.</p>
    <p data-bind="visible: isSiteAdmin" style="display:none">You are an administrator
for this site.</p>

        <h2>Faculty Members</h2>
        <table border="1" cellspacing="0" cellpadding="10">
            <thead style='background-color:gray;color:white'>
                <tr>
                    <th>Name</th>
                    <th>Login</th>
                </tr>
            </thead>
            <tbody data-bind="foreach: faculty">
                <tr>
                    <td data-bind="text: name"></td>
                    <td data-bind="text: email"></td>
                </tr>
            </tbody>
        </table>

        <h2>Students</h2>
        <table border="1" cellspacing="0" cellpadding="10">
            <thead style='background-color:gray;color:white'>
                <tr>
                    <th>Name</th>
                    <th>Login</th>
                </tr>
            </thead>
            <tbody data-bind="foreach: students">
                <tr>
                    <td data-bind="text: name"></td>
                    <td data-bind="text: email"></td>
                </tr>
            </tbody>
        </table>
    </asp:Content>
```

Knockout bindings on this page control the visibility of the messages at the top of the page. The `foreach` binding is used to generate the tables.

14. Run the app and view the roster page (see Figure 6-10).

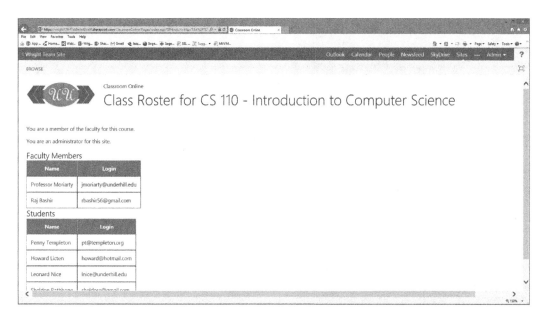

Figure 6-10. *The roster page*

The page displays the members of the groups configured to contain the students and faculty. We still need to be sure to set the SharePoint permissions for these groups. The end-user can always access the contents of our site directly if they know the correct URL of the list or other resource.

Using Remote Web Resources

Up to this point, we have been dealing with apps that run all of their logic in the client web browser. These are known as *SharePoint-hosted* apps. While the enhanced client-side object models for SharePoint 2013 make this a viable solution in many cases, there are still situations where logic needs to be kept on the server. This may be because of specialized resources that can only be accessed from a specific server. It could also be necessary because of custom security requirements or proprietary algorithms that cannot be publically exposed as client side JavaScript.

For cases like these, the Cloud App Model includes two additional hosting options: auto-hosted and provider-hosted. Both of these architectures permit the use of server-side code by creating a separate ASP.NET application that is hosted outside of SharePoint, as illustrated in Figure 6-11. Note that the remote web does not have to be an ASP.NET application. The Visual Studio project templates create an ASP.NET project, but any web stack can be used.

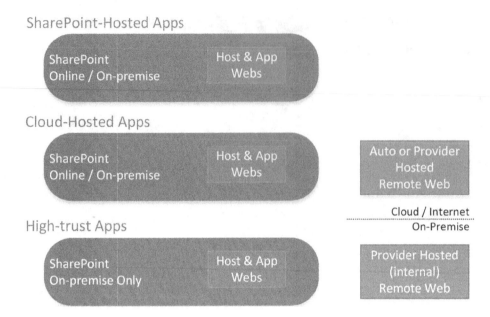

SharePoint-Hosted Apps

Cloud-Hosted Apps

High-trust Apps

Figure 6-11. Remote web access to SharePoint resources

Auto-hosted apps deploy their remote web components directly to the Windows Azure cloud. The ASP.NET components are bundled into the app's deployment file (.APP). When the app is deployed from the Office Store or an App Catalog, the remote web is automatically provisioned in Azure. The connection between the app instance in SharePoint and the corresponding web application running in Azure is configured automatically as well.

Provider-hosted apps are very similar to auto-hosted apps except that their remote web components are not automatically provisioned. It is the responsibility of the app publisher to deploy the remote web and include the connection information in the app's configuration. When the app is deployed to a SharePoint site, the app's remote web is already available on the network. The remote web can be deployed on-premise, in Azure, or in any other hosting or cloud environment as long as it is accessible on the network.

■ **Tip**   You may have already used a provider-hosted app without realizing it. Microsoft's Napa development tool is actually a provider-hosted SharePoint app. When you launch Napa within a SharePoint site, you are automatically redirected to `https://www.napacloudapp.com`. This is the cloud-hosted remote web site for Napa.

The problem with using remote web applications, and allowing them to access SharePoint resources, is how to ensure secure authentication and authorization. There are two different solutions to this problem, depending on the environment in which your app will run. For apps that will, or might, run in the cloud, Microsoft has created the Windows Azure Access Control Service (ACS) to facilitate this communication. For apps that will run only behind an organization's firewall, SharePoint Server 2013 contains a Security Token Service (STS) component that can take the place of ACS for trusted internal applications. Because these apps are identified by client certificates instead of a trusted third-party such as ACS, these apps are referred to as high-trust apps.

A secure connection using Secure Socket Layer (SSL) or an equivalent protocol is assumed and required by SharePoint. This prevents information from being intercepted and reused without the app's knowledge. SharePoint contains options to allow remote access without SSL, but this is not recommended in a production app and is prohibited in the Azure cloud. In the next two sections, we will walk through the messages passed between the various components of the application to ensure secure communication.

Cloud-Hosted Remote Webs

The basic task to be accomplished with these protocols is to establish the identity of both the app and the user in a way that is confidential and can be verified. When an app is running in the cloud, it needs a means of identifying itself to SharePoint, verifying the identity of the SharePoint instance, and requesting access to SharePoint's resources. This is accomplished using the OAuth 2.0 protocol, as described in Chapter 1.

Figure 6-12 lays out the various requests and responses that go into satisfying a request that is processed in a remote web component. Each step in the process passes tokens that contain encrypted information concerning what is known about the request at that point in the process.

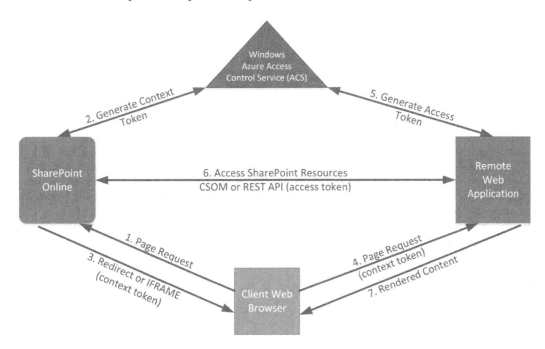

Figure 6-12. *Authorization in cloud-based apps*

The steps involved in Figure 6-12 are as follows:

1. The client browser requests a page from SharePoint. SharePoint processes the request and determines that an app will be involved in completing the response. SharePoint either needs to redirect the browser to a remote web site page or create an app part (using an IFRAME tag) on the SharePoint page that will contain content rendered by the remote web site.

2. SharePoint requests a context token from ACS. ACS is a third party that is trusted by both SharePoint and the remote web app. ACS creates the encrypted context token and returns it to SharePoint. The context token identifies the SharePoint instance that triggered the request, including the identity of the user, the SharePoint web where the request originated, and whatever other claims are being made by the SharePoint server.

3. SharePoint includes the context token in the response to the client browser as part of the redirect or IFRAME URL.

4. The client browser makes a web request using the URL provided by SharePoint. This passes the context token to the remote web.

5. The remote web application decodes the context token and uses it to construct a request to ACS for an access token. The access token indicates what resources the remote web wishes to access within SharePoint. ACS creates the token and returns it to the remote web app.

6. The remote web application creates a request for SharePoint using one of the client-side APIs provided (CSOM or REST). The access token is included in the request allowing SharePoint to verify the identity of the caller. SharePoint processes the request, doing any necessary permission checks based on the user and app identities in the access token. The results are then passed back to the remote web.

7. Finally, the remote web uses the information provided by SharePoint to render the HTML content for the web page. The response is sent to the client browser and presented to the end-user.

High-Trust Apps

The scenario described in the previous section assumes that the app is running in the cloud and is registered with ACS to handle authorization. For apps running within an organization's firewall, this is not necessarily the case. High-trust apps are designed to provide the same level of security without the need to involve a trusted third party, like ACS.

SharePoint Server 2013 contains a Security Token Service (STS) that can provide some of the functionality provided by ACS. Instead of sharing a security secret with ACS, a client certificate is configured within SharePoint to identify the app. In this case, there is no context token involved. The OAuth access token is created directly within the remote web application using the private key of the client certificate. This identifies the remote web as belonging to a trusted application. However, it does not identify the user in a secure way because there was no context token. The remote web is responsible for determining and supplying the user's identity when making requests into SharePoint (see Figure 6-13).

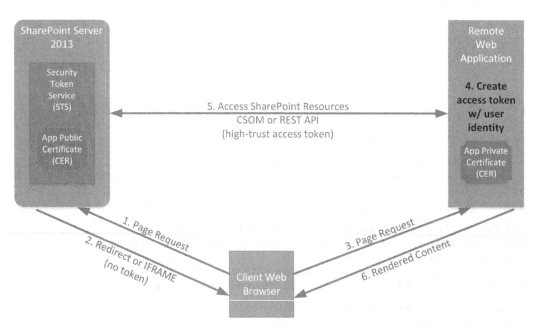

Figure 6-13. *Authorization in high-trust apps*

The sequence of messages in a high-trust app are similar to those in a cloud-based app except that there is no context token and no requests are made to ACS. The steps involved in Figure 6-13 are as follows:

1. The client browser requests a page from SharePoint. SharePoint processes the request and determines that an app will be involved in completing the response. SharePoint either needs to redirect the browser to a remote web site page or create an app part (using an IFRAME tag) on a SharePoint page that will contain remote web rendered content.

2. SharePoint includes partial context information (such as the host web URL) in the response to the client browser as part of the redirect or IFRAME URL, but not a context token.

3. The client browser makes a web request using the URL provided by SharePoint. This passes control to the remote web without a context token.

4. The remote web application uses its client certificate to construct its own access token for the request. This happens in the TokenHelper utility, described later in this chapter.

5. The remote web application creates a request for SharePoint using one of the client-side APIs provided (CSOM or REST). The access token is included in the request. The STS is used to decode the access token using the app's public certificate. This allows SharePoint to verify the identity of the calling app and retrieve the user identity provided by the remote app. SharePoint processes the request, doing any necessary permission checks, based on the user and app identities received. The results are then passed back to the remote web.

6. Finally, the remote web uses the information provided by SharePoint to render the requested web content. The response is sent to the client browser and presented to the end-user.

The most important things to remember when working with a high-trust app is that there is no context token and the user's identity is ensured by the remote web application, not ACS or SharePoint. A high-trust app has no more access to the SharePoint environment than any other app, except that it has the ability to impersonate any user.

Understanding the TokenHelper Utility

The various tokens we need in order to access SharePoint resources remotely can be very complicated to manage. They each have different sources, durations, and uses. To assist in managing tokens, a code file is added to the remote web site project when a new app is created using either auto or provider hosting. The file is called `TokenHelper.cs`, or `TokenHelper.vb` if you are using Visual Basic.NET.

TokenHelper contains four .NET framework classes that represent and manage tokens for your remote web. The TokenHelper class contains the public token-handling methods.

Table 6-4. *Important TokenHelper Public Methods*

Method	Description
GetContextTokenFromRequest *(request)*	This method extracts the context token from the current HTTP request object. The token should have been posted to the page or included in the query string.
ReadAndValidateContextToken (tokenString, *appHostName*)	This method verifies that the context token is properly formatted and was intended for this site.
GetAccessToken (*contextToken, targetHost*)	This method converts a context token into an access token for the target site. The access token is issued by ACS. Other variations of this method use other values (authorization code or refresh token) to request an access token.
CreateRemoteEvent ReceiverClientContext(*properties*)	This method creates a CSOM client context object, based on the properties provided, to a remote event handler.
CreateAppEventClientContext (*properties*)	This method creates a CSOM client context object, based on the properties provided, to an app event handler (install, upgrade, or uninstall).
GetS2SAccessTokenWith WindowsIdentity (*targetApplicationUri, identity*)	***High-trust apps only:*** This creates an access token for use with a server-to-server OAuth connection to SharePoint.
GetS2SClientContext WithWindowsIdentity (*targetApplicationUri,* identity)	***High-trust apps only:*** This creates a CSOM client context for use with a server-to-server OAuth connection to SharePoint.

The TokenHelper source code files demonstrate how many of the tokens and protocols associated with remote site calls work. It can be instructive to read through these methods to understand how the various concepts are related.

EXERCISE 6.4

In this exercise, we will disassemble the TokenHelper utility and take a look inside. We will see how the utility is used to simplify our access of SharePoint from a remote web site. We will also pull out some of the values it uses. This will help us understand how the connection is constructed and aid us in debugging problems later.

Specifically, we will create a simple auto-hosted app that reads data from the associated SharePoint server using the TokenHelper utility and displays it on the page. We will also add logic to the page to dump many of the token values to the page so that we can see their contents.

This code will be put into a separate Visual Studio project, since it will not be a part of the Classroom Online app.

1. Open Visual Studio 2012.

2. Create a new C# SharePoint app project called RemoteWebApp. If you prefer to use VB.NET, you will need to convert the code provided later in this exercise to VB.

3. Select Autohosted for the hosting option (this is the default).

The project generated contains two projects. The first is for the SharePoint app web, and the second is for the remote web site. When debugging, the remote web app will run on a local copy of IIS Express. When deployed through the Office Store or an App Catalog, the remote web will be deployed to the Azure cloud.

4. Press F5 to compile and run the app.

The page will simply query the host web site's title and write it to the page. It only take a few lines of code to do this because of the TokenHelper utility. We are going examine what the utility is doing under the covers to better understand the process.

5. Stop the debugger.

6. Open the code-behind file for the Default.aspx page (Default.aspx.cs).

7. Comment out the existing code in the Page_Load() method.

8. Add the following using statements to the top of the source file. These namespaces contain the objects we will be using.

```
using System.Data;
using System.Globalization;
using System.Web.Configuration;
using Microsoft.IdentityModel.S2S.Protocols.OAuth2;
using Microsoft.SharePoint.Client;
```

9. Add the following code to the Page_Load() method:

```
// get app info from web.config
string clientID =
    string.IsNullOrEmpty(WebConfigurationManager.AppSettings.Get("ClientId"))
        ? WebConfigurationManager.AppSettings.Get("HostedAppName")
        : WebConfigurationManager.AppSettings.Get("ClientId");

string clientSecret =
    string.IsNullOrEmpty(WebConfigurationManager.AppSettings.Get("ClientSecret"))
        ? WebConfigurationManager.AppSettings.Get("HostedAppSigningKey")
        : WebConfigurationManager.AppSettings.Get("ClientSecret");
```

The client ID and secret are read from the remote web's configuration file. The ID identifies the app and the secret is a shared secret used to create access tokens.

10. Add the following code to the Page_Load() method:

```
// get values from Page.Request
string reqAuthority = Request.Url.Authority;
string hostWeb = Page.Request["SPHostUrl"];
string hostWebAuthority = (new Uri(hostWeb)).Authority;
```

These lines get the URL authority names for the host web and the remote web site. The host web's URL was passed in the request for the page. It is usually passed on the query string, but it can also be posted as part of a form.

11. Add the following code to the Page_Load() method:

```
// get context token
string contextTokenStr = TokenHelper.GetContextTokenFromRequest(Request);
SharePointContextToken contextToken =
    TokenHelper.ReadAndValidateContextToken(contextTokenStr, reqAuthority);
```

```
// read data from the context token
string targetPrincipalName = contextToken.TargetPrincipalName;
string cacheKey = contextToken.CacheKey;
string refreshTokenStr = contextToken.RefreshToken;
string realm = contextToken.Realm;
```

SharePoint also passed the context token in an encoded form. The ReadAndValidateContextToken() function converts the encoded string into a SharePointContextToken object for easy access to its contents. Validating the token refers to verifying that the context token is addressed to this app running in this realm. The remaining lines of code pull out some key values from the token.

12. Add the following code to the bottom of the Default page class. This routine was copied from the TokenHelper.cs file. We did this because it is declared as private in TokenHelper.

```
private static string GetFormattedPrincipal
              (string principalName, string hostName, string realm)
{
    if (!String.IsNullOrEmpty(hostName))
    {
        return String.Format(CultureInfo.InvariantCulture,
                             "{0}/{1}@{2}", principalName, hostName, realm);
    }
    else
    {
        return String.Format(CultureInfo.InvariantCulture,
                             "{0}@{1}", principalName, realm);
    }
}
```

13. Add the following code to the Page_Load() method:

```
// create principal strings
string targetPrincipal =
        GetFormattedPrincipal(targetPrincipalName, hostWebAuthority, realm);
string appPrincipal =
        GetFormattedPrincipal(clientID, null, realm);
```

The app principal identifies the app installation that is making the request. The target principal identifies the application, host, and realm that will be receiving the request.

14. Add the following code to the Page_Load() method:

```
// request an access token from ACS
string stsUrl = TokenHelper.AcsMetadataParser.GetStsUrl(realm);

OAuth2AccessTokenRequest oauth2Request =
    OAuth2MessageFactory.CreateAccessTokenRequestWithRefreshToken(
        appPrincipal, clientSecret, refreshTokenStr, targetPrincipal);

OAuth2S2SClient client = new OAuth2S2SClient();
OAuth2AccessTokenResponse oauth2Response =
    client.Issue(stsUrl, oauth2Request) as OAuth2AccessTokenResponse;

string accessTokenStr = oauth2Response.AccessToken;
```

This is the key to connecting back to the host web. This code formats a request for an OAuth access token and sends it to the Access Control Service (ACS). ACS issues the access token and returns it to the remote web. This call can be made synchronously because we are in server-side code running outside of SharePoint.

15. Add the following code to the Page_Load() method:

```
// build the CSOM context with the access token
ClientContext clientContext =
    TokenHelper.GetClientContextWithAccessToken(hostWeb, accessTokenStr);
clientContext.Load(clientContext.Web, web => web.Title);
clientContext.ExecuteQuery();
```

Here we use the access token to create a CSOM client context that can be used to make requests of SharePoint. Again, we are able to make the synchronous ExecuteQuery() call because this is server-side code.

16. Add the following code to the Page_Load() method:

```
// dump values to the page
DataTable dt = new DataTable();
dt.Columns.Add("Name");
dt.Columns.Add("Value");

dt.Rows.Add("QueryString", Request.QueryString);
dt.Rows.Add("clientID", clientID);
dt.Rows.Add("clientSecret", clientSecret);
dt.Rows.Add("hostWeb", hostWeb);
dt.Rows.Add("contextTokenStr", contextTokenStr);
dt.Rows.Add("contextToken", contextToken);
dt.Rows.Add("targetPrincipalName", targetPrincipalName);
dt.Rows.Add("cacheKey", cacheKey);
dt.Rows.Add("refreshTokenStr", refreshTokenStr);
dt.Rows.Add("realm", realm);
dt.Rows.Add("targetPrincipal", targetPrincipal);
dt.Rows.Add("appPrincipal", appPrincipal);
dt.Rows.Add("stsUrl", stsUrl);
dt.Rows.Add("oauth2Request", oauth2Request);
dt.Rows.Add("client", client);
dt.Rows.Add("oauth2Response", oauth2Response);
dt.Rows.Add("accessTokenStr", accessTokenStr);
dt.Rows.Add("Host Web Title", clientContext.Web.Title);
grd.DataSource = dt;
grd.DataBind();
```

This code binds the values we have retrieved to a data grid in the page so that they can be displayed on the page.

17. Open the Default.aspx page in the source editor.

18. Replace the body of the page with this markup:

```
<h2>Remote Web Tokens and Values</h2>
<form id="Form1" runat="server">
    <asp:GridView ID="grd" runat="server" CellPadding="4"
            ForeColor="#333333" GridLines="None" AutoGenerateColumns="True"
            Width="100%">
```

```
                <AlternatingRowStyle BackColor="White" />
                <EditRowStyle BackColor="#2461BF" />
                <FooterStyle BackColor="#507CD1" Font-Bold="True" ForeColor="White" />
                <HeaderStyle BackColor="#507CD1" Font-Bold="True" ForeColor="White" />
                <PagerStyle BackColor="#2461BF" ForeColor="White" HorizontalAlign="Center" />
                <RowStyle BackColor="#EFF3FB" />
                <SelectedRowStyle BackColor="#D1DDF1" Font-Bold="True" ForeColor="#333333" />
                <SortedAscendingCellStyle BackColor="#F5F7FB" />
                <SortedAscendingHeaderStyle BackColor="#6D95E1" />
                <SortedDescendingCellStyle BackColor="#E9EBEF" />
                <SortedDescendingHeaderStyle BackColor="#4870BE" />
            </asp:GridView>
        </form>
```

19. Press F5 to run the app.

The app displays the default page on the remote site (see Figure 6-14) displaying the values of the tokens for this site. Becoming familiar with the appearance, format, and purpose of these tokens will make debugging your apps much easier.

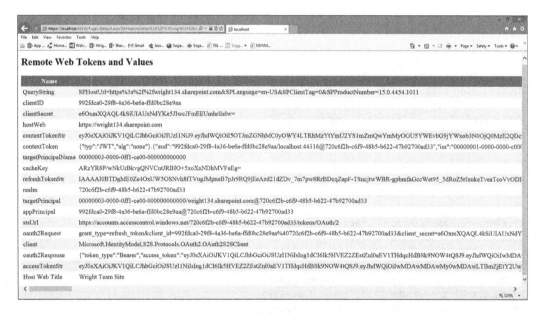

Figure 6-14. *Remote web tokens*

Summary

In this chapter, we have examined the security framework on which SharePoint apps are built. We have explored the authorization and authentication systems in both SharePoint and Windows Azure. The ability to protect the integrity and privacy of data within SharePoint is a key requirement in providing a robust platform for developing mission-critical applications.

Next, we will begin looking at the ways we can use resources securely across the Internet. In Chapter 7, we will look at connecting to web services, as well as SharePoint, using the REST API instead of the client-side object model.

CHAPTER 7

Web Services with REST and OData

In Chapter 5, we learned how to use the SharePoint 2013 Client-Side Object Model (CSOM) to access SharePoint data from client applications and remote web servers. We will now use another style of interface to accomplish the same tasks using the SharePoint 2013 REST API. In this chapter, we will go over the following points:

- How the SharePoint 2013 REST web service interface allows us to access SharePoint from a client application without the need to include custom libraries or code modules.

- The roles played by the various components that make up a SharePoint REST request and how these components map to objects in the SharePoint environment.

- How to choose a client-side library with which to access the REST API.

- When it is necessary to include security information, such as access tokens and form digests, in a REST request.

- How to read, create, update, and delete SharePoint objects using REST.

The SharePoint 2013 REST API

The SharePoint 2013 REST API is an alternative to the Client-Side Object Model (CSOM) discussed in Chapter 5. REST stands for *Representational State Transfer* and describes an architectural pattern that is common in web-based applications.

A REST interface consists of a web service that implements a set of *endpoints* that accept requests and deliver responses to client applications. A REST endpoint is a URL that is constructed to indicate the object to be accessed or action to be performed. These requests and responses are formatted as standard HTTP interactions. Therefore, unlike when using CSOM, there is no need for the client to use a proprietary library of scripts or classes when accessing the service.

The SharePoint 2013 REST API is a set of REST endpoints that allow client applications to perform almost any action supported by any of the CSOM libraries. This includes create, read, update, and delete (CRUD) operations on SharePoint's lists and libraries. There are also REST endpoints for accessing SharePoint services such as search and user profiles.

The REST architecture requires that a service provider, such as SharePoint Server, make a series of decisions concerning security, data formats, and transmission protocols. SharePoint 2013 implements REST using the OData and OAuth standards for these features. As shown in Figure 7-1, the SharePoint REST API is implemented using the same web service interface (`client.svc`) used to process requests created by the CSOM libraries.

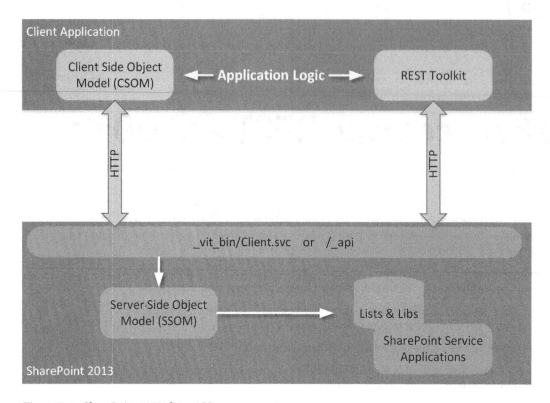

Figure 7-1. SharePoint 2013 client APIs

REST requests are created using all of the elements available in an HTTP web request. The URL indicates the endpoint and many of the parameters to be used to when performing the requested actions. The HTTP headers contained in the request provide additional information required to process the request, such as security tokens, data format specifications, and data consistency check information. In some cases, additional objects are posted to the service in the body, or payload, of the HTTP request message. Query results and status information are returned in the HTTP response message.

Because REST and OData are general-purpose protocols, they do not support all of the rich functionality of a custom-coded object model like the CSOM. The primary limitations of the REST API relative to the CSOM libraries are as follows:

1. The REST API does not support batching requests. Whereas a number of requests can be performed as a unit using CSOM, each REST API operation must be submitted as a separate request and response message to the server.

2. The REST API returns only standard OData exception information. This information is generally not as detailed as that which can be obtained using the CSOM libraries.

3. The CSOM libraries contain the conditional scope object. This object allows the client application to specify that certain requests in a batch should only be executed if certain conditions are met based on the results of previous steps. Since the REST API does not support request batches, conditional scopes are not available either.

The lack of batching support in the REST API may not be relevant for many situations where only a few operations are required. When multiple complex requests need to be performed, using the REST interface may cause performance and scalability problems for heavily used applications.

Anatomy of a REST Request

In this section, we will look at the parts of a REST request and for what behaviors they are used. Remember that a REST request is nothing more than an ordinary HTTP web request containing a URL, headers, and a payload which can contain data objects or other information to be posted to the service.

Constructing SharePoint REST URLs

The most important piece of information used to access anything on the Internet is, of course, the Uniform Resource Locator (URL). This is the address used to route the request to the correct server on the network and the correct service on that server. In the case of URLs used for accessing REST services, the URL can be broken down into three major components, as shown in Figure 7-2.

Figure 7-2. REST URL components

The first part of the URL is the *service root*. The service root indicates how to access the service to be used. The first portion is the *schema*, which is either `http` or `https` when using REST. Since most SharePoint apps access data that should be kept private, SSL is generally used so the schema would be `https`. The next part of the service root is the server and domain name with an optional port number. This is used to route the request to the correct server. Finally, the service on the server is specified. In SharePoint REST calls, this takes the form of a path to a specific SharePoint site, followed by either `/_vti_bin/client.svc` or `/_api`. These both refer to the same service.

The second component of the URL is the *resource path*. This tells the client service what resource within SharePoint will be used. The resource path begins by specifying which endpoint will be used. This can be stated explicitly, as `SP.AppContextSite` in Figure 7-2, or it can be implied by referencing the local context for the web being accessed. For example, `/_api/web` accesses the current web where the service resides. `SP.AppContextSite(@target)` uses the `SP.AppContextSite` endpoint to create a reference to the app's context site with a URL specified by the `@target` parameter. As a general rule, the REST endpoint corresponding to an object in the client-side object model will have the same name as the object. A list of the commonly used SharePoint 2013 REST endpoints will be presented in Table 7-4, later in this chapter.

The final portion of the URL is the query string. In a REST request, the query string is used to pass parameter and option values to the service.

Passing Parameters to the REST API

The most common type of parameter used in the SharePoint REST API is one that specifies a member in one of SharePoint's collections. These are passed using parenthesis after the collection or in one of the collection's access methods.

For example, to access a particular list, you could pass the lists globally unique identifier (GUID) using `/_api/web/lists('<guid>')`. This assumes that the client already has the GUID of the list when making the request. If not, the list can also be retrieved using the `getByTitle()` access method, as in `/_api/web/lists/getByTitle('MyList')`. Different collections have different types of access methods depending on their contents.

■ **Tip** The URLs used in the REST API are not case sensitive. Therefore, `getByTitle` is equivalent to `getbytitle`.

When a method requires more than one parameter, these can be passed as name-value pairs separated using commas, such as /_api/web/getAvailableWebTemplates (lcid=1033,includeCrossLanguage=false).

The OData standard also allows for parameter aliasing. When a parameter alias is used, a placeholder appears in the resource path portion of the URL. The value for the placeholder is then specified in the query string. The placeholder is identified using an at (@) sign prior to the name. In Figure 7-2, @target was used as an alias for the URL of the app context site to be specified. The value of @target was then included in the query string.

The complexity of the data values that can be specified in the URL is limited. More complex parameters should be included in the body of the request. For example, when creating a new list item, the values of the properties for the item are passed as an object in the body of the request.

Some REST URLs specify actions to be taken using a method call. In this case, the parameters for the call can be passed as simple variables on the query string. For example, to ensure that a user is a member of a site, you could use /_api/web/ensureUser?logonName="MyDomain\MyUser". Alternatively, /_api/web/ensureUser("MyDomain\MyUser") would be valid as well.

OData Query Operators

The SharePoint REST service supports a wide range of options on the URL, known as *query operators,* which are defined by the OData standard. However, not all OData query operators are supported. Table 7-1 lists the supported query operators and some of the limitations of that support.

Table 7-1. *Supported OData Query Operators*

Operator	Description	Samples
$select	This operator is used to specify a subset of fields to be returned. If not specified, SharePoint will return all fields except those deemed too resource intensive. Those values must be explicitly requested.	$select=Title,ID
$expand	This operator is used in conjunction with the $select operator to cause certain properties of child elements of the items to be returned as well. These are referred to as *projected properties.*	$select=Title,Members &$expand= Members/FirstName, Members/LastName
$filter	This operator specifies a query to be used to limit the items returned. The conditions used can include comparisons of the values of item properties, string comparisons, and date/time comparisons. There are some OData comparisons that are not supported by SharePoint. See the reference link in the Caution point following this table.	$filter=Title eq 'Huckleberry Finn'
$orderby	This operator sorts the items returned by a property value. asc and desc can be used to sort in ascending or descending order, respectively.	$orderby=Modified desc
$top	This operator limits the number of items returned.	$top=100
$skip	This operator is used when paging through a long list of items. It specifies how many items show be discarded before beginning to return data.	$skip=0&$top=100 $skip=100&$top=100 $skip=200&$top=100

■ **Caution**   As previously noted, not all operators defined by the OData standard are supported by the SharePoint REST API. For a list of the supported options, see http://msdn.microsoft.com/en-us/library/fp142385.aspx.

Choosing an HTTP Method

Each HTTP request contains a *method*, or *verb*, that describes the purpose of the request. The most common verbs in use are GET and POST. GET is typically used to retrieve a web page. POST is used to send information to a web server. This information is included in the body of the request and usually contains the values of form elements, such as text boxes, check boxes, or drop-down lists.

In OData requests, the URL indicates which object is being accessed and the HTTP method is used to determine what type of action is being requested. Table 7-2 lists the methods used by the SharePoint REST API.

Table 7-2. *OData HTTP Methods*

Method	Uses	Behavior
GET	Read operations	The URL indicates the item(s) to be returned in the payload of the response.
POST	Create objects	The URL indicates the collection into which the object will be placed. The request body contains the values to set on the object.
PUT	Overwrite an object	The URL specifies the object. The request body contains the values to set on the object. Any properties not specified are set to their DEFAULT values.
PATCH	Update an object	The URL specifies the object. The request body contains the values to set on the object. Any properties not specified are left UNCHANGED. Equivalent to MERGE in previous versions of the OData standard. MERGE is still supported.
DELETE	Delete an object	The URL specifies the object. If the object can be put into SharePoint's recycle bin it is. Otherwise, it is permanently deleted.

It is standard in the HTTP protocol to include the verb in the initial line of the request. For example, to retrieve the properties of a web, the request might be GET /_api/web HTTP/1.1. While HTTP allows the creation of additional verbs, such as those listed in Table 7-2, most web firewalls block any verbs except GET and POST. This is because of certain types of web attacks that use non-standard HTTP verbs as a means of circumventing web site security. To avoid having these requests blocked, OData and SharePoint use the concept of *method tunneling*.

Instead of using these non-standard verbs in the HTTP request directly, they are included in a custom request header called *X-HTTP-Method*. When one of the verbs other than GET or POST must be used, the request is formatted as a POST with the X-HTTP-Method header containing the real method to be used. We will explain the use of request headers in the next section. The exercises later in this chapter will demonstrate how and when to use them.

Configuring Request Headers

Each HTTP request contains a set of optional header values. These headers control various aspects of the handling of the request. Typical uses of request headers include security and data formatting control. Table 7-3 lists the various headers relevant to the sending of requests to the SharePoint REST web service.

Table 7-3. *SharePoint REST API Headers*

Header	Description	Values/Formatting	When to Use
Accept	Specifies the requested format for the response.	application/atom-xml (default) application/json	Any.
Authorization	Used to pass the access token.	Encoded access token string	Only required when making a request across domains.
X-HTTP-Method	Used to tunnel the HTTP method value. Used in conjunction with a POST request.	PUT PATCH MERGE DELETE	Only required when making a PUT, PATCH, MERGE, or DELETE request.
X-RequestDigest	Used to ensure the context of any operation that updates data. Included in the original request from SharePoint to the app.	Encoded digest value	Not required for GET request. Not required when using OAuth server-to-server sessions. See the section, "The TokenHelper and HTTPWebRequest Objects," later in this chapter.
Content-type	Specifies the format of the data included in the body of the request.	Application/atom-xml;type=entry Application/atom-xml;type=feed Application/json;odata=verbose	Used whenever data is passed in the body of the request.
Content-length	Gives the number of bytes in the request body.	Integer	Used whenever data is passed in the body of the request.
IF-MATCH	Used to check for concurrency violations using ETags. See the section, "Ensuring Consistent Updates with ETags," later in this chapter.	ETag Value or * (default)	Used on PUT, PATCH, MERGE, and DELETE requests. The asterisk (*) indicates that no check is required. If the header is omitted, no check is performed.

SharePoint 2013 REST Endpoints

As mentioned earlier, most of the REST service endpoints in SharePoint correspond to objects in the client-side object model. Table 7-4 contains a listing of the most commonly used of these endpoints and what each represents within SharePoint.

Table 7-4. *SharePoint REST Endpoints*

Resource	Description
SP.Site	A SharePoint site collection
SP.Web	A SharePoint site
SP.List	A list or library
SP.ListItem	An item or document in a list or library
SP.Field	A field containing a property of a list item
SP.File	A physical file stored in SharePoint, either in a web site or in a document library
SP.Folder	A named container of SP.File objects
SP.User	A SharePoint user
SP.Group	A SharePoint group of users
SP.RoleAssignment	Represents the assignment of permissions to a user or group for a particular securable object, such as a web, list, or list item
SP.RoleDefinition	A named collection of permissions that can be used in multiple assignments; also known as a *permission level*

Notice that most of these objects also have container objects that include the Collection suffix to the name. For example, the lists in a web are accessed through the web's lists property, which is of type SP.ListCollection and contains a set of SP.List objects.

In addition to endpoints, the SharePoint REST API implements a set of *access points* that represent the instance of an object or service that is implied by the current context of the request. These are listed in Table 7-5.

Table 7-5. *SharePoint REST Access Points*

Access Point	Description
/_api/web	The web object in the current context
/_api/site	The site collection containing the current web object
/_api/SP.UserProfiles.PeopleManager	An object used to access the User Profile service for the current web site
/_api/search	An object used to access the Search service for the current web site

Choosing a Client-Side Library

Before using the SharePoint REST API, the client developer must determine how they will create their REST requests. Writing raw HTTP requests is difficult and error prone. This is not something that an ordinary web developer should consider doing in most cases. There are also the response messages to be considered. The interpreting of response data and error information coming from the REST service can also be very difficult. As a result, almost all users of the REST interface will use a utility library of some sort to simplify this type of coding.

There are three libraries provided with SharePoint 2013 and the Microsoft .NET Framework for handling this type of request. Each of these libraries is most useful in different situations. In the following sections, we will examine each library and do an exercise to demonstrate its use. We will do the same basic exercise with each library to make the similarities and differences clear.

SharePoint REST Access with JQuery

The first technique we will examine uses only JQuery. SharePoint 2013 includes the JQuery library to enable simple client-side coding in JavaScript (as described in Chapter 4). One of the features of JQuery is the ajax() function.

Ajax stands for *Asynchronous JavaScript and XML*. Like REST, Ajax is not a standard or a protocol but an architectural pattern. In the Ajax pattern, JavaScript code running in a web browser sends a web request to a web server. The response is processed asynchronously when it arrives, usually in XML format. The JQuery ajax() function provides a means to create and send these requests and handles the formatting of the responses. The function takes an object as a parameter that contains the settings to be used when making the call. Since the ajax() function is a standard part of the JQuery library and that library is included with the default SharePoint app templates, it is quite simple to access in your code.

The JQuery Ajax technique is useful when you have the following situations:

1. The REST API will be accessed from within the web browser.

2. There is a desire to avoid including any additional libraries, such as CSOM, in the solution.

3. There is no need to cross domains, such as from a remote web page to the SharePoint app web.

When using this technique to access SharePoint from within the same domain, it is not necessary to include the authorization header. When crossing domains, the authorization header should be added to include a valid access token for the site being accessed.

EXERCISE 7-1

In this exercise, we will use the JQuery AJAX function to send a REST request and view the response. To help us explore the REST interface, we will add input elements to the page to enable the page's user to interactively enter a REST URL to be queried. This will allow us to experiment with constructing URLs to retrieve information from SharePoint.

First, we will create a SharePoint-hosted app. Then we will add input controls to the app's default page. Finally, we will add a view-model to process the REST request and display the results.

We will start by creating a new SharePoint-hosted app to use as a test bed.

1. Start Visual Studio 2012.

2. Create a new SharePoint 2013 app.

3. Name it Exercise 7-1 and select SharePoint-hosted for the hosting option, as shown in Figure 7-3.

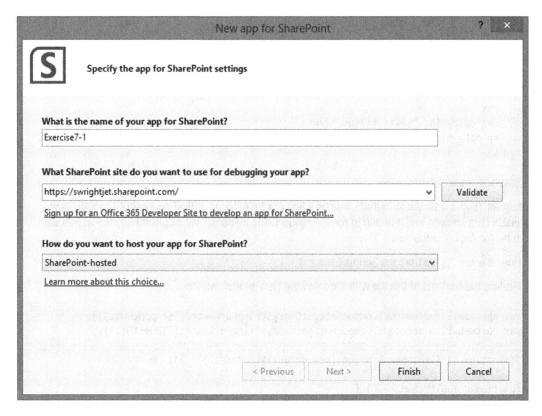

Figure 7-3. *Create a SharePoint-hosted app*

4. Open the Default.aspx page from the Pages folder.

5. Add a script reference to the Knockout library.

```
<script type="text/javascript"
        src="https://ajax.aspnetcdn.com/ajax/knockout/knockout-2.2.1.js" ></script>
```

6. Replace the contents of the PlaceHolderMain content area with the following markup:

```
<div>
    <input type="text" data-bind="value: url" size="100" />
    <br />
    <br />
    <select data-bind="value: format">
        <option value="application/json;odata=verbose">
            application/json;odata=verbose
        </option>
        <option value="application/atom-xml">
            application/atom-xml
        </option>
    </select>
```

```
                    <br />
                    <br />
                    <input data-bind="click: onRunRequest"
                            type="button"
                            value="Execute the REST Request" />
                    <br />
                    <br />
                    <h1 data-bind="text: status"></h1>
                    <p data-bind="text: message" />
            </div>
```

7. Save and close Default.aspx.

This markup will render a simple form that contains a text box for entering a REST request URL, a drop-down list of available data formats, and a button to run the request. The response will be placed into the header and paragraph tag for display to the user.

8. Open the App.js file from the Scripts library.

9. Replace the contents of this file with the following view-model definition:

```
var appweburl = decodeURIComponent(getQueryStringParameter("SPAppWebUrl"));
var hostweburl = decodeURIComponent(getQueryStringParameter("SPHostUrl"));

$(function () { ko.applyBindings(new defaultViewModel()); });

function defaultViewModel() {
    var self = this;

    self.status = ko.observable();
    self.message = ko.observable();
    self.url = ko.observable("/_api/web");
    self.format = ko.observable();

    self.result = null;

    self.onRunRequest = function () {
        jQuery.ajax({
            url: appweburl + self.url(),
            type: "GET",
            headers: {
                "accept": self.format(),
            },
            success: Function.createDelegate(self, self.onComplete),
            error: Function.createDelegate(self, self.onComplete)
        });
    };

    self.onComplete = function (data, status) {
        self.status(status);
```

```
                if (self.format() == 'application/atom-xml') {
                    self.result = data;
                    self.message((new XMLSerializer()).serializeToString(data));
                } else {
                    self.result = data.d;
                    self.message(JSON.stringify(data));
                }
            }
        }

        // utility routine
        function getQueryStringParameter(paramToRetrieve) {
            var params =
                document.URL.split("?")[1].split("&");
            var strParams = "";
            for (var i = 0; i < params.length; i = i + 1) {
                var singleParam = params[i].split("=");
                if (singleParam[0] == paramToRetrieve)
                    return singleParam[1];
            }
        }
```

The onRunRequest() function initiates the asynchronous REST request. The settings provided are used to format the request.

```
        jQuery.ajax({
            url: appweburl + self.url(),
            type: "GET",
            headers: {
                "accept": self.format(),
            },
            success: Function.createDelegate(self, self.onComplete),
            error: Function.createDelegate(self, self.onComplete)
        });
```

- url—This is set to access the app web. Since this page is running in the same domain as the app web, this is not a cross-domain call.

- type—This specified that this is a GET operation, not a POST.

- headers—We include the "accept" header to indicate the format in which we wish to receive the response data.

- success—This specifies the event handler to be called if the request completes successfully.

- error—This specifies the event handler to be called if the request completes with an error.

The onComplete() function handles both error and non-error responses in this case.

```
    self.onComplete = function (data, status) {
        self.status(status);
```

```
        if (self.format() == 'application/atom-xml') {
            self.result = data;
            self.message((new XMLSerializer()).serializeToString(data));
        } else {
            self.result = data.d;
            self.message(JSON.stringify(data));
        }
    }
}
```

The JQuery library returns two pieces of data as parameters to the event handler. The first item is the response data formatted as either an XML DOM object or a native JavaScript object, depending on which format was requested. Note that in the case of a native JavaScript object, the data is actually returned as the d property of the response object.

10. Save and close the App.js file.

11. Execute the project with F5 to start debugging.

12. When the Default.aspx page is rendered, press the execute button to see the JSON formatted response. (see Figure 7-4).

Figure 7-4. *JSON response data*

Many of the properties of the object returned are in the form of a _deferred property. These properties values were not selected in the query but can be retrieved using the REST request URL in the deferred property.

13. Select application/atom-xml from the drop-down list.

14. Press the execute button again (see Figure 7-5).

196

Figure 7-5. *ATOM XML response data*

In this case, the data was returned as an ATOM entry element. This is because only a single object, a web, was being returned. If the URL was set to /_api/web/lists, the response would have been in the form of an ATOM feed. A feed is an XML element that contains a set of entry elements. The client service returns an entry or a feed as appropriate to the request.

Try experimenting with other REST URLs to see how the data returned varies.

The SharePoint Cross-Domain Library

Although the JQuery library can be used across domains, by including the authorization header, SharePoint offers an easier solution. The cross-domain library can be used to access services including the REST API across domains. These calls can be made to web services outside of SharePoint using a standard proxy built into SharePoint. In this case, we will use it to access SharePoint from the remote web site in an auto-hosted app.

The cross-domain library is implemented using the SP.RequestExecutor object. This object is contained in a separate JavaScript library from the rest of the client-side object model. The use of the RequestExecutor object is very similar to the JQuery ajax() function. The object manages the formatting of requests and responses in JavaScript code. In fact, the RequestExecutor can be used in place of the JQuery technique, since it will work perfectly well even when a call does not cross domains.

The RequestExecutor is useful when you have the following situations:

1. The REST API will be accessed from within the web browser.

2. There is a need to cross domain boundaries, such as from a remote web page to the SharePoint app web.

3. There is a need to access a web service outside of the SharePoint server farm.

When using the RequestExecutor to access external web services, the remote web service should be registered in the AppManifest file. This allows the user to grant access to the service when the app is installed. In this case, the RequestExecutor does not access the service directly. It makes a call to a proxy page built into SharePoint that forwards the request to the service and routes the response back to the calling page. This allows the JavaScript to make a cross-domain web service call that would otherwise be blocked by the web browser.

EXERCISE 7-2

In this exercise, we re-create the app in Exercise 7-1 using the cross-domain library. To show the library crossing domains, we will create the page in the remote web of an auto-hosted app. Otherwise, the two apps will perform identically for the user.

First, we will create an auto-hosted app. Then we will add input controls to the app's default page. Finally, we will add a view-model to process the REST request and display the results.

We will start by creating a new auto-hosted app to use as a test bed.

1. Start Visual Studio 2012.

2. Create a new SharePoint 2013 app.

3. Name it Exercise 7-2 and select auto-hosted for the hosting option.

4. Open the `Default.aspx` page from the `Pages` folder.

5. Add a script reference for the Microsoft AJAX toolkit library. This library is used by the `SP.RequestExecutor` object.

    ```
    <script type="text/javascript"
            src="//ajax.aspnetcdn.com/ajax/4.0/1/MicrosoftAjax.js"></script>
    ```

6. Add script references for JQuery and Knockout.

    ```
    <script type="text/javascript"
            src="../Scripts/jquery-1.7.1.min.js"></script>
    <script type="text/javascript"
            src="//ajax.aspnetcdn.com/ajax/knockout/knockout-2.2.1.js" ></script>
    ```

7. Replace the contents of the `<form>` tag with the same HTML markup used in Exercise 7-1.

8. Save and close `Default.aspx`.

9. Open the `Default.aspx.cs` code-behind file.

10. Remove the code within the `Page_Load` routine.

11. Save and close the `Default.aspx.cs` file.

12. In the remote web site project, create a new JavaScript file called `App.js` in the Scripts library.

13. Replace the contents of this file with the following view-model definition

```
var appweburl = decodeURIComponent(getQueryStringParameter("SPAppWebUrl"));
var hostweburl = decodeURIComponent(getQueryStringParameter("SPHostUrl"));

$().ready(function () {
    $.getScript(hostweburl + '/_layouts/15/sp.runtime.debug.js',
        function () {
            $.getScript(hostweburl + '/_layouts/15/sp.debug.js',
                function () {
                    $.getScript(hostweburl + '/_layouts/15/sp.RequestExecutor.js',
                        function () {
                            ko.applyBindings(new defaultViewModel());
                        });
                })
        })
});

function defaultViewModel() {
    var self = this;

    self.status = ko.observable();
    self.message = ko.observable();
    self.url =
        ko.observable("/_api/SP.AppContextSite(@target)/web/lists?@target='"
                        + hostweburl + "'");
    self.format = ko.observable();

    self.result = null;

    self.onRunRequest = function () {
        var executor = new SP.RequestExecutor(appweburl);
        executor.executeAsync(
            {
                url: appweburl + self.url(),
                method: "GET",
                headers: {
                    "accept": self.format(),
                },
                success: Function.createDelegate(self, self.onComplete),
                error: Function.createDelegate(self, self.onComplete)
            }
        );
    };

    self.onComplete = function (data) {
        self.status(data.statusText);
        self.message(data.body);
```

```
                    if (self.format() == 'application/atom-xml')
                        self.result = $(data.body)[1];
                    else
                        self.result = JSON.parse(data.body).d;
                }
            }

            // utility routine
            function getQueryStringParameter(paramToRetrieve) {
                var params =
                    document.URL.split("?")[1].split("&");
                var strParams = "";
                for (var i = 0; i < params.length; i = i + 1) {
                    var singleParam = params[i].split("=");
                    if (singleParam[0] == paramToRetrieve)
                        return singleParam[1];
                }
            }
```

This code begins by loading three JavaScript libraries from SharePoint. These libraries could not be included in the script references in the ASPX file because they reside on SharePoint. This page runs outside of the SharePoint app web and therefore cannot reference these files using a relative URL. Instead, the URL for each file is calculated as it is loaded. Once all of the scripts needed are loaded, the view-model object is created and bound to the form as before.

The next change is in the default REST URL being supplied in the URL text box.

```
self.url =
    ko.observable("/_api/SP.AppContextSite(@target)/web/lists?@target='"
                    + hostweburl + "'");
```

This line is formatting the URL to access the list collection in the host web site using the SP.AppContextSite endpoint.

The onRunRequest() function looks very similar to its JQuery counterpart except for the need to create the SP.RequestExecutor object. The constructor for this object takes a URL, which refers to the site where the request will be submitted by the cross-domain library.

```
var executor = new SP.RequestExecutor(appweburl);
```

When accessing the SharePoint REST API from with our app, we will use the app web for the destination. This only indicates where the request should be sent, not its ultimate destination. In our case, we will be using the SP.AppContextSite object to access the host site. If the URL provided in the executeAsync() function call had been outside of SharePoint, the cross-domain proxy on the app web would be used to forward the request.

■ **Tip**   It is possible to code a custom proxy page on the remote web site for the cross-domain library to use. This might be necessary if the target web service required some special formatting or security information. In that case, it would be the URL of the remote web that would be specified in the constructor. The custom proxy page would also need to be configured in the `iFrameSourceUrl` property of the `RequestExecutor` object. Details on building custom proxies can be found at `http://msdn.microsoft.com/en-us/library/fp161183.aspx`.

The `onComplete()` function receives slightly different parameters than it did from the JQuery library.

```
self.onComplete = function (data) {
    self.status(data.statusText);
    self.message(data.body);

    if (self.format() == 'application/atom-xml')
        self.result = $(data.body)[1];
    else
        self.result = JSON.parse(data.body).d;
}
```

The `RequestExecutor` returns a JavaScript object that contains the status and body of the response in two different properties of the same object. The response is presented in string form regardless of the format requested from the service. The data in the string is either a serialized JSON object or XML document.

14.   Save and close the `App.js` file.

If we ran this solution in its current state, it would fail because it would not be able to find the app web. An app web is only created if one is needed. Since we created an auto-hosted app and have not added any lists or other objects to the app web project, no app web will be created when the app is installed. Since we need to access the REST API from within the app web, this would not work. To force the creation of a minimal app web, we will add an empty element file to the project.

15.   Right-click on the Exercise 7-2 SharePoint project in the Solution Explorer.

■ **Caution**   Do not select the Exercise 7-2 Web project by mistake in the previous step.

16.   Select Add ➤ New Item….

17.   Select the Empty Element item and click Add. The name of the new element is not important.

18.   Execute the project with F5 to start debugging.

Except for some missing menus and icons, the resulting page looks exactly the same as the one we created in Exercise 7-1. The important difference to note is that this request is now executing in a remote web app completely outside of the SharePoint farm. The header associated with the access token was added automatically by the cross-domain library.

The TokenHelper and HTTPWebRequest Objects

The first two libraries used to access the REST API were both JavaScript based and ran within the web browser. The last technique is used by server-side code running in a remote web site that needs to access SharePoint.

■ **Note** Technically, the only scenario that uses the full OAuth protocol is when there is server-to-server (S2S) communication between servers in different security domains. That is the case when an app's remote web site accesses the REST service within the app's app web. That is the case we are dealing with here.

This code runs within the web server process running an ASP.NET web site. The code components exist in either the .NET Framework or the web site's own codebase.

- The TokenHelper.cs (or .vb) file that is included in the project template is used to manage the tokens used.

- The HttpWebRequest object is used to format and send web requests.

- The HttpWebResponse object is used to interpret the responses from the REST API.

EXERCISE 7-3

In this exercise, we will create the same functionality as in the previous two exercises using server-side ASP.NET code.

We will create an auto-hosted app and add ASP.NET controls to the app's default page. Then we will add server-side code to process the REST request and display the results.

We will start by creating a new auto-hosted app to use as a test bed.

1. Start Visual Studio 2012.

2. Create a new SharePoint 2013 app.

3. Name it Exercise 7-3 and leave auto-hosted selected for the hosting option.

4. Open the Default.aspx page from the Pages folder.

5. Replace the contents of the <form> tag with the following HTML markup:

```
<asp:HiddenField ID="SPAppToken" runat="server" />
<div>
    <table>
        <tr>
            <td>REST Path:</td>
            <td>
                <asp:TextBox ID="txtREST" runat="server" Width="700">
                    /_api/web/lists
                </asp:TextBox>
            </td>
        </tr>
    </table>
```

```
            <tr>
                <td>Format:</td>
                <td>
                    <asp:DropDownList ID="ddlFormat" runat="server">
                        <asp:ListItem Value="application/json;odata=verbose">
                            application/json;odata=verbose
                        </asp:ListItem>
                        <asp:ListItem Value="application/atom-xml">
                            application/atom-xml
                        </asp:ListItem>
                    </asp:DropDownList>
                </td>
            </tr>
        </table>
        <asp:Button ID="cmdRunRequest" runat="server"
                Text="Execute the REST Request"
                OnClick="cmdRunRequest_Click" />
    </div>

    <h2><asp:Label ID="lblStatus" runat="server" Text=""></asp:Label></h2>
    <asp:Label ID="lblOutput" runat="server" Text=""></asp:Label>
```

This markup generates a UI similar to the previous two exercises except that it uses ASP.NET server controls instead of HTML input elements. Instead of processing the request within the client browser, clicking the button will cause an ASP.NET postback to occur.

<asp:HiddenField ID="SPAppToken" runat="server" />

This field in the form is not visible to the user. It will contain the context token for the page. This field has been added to the page because we must have the context token available in order to make the call into SharePoint when the postback occurs.

As an alternative, we could have placed the context token into session state on the web server. This involves a trade-off. Storing session state data can cause scalability problems. Including the context token in the form could allow it to be intercepted if the page does not use SSL. In this case, the page will use SSL, so placing the token in the page is appropriate. In fact, the token was originally posted to the page in the same manner.

6. Save and close Default.aspx.

7. Open the Default.aspx.cs code-behind file.

8. Add the following lines at the top of the file:

```
using System.Net;
using System.IO;
```

9. Replace the `Page_Load` routine with the following code. This code copies the provided context token into the form.

```
protected void Page_Load(object sender, EventArgs e)
{
    // This copies the context token that is originally posted to the page into a
    // hidden field on the form so that it is available during event handler
    // routines executed during a postback.
    if (!IsPostBack)
        SPAppToken.Value = TokenHelper.GetContextTokenFromRequest(Request);
}
```

10. Add an event handler for the command button, as follows:

```
protected void cmdRunRequest_Click(object sender, EventArgs e)
{
    // For testing only!
    // Remove this line before releasing to production.
    TokenHelper.TrustAllCertificates();

    Uri appWebUrl = new Uri(Request.QueryString["SPAppWebUrl"]);

    // The context token is retrieved from the SPAppToken field
    // in TokenHelper.GetContextTokenFromRequest().
    SharePointContextToken contextToken =
            TokenHelper.ReadAndValidateContextToken(
                        TokenHelper.GetContextTokenFromRequest(Request),
                        Request.Url.Authority);

    string accessToken =
            TokenHelper.GetAccessToken(contextToken,
                                    appWebUrl.Authority).AccessToken;

    HttpWebRequest req =
            (HttpWebRequest)HttpWebRequest.Create(
                        Request.QueryString["SPAppWebUrl"] + txtREST.Text);
    req.Method = "GET";
    req.Accept = ddlFormat.SelectedValue;
    req.Headers.Add("Authorization", "Bearer " + accessToken);

    HttpWebResponse resp = (HttpWebResponse)req.GetResponse();
    lblStatus.Text = resp.StatusDescription;

    StreamReader st = new StreamReader(resp.GetResponseStream());
    lblOutput.Text = WebUtility.HtmlEncode(st.ReadToEnd());
}
```

11. Save and close the `Default.aspx.cs` file.

This routine performs a series of steps to execute the REST request. First, the context token is retrieved from the page and an access token is generated by making a call to the Access Control Service in Windows Azure.

```
SharePointContextToken contextToken =
        TokenHelper.ReadAndValidateContextToken(
                        TokenHelper.GetContextTokenFromRequest(Request),
                        Request.Url.Authority);

string accessToken =
        TokenHelper.GetAccessToken(contextToken,
                                appWebUrl.Authority).AccessToken;
```

Next, the request object is created using the URL and header information required. Note that the access token generated by ACS is added to the authorization header.

```
HttpWebRequest req =
        (HttpWebRequest)HttpWebRequest.Create(
                        Request.QueryString["SPAppWebUrl"] + txtREST.Text);
req.Method = "GET";
req.Accept = ddlFormat.SelectedValue + "; odata=verbose";
req.Headers.Add("Authorization", "Bearer " + accessToken);
```

Finally, the request is executed and the web response object is created.

```
HttpWebResponse resp = (HttpWebResponse)req.GetResponse();
lblStatus.Text = resp.StatusDescription;

StreamReader st = new StreamReader(resp.GetResponseStream());
lblOutput.Text = WebUtility.HtmlEncode(st.ReadToEnd());
```

As we saw in the last exercise, if we ran this solution in its current state, it would fail because there would be no app web. To force the creation of a minimal app web, we will add an empty element file to the project.

12. Right-click on the Exercise 7-3 SharePoint project in the Solution Explorer.

Caution Do not select the Exercise 7-3 Web project by mistake in the previous step.

13. Select Add ➤ New Item….

14. Select the Empty Element from Office/SharePoint Items and click Add. The name of the new element is not important.

15. Execute the project with F5 to start debugging.

Cosmetically, the page looks and behaves the same as in the previous exercise. The difference is that, in this case, pressing the button causes the browser to send a new request to the web browser and re-render the entire page. No logic is performed within the client web browser.

Choosing the Appropriate Library

There is no one right answer for which library to use. It depends on the situation. The key considerations are as follows:

1. Where will the code run—in the web browser or in ASP.NET server-side code?

2. Will the call cross domains? Remember, the host, app, and remote webs within a single SharePoint app each reside in separate domains.

3. Will the call access a web service outside of the SharePoint app?

Figure 7-6 depicts the various types of REST calls that an app might be required to make.

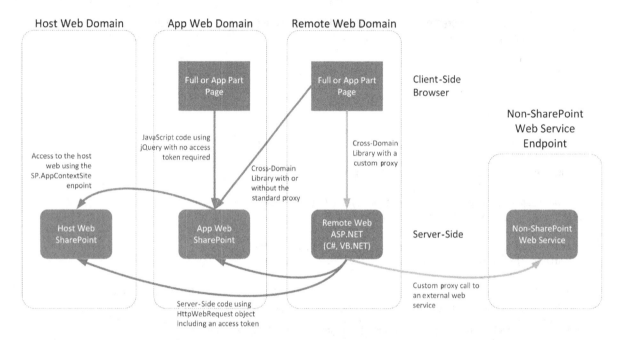

Figure 7-6. *REST library scenarios*

Each arrow in Figure 7-6 is labeled with the most appropriate library to use in each situation. This is not to say that other options are not possible. For example, both the JQuery and cross-domain libraries can be used to perform any web service call from client JavaScript code. They each have strengths in different situations.

Table 7-6 describes the strengths and weaknesses of each library. Use this table to help understand when to use each library. When evaluating other libraries that may be available to you, try to keep these points in mind.

Table 7-6. *Web Service Library Properties*

Library	Strengths	Limitations
JQuery (ajax() function)	Simple to use. Requires no SharePoint libraries. Used in client script in a web page. Easy calling within the page's domain.	To cross domains, an access token must be supplied manually. No server-side proxy support.
Cross-Domain Library (RequestExecutor)	Used in client script in a web page. Used when calling across domains. Automatic token handling. Used when a server side proxy is required. Used when calling external web services.	Custom SharePoint libraries required.
HTTPWebRequest and TokenHelper objects	Used in server-side ASP.NET code. Supports browsers with no JavaScript. Can access server-side resources directly.	Requires requests to be posted to the web server. Requires an IIS hosting environment.

Managing Data in SharePoint

In the previous section, we examined the libraries used to read data from the SharePoint REST API. The same libraries are used when performing create, update, and delete operations. However, they are used somewhat differently because of the need to pass additional types of data to the service.

In this section, we will cover the techniques used to update data in SharePoint. This will include implementing security and consistency protections for our requests. In CSOM, these are handed by the client object library, but in REST we have to supply this information ourselves.

Passing the Request Digest

Each time ASP.NET renders a form that will return data, it embeds a *request digest* in the page. The specific contents of the digest are not important to us. The purpose of the digest is to ensure that when the form is submitted back to the web server, it has not been altered in a way that may violate the security of the web site. When making a call to update data in SharePoint, the request digest is included in the X-RequestDigest header in the request to verify the validity of the request.

The primary type of attack prevented using the request digest is a *replay attack*. In this type of attack, data is gathered from the network by an attacker and is later sent back into the application in an attempt to bypass some type of security check. For example, imagine submitting a cash transfer request to your bank's web site asking for funds to be transferred from your savings to checking account. What if someone intercepted this traffic, altered the account number of the destination account, and resubmitted the request to the server. You have suddenly been robbed. Of course, this attack might, and should, be prevented by using an SSL connection between the browser and the server. The request digest simply provides another layer of protection.

The request digest is included in an ASP.NET form as a hidden field called __REQUESTDIGEST (note there are *two* leading underscores). In the JQuery script associated with such a form, you can use $("#__REQUESTDIGEST").val() to retrieve the value. In some cases, there may be a legitimate reason why the request digest value is not available to your client code. For these instances, the SharePoint REST API contains an access point designed to return this information along with other fields relating to the context of a request. The contextinfo access point returns an SP.ContextWebInformation object that contains this information.

■ **Tip**   When calling the `contextinfo` access point, be sure to use a POST operation, not a GET. Contextinfo responds only to a POST.

A request digest is not required on all REST requests. For example, none of the previous exercises in this chapter specified a digest value. This is because all of these were GET requests. The request digest only applies to POST type requests. The request digest is also not required when posting information on a validated OAuth connection. This is the case when server-side ASP.NET code calls into SharePoint using the TokenHelper library. All browser-based JavaScript POST requests require the request digest to be included.

Ensuring Consistent Updates with ETags

The OData protocol defines a consistency checking mechanism called *ETags*. An ETag can be thought of as a version number for a list or list item object in SharePoint. This version number is then supplied in any future update of that object to ensure that the version that was read is still current when it is updated. If the version number in SharePoint has changed, the new update request will fail (with HTTP status code 412) to avoid losing changes. This is known as *optimistic locking*.

When an object is read from SharePoint, the JSON or XML object returned from the REST API will contain an ETag value. This value can then be included in the IF-MATCH header in the update request.

ETag checking is only relevant to update and delete operations (PUT, PATCH, MERGE, or DELETE). Operations that create SharePoint objects (POST) do not use ETags because there is no previous version of the object to check. ETags are only used for lists, libraries, list items, and document objects. They do not apply to objects such as webs or content types.

Unlike the request digest, an ETag is never required. If no consistency checking is desired, the header can be passed with a * wildcard value or it can be omitted altogether. If no ETag value is supplied, no check will be made and the update will complete as though the check had been successful. Using ETags may require an extra request to be made to read the object from the server to retrieve the ETag value. This may not always be necessary if the item is known to be unchanged through some other mechanism. It may also be decided that the likelihood to an update collision is remote enough to be ignored.

The Classroom Online Gradebook

Throughout the remainder of this section, we will create a page for our Classroom Online app that allows a faculty member to enter grades for each student and display those grades to the student when they view the page. The form will support basic CRUD operations in a standard data grid. We will use the REST API behind the scenes to handle all of the interactions with SharePoint.

EXERCISE 7-4

This exercise will lay down the outline of the page and set up the script files we will use. In the following sections, we will add the functionality to create, update, and delete rows from the gradebook.

We will add a "Grades" list to the app web to store the gradebook. We will also create a page to host the gradebook's view, and create a model object to handle CRUD operations for grade entries. Finally, we will create a view-model object to manage the page.

Since we will be adding this page to the Classroom Online app, we will start with the project files as they were at the end of Chapter 6. You can download these from the book's web site if you need them, available from the Source Code/Download area of the Apress web site (www.apress.com).

1. Open Visual Studio 2012.

2. Open the Classroom Online solution.

3. Right-click the app project file and select Add ➤ New Item....

4. Select List from the templates and name the list Grades.

5. On the next dialog, leave all of the defaults and click Finish.

6. In the list designer, rename the Title field to Assignment Title.

7. Add the other fields shown in Figure 7-7.

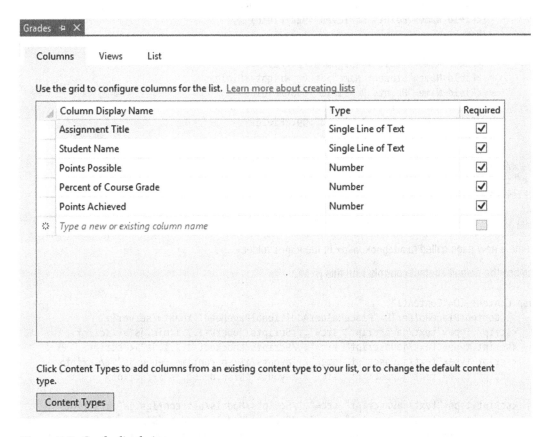

Figure 7-7. *Grades list designer*

8. Save and close the list designer.

To make debugging easier, we will add a few grades to the default gradebook.

9. Open the Elements.xml file under the Grades ➤ GradesInstance node in the Solution Explorer.

10. Replace its contents with the following XML. If you replace the student name with yours, you can test the project as a student and see your grades.

```xml
<?xml version="1.0" encoding="utf-8"?>
<Elements xmlns="http://schemas.microsoft.com/sharepoint/">
  <ListInstance Title="Grades" OnQuickLaunch="FALSE"
            TemplateType="10001" Url="Lists/Grades"
            Description="Course gradebook">
    <Data>
      <Rows>
        <Row>
          <Field Name="Title">Assignment 1</Field>
          <Field Name="Student Name">Steve Wright</Field>
          <Field Name="Points Possible">100</Field>
          <Field Name="Percent of Course Grade">10</Field>
          <Field Name="Points Achieved">92</Field>
        </Row>
        <Row>
          <Field Name="Title">Assignment 2</Field>
          <Field Name="Student Name">Steve Wright</Field>
          <Field Name="Points Possible">100</Field>
          <Field Name="Percent of Course Grade">5</Field>
          <Field Name="Points Achieved">99</Field>
        </Row>
      </Rows>
    </Data>
  </ListInstance>
</Elements>
```

11. Save and close the `Elements.xml` file.

12. Create a new page called `Gradebook.aspx` in the `Pages` folder.

13. Replace the default content controls with this HTML:

```html
<asp:Content ID="Content1"
        ContentPlaceHolderID="PlaceHolderAdditionalPageHead" runat="server">
    <script type="text/javascript" src="../Scripts/jquery-1.7.1.min.js"></script>
    <script type="text/javascript" src="../Scripts/knockout-2.2.1.js"></script>
    <script type="text/javascript" src="/_layouts/15/sp.runtime.debug.js"></script>
    <script type="text/javascript" src="/_layouts/15/sp.debug.js"></script>

    <script type="text/javascript" src="../Scripts/Models/siteconfigs.js"></script>
    <script type="text/javascript" src="../Scripts/Models/grades.js"></script>
    <script type="text/javascript" src="../Scripts/ViewModels/gradebook.js"></script>
</asp:Content>

<asp:Content ID="Content2"
        ContentPlaceHolderId="PlaceHolderPageTitleInTitleArea" runat="server">
    Course Gradebook
</asp:Content>

<asp:Content ID="Content3" ContentPlaceHolderID="PlaceHolderMain" runat="server">
    <table border="1" cellspacing="0" cellpadding="5">
```

```
        <thead style='background-color:gray;color:white'>
            <th>Student</th>
            <th>Assignment</th>
            <th>Points Possible</th>
            <th>Course Weight (%)</th>
            <th>Points Acheived</th>
            <th class='buttonColumn'></th>
        </thead>
        <tbody data-bind="foreach: gradebookEntries()">
            <tr>
                <td data-bind="text: studentName"></td>
                <td data-bind="text: assignmentTitle"></td>
                <td data-bind="text: pointsPossible"></td>
                <td data-bind="text: percentOfGrade"></td>
                <td data-bind="text: pointsAchieved"></td>
                <td class='buttonColumn'>
                    <a href="#" data-bind="click: $root.onEdit">Edit</a>
                    <a href="#" data-bind="click: $root.onDelete">Delete</a>
                </td>
            </tr>
            <tr style="display:none">

                <td><input data-bind="value: studentName" /></td>
                <td><input data-bind="value: assignmentTitle" /></td>
                <td><input data-bind="value: pointsPossible" /></td>
                <td><input data-bind="value: percentOfGrade" /></td>
                <td><input data-bind="value: pointsAchieved" /></td>
                <td class='buttonColumn'>
                    <a href="#" data-bind="click: $root.onSave">Save</a>
                    <a href="#" data-bind="click: $root.onCancel">Cancel</a>
                </td>
            </tr>
        </tbody>
        <tfoot id="addLine">
            <tr data-bind="with: addItem">
                <td><input data-bind="value: studentName" /></td>
                <td><input data-bind="value: assignmentTitle" /></td>
                <td><input data-bind="value: pointsPossible" /></td>
                <td><input data-bind="value: percentOfGrade" /></td>
                <td><input data-bind="value: pointsAchieved" /></td>
                <td class='buttonColumn'>
                    <a href="#" data-bind="click: $root.onAdd">Add</a>
                </td>
            </tr>
        </tfoot>
    </table>
</asp:Content>
```

14. Save and close the page.

A quick look at this code will show that it includes the JQuery and Knockout libraries along with the SharePoint JSOM libraries and the `siteconfigs.js` file from previous chapters. The other included script files are for our model and view-model objects that we will create shortly.

■ **Tip**   Since we will be making REST calls only within the app web domain, we will use the `JQuery.ajax()` function. Therefore, this page does not need to include the JSOM libraries for its own use. However, since we will be including the `siteconfigs.js` file, we still need to include JSOM in this case.

The rest of the HTML page renders a very simple table that uses Knockout to bind our data. Each row in the table has a read-only and a read-write set of controls. In read-only mode, the user can delete the line or start editing it. In read-write mode, the user can save their changes or cancel the editing. There is also a row at the bottom to allow new rows to be entered. The completed page can be seen in Figure 7-8.

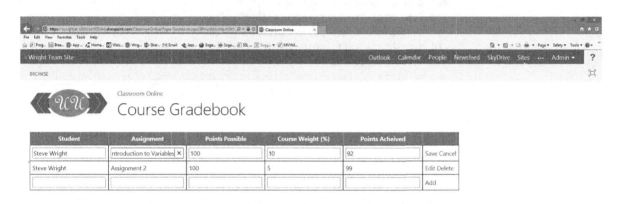

Figure 7-8. *Gradebook page in faculty edit mode*

15.   Create a new JavaScript file in the `Scripts/ViewModels` folder called `gradebook.js`.

16.   Add this JavaScript to the file:

```
$(function () {
    CO.Configs.ensureConfigs(
        function () {
            ko.applyBindings(new gradebookViewModel(!CO.Configs.isCurrentUserSiteAdmin));
        });
})

function gradebookViewModel(viewAsStudent) {
    var self = this;
```

```
self.model = new CO_Grades();
self.eventItem = null;
self.eventTarget = null;

self.viewAsStudent = viewAsStudent;
self.gradebookEntries = ko.observableArray();
self.addItem = ko.observable(new gradebookEntry('', '', '', '', '',0,''));

self.onLoad = function () {
    // render a read-only version of the form for students
    if (self.viewAsStudent) {
        $('.buttonColumn').hide();
        $('#addLine').hide();

        self.model.getGrades(
            Function.createDelegate(self, self.onLoadComplete),
            CO.Configs.currentUser.name);
    }
    else // render all grades for the faculty
        self.model.getGrades(
            Function.createDelegate(self, self.onLoadComplete),
            null);
};
self.onLoadComplete = function (gradeList) {
    for (var i = 0; i < gradeList.length; i++)
        self.gradebookEntries.push(
            new gradebookEntry(gradeList[i].StudentName,
                               gradeList[i].Title,
                               gradeList[i].PointsPossible,
                               gradeList[i].PercentofCourseGrade,
                               gradeList[i].PointsAchieved,
                               gradeList[i].Id,
                               gradeList[i].__metadata.etag));
}

self.onAdd = function (sender, e) {
    // TBD
};

self.onEdit = function (sender, e) {
    // TBD
};

self.onDelete = function (sender, e) {
    // TBD
};

self.onSave = function (sender, e) {
    // TBD
}
```

```
            self.onCancel = function (sender, e) {
                // TBD
            };

            self.onLoad();
        }

        function gradebookEntry(studentName, assignmentTitle, pointsPossible,
                            percentOfGrade, pointsAchieved, id, etag) {
            var self = this;
            self.studentName = ko.observable(studentName);
            self.assignmentTitle = ko.observable(assignmentTitle);
            self.pointsPossible = ko.observable(pointsPossible);
            self.percentOfGrade = ko.observable(percentOfGrade);
            self.pointsAchieved = ko.observable(pointsAchieved);
            self.id = id;        // Not bound to an HTML element.
            self. etag = etag;   // Not bound to an HTML element.

            self.isValid = function () {
                if (self.studentName() == '')
                    { alert("Please enter the student's name."); return 0; }
                if (self.assignmentTitle() == '')
                    { alert("Please enter the assignment's title."); return 0; }
                if ((self.pointsPossible() == '')
                        || (self.pointsPossible() != parseInt(self.pointsPossible())))
                    { alert("Please enter a valid number of points possible."); return 0; }
                if ((self.percentOfGrade() == '')
                        || (self.percentOfGrade() != parseFloat(self.percentOfGrade())))
                    { alert("Please enter a valid percentage."); return 0; }
                if ((self.pointsAchieved() == '')
                        || (self.pointsAchieved() != parseInt(self.pointsAchieved())))
                    { alert("Please enter a valid number of points achieved."); return 0; }
                return 1;
            }

            self.backupValues = function () {
                self._studentName = self.studentName();
                self._assignmentTitle = self.assignmentTitle();
                self._pointsPossible = self.pointsPossible();
                self._percentOfGrade = self.percentOfGrade();
                self._pointsAchieved = self.pointsAchieved();
            }

            self.restoreValues = function () {
                self.studentName(self._studentName);
                self.assignmentTitle(self._assignmentTitle);
                self.pointsPossible(self._pointsPossible);
                self.percentOfGrade(self._percentOfGrade);
                self.pointsAchieved(self._pointsAchieved);
            }
        }
```

This will be the view-model for the page. We start by loading the site configurations and then we bind the view-model to the page. The view-model function takes a parameter that indicates what mode the page will be in. A `true` value indicates that the page is being viewed by a student.

```
$(function () {
    CO.Configs.ensureConfigs(
        function () {
            ko.applyBindings(new gradebookViewModel(!CO.Configs.isCurrentUserSiteAdmin));
        });
})
```

The view-model creates an instance of the model object `CO_Grades()` to use when accessing SharePoint.

```
self.model = new CO_Grades();
```

The table's rows are bound to Knockout observable objects.

```
self.gradebookEntries = ko.observableArray();
self.addItem = ko.observable(new gradebookEntry('', '', '', '', '',0,''));
```

When the page loads, a call is made to the model object to retrieve the data from SharePoint asynchronously.

```
self.onLoad = function () {
    // render a read-only version of the form for students
    if (self.viewAsStudent) {
        $('.buttonColumn').hide();
        $('#addLine').hide();

        self.model.getGrades(
            Function.createDelegate(self, self.onLoadComplete),
            CO.Configs.currentUser.name);
    }
    else // render all grades for the faculty
        self.model.getGrades(
            Function.createDelegate(self, self.onLoadComplete),
            null);
};
```

We pass a delegate that the model will call when the data is available and, optionally, the name of a student if we need to filter the items returned.

The callback routine accepts the array of JavaScript objects returned by the REST service. The properties of these objects are used to create a set of `gradebookEntry` objects that are added to an observable array bound to the grid in the view.

```
self.onLoadComplete = function (gradeList) {
    for (var i = 0; i < gradeList.length; i++)
        self.gradebookEntries.push(
            new gradebookEntry(gradeList[i].StudentName,
                               gradeList[i].Title,
                               gradeList[i].PointsPossible,
```

```
                                   gradeList[i].PercentofCourseGrade,
                                   gradeList[i].PointsAchieved,
                                   gradeList[i].Id,
                                   gradeList[i].__metadata.etag));
}
```

Aside from the five fields that make up our list items, we receive two other items that we need to hold on to. The `Id` field contains the ID of the list item in SharePoint. We will use this to identify the item when we update or delete it. The `__metadata` property (be sure to include two underscores in the name) contains control information about the SharePoint object returned from the service. In this case, we are interested in the `etag` field, since we will implement optimistic locking.

We will fill in the other functions in the view-model in later exercises.

17. Save and close the `gradebook.js` file.

18. Create a new JavaScript file in the `Scripts/Models` folder called `grades.js`. This will contain our model object.

19. Add this JavaScript to the file:

```javascript
// Data Model Object for the gradebook
CO_Grades = function () {
    var self = this;

    self.getGrades = function (callback, studentName) {
        var restUrl = CO.Configs.SPAppWebUrl
                    + "/_api/web/lists/getbytitle('Grades')/items"
                    + "?$orderby=Created desc"
      + "&$select=ID,StudentName,Title,PointsPossible,PercentofCourseGrade,PointsAchieved";

            // if a student is given, read only their grades
            if (studentName)
                restUrl += '&$filter=StudentName eq \'' + studentName + '\'';

            // query the grade list for the grades to display/edit
            jQuery.ajax({
                url: restUrl,
                type: "GET",
                headers: {
                    "accept": 'application/json;odata=verbose',
                },
                success: function (data) {
                    callback(data.d.results);
                },
                error: function () {
                    alert('Unable to load grades.');
                }
            });
    };
}
```

At this point, the model contains only a single method used for reading the grades from SharePoint. We will add more methods in later sections. We use a simple GET request on the list. The resulting list item array is passed into the callback function.

```
var restUrl = CO.Configs.SPAppWebUrl
        + "/_api/web/lists/getbytitle('Grades')/items"
        + "?$orderby=Created desc"
+ "&$select=ID,StudentName,Title,PointsPossible,PercentofCourseGrade,PointsAchieved";

    // if a student is given, read only their grades
    if (studentName)
        restUrl += '&$filter=StudentName eq \'' + studentName + '\'';
```

The REST URL we are using contains multiple query options. We are ordering the results by the Created date field. We are selecting only those fields that we will need. If we are given a student's name, we use it to filter the items returned.

If you run the app at this point, you will see that the default list items are shown, but none of the links are active.

Creating Objects in SharePoint

To create a new object in SharePoint using the REST API, we have to provide the values of any necessary properties. Doing this in the URL is not practical, so this data is sent in the body of the request. In order to pass information this way, it is necessary to use a POST request instead of a GET. While REST supports posting this information in ATOM-XML form, it is usually easier to work with JSON objects, especially when calling REST from JavaScript.

It is not necessary, or even possible, to post every property that makes up a SharePoint object. For example, the object's ID value will be assigned by SharePoint and cannot be specified in the request. To create a new object, it is only necessary to specify any property that is not set by SharePoint and does not have a default value.

SharePoint stores objects in collection objects like SP.ListCollection or SP.ListItemCollection. To add an item to the collection, we will invoke the Add() method of the collection object. The inputs to the add method vary depending on the requirements of the item being created. For example, when creating an SP.Web object, the add method takes an SP.WebInfoCreationInformation object. This is an object that encapsulates the parameters used to create a new SharePoint site. When adding items to a list, the object passed in the request body corresponds to the content type of the item to be created. Always refer to the documentation for the add method you are using to determine what the correct parameters are.

EXERCISE 7-5

This exercise will add logic to the gradebook page to allow a new grade to be entered. The data fields will be passed to the REST API to add a new list item to the Grades list.

We will add a method to the model object to create a new gradebook entry. We will also add event handlers to the view-model to handle the add event, and update the UI with the result of the operation.

First, we will add the create method to the modelOpen the grades.js file in the Scripts/Models folder.

1. Add the following code to the CO_Grades constructor function. Note that this is only the first half of the function. The rest will be added in a moment.

```
self.addGrade = function (studentName, assignmentTitle, pointsPossible,
                          percentofCourseGrade, pointsAchieved, callback) {
    var body = {
        '__metadata': { 'type': 'SP.Data.GradesListItem' },
        'Title': assignmentTitle,
        'StudentName': studentName,
        'PointsPossible': pointsPossible,
        'PercentofCourseGrade': percentofCourseGrade,
        'PointsAchieved': pointsAchieved
    };
    body = JSON.stringify(body);
```

This JavaScript creates the `addGrade` method in the model and formats an object to use as the body of the REST request. Note that the property names are exactly as we declared them, except that the spaces were removed. The `__metadata` child object specifies the type of object being created. Because we created this list in the designer, without building a separate content type, the type name for the list items is `SP.Data.GradesListItem`. The `JSON.stringify()` function is used to convert the object to a string in JSON format.

2. Add the rest of the `addGrade` method.

```
jQuery.ajax({
    url: CO.Configs.SPAppWebUrl + "/_api/web/lists/getbytitle('Grades')/items",
    type: "POST",
    data: body,
    headers: {
        "X-RequestDigest": $("#__REQUESTDIGEST").val(),
        "accept": "application/json;odata=verbose",
        "content-type": "application/json;odata=verbose",
        "content-length": body.length
    },
    success: function (data) {
        callback(data.d.Id, data.d.__metadata.etag);
    },
    error: function (err) {
        alert('Unable to add the grade.');
    }
});
}
```

Using the JQuery ajax function, we are posting the body object we created in the data area of the request. Note the headers we are including. The request digest was created as part of the form. The content type and length describe the body of the message.

Notice that when we call the callback function, we pass two pieces of information received from SharePoint. `data.d.id` contains the new ID for the list item we just created. `data.d.__metadata.etag` contains the ETag value that we will need if we later wish to update the item. The ETag value returned will always be 1 since we just created the item, but it is best not to assume that.

3. Save and close the `grades.js` file.

4. Open the `gradebook.js` file in the `Scripts/ViewModels` directory.

5. Replace the `self.onAdd` handler with this code:

```
self.onAdd = function (sender, e) {
    if (self.addItem().isValid()) {
        self.model.addGrade(sender.studentName(),
                            sender.assignmentTitle(),
                            sender.pointsPossible(),
                            sender.percentOfGrade(),
                            sender.pointsAchieved(),
                            Function.createDelegate(self, self.onAddComplete));
    }
};
```

The event handler gets two parameters. The first is the observable Knockout object that is bound to the relevant part of the form. In this case, that is the object referenced by `self.addItem()`.

The second parameter is the JQuery event object. The most important property we will use from that object is the `target` property, which specifies the HTML element that received the event.

6. Add the callback routine that will run when the item has been successfully added to the list.

```
self.onAddComplete = function (id, etag) {
    // Copy the new ID and etag so that future updates can occur.
    self.addItem().id = id;
    self.addItem().etag = etag;

    var item = self.addItem();
    self.addItem(new gradebookEntry('', '', '', '', '', 0, ''));
    self.gradebookEntries.push(item);
}
```

The ID and ETag values provided by SharePoint are added to our view-model object. Then we move the new entry into the main grid and create a new item to be used for any further new items.

Updating Objects

When updating an existing object in SharePoint, there are two different types of operations that we can perform. If we wish to replace all of the writable properties of an object, that is to overwrite the object completely, we would use a PUT operation. If we wish to only update certain fields, then we would use a PATCH. These options are put into the X-HTTP-Method header. The REST request is sent as a POST.

■ **Tip** The SharePoint REST API also supports the MERGE operation, which is functionally equivalent to the PATCH method. MERGE is an older OData option that has been superseded by PATCH.

Formatting an update request is similar to creating an object. The REST URL is used to identify the object to be updated. The new property values are specified in an object included in the body of the request message. An ETag header should also be included in most cases to perform optimistic locking.

EXERCISE 7-6

In this exercise, we add logic to the gradebook page to allow an existing grade to be modified. We will use the PATCH method even though we are updating all of the custom fields in the list item. This is because the SP.ListItem object does not support the PUT method.

We will add a method to the model object to update a gradebook entry. We will also add event handlers to the view-model to handle the edit, save, and cancel events. Then, we will update the UI with the result of the save operation.

First, we will add the update method to the model.

1. Open the grades.js file in the Scripts/Models folder.

2. Add the following code to the CO_Grades constructor function. Note that this is only the first half of the function. The rest will be added in a moment.

```
self.updateGrade = function (studentName, assignmentTitle, pointsPossible,
                             percentofCourseGrade, pointsAchieved,
                             id, etag, callback) {
    var body = {
        '__metadata': { 'type': 'SP.Data.GradesListItem' },
        'Title': assignmentTitle,
        'StudentName': studentName,
        'PointsPossible': pointsPossible,
        'PercentofCourseGrade': percentofCourseGrade,
        'PointsAchieved': pointsAchieved
    };
    body = JSON.stringify(body);
```

This JavaScript is very similar to the beginning of the addGrade method we created in the previous exercise. The only difference is that the updateGrade method accepts the id and etag parameters.

3. Add the rest of the updateGrade method.

```
jQuery.ajax({
    url: CO.Configs.SPAppWebUrl
            + "/_api/web/lists/getbytitle('Grades')/items/getbyid('"
            + id.toString() + "')",
    type: "POST",
    data: body,
    headers: {
        "X-Http-Method": "PATCH",
        "X-RequestDigest": $("#__REQUESTDIGEST").val(),
        "IF-MATCH" : etag,
        "accept": "application/json;odata=verbose",
        "content-type": "application/json;odata=verbose",
        "content-length": body.length
    },
    success: function (data,status,resp) {
        callback(id, resp.getResponseHeader("ETAG"));
    },
```

```
        error: function (err) {
            alert('Unable to update the grade.');
        }
    });
}
```

Using the JQuery ajax function, we post the body object to a REST URL that identifies the object to be updated. Again, we include the request digest and content headers as we did when creating the item. Note that the type of the request is POST and the X-Http-Method header is PATCH. We are also including the IF-MATCH header with the current ETag value for the item.

When we call the callback function, we pass id and etag values, as we did in the create case. The id won't change in this case. The etag value is returned in the response message's ETAG header.

4. Save and close the grades.js file.

5. Open the gradebook.js file in the Scripts/ViewModels directory.

6. Replace the self.onEdit and self.onCancel handlers with this code:

```
self.onEdit = function (sender, e) {
    sender.backupValues();
    $(e.target).parent().parent().hide().next().show();
};

self.onCancel = function (sender, e) {
    sender.restoreValues();
    $(e.target).parent().parent().hide().prev().show();
};
```

These methods handle enabling and disabling editing for a line in the grid. The Knockout template for each item contains one row for viewing and one row for editing. The field values are bound to both rows. This code simply swaps which row is visible.

7. Replace the self.onSave event handler with this code:

```
self.onSave = function (sender, e) {
        if (sender.isValid()) {
            self.eventItem = sender;
            self.eventTarget = e.target;

            self.model.updateGrade(sender.studentName(),
                                   sender.assignmentTitle(),
                                   sender.pointsPossible(),
                                   sender.percentOfGrade(),
                                   sender.pointsAchieved(),
                                   sender.id,
                                   sender.etag,
                                   Function.createDelegate(self, self.onSaveComplete));
        }
    };
```

This method invokes the model object's update method. Note that since this is done asynchronously, it is necessary to retain the context of the event in the `eventItem` and `eventTarget` variables in the view-model. These will be used in the callback routine.

8. Add the callback routine that will run when the item has been successfully updated.

```
self.onSaveComplete = function (id, etag) {
    // Copy the ETag so that future updates can occur. The ID didn't change.
    self.eventItem.etag = etag;

    $(self.eventTarget).parent().parent().hide().prev().show();
}
```

The ETag value provided by SharePoint is updated in our view-model object. Then we restore the row to view mode.

Deleting Objects

The last of the CRUD operations to examine is the `delete` operation. To perform a `delete`, the REST URL only needs to identify the object to be deleted. You can, and should, include an ETag value to ensure consistent changes are being made, but this is optional.

EXERCISE 7-7

In this exercise, we will add logic to the gradebook application to allow an existing grade to be removed.

We will add a method to the model object to delete a gradebook entry. We will also add an event handler to the view-model to handle the `delete` event. Then, we will update the UI with the result of the `delete` operation.

First, we will add the `delete` method to the model.

1. Open the `grades.js` file in the `Scripts/Models` folder.

2. Add this code to the `CO_Grades` constructor function:

```
self.deleteGrade = function (id, etag, callback) {
    jQuery.ajax({
        url: CO.Configs.SPAppWebUrl
                + "/_api/web/lists/getbytitle('Grades')/items/getbyid('"
                    + id.toString() + "')",
        type: "POST",
        headers: {
            "X-Http-Method": "DELETE",
            "X-RequestDigest" : $("#__REQUESTDIGEST").val(),
            "IF-MATCH" : etag
        },
        success: function () {
            callback();
        },
```

```
            error: function (err) {
                alert('Unable to delete the grade.');
            }
        });
    }
```

Using the JQuery ajax function, we send a `DELETE` request to the REST URL representing the object to be deleted. There is no body object to be included in this case. We are also supplying the current ETag value for the object.

Note that the callback routine receives no parameters. The `delete` operation returns no information other than an indication of success or failure for the operation.

3. Save and close the `grades.js` file.

4. Open the `gradebook.js` file in the `Scripts/ViewModels` directory.

5. Replace the `self.onDelete` handler with this code:

```
self.onDelete = function (sender, e) {
    self.eventItem = sender;
    self.eventTarget = e.target;

    self.model.deleteGrade(sender.id, sender.etag,
                        Function.createDelegate(self, self.onDeleteComplete));
};
self.onDeleteComplete = function () {
    self.gradebookEntries.remove(self.eventItem);
}
```

6. Press F5 to execute the app.

7. Click the Delete button next to one of the entries in the grid and it should be removed.

The `onDelete` method sends the `id` and `etag` value to the model object. The event item and target element are retained so that the callback routine can remove the item from the grid.

Summary

In this chapter, we explored the SharePoint REST API. We deconstructed the requests and responses used to access the SharePoint environment from a client browser or web site. We reviewed the different security scenarios that may need to be addressed in an app when crossing domains or leveraging server-side ASP.NET code. We learned the techniques for using REST to create, read, update, and delete objects in SharePoint web sites and collections.

In Chapter 8, we will move on to accessing business data that is stored outside of SharePoint's lists and libraries. We will use Business Connectivity Services (BCS) to expose line-of-business data to our SharePoint apps. BCS allows us to read and update information within the enterprise programmatically from our aps in a secure, manageable way.

■ ■ ■

CHAPTER 8

Business Connectivity Services

So far, all of the data used by our apps has resided in SharePoint. There are situations where this is not practical or desirable. For example, when our data exists in a line-of-business application such as a CRM or enterprise data warehouse, moving or replicating this data in SharePoint would be cumbersome and unreliable. Also, given the fact that our apps may be deployed in many different sites or farms, it may be difficult to access a central copy of the data in SharePoint. This situation calls for a means of accessing data stored outside of SharePoint in a way that allows our apps to provide a rich user experience while maintaining data security.

In this chapter, we will go over the following points:

- How Business Connectivity Services (BCS) provides secure access to external systems.

- How SharePoint 2013 has been enhanced to support ODataservices for accessing data through BCS.

- The new features that have been added in SharePoint 2013 to support events and notifications for BCS data.

- How to create a centralized OData service that can be shared by various instances of a SharePoint app.

- How app-scoped external content types provide a simple means for SharePoint apps to access centralized data sources.

Business Connectivity Services Overview

Business Connectivity Services (BCS) is a set of features in SharePoint 2013 that supports exposing external, line-of-business data within SharePoint. This data may be stored in a relational database such as SQL Server or Oracle, an enterprise application such as a CRM or ERP system, or a custom-developed application. BCS provides an integration mechanism that allows this data to be used like standard office data elements such as tasks or contacts. Office applications including Excel, Access, and Outlook can use this data through SharePoint without the need to integrate each source system with each office application.

BCS has evolved over the last three versions of SharePoint to include an array of components that work together to support many different uses. The key to interacting with business entities in BCS is the creation of the Business Data Connectivity model. A BDC model is an XML document that describes the interface to be used between BCS and the line-of-business application. The model encapsulates the unique aspects and capabilities of the LOB application in a standard way that can be utilized by BCS.

Some of the features that are enabled by the components that make up BCS include the following:

- Create, read, update, and delete (CRUD) operations can be performed on LOB data through BCS.

- Endusers can be given the ability to create mash-up type applications using LOB data within the SharePoint environment without the need to write custom code.

- BCS data can be taken offline and be updated while disconnected.

- The business data in BCS can be added to the SharePoint Search service and be returned in search results.

- All of the security restrictions of the LOB application are obeyed and enforced by SharePoint. Additional security constraints can be managed within SharePoint web sites.

BCS Architecture

BCS is actually a set of components that exist within SharePoint 2013. The most important of these is the Business Data Connectivity (BDC) service. Introduced in SharePoint 2007, the BDC service is a SharePoint service application that resides on the server farm to process business entity requests.

As shown in Figure 8-1, the BDC service accesses line-of-business data through a layer of components called the *BCS Connector Framework*. BCS connectors are components that use the BDC model to access a specific type of back-end system. In SharePoint 2013, the available connector types are the following:

- *SQL*—This connects BCS directly to a SQL Server database.

- *WCF*—This connector maps the exposed methods on a Windows Communication Foundation web service to operations on a business entity.

- *.NET Framework*—This type of connector allows custom-coded .NET assemblies to be used to connect to line-of-business data.

- *OData*—New in SharePoint 2013, this connector allows for connections to standard OData service endpoints.

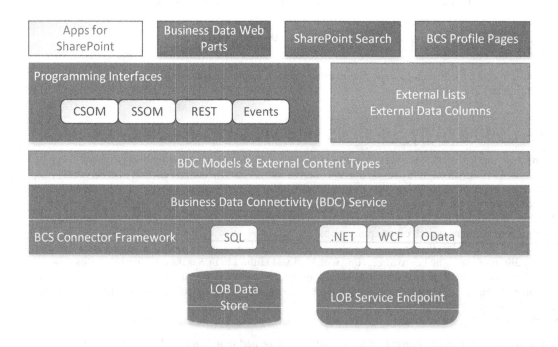

Figure 8-1. *Business Connectivity Services architecture*

The BDC service exposes modeled business entities as *external content types* in the SharePoint environment. External content types (ECTs) can be used to create external lists and data columns for use by users within SharePoint web sites. Through various APIs, ECTs can be accessed directly by server-side code and apps for SharePoint. External content types will be explained in more detail later in this chapter.

The business data exposed through BCS can be used in a variety of ways in SharePoint. The most basic use is through an external list in a web site. This type of list appears just like an ordinary SharePoint list, but the underlying data is stored in the back-end line-of-business system. SharePoint also contains a set of web parts specifically designed to query and present BCS data. These are called the Business Data Web Parts. SharePoint Search can be used to search and retrieve business data in BCS. BCS data can also be accessed by Office applications such as Outlook and Excel. Finally, and most importantly for us, BCS provides a robust means of integrating line-of-business data with our custom apps for SharePoint.

The following links provide more detailed technical information for creating BDC models and writing code against BCS:

- ***BDC Model Schema Reference***—http://msdn.microsoft.com/en-us/library/jj163906.aspx

- ***BCS Client Object Model Reference***—http://msdn.microsoft.com/en-us/library/ jj164116.aspx

- ***BCS REST Interface***—http://msdn.microsoft.com/en-us/library/jj163227.aspx

External Content Types

External content types are the building blocks for solutions using Business Connectivity Services. An ECT provides a detailed description of an interface with a back-end system that is used to manage business data.

In previous versions of SharePoint Server, external content types were always managed at the farm level. This meant that they could only be deployed and managed by a user with at least some farm-level privileges. The advantage to deploying them at the farm level is that they can be reused anywhere in the farm (see Figure 8-2). SharePoint 2013 still supports this style of BCS type management, but there are now additional ways to deploy ECTs as well.

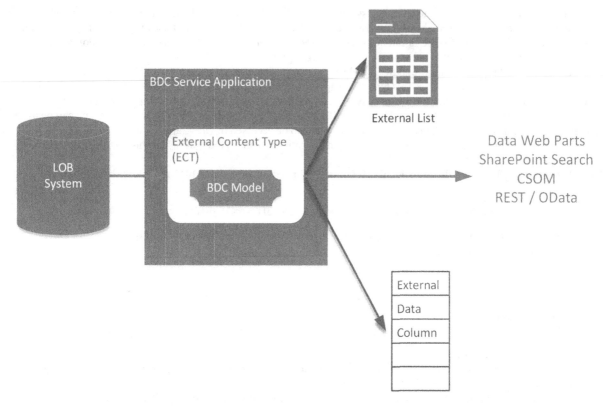

Figure 8-2. *External content type uses*

App-scoped external content types are definitions for BCS connections that can be included in an app for SharePoint package. An ECT deployed in this manner is only accessible by the app that created it. This provides greater flexibility for the enduser since no farm administrator needs to be involved in managing the type definition. As a result, this type of ECT is ideal for cloud-based apps where farm administrator support is minimal at best. Later in this chapter, we will create an app-scoped ECT and add it to our Classroom Online solution.

The interface between an external content type and the line-of-business system is defined by a *Business Data Connectivity (BDC) Model*. A model consists of an XML document that specifies how the LOB system is going to be accessed and what operations are supported. The major parts of a BDC model are as follows:

- IP or web addresses for accessing the LOB system.

- Security parameters for passing user identity information.

- Access control lists (ACLs) for defining the rights to be granted to the users.

- The business entities and properties to be managed.

- A set of operations (a.k.a. methods) supported by each entity. These may include queries and CRUD operations.

In SharePoint 2007, BDC models had to be coded by hand or through the use of a third-party tool. With SharePoint 2010 Server, Microsoft enhanced the SharePoint Designer tool to include the ability to create simple BDC models. Visual Studio can also be used to author BDC models for use with SharePoint apps.

■ **Note**　The terminology around BCS can be confusing. In Microsoft Office SharePoint Server (MOSS) 2007, *BDC* stood for the *Business Data Catalog*. There was no *BCS* in MOSS. Since SharePoint 2010, the term *Business Connectivity Services (BCS)* is used to describe the entire set of features associated with BCS. *BDC*, which now stands for *Business Data Connectivity*, is used to describe the XML models for external content types (BDC models) and the SharePoint service application that manages BCS data (the BDC Service).

The Open Data Protocol (OData) Connector

In Chapter 7, we examined how SharePoint exposes information using REST-style interfaces that follow the OData standard. SharePoint also has the ability to consume an OData service using BCS. The OData connector allows data exposed by an OData service to be used as the source for an external content type. This new feature in SharePoint 2013 is a key enabler for accessing external data in SharePoint apps.

Here are some examples of back-end systems that expose OData interfaces that can be consumed by BCS:

- SharePoint Server 2010, 2013, and SharePoint Online

- SQL Server and SQL Azure

- SQL Server Reporting Services (SSRS)

- ERP and CRM systems,such as MS Dynamics

- Windows Azure cloud table storage

- WCF Data Services

BCS Events and Notifications

Another new feature in SharePoint 2013 is the ability of BCS external lists to support event handlers and alerts.

An event is an action taken on a site, list, or item in SharePoint. The event handler is a piece of code that is run in response to an event. Alerts in SharePoint allow the user to be notified automatically when an event occurs. Prior to SharePoint 2013, external lists could not support event handlers because the data resides outside of SharePoint. SharePoint had no way of knowing when an event occurred in the LOB system. A new interface has been introduced in the BDC model that allows an external list to subscribe to events in the LOB system using remote event receivers.

A *remote event receiver* is a piece of code that is triggered by the LOB system when an event occurs. When an external list is created, SharePoint subscribes to notifications from the LOB system. When a change occurs, the LOB system sends the notification to a REST/OData service hosted within SharePoint. SharePoint can then trigger the necessary event handling within the SharePoint environment. Remote event receivers will also be used to forward SharePoint events to SharePoint apps. We will look at remote event receivers in Chapter 9.

Of course, not all line-of-business applications will be able to support BCS notifications. There must be a subscription service in the application and the ability to send OData notifications to SharePoint.

Creating an OData Endpoint

Because of the isolated nature of an app-scoped external content type, the only valid BCS connector for SharePoint apps is the OData connector. In some cases, the data to be exposed through BCS is already available in an OData service. When there is no existing OData service, it may be necessary to create one.

Microsoft's .NET Framework contains a set of classes that make creating an OData endpoint reasonably painless. Visual Studio can be used to create a Windows Communication Foundation (WCF) Data Service, formerly called an ADO.NET Data Service. A *WCF Data Service* provides an OData-compatible interface for a set of business entities modeled using an Entity Data Model (EDM) in an ASP.NET web site.

EXERCISE 8-1

In Chapter 7, the Classroom Online gradebook was implemented using a custom list in the local app web. This has certain limitations. Grade data is not retained after the app is uninstalled or the host site is deleted. There is also no way to centrally access all of the grades across the app's installed base. All grades must be accessed site by site. Imagine trying to create a transcript for a student with their grades spread all over a SharePoint farm or the Internet (assuming they haven't been accidently deleted).

To solve this problem, we will move the gradebook data store from the app web to a centralized relational database. For our example, we will use a table in SQL Azure, but a SQL Server running behind an organization's firewall would work just as well.

In this exercise we will create the Grade table in SQL Azure, and create an Entity Data Model for the Grade table. We will also create a WCF Data Service to host the OData endpoint, and deploy the ASP.NET site to Windows Azure.

Prerequisites

In order to complete this exercise, as written, you will need to have the following items already configured:

- A Windows Azure account with a publishing profile that can be used to publish a small ASP.NET web site to the Internet.

- A SQL Azure data server containing a database where a table can be placed and accessed from the ASP.NET web site.

■ **Tip** Visit http://www.windowsazure.com to sign up for an Azure account.

---

1. Open Visual Studio 2012.

2. Open the Classroom Online solution as it was at the end of Chapter 7. These files can be downloaded from the Source Code/Download area of the Apress web site (www.apress.com).

3. Open the Server Explorer window.

4. Create a new Data Connection for your SQL Azure database.

5. Choose the Microsoft SQL Server data provider (see Figure 8-3).

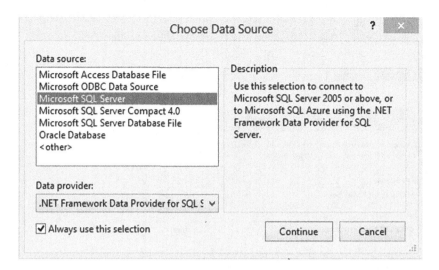

Figure 8-3. *Choose a data source type*

6. Connect to the SQL Azure database using the virtual database server name provided by Azure and the database name (see Figure 8-4).

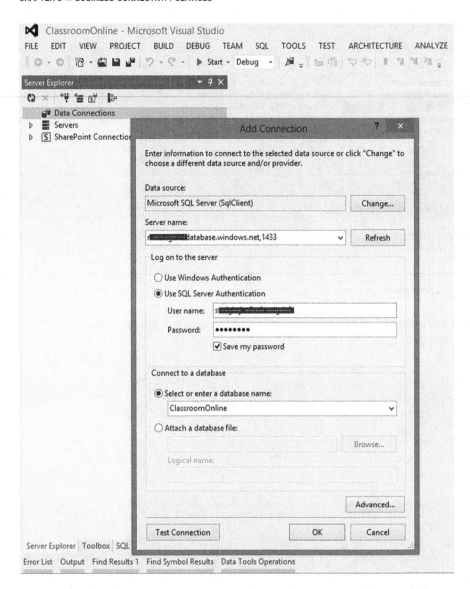

Figure 8-4. *Create SQL Azure connection*

7. In the database, create a Grade table using this T-SQL or an equivalent table using the designer in Visual Studio.

```
CREATE TABLE [dbo].[Grade] (
    [GradeID]              INT            IDENTITY (1, 1) NOT NULL,
    [ClassroomURL]         NVARCHAR (500) NOT NULL,
    [AssignmentTitle]      NVARCHAR (100) NOT NULL,
    [StudentName]          NVARCHAR (100) NOT NULL,
    [PointsPossible]       DECIMAL (18, 2) NOT NULL,
    [PercentOfCourseGrade] DECIMAL (18, 2) NOT NULL,
```

```
    [PointsAchieved]       DECIMAL (18, 2) NOT NULL,
    [EnteredBy]            NVARCHAR (200)  NOT NULL,
    [EnteredDate]          DATETIME        NOT NULL,
    PRIMARY KEY CLUSTERED ([GradeID] ASC)
);
```

This table will hold all of the grades entered in any site running Classroom Online. In a real-life scenario, this database would be part of Underhill University's transcript system of record. Go ahead and add a few grades to the table as test data.

8. Add a new project to the Classroom Online solution.

9. Select the Visual C# ➤ Web ➤ ASP.NET Empty Web Application project template.

10. Name the new project UnderhillIntegration.

11. In the UnderhillIntegration project, add a new item.

12. Select Visual C# ➤ ADO.NET Entity Data Model.

13. Name the model GradeModel.edmx (see Figure 8-5).

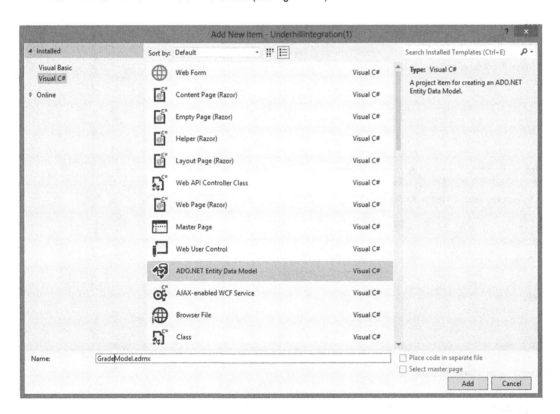

Figure 8-5. *Create an ADO.NET Entity Data Model*

14. Click Add.

15. Select the Generate from database option.

16. Click Next.

17. Select Yes, include the sensitive data in the connection string. This is only for demo purposes.

18. Click Next.

19. Select the Grade table to be included in the model (see Figure 8-6).

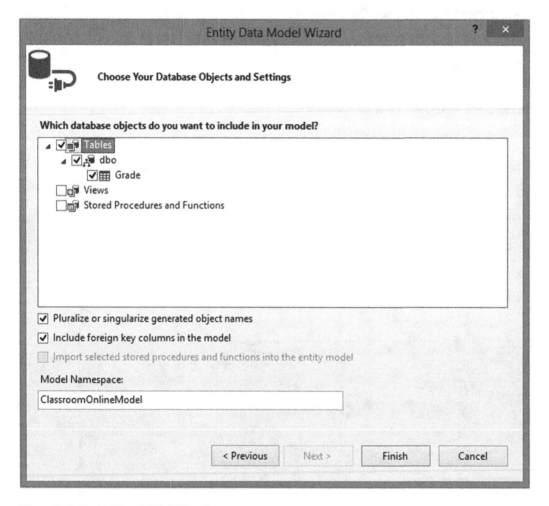

Figure 8-6. Entity Data Model Wizard

20. Click Finish.

21. Save and close the EDM window.

We now have an entity data model that connects to our SQL Azure table. Next, we will create a WCF service that will expose the model through an OData interface.

22. In the `UnderhillIntegration` project, add a new item.

23. Select Visual C# ➤ WCF Data Service.

24. Name the new service `GradeService.svc`.

25. Replace the template declaration for the class with `DataService<ClassroomOnlineEntities>`.

26. Add the following line of code to the beginning of the `InitializeService()` method in the `GradeService` class:

    ```
    config.SetEntitySetAccessRule("Grades", EntitySetRights.All);
    ```

27. Save and close the `GradeService.svc.cs` file.

The finished ASP.NET web site is ready to be deployed to Windows Azure.

28. Right-click on the `UnderhillIntegration` web project and select Publish....

29. Select your publishing profile. This is a file provided by Windows Azure that has a PUBLISHSETTINGS filename extension.

■ **Tip** To retrieve your publishing profile, go to the Windows Azure Management Portal for your account. Select the web site to which you wish to publish. Look for the Download the Publish Profile link under Quick Glance to the right of the page.

---

30. Click Next.

31. Test the connection to Windows Azure by clicking Validate Connection.

32. If the connection is successful, click Next.

33. Select the connection string for the `ClassroomOnlineEntities` database. This string is available in the drop-down list (see Figure 8-7).

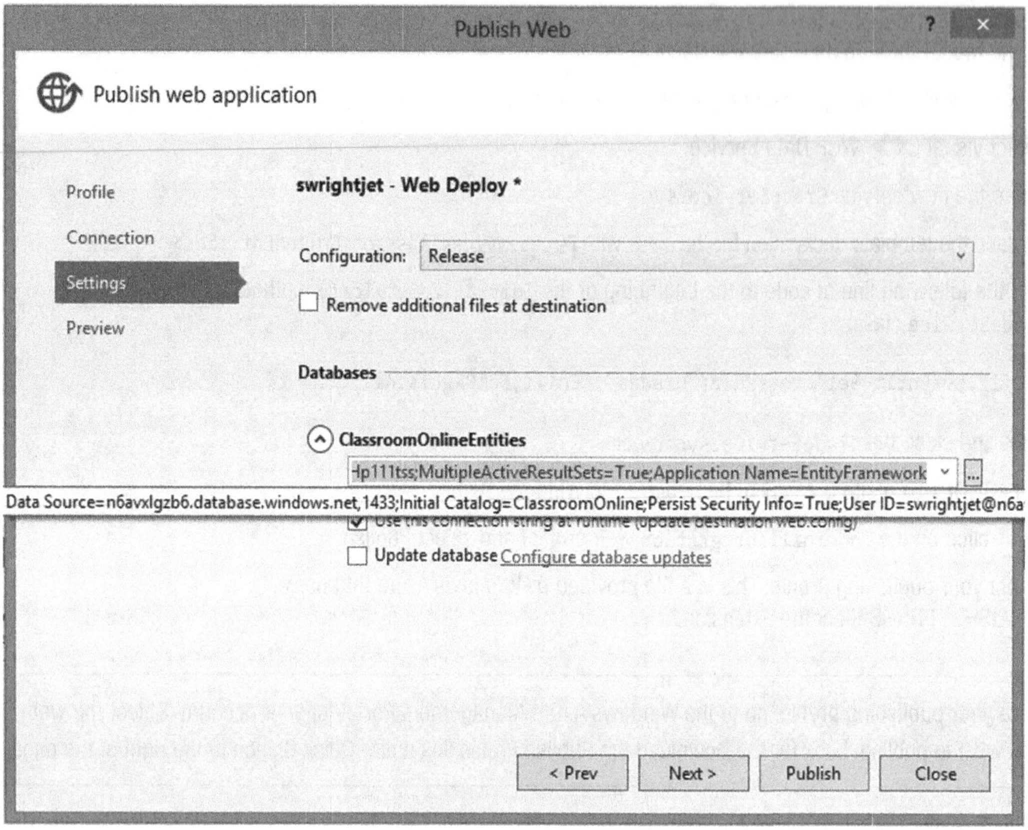

Figure 8-7. *Publish Web wizard (set connection string)*

34.　Click Next.

35.　Click Publish.

At this point, Visual Studio will compile and deploy your web site to Windows Azure.

To test the site and the OData service, navigate your browser to the Azure web site and add /GradeService.svc/Grades to the URL. You should see a feed page similar to Figure 8-8. This page is generated by Internet Explorer in response to the ATOM XML feed document that was returned by the grade service.

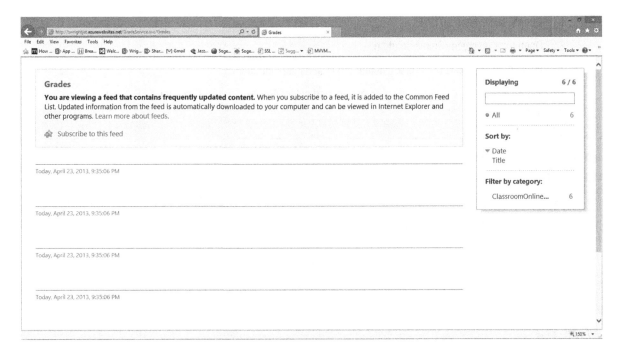

Figure 8-8. *GradeService feed page for Grades*

Creating App-Scoped External Content Types

An app-scoped external content type allows an app to access external data without requiring the intervention of a farm administrator. There are some restrictions to remember when creating this type of ECT, including the following:

- The only valid BCS connector for an app-scoped ECT is the OData connector. The external data to be accessed must be visible through an OData-compliant web service.

- An app-scoped ECT can only be used by the app that installs it. Other apps can contain their own ECTs that connect to the same data source, but they cannot use one deployed by a different app.

- Only one BDC model file can be included in a single app for SharePoint. If multiple business entities are required, they should be placed into a single BDC model.

EXERCISE 8-2

In the last exercise, we created an OData service that exposes a business entity called Grades. Now we need to update the Classroom Online app to access that service, via BCS, instead of a local SharePoint list.

In this exercise, we will create an app-scoped external content type in the Classroom Online app. We will also create an external list for the ECT. In addition, we will update the JavaScript in Classroom Online that reads and updates the gradebook.

We will start with the Classroom Online app in the state we left it at the end of the previous exercise. That exercise did not change anything in the app itself. It just created a new WCF data service and deployed it to the Windows Azure cloud. We will use that service in this exercise.

---

1. Open Visual Studio 2012.

2. Open the Classroom Online solution.

3. In the `ClassroomOnline` project, delete the `Grades` list definition.

4. Right-click on the `ClassroomOnline` project and select Add ➤ Content Types for an External Data Source.

■ **Note** We are not using the normal Add Item wizard as we have in the past. External content types are created directly from the Add context menu.

---

5. On the wizard dialog that appears, specify the URL for the OData service you created in Exercise 8-1.

6. Set the Data Source Name to `Grades` (see Figure 8-9).

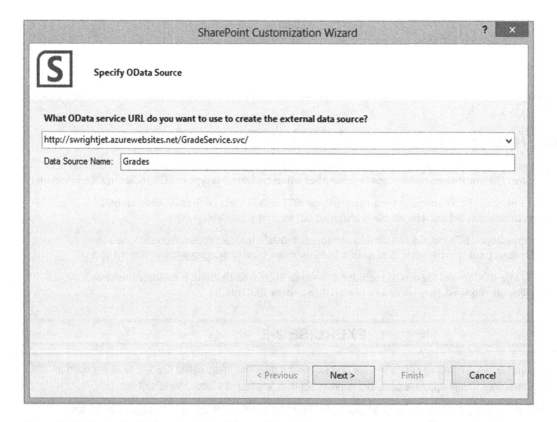

Figure 8-9. Create the Grades app-scoped external content type

7. Click Next.

At this point, the wizard will contact the web service to retrieve the details of its interface. On the next page of the wizard, you will specify which entities exposed by the OData service are to be included in the BDC model.

8. Check the box next to Grades (see Figure 8-10) and click Finish.

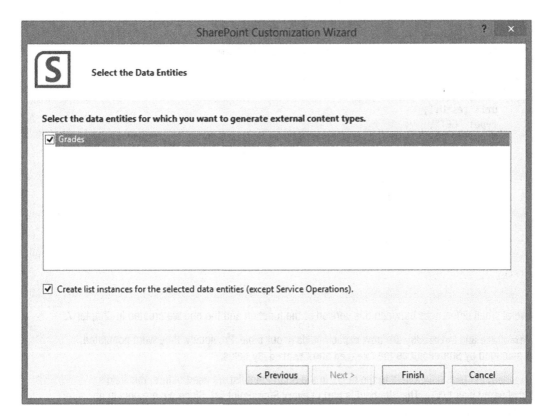

Figure 8-10. *Add business entities to the ECT*

The result is to add several new nodes to the ClassroomOnline project. The most important of these is the Grades.ect file that contains the BDC model for the service. An external list instance called Grades was also added to the app web.

Now we are going to update the model object for grades. This will involve slight changes to the grades.js file. You may be surprised by how little of the code actually changes. Remember, we have gone from accessing a normal SharePoint list called Grades in our app web to accessing an external list called Grades in our app web. We will continue to use the REST interface to access the list, as we did in Chapter 7. There are some code differences but, overall, the process will be very familiar.

9. Open the grades.js file in the Scripts/Models directory in the ClassroomOnline project.

10. Replace the getGrades() function with the following JavaScript:

```
self.getGrades = function (callback, studentName) {
    var restUrl = CO.Configs.SPAppWebUrl
        + "/_api/web/lists/getbytitle('Grades')/items"
```

```
            + "?$orderby=EnteredDate desc"
            + "&$select=GradeID,StudentName,AssignmentTitle,PointsPossible,"
            + "PercentOfCourseGrade,PointsAchieved,ClassroomURL"
            + '&$filter=ClassroomURL eq \'' + CO.Configs.SPHostUrl + '\'';

        // if a student is given, read only their grades
        if (studentName)
            restUrl += ' and StudentName eq \'' + studentName + '\'';

        // query the grade list for the grades to display/edit
        jQuery.ajax({
            url: restUrl,
            type: "GET",
            headers: {
                "accept": 'application/json;odata=verbose',
            },
            success: function (data) {
                callback(data.d.results);
            },
            error: function (a,b,c) {
                alert('Unable to load grades.');
            }
        });
    };
```

There are several small differences between this version of the function and the one we created in Chapter 7.

- `EnteredDate` and `EnteredBy` are now explicit fields in our table. Previously, they were populated and managed by SharePoint as the `Created` and `Created By` fields.

- `AssignmentTitle` is now a field in the table. In the SharePoint list we used before, this field's internal name was `Title`. The title field is part of every SharePoint list. Since we are now in an external table, we can call it whatever we like.

- `PercentOfCourseGrade` now contains a capitalized `Of` because it is the name of the field in the table. In the previous version, this field name was created by SharePoint by removing the spaces from the field's display name which was `Percent of Course Grade`.

Aside from these minor differences in the field names, the only difference in this function is the inclusion of a filter for the `ClassroomURL`. This is the URL of the host site in which our app is installed. This URL is used to filter the contents of the table in Azure.This ensures that each site on which our app is installed only sees its own data.

11. Replace the `addGrade()` function with the following JavaScript:

```
self.addGrade = function (studentName, assignmentTitle, pointsPossible,
percentofCourseGrade, pointsAchieved, callback) {
    var d = new Date();
    d = (d.getMonth() + 1).toString()
        + "/" + d.getDate().toString()
        + "/" + d.getFullYear().toString()
        + " " + d.getHours().toString()
        + ":" + d.getMinutes().toString()
        + ":" + d.getSeconds().toString();
```

```
    var body = {
        '__metadata': { 'type': 'SP.Data.GradesListItem' },
        'ClassroomURL': CO.Configs.SPHostUrl,
        'AssignmentTitle': assignmentTitle,
        'StudentName': studentName,
        'PointsPossible': pointsPossible,
        'PercentOfCourseGrade': percentofCourseGrade,
        'PointsAchieved': pointsAchieved,
        'EnteredBy': CO.Configs.currentUser.name,
        'EnteredDate': d
    };
    body = JSON.stringify(body);

    jQuery.ajax({
        url: CO.Configs.SPAppWebUrl + "/_api/web/lists/getbytitle('Grades')/items",
        type: "POST",
        data: body,
        headers: {
            "X-RequestDigest": $("#__REQUESTDIGEST").val(),
            "accept": "application/json;odata=verbose",
            "content-type": "application/json;odata=verbose",
            "content-length": body.length
        },
        success: function (data) {
            callback(data.d.__metadata.uri, '*');
        },
        error: function (err) {
            alert('Unable to add the grade.');
        }
    });
}
```

There are several differences in this function, including the following:

- `EnteredDate` and `EnteredBy` must be supplied for our table because SharePoint does not provide these fields for an external list. This could also have been handled with defaults in the database.

- `ClassroomURL` is added to the table using the host site's URL.

- `AssignmentTitle` is no longer called `Title`, as it was in the internal list.

- In the callback routine, we are passing different values.

  - `ID`—We are using the URI provided by REST as the ID for the item. This will allow us to retrieve the item more easily later.

  - `ETag`—We are passing the wildcard character for the `ETag` because `ETag` values are not generated for external list items. If needed, we would need to perform any optimistic locking checks manually.

12. Replace the `updateGrade()` function with the following JavaScript:

```javascript
self.updateGrade = function (studentName, assignmentTitle, pointsPossible,
percentofCourseGrade, pointsAchieved, id, etag, callback) {
    var d = new Date();
    d = (d.getMonth() + 1).toString()
            + "/" + d.getDate().toString()
            + "/" + d.getFullYear().toString()
            + " " + d.getHours().toString()
            + ":" + d.getMinutes().toString()
            + ":" + d.getSeconds().toString();

    var body = {
        '__metadata': { 'type': 'SP.Data.GradesListItem' },
        'ClassroomURL': CO.Configs.SPHostUrl,
        'AssignmentTitle': assignmentTitle,
        'StudentName': studentName,
        'PointsPossible': pointsPossible,
        'PercentOfCourseGrade': percentofCourseGrade,
        'PointsAchieved': pointsAchieved,
        'EnteredBy': CO.Configs.currentUser.name,
        'EnteredDate': d
    };
    body = JSON.stringify(body);

    jQuery.ajax({
        url: id,
        type: "POST",
        data: body,
        headers: {
            "X-Http-Method": "PATCH",
            "X-RequestDigest": $("#__REQUESTDIGEST").val(),
            "IF-MATCH" : etag,
            "accept": "application/json;odata=verbose",
            "content-type": "application/json;odata=verbose",
            "content-length": body.length
        },
        success: function (data,status,resp) {
            callback(id, '*');
        },
        error: function (err) {
            alert('Unable to update the grade.');
        }
    });
}
```

The changes in this function are almost the same as in the previous function. Notice that instead of creating the REST URL from scratch, we are just supplying the `id` that was provided when the data was loaded. Again, the `ETag` is hard-coded in the callback.

13. Replace the deleteGrade() function with the following JavaScript:

```
self.deleteGrade = function (id, etag, callback) {
    jQuery.ajax({
        url: id,
        type: "POST",
        headers: {
            "X-Http-Method": "DELETE",
            "X-RequestDigest" : $("#__REQUESTDIGEST").val(),
            "IF-MATCH" : etag
        },
        success: function () {
            callback();
        },
        error: function (err) {
            alert('Unable to delete the grade.');
        }
    });
}
```

The only alteration needed by this function is to replace the REST URL with the URI now used for the id.

14. Save and close the grade.js file.

15. Open the gradebook.js file in the Scripts/ViewModels folder.

16. Replace the onLoadComplete() function with the following JavaScript:

```
self.onLoadComplete = function (gradeList) {
    for (var i = 0; i < gradeList.length; i++)
        self.gradebookEntries.push(
            new gradebookEntry(gradeList[i].StudentName,
gradeList[i].AssignmentTitle,
gradeList[i].PointsPossible,
                               gradeList[i].PercentOfCourseGrade,
gradeList[i].PointsAchieved,
                               gradeList[i].__metadata.uri,
                               '*'));
}
```

17. Save and close the gradebook.js file.

18. Press F5 to run the app.

This completes the changes that allow the app to use the SQL Azure table as its data store. From the user's perspective the app works exactly as it did before. However, if you look at the contents of the table, you will see that the entries added or updated on the grade book page are now reflected in SQL Azure, outside of SharePoint.

Summary

In this chapter, we have explored how Business Connectivity Services can be used within apps for SharePoint to provide access to line-of-business data that resides external to the local SharePoint farm. SharePoint 2013 includes the new OData Connector Framework for BCS, allowing an OData service to be used as a BCS data source. There is also new support for notifications and remote event receivers in SP 2013. The ability to include app-scoped external content types within a SharePoint app allows designers to use the features of BCS without requiring the involvement of farm or tenant administrators.

In Chapter 9, we will move away from the data tier of our app and begin looking at the tools we have for creating rich application logic. We will look at how we can use remote event receivers to handle events generated by SharePoint. We will also look at using the Azure workflow engine to automate the logic of our app.

■ ■ ■

CHAPTER 9

App Logic Components

Now that we understand how to store, access, and manage back-end data through our SharePoint apps, let's move up a level in our solution. Let's now look at how to build the middle tier of our application. This is the level that sits between our data and the user interface and provides the business logic for our app. In this chapter, we will go over the following points:

- How to organize the app logic to allow maximum flexibility in our design.

- What the events are that will be generated by SharePoint and how our app can respond to them.

- How to code remote event receivers into our apps to provide logic that runs in the background on the server.

- The components that make up the SharePoint 2013 workflow infrastructure and how they interact.

- How to create workflow definitions that can be deployed with and act as a part of an app for SharePoint.

Middle-Tier Concepts

Take a moment to consider all of the components that go into an application. Not just a SharePoint app, but any software application. Conceptually, an application can be divided into three layers that provide three distinct sets of services. The top layer is the user interface (UI). This is the layer that interacts directly with the user. The bottom layer is the data that the application creates or uses to perform its function. The logic for reading and writing this data is often considered part of this layer as well and is often referred to as a *data access layer*. The CSOM and REST APIs for SharePoint 2013 act as a data access layer for SharePoint. Between the UI and data layers is the middle tier (see Figure 9-1).

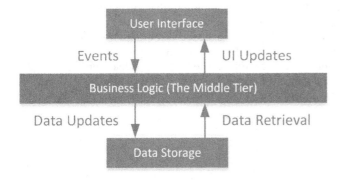

Figure 9-1. *The conceptual tiers of an application*

The purpose of the middle tier is to control the interactions between the other two tiers and to implement the business logic of the application. The middle tier often contains the most critical and complex logic in the application. This is where the real work gets done. This chapter is all about how we can build a decoupled, scalable middle tier for apps for SharePoint.

ABOUT DESIGN PATTERNS

In this discussion, we are treating the app as having three layers: UI, middle tier, and data layer. This is not to say that this is how we will **build our app**. The three tiers in this section are only a *conceptual model* for categorizing the components that make up the app.

There is extensive literature on code design patterns and application architectures. These include patterns like the one we are using in our examples, the *Model-View-ViewModel (MVVM)*, and other common patterns like the *Model-View-Controller (MVC)*. Many of these patterns may be more appropriate for building apps for SharePoint than implementing design components in three physical tiers.

The middle tier of any application is primarily driven by events. These events can be anything from mouse clicks in the UI to data updates that occur in the middle of the night. Any of these events may require that custom logic in the app be triggered. As we have seen in previous chapters, implementing UI-driven events that have an immediate effect on data is relatively straightforward using tools like JQuery and Knockout. Handling events that occur outside of the control of the user interface requires a different set of tools.

SharePoint 2013 apps can leverage two useful techniques for handling this kind of event: remote event receivers (RER) and workflows. In this chapter, we will learn about using RERs and workflows to implement middle-tier logic in our apps.

Remote Event Receivers

Event receivers are used to handle events that occur within the SharePoint environment. These events include modifying lists, list items, web sites, or security settings. In traditional SharePoint development using full-trust solutions, these events are handled by coding an event receiver class, compiling it into a .NET assembly, installing the assembly on the SharePoint farm, and then registering the event receiver with SharePoint for the object whose events are to be received. Obviously, this approach is not appropriate for an app using the Cloud App Model because it requires executable code to run within SharePoint.

SharePoint 2013 has introduced the concept of a remote event receiver (RER). An RER is an event receiver that runs outside of the SharePoint farm. We saw an example of an RER in Chapter 3 when we looked at handing the installation, upgrade, and uninstallation events for an app. There are many other events that can be handled in the same way. A listing of these events is included in the next section, "Remote Event Types."

Instead of calling a .NET class in an assembly, a remote event is passed to the receiver using a web service call, as shown in Figure 9-2. This call contains all of the security and context information necessary to allow the web service to make CSOM or REST calls back into SharePoint. Using these APIs, the developer can create almost any logic in a remote receiver that could be created using a local event receiver. Server-to-server security using OAuth allows this interaction to happen securely even when the events occur outside of the context of any particular user's session.

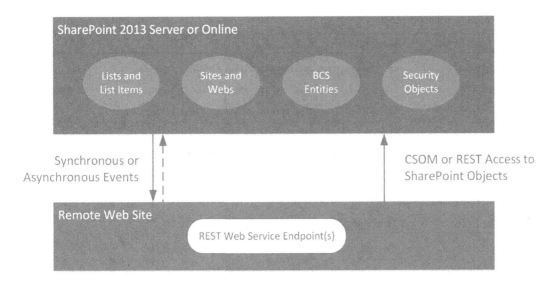

Figure 9-2. *Remote event receiver (RER)*

There are two categories of remote event types. The first type is synchronous, or two-way, events. Two-way events occur before the action has occurred in SharePoint. The web service call behind a two-way event is synchronous in that SharePoint will wait for the web service to complete before completing the server-side event. This allows the event receiver to cancel the event or throw an error if needed. Two-way event receivers can impact the apparent performance of SharePoint if they perform long-running tasks. Therefore, these event types should be used only when there is a need to pass status information back to SharePoint that may include errors or canceling the event. You can identify two-way events because they always include "ing," as in `ItemAdding` or `ItemCheckingIn`.

The other type of remote event is an asynchronous, or one-way, event. A one-way event results in a request being sent to the remote event receiver, but no status or error information can be returned to SharePoint. These events occur after the event has taken place in more of a "fire-and-forget" fashion. Because they occur after the event and no status information will be returned, SharePoint does not have to wait for the web service to complete before continuing with other processing. One-way events do not provide the control that two-way events allow, but they do not tend to impact performance much, if at all. As a result, one-way events should be used unless there is a need for the control associated with a two-way event. One-way events always include "ed" in the name, as in `ItemAdded` or `ItemCheckedIn`.

Most SharePoint events come in both one- and two-way varieties. In a few cases, one or the other option may not be available. These cases occur because an event receiver would not make sense in that case. For example, there is an `AppInstalled` (after) event, but no `AppInstalling` (before) event. This makes sense when you consider that it would be quite difficult to call a web service in the remote web site associated with an app that has not yet been installed.

Remote Event Types

In this section, we will list and briefly describe each of the remote events that can be handled by a remote event receiver in an app for SharePoint.

Table 9-1 lists the app-related events that we examined in Chapter 3. Note that all of these events have only a one-way or two-way version. This is because app logic cannot be executed before it is installed, nor after it has been uninstalled.

Table 9-1. *Remote App Management Events*

Before Event	After Event	Description
	AppInstalled	Occurs when an app is installed on a SharePoint site.
	AppUpgraded	Occurs when an installed app is upgraded from one version to another.
AppUninstalling		Occurs before an app is removed from a SharePoint site.

Table 9-2 lists the events that are triggered when SharePoint site collections or sub sites (a.k.a. webs) are created, updated, or destroyed.

Table 9-2. *Remote Site Management Events*

Before Event	After Event	Description
SiteDeleting	SiteDeleted	Occurs when a SharePoint site collection is deleted.
WebAdding	WebProvisioned	Occurs when a SharePoint site is created.
WebMoving	WebMoved	Occurs when a SharePoint site is moved from one location to another.
WebDeleting	WebDeleted	Occurs when a SharePoint site is deleted.

Table 9-3 lists the events that are triggered when lists within a site are added, updated, or removed.

Table 9-3. *Remote List Events*

Before Event	After Event	Description
ListAdding	ListAdded	Occurs when a new list is added to a site.
ListDeleting	ListDeleted	Occurs when a list is deleted from a site.
FieldAdding	FieldAdded	Occurs when a new field, or attribute, is added to a list.
FieldUpdating	FieldUpdated	Occurs when a field definition is modified.
FieldDeleting	FieldDeleted	Occurs when a field is deleted from a list.

Table 9-4 lists the events that are triggered when list items or their associated files are added, updated, or deleted.

Table 9-4. *Remote List Item Events*

Before Event	After Event	Description
ItemAdding	ItemAdded	Occurs when a new list item is created.
ItemUpdating	ItemUpdated	Occurs when a list item is modified.
ItemDeleting	ItemDeleted	Occurs when a list item is deleted.
ItemCheckingOut	ItemCheckedOut	Occurs when a list item is checked out for editing.
ItemUncheckingOut	ItemUncheckedOut	Occurs when a list item that has previously been checked out is released without new changes being checked in.

(continued)

Table 9-4. (*continued*)

Before Event	After Event	Description
ItemCheckingIn	ItemCheckedIn	Occurs when changes to a list item are checked in.
ItemVersionDeleting	ItemVersionDeleted	Occurs when a previous version of a list item is purged from the item's version history.
ItemAttachmentAdding	ItemAttachmentAdded	Occurs when a new file is attached to a list item.
ItemAttachmentDeleting	ItemAttachmentDeleted	Occurs when a file attached to a list item is removed.
	ItemFileConverted	Occurs after a file is converted from one format to another by SharePoint.
ItemFileMoving	ItemFileMoving	Occurs when a file is moved from one location to another.

Table 9-5 lists the events that are triggered when a line-of-business application reports an event concerning a business entity registered in BCS. Note that these events are all one-way events and only occur after the entity has been altered. This is because the event is occurring outside of SharePoint and is only reported to SharePoint after the fact.

Table 9-5. *Remote BCS Events*

Before Event	After Event	Description
	EntityInstanceAdded	Occurs after a line-of-business application reports the creation of a new business entity.
	EntityInstanceUpdated	Occurs after a line-of-business application reports the update of a business entity.
	EntityInstanceDeleted	Occurs after a line-of-business application reports the deletion of a business entity.

Table 9-6 lists the events that are triggered when any of the objects that control permissions within SharePoint are modified.

Table 9-6. *Remote Security Object Events*

Before Event	After Event	Description
GroupAdding	GroupAdded	Occurs when a new SharePoint group is added.
GroupUpdating	GroupUpdated	Occurs when a SharePoint group is modified.
GroupDeleting	GroupDeleted	Occurs when a SharePoint group is deleted.
GroupUserAdding	GroupUserAdded	Occurs when a user is added to a SharePoint group.
GroupUserDeleting	GroupUserDeleted	Occurs when a user is removed from a SharePoint group.
RoleDefinitionAdding	RoleDefinitionAdded	Occurs when a new role definition (a.k.a. permission level) is created in a site collection.

(*continued*)

Table 9-6. *(continued)*

Before Event	After Event	Description
RoleDefinitionUpdating	RoleDefinitionUpdated	Occurs when a role definition (a.k.a. permission level) is modified.
RoleDefinitionDeleting	RoleDefinitionDeleted	Occurs when a role definition (a.k.a. permission level) is removed from a site collection.
RoleAssignmentAdding	RoleAssignmentAdded	Occurs when a new role assignment is created.
RoleAssignmentDeleting	RoleAssignmentDeleted	Occurs when a role assignment is removed.
InheritanceBreaking	InheritanceBroken	Occurs when the inheritance of permissions between an item and its container is broken.
InheritanceResetting	InheritanceReset	Occurs when the inheritance of permissions between an item and its container is reestablished and any custom permissions for the item are discarded.

Programming Interfaces

Creating a remote event receiver is not very different from creating a traditional event receiver in SharePoint. The difference is that instead of being compiled into an assembly as a .NET class, the RER is placed into an ASP.NET application as a WCF web service.

■ **Note** A remote event receiver does not have to be implemented using ASP.NET. It can be implemented in any OData-compatible web service. Visual Studio 2012 contains wizards and templates for creating RERs in ASP.NET, so that will be the technology used in our exercises.

Adding a remote event receiver to an existing app is a simple process.

1. Add remote event receiver item to the app project in the same way you would add any other type of component.

2. You will select whether to create a receiver to handle list events or list item events. Other event types are not supported by the wizard and must be coded by hand.

3. Depending on your selections, you will see a list of events that can be handled. Check each event you are interested in.

4. If your app does not already include a remote web site, one will be added in auto-hosted mode.

5. A new WCF service is created in the app's remote web site that implements the IRemoteEventService interface.

IRemoteEventService Interface

The `IRemoteEventService` interface defines the methods that SharePoint will call when an event occurs (see Table 9-7).

Table 9-7. `IRemoteEventService` Interface Methods

Method Name	Inputs	Outputs	Description
ProcessEvent	SPRemoteEventProperties	SPRemoteEventResult	Processes two-way (-ing) events before the event is completed.
ProcessOneWayEvent	SPRemoteEventProperties	None	Processes one-way (-ed) events after the event is completed.

The code placed into these methods is run once for each event that occurs. Each type of event, one or two-way, is routed only to the corresponding method.

Both of these methods take an `SPReportEventProperties` object as their input parameter. This object encapsulates all of the details of the event. All events provide the following basic properties:

- **EventType** —This indicates what type of event has occurred. See the list of event types in the previous section, "Remote Event Types."

- **ContextToken**—This is the token needed to establish a server-to-server OAuth connection back to SharePoint.

- **CorrelationID**—This ID allows all of the actions triggered by one event to be logged together in SharePoint. It should be included in any error messages provided to the user. This will allow the farm administrator to find the relevant parts of the SharePoint server logs.

The remaining properties in this object provide properties that are specific to the type of event that occurred.

- **AppEventProperties**—App install, upgrade, and uninstall events

- **ItemEventProperties**—List item–related events

- **ListEventProperties**—List management events

- **EntityInstanceEventProperties**—BCS business entity events

- **SecurityEventProperties**—Permissions-related events

- **WebEventProperties**—Site and site collection events

SPRemoteEventResult Object

For two-way events that use the `ProcessEvent()` method, an `SPRemoteEventResult` object is returned by the web service to provide status and error information to SharePoint. This object contains only a few fields.

- **Status**—Indicates the result of the web service call.

  - Continue—Informs SharePoint that it should continue processing any other event handlers that may exist for this event.

  - CancelNoError—Informs SharePoint that it should stop processing any further event handlers.

  - CancelWithError—Informs SharePoint that an error has occurred and the processing should stop.

- **ErrorMessage**—Contains any error message string to be returned to SharePoint.

- **ChangedItemProperties**—Used to communicate property changes for the item associated with the event.

Debugging Event Receivers

Debugging remote event receivers, especially in the cloud, can be very challenging. Think about the messages that are being sent and received when a remote event receiver is called. The SharePoint server sends a message to the remote web site for the app. The remote web site may or may not exchange client requests and responses with SharePoint. Finally, in the case of two-way events, a response is generated to the original event message.

The problem is that at no point does this process involve a client browser or the developer's workstation. If the remote web site is auto-hosted, instead of provider-hosted, the developer will not even know the URL of the remote web site in advance. There is no server to attach a debugger to or messages to be intercepted. The interaction is going on completely outside of the developer's view.

If the app is running on-premise instead of in the cloud, these problems are lessened but not removed. Attaching the Visual Studio debugger to the remote web site will allow debugging of the event receiver code in the ASP.NET web site. However, this can cause unexpected behaviors when SharePoint is waiting for a response from a web service that is stopped in the debugger.

In order to properly support remote event debugging, Visual Studio 2012 has added support for debugging this type of app using the Azure Service Bus. The service bus is used to route remote events from SharePoint to the corresponding event receiver. By tapping into this message flow, Visual Studio can attach the debugger remotely. We will not walk through the entire process, but here is a summary.

1. The developer must register for a Windows Azure account.

2. Within Azure, the service bus uses namespaces to organize traffic. A new namespace should be created for debugging the app.

3. Creating the namespace creates a connection string that looks like this:
   `Endpoint=sb://sp2013apps.servicebus.windows.net/;SharedSecretIssuer=owner;SharedSecretValue=bX+eW/lypy+jppYRctkJJyVpS9eTpuEetRkrR2EpSfc=`

4. Open the property pages for the SharePoint app. On the SharePoint tab, enable remote event debugging and supply the service bus connection string.

With this configuration completed, you can now debug remote events. One important thing to remember is that using the Azure Service Bus in this way is not free. The components used for debugging are not part of the normal auto-hosting support for apps. You should research the costs for using the service bus before doing any heavy debugging using it. Microsoft has various programs and discounts, especially for developers.

EXERCISE 9-1

In this exercise, we will create a remote event receiver that processes events generated by our Classroom Online app. A common use of event handlers like these is to record event information for later auditing. In previous chapters, we implemented a custom list for storing student grades. Now we will create an audit trail for this list. Each time a grade is entered, updated, or deleted, an entry will be added into another list to keep a record of each change.

First we will create a new list (GradeHistory) to contain the audit trail. Then we will add a remote event receiver to the Grades list. Finally, we will add code to record each event in the Grades list as a new item in the GradeHistory list.

We will add these items to the Classroom Online app as it existed at the end of Chapter 7. Note that we are not using the changes we introduced to Classroom Online in Chapter 8. The Chapter 7 Classroom Online source files can be downloaded from the Source Code/Download area of the Apress web site (www.apress.com).

1. Open Visual Studio 2012.

2. Open the Classroom Online solution as it was at the end of Chapter 7.

3. Add a new default custom list to the ClassroomOnline project named GradeHistory.

4. In the list designer, change the name of the Title field to EventType.

5. Add an EnteredDate field with a type of Date and Time.

6. Add an EnteredBy field with a type of Single Line of Text.

7. Add an AuditData field with a type of Single Line of Text.

The list designer should now contain the list definition shown in Figure 9-3.

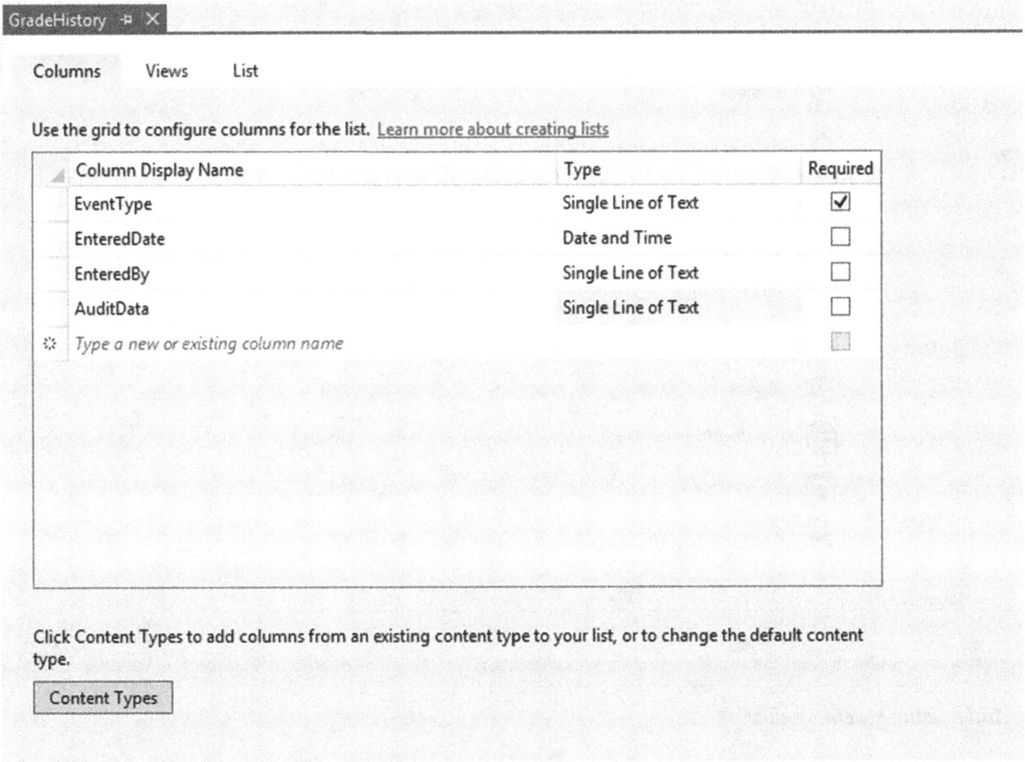

Figure 9-3. GradeHistory *list designer*

8. Save and close the GradeHistory list.

To make this list easy to get to, we will add a link to it on the gradebook page.

9.   Open the Gradebook.aspx page from the Pages folder.

10. Find the PlaceHolderMain content control and add the following HTML markup as the first item in the control:

```
<p><a href="../Lists/GradeHistory">View Gradebook History List...</a></p>
```

11. Right-click the ClassroomOnline project and select Add ➤ New Item.

12. From the list, select the C# Remote Event Receiver template (see Figure 9-4).

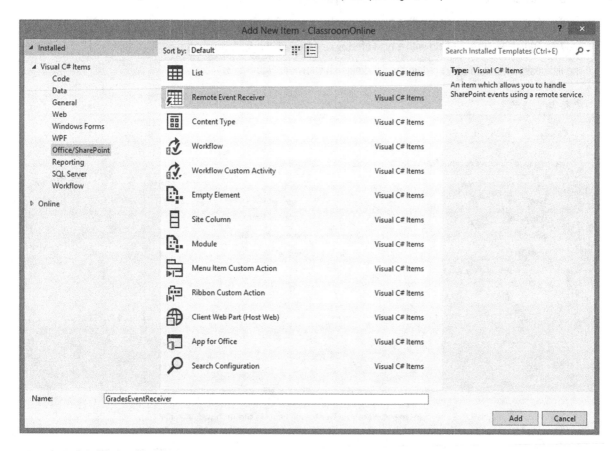

Figure 9-4. *Add a remote event receiver*

13. Set the name to GradesEventReceiver.

14. Click Add.

15. On the following screen, select List Item Events for the type of event receiver to create.

16. Select the Grades list as the event source.

17. Select all of the events listed (see Figure 9-5).

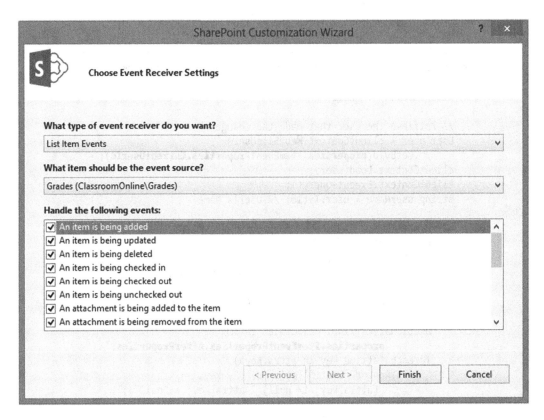

Figure 9-5. *Configure the remote event receiver*

18. Click Finish.

Since our app already had a remote web site, the new WCF service was added to it. A class was created that implements the IRemoteEventService interface. We will replace the default code in the template with code that will record events as they occur.

19. Replace the methods inside the class with the following C# code.

```
public SPRemoteEventResult ProcessEvent(SPRemoteEventProperties properties)
{
    LogAuditRecord(properties);
    return new SPRemoteEventResult();
}

public void ProcessOneWayEvent(SPRemoteEventProperties properties)
{
    LogAuditRecord(properties);
}
```

```
private void LogAuditRecord(SPRemoteEventProperties properties)
{
    using (ClientContext clientContext =
        TokenHelper.CreateRemoteEventReceiverClientContext(properties))
    {
        if (clientContext != null)
        {
            // retrieve the user that made the change
            User user = clientContext.Web.SiteUsers
                .GetById(properties.ItemEventProperties.CurrentUserId);
            clientContext.Load(user);
            clientContext.ExecuteQuery();
            string userName = user.Title; // User's Name

            // format ID and attributes for auditing
            StringBuilder sb =
                new StringBuilder("'ListItemID':'"
                + properties.ItemEventProperties.ListItemId.ToString()
                + "',");
            if (properties.ItemEventProperties.AfterProperties != null)
            {
                Dictionary<string, object> attrs =
                        properties.ItemEventProperties.AfterProperties;
                foreach (string key in attrs.Keys)
                    sb.AppendFormat("'{0}':'{1}',", key,
                        (attrs[key] != null) ? attrs[key] : "null");
            }
            sb.Remove(sb.Length - 1, 1);
            string auditData = "{" + sb.ToString() + "}";

            // create a new entry in the audit trail
            List gradeHistory =
                clientContext.Web.Lists.GetByTitle("GradeHistory");
            ListItemCreationInformation ici =
                new ListItemCreationInformation();
            ListItem newItem = gradeHistory.AddItem(ici);
            newItem["Title"] = properties.EventType.ToString();
            newItem["EnteredDate"] = DateTime.Now;
            newItem["EnteredBy"] = userName;
            newItem["AuditData"] = auditData;
            newItem.Update();

            clientContext.ExecuteQuery();
        }
    }
}
```

First, we need to remember that this is server-side code running within our remote web site. This code is invoked when SharePoint publishes an event for an item in the Grades list. It is not running on the SharePoint server.

```
public SPRemoteEventResult ProcessEvent
                              (SPRemoteEventProperties properties)
{
    LogAuditRecord(properties);
    return new SPRemoteEventResult();
}
```

Both event processing methods are going to call a single routine passing in their event properties. The return statement in ProcessEvent()returns a default result object. This object returns a status of continue with no changes and no errors.

```
using (ClientContext clientContext =
            TokenHelper.CreateRemoteEventReceiverClientContext(properties))
```

The TokenHelper handles all of the messaging and token parsing necessary to set up a server-to-server OAuth connection between the remote web site and the SharePoint farm. This call creates a client context object that will allow us to make CSOM calls back into the SharePoint site that triggered this event receiver.

```
User user = clientContext.Web.SiteUsers
            .GetById(properties.ItemEventProperties.CurrentUserId);
```

Because our event receiver is designed to receive list item events, we will find our event-specific properties in the ItemEventProperties field in the event properties object. In the previous code, we are using the CurrentUserId value to lookup the current user's information, such as their login, e-mail address, and name.

```
Dictionary<string, object> attrs =
            properties.ItemEventProperties.AfterProperties;
```

The event properties also include the properties of the list item before and after the event. These properties are stored in a dictionary object that is indexed by the name of the property.

If we simply run the app now, the event receiver will probably fail to work properly. When you debug an auto-hosted app in Visual Studio, the remote web site runs on the developer's workstation using a URL such as http://localhost:23414. Unless you are developing on the same SharePoint server you are deploying to, this will not work. In order to give SharePoint the ability to connect to the auto-hosted site, we need to deploy our app through the app catalog.

20. Right-click on the ClassroomOnline project and select Publish....

21. In the publishing wizard, click Finish.

22. In a web browser, navigate to your App Catalog site.

23. Upload the .app file created by Visual Studio.

24. Navigate to your test site.

25. Click on Site Contents.

26. Click on Add an app.

27. Click on the Classroom Online tile.

28. Click Trust It to begin the installation.

■ **Tip** It sometimes takes a few minutes for Azure to get the remote web site configured properly to receive event notifications. If you attempt to continue with the exercise immediately, you may notice that some events do not get logged.

29. After the installation is complete, use the gradebook page to add, update, and delete some grades.

30. When finished, click on the View Grade History List… link to see the events that have been recorded (see Figure 9-6).

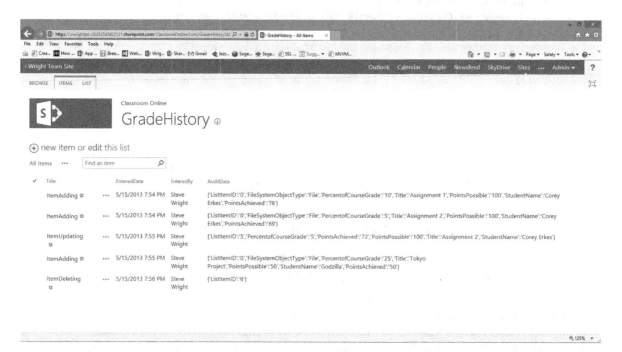

Figure 9-6. *Grade history list*

The app is now recording each event that is reported to it. In the next section, we will look at ways to perform similar processes when they have multiple steps or require human interaction.

Workflows in Apps for SharePoint

Remote event receivers, and event receivers in general, are a good way to handle events that occur in isolation from other business processes. An event receiver receives control when needed, performs its function, and then terminates. What if we need to coordinate a chain of events to orchestrate a complete business process?

One solution would be to create a group of related event receivers that are triggered at different points in the business process. These receivers could check the state of the related SharePoint objects to determine where in the process we are and which step should come next. This solution has several limitations. How does one step in the process communicate with the next without adding unneeded, and perhaps sensitive, information to the SharePoint items being processed? How do we handle steps that need to be repeated or processed in a loop? How do we cancel, restart, and keep track of these processes as they are running?

Obviously, using individual event receivers for implementing complex business processes is problematic at best. What is needed is a means of specifying the entire flow of a business process in one place. This information could be compiled into a process definition that would specify the steps of the process, any data that needs to be passed between the steps, and any other communication that needs to take place outside of the process. A piece of software designed to read this process definition can then ensure that each step in the process occurs in the correct order. This software is called the *workflow engine* in Windows Workflow Foundation (WF).

SharePoint 2013 Workflows

Microsoft has created the Windows Workflow Foundation (abbreviated WF, *not* WWF, for copyright reasons) to provide a solution to this problem. WF is a set of components that are part of the .NET framework starting in version 3.0. In SharePoint 2007, Microsoft introduced features that allowed SharePoint Server to act as a host for running the WF3 workflow engine. SharePoint 2010 greatly improved this support and also upgraded the workflow host to version 3.5 of the .NET Framework. In Windows Workflow Foundation 4 and SharePoint 2013, the workflow engine has been redesigned with the cloud in mind.

A workflow definition is an XML document that defines a business process. This process is broken down into steps called *activities*. An activity defines some action the workflow should take, such as sending an e-mail or updating a SharePoint list item. The activities in a workflow can be executed sequentially, repeatedly in loops, or use a more fluid structure called a state-machine or stages.

The workflow definition is installed in SharePoint by creating an *association*. An association connects a workflow with a SharePoint list or web site. A workflow associated with a web site responds to events that affect the web site, such as lists being added or removed. A list workflow responds to events that affect the items in a list.

The changes to the workflow engine in SharePoint 2013 are extensive and fundamental. Developers familiar with using workflows in previous versions should look at SharePoint 2013 as an entirely new workflow engine. While many of the concepts have been retained, the architecture and behavior are very different.

Windows Workflow Foundation 4

SharePoint 2013 workflows are built using Windows Workflow Foundation version 4. This version of WF introduces a new engine and a new style of workflow communication.

In .NET 3.0 and 3.5, workflows were implemented using .NET assemblies. A workflow definition was compiled into a .NET assembly that called other assemblies containing workflow activities. This created an efficient but tightly-coupled calling structure.

In contrast, WF4 uses a loosely coupled calling structure based on the Windows Communication Foundation (WCF). WCF is used to perform remote web service calls instead of directly calling activities classes. The messaging patterns available in WCF and SharePoint allow for the integration of services without the need to create tightly bound, compiled executables.

WF4 also contains improvements in how workflows are defined. There is a new stage concept that allows a workflow to be broken down into discrete pieces or stages. A *stage* has a single entry point and a single exit point. No transitions are allowed outside of the stage except through these points. The entire workflow consists of a starting point, followed by one or more stages. Stages can be selected for execution using conditions within the workflow, but no activities can occur outside of a stage. Stages serve the same purpose as state-machine workflows did in previous versions. However, since stages are just shapes in a normal workflow definition, the distinction between sequential and state-machine workflows is no longer relevant.

Workflow Hosting and Interoperability

In SharePoint 2007 and 2010, SharePoint acted as the host process for the Windows Workflow engine. Workflow assemblies were loaded and run within the SharePoint process allowing for direct communication between them and SharePoint. SharePoint, .NET and custom-coded activity assemblies also ran in this process. This arrangement can cause problems in multiple ways. First, a poorly written activity class can degrade performance or even cause the host process to crash. This leads to stability problems in SharePoint farms that rely heavily on workflows. Also, the fact that even well-behaved workflows and activities consume resources on the SharePoint server farm means that the performance and scalability of the farm will be degraded to some extent.

SharePoint 2013 was designed to operate in a cloud environment where such stability issues and scalability limitations cannot be allowed. As a result, Microsoft has redesigned the architecture supporting workflows in SharePoint. This architecture will be described in more detail shortly. The most important change is that workflows no longer execute within any SharePoint process. As we have seen with apps for SharePoint, workflows are now designed to execute entirely outside the SharePoint environment. Instead, it communicates with an external service that hosts workflows on SharePoint's behalf.

Because of the significant changes in the workflow engine in SharePoint 2013, and the large numbers of existing workflows in previous versions, Microsoft has chosen to continue supporting SharePoint 2010-style workflows in the 2013 release of SharePoint. In fact, SharePoint 2013 Server contains two entirely separate workflow engines. SharePoint 2010 workflows can still be hosted within SharePoint using the same architecture and components that existed in SharePoint 2010 Server. SharePoint 2013 workflows run under the new workflow system. There are new workflow activities that allow control to be passed between 2010 and 2013 workflows, allowing them to be integrated. This feature allows organizations to upgrade to SharePoint 2013 Server without having to convert all of their existing workflows to the new design first.

Workflow Authoring

As in previous versions of SharePoint, there are two primary tools used for authoring workflow definitions: SharePoint Designer and Visual Studio. The difference is that there is now much more parity between these tools.

SharePoint Designer 2013 has been enhanced to support all of the new features of WF4 workflows. It also contains an editor for SharePoint 2010 workflows as well. This means that it is not necessary to load both versions of SharePoint Designer in order to author both types of workflows. SharePoint Designer integrates with the Visio client application in Microsoft Office. A business user can create a workflow diagram in Visio and provide it to the workflow author. That diagram can be imported into SharePoint Designer as a starting point for authoring the final workflow. Unlike in previous versions, SharePoint Designer 2013 has the ability to create advanced workflows that include stages, steps, and looping constructs.

Visual Studio 2012 has also been upgraded to support 2013-style workflows. One of the most striking differences for experienced Visual Studio workflow developers is the lack of coding. Workflows in WF4 do not support the inclusion of embedded .NET code. All logic is represented declaratively in the workflow XML definition. In cases where custom-coded logic is absolutely required, there are a few options. If your workflows will be running within your own servers, you can code custom activities to include in your workflows. For cloud-based solutions, the best option is to create custom web services that can be called from within your workflows.

Developing Workflow Components

In addition to creating custom activities, SharePoint 2013 creates other development opportunities around workflows.

Because WF4 workflows are based on the WCF framework, there is built-in support for many standard protocols. These include HTTP, SOAP, REST, and OData. These technologies enable messages to be passed both into and out of workflows. You can submit event notifications into a running workflow or receive information from it via web service calls.

Workflows often present user interface forms to collect information from users. These forms fall into three categories.

- *Association forms* are displayed when a user uses the SharePoint web interface to link a workflow definition to a web or list in SharePoint.

- An *initiation form* is displayed when a user manually starts a workflow through the web interface. Both association and initiation forms collect parameters that are passed into the workflow when it begins executing.

- The third type of form is a *task form*. During the execution of a workflow, a common action is to assign a task to a user. This could be a request for approval or feedback on a list item, for example. In some cases, it is necessary to collect information from the user during their completion of a task. A task form collects that information and makes it available to the workflow.

Like SharePoint 2010, SharePoint 2013 still uses each of these types of forms, but the implementation of them has changed dramatically. In SharePoint 2010, workflow forms were based on InfoPath forms. InfoPath is a Microsoft Office application that is used to create a form definition. When the user fills out the form, the information is stored in XML format. InfoPath forms can be rendered as web pages using InfoPath Forms Services in SharePoint Server. There are limitations to these forms when used as web pages. Authoring InfoPath forms can be difficult and, since they are not based on a web standard like HTML, their use is not consistent with the other design decisions made with regard to the new workflow architecture.

In SharePoint 2013, Microsoft has shifted its strategy for these forms. Instead of using InfoPath, workflows will now use web pages for forms. Typically, a workflow form will be implemented using an ASP.NET web form. The form can take inputs from the user and use one of the SharePoint client APIs (see Chapters 5 and 7) to update the information in the workflow or in SharePoint.

The most important new feature in SharePoint 2013 workflows (for the purposes of this book anyway) is the ability to embed workflows within apps for SharePoint using the Cloud App Model. As we will see later in this chapter, we can create workflows in Visual Studio that can interact with the other elements of our app. This will allow us to model business processes as workflows that will automate the behavior of our apps.

Architecture

The new workflow engine architecture of SharePoint 2013 Server (or SharePoint Online) is shown in Figure 9-7. We will start at the left of the diagram and move to the right.

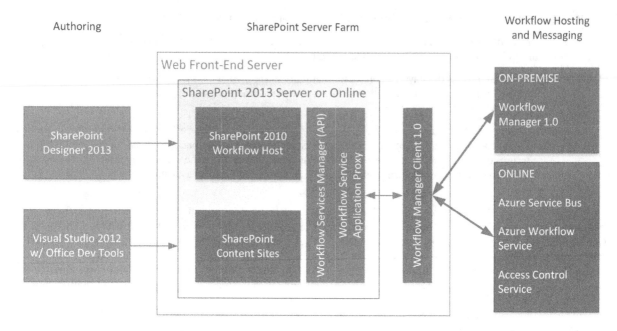

Figure 9-7. SharePoint 2013 workflow engine

The first layer of components is the authoring tools. SharePoint Designer 2013 is the tool-of-choice for business and power users. This is a free client application that can be downloaded from Microsoft's web site at http://www.microsoft.com/en-us/download/details.aspx?id=35491. Designer contains authoring tools for both SharePoint 2010 and 2013 workflows. Microsoft Office Visio can be used to visually diagram workflows for use in SharePoint Designer.

The other authoring tool is Visual Studio 2012. This is the latest edition of Microsoft's main integrated development environment (IDE) for professional developers. Visual Studio contains all of the tools needed to create and package workflows for SharePoint apps. This is the tool we will use for creating workflows.

The center of Figure 9-7 represents the components that exist within the SharePoint server farm. Within the SharePoint product itself are the components for managing workflow definitions and associations.

- **SharePoint Content Sites**—These are the SharePoint webs, lists, and libraries that can be associated with workflow definitions. These items create events that trigger the execution of workflows.

- **SharePoint 2010 Workflow Host**—This is a service application that can be used to host SharePoint 2010–style workflows using the old workflow architecture. This is available for backward compatibility. SharePoint 2010 workflows can exchange information and control with SharePoint 2013 workflows.

- **Workflows Services Manager**—WSM is a set of classes within the SharePoint object model that allow client- or server-side code to interact with the workflow engine in SharePoint. The main functional areas in the WSM objects are for managing workflow definitions and associations, running workflow instances, routing messages, and interoperating with SharePoint 2010 workflows.

- **Workflow Service Application Proxy**—This proxy is configured in SharePoint as a pass-through component for the workflow service. It is responsible for routing workflow traffic from SharePoint to the service that is hosting the workflows outside of SharePoint.

The next component in Figure 9-7 is the Workflow Manager Client 1.0. WMC resides on the SharePoint servers in the farm and provides a software interface to the service that is actually hosting the workflows. Depending on the environment in which you are running, this library acts as a proxy for a copy of the Workflow Manager Service or the Azure Workflow Service.

For on-premise SharePoint deployment, Workflow Manager 1.0 provides a host application for workflows. This service can be run within the SharePoint farm, but for maximum scalability, it should run on its own server farm. WM uses a local installation of the Windows Azure Service Bus to route messages from SharePoint Server to the workflow engine.

When using SharePoint Online, workflows are hosted in the Azure Workflow Service. The Azure Service Bus is used to route messages to workflows, and REST endpoints are used to send information back to SharePoint Online.

Subscriptions and Associations

Subscriptions and associations are related concepts in Windows Workflow Foundation (WF) and SharePoint 2013 Server, respectively.

Subscriptions are used within WF to control the routing of messages and events between workflows and the applications that interact with them. When a workflow is created that should be triggered when a certain event is received, a subscription is created. A subscription can also be used to wait for messages or events during the execution of a workflow. A subscription describes when events are of interest to the workflow and what action should be taken when those events arrive.

Associations within SharePoint create a connection between a workflow definition and a list or web site within SharePoint. Associations can be used to trigger a workflow automatically when an item is created or modified, or it may simply allow a user to manually initiate a workflow. For example, an approval workflow might be associated with the items in a form library. When a new form is received, it could automatically start a workflow that will perform approval on the form.

SharePoint 2013 uses subscriptions in WF to implement associations in SharePoint. The Windows Azure Service Bus contains a subsystem that manages subscriptions and routes notifications when an event is published. This is called the publication/subscription server, or just PubSub. The Windows Azure Service Bus can exist either on-site or in the Azure cloud. Either way, the PubSub feature is responsible for triggering workflows in the workflow management service. It also handles routing messages to active workflow instances.

The *publish/subscribe architectural pattern* has been used for many years to handle flexible, event-driven routing of messages between loosely coupled asynchronous senders (publishers) and receivers (subscribers). The PubSub service implements this pattern for messages traveling across the Azure Service Bus.

Here is a typical PubSub scenario:

1. A workflow definition is associated with an object in SharePoint.

2. A subscription is created in the PubSub service.

3. An event occurs that generates an event against the SharePoint object.

4. A message is published to the service bus.

5. The PubSub service determines the list of subscribers for the event.

6. The message is forwarded to the workflow hosting service.

7. The workflow service initiates a new instance of the workflow for the object.

The PubSub technique does not require the publisher or subscriber to have any direct knowledge of or contact with one another. A single message may be routed to a single subscriber, many subscribers, or none. This design allows the publishers, subscribers, and the PubSub service itself to be implemented across many servers with great scalability.

Associations in SharePoint implement a concept that is not relevant to workflows. That is the concept of a scope. An *association scope* defines the type of object that the workflow is bound to. This controls the types of events the workflow can respond to. The scopes in SharePoint 2013 are as follows:

- *SPWeb*—Associated with site-wide events, such as creating lists.

- *SPList*—Associated with changes to list items within a list.

- *Custom*—See the following discussion.

Those familiar with SharePoint 2010 workflows will notice an item missing from this list. SharePoint 2010 introduced reusable workflows that could be attached to a SharePoint content type. This allows the workflow to be automatically associated with any item of that type, no matter what list it resides in. The SharePoint 2013 workflow engine does not support reusable workflows. This makes sense if you consider that the Windows Workflow Foundation 4 was not designed with SharePoint in mind, but rather as a general solution for handling workflows. This is where the custom scope comes into play.

A custom-scoped association is basically a subscription that is created programmatically using the Workflow Services Manager components in the SharePoint object model. A workflow subscription is created using a unique event source identifier (a GUID). The subscription is not associated with a list or web site, just the event source GUID value, so SharePoint will never trigger the subscription on its own. Instead, some piece of code will have to make a call to the PublishEvent() method in the Workflow Services Manager API. This call produces a message to the PubSub service that gets routed to the workflow host to initiate a new workflow instance. When you consider that both SharePoint webs and lists have a unique GUID associated with them, it makes sense that custom events would be published in this way.

Alternatives to Writing Code

Workflows in SharePoint 2013 no longer support adding .NET code directly into a workflow definition. As mentioned before this can be handled in multiple ways, including writing web services or custom activities. The new workflow system also supports new features that make writing code less necessary. This includes a new way of writing expressions and new data types.

Two of the most common reasons for resorting to coding in workflows have been performing complex calculations and representing complex data types. Workflow Foundation 4 has features to help with these tasks.

The first of these features is designed to make configuring workflow activities more flexible. Instead of hard-coding a value into an activity property, you put in a C# (or VB.NET) expression. This expression is evaluated at runtime and the result is used in the activity. These expressions can make use of the workflow's variable values. This makes performing complex calculations in workflows no more difficult than in C# or VB.NET. While code *statements* are not legal in a workflow, *expressions* work just as they do in any .NET language.

There are also new data types available within workflows. There are special activities in WF4 that allow for the creation, update, and use of these data structures. The values are stored as variables within the workflow and can be passed into and out of various activities.

- **Collection<T>**—This is a collection that holds a list of elements of a certain type. T is a generic parameter that represents the type of the elements in the collection.

- **Dictionary<TKey,TValue>**—This is a dictionary object that holds a set of values of one type (TValue) indexed by values of another type (TKey). For example, a variable of this type could be used to store name-value pairs.

- *Dynamic Values*—This structure is created and consumed by several different activities. It functions similar to a dictionary except that the keys are always strings and the values are passed through to other variables in the workflow. Essentially, a variable of this type is a mapping from a set of properties to a set of variables for those properties. This data type is used to store sets of properties being passed into and out of activities like LookupSPListItem, LookupSPUser, and CreateListItem.

SharePoint App Workflow Activities

The SharePoint 2013 workflow engine supports a large number of activities. These are listed in the Toolbox panel in Visual Studio when designing a workflow. The following lists describe the most commonly used activities in SharePoint apps. This is not an exhaustive list of all activities that are available. These can be found online in the MSDN library (`msdn.microsoft.com`).

Control Flow Activities

Control flow activities are used to control the execution sequence of other activities in the workflow. This includes branching and looping constructs, as well as creating parallel execution paths.

- **Sequence**—Acts as a container for a set of activities that are executed sequentially.
- **If**—Evaluates a condition and executes one of two branches, depending on its value.
- **Switch<T>**—Evaluates an expression and executes one of several branches, depending on its value.
- **While/DoWhile**—Executes a sequence of activities as long as a condition evaluates to `true`. `While` checks the condition before each loop. `DoWhile` checks it afterward.
- **ForEach<T>**—Executes a loop for each element in the result of an expression.
- **Parallel**—Allows multiple branches of a workflow to be executed simultaneously.
- **ParallelForEach<T>**—Equivalent to the `ForEach` activity except that all iterations of the loop body are executed at the same time.

Current Context Activities

Each workflow instance has an associated context object that stores details of the particular instance. These activities allow a workflow to retrieve this information.

- **GetCurrentItemId**—Gets the Int32 ID value for the list item associated with the workflow instance.
- **GetHistoryListId**—Gets the GUID ID value for the history list for the workflow.
- **GetTaskListId**—Gets the GUID ID value for the task list for the workflow.
- **LookupWorkflowContextProperty**—Retrieves a property from the workflow instance context object. Properties available include associator, initiator, association name, instance ID, site URL, item URL, list name, and list ID.
- **WebUri**—Get the string value of the URL for the site running the workflow.

List Item Activities

These activities act upon a single list item in SharePoint.

- **CheckInItem/CheckOutItem/UndoCheckOutItem**—Manages the check-out status of the item.
- **CreateListItem**—Creates a new item.
- **UpdateListItem**—Updates an existing item.

- **DeleteListItem**—Removes an item from a list.

- **CopyItem**—Copies the contents of a list item into a different list.

- **LookupSPListItem**—Retrieves a specified set of attributes from a list item.

- **WaitForFieldChange**—Waits for a field on a list item to be changed to a certain value.

- **WaitForItemEvent**—Waits for a list item to added or updated.

Task Activities

One of the most common actions taken by workflows is to assign tasks to users. The user can be notified of the task via e-mail or by viewing their assigned tasks in a SharePoint site. When the user responds to the task, the workflow continues.

- **SingleTask**—Assigns a single task to a SharePoint user to group.

- **CompositeTask**—Assigns multiple tasks to be performed sequentially or in parallel. The activity completes when a completion criteria is met. This may include receiving one, all, or a percentage of task responses.

User and Group Activities

These activities allow a workflow to retrieve information about SharePoint users and groups.

- **LookupSPUser**—Loads a set of properties for a SharePoint user into a dynamic value, based on the user's principal ID.

- **LookupSPGroupMembers**—Loads the members of a SharePoint group into a dynamic value, based on the user's principal ID.

- **LookupSPPrincipal**—Loads a set of properties for a SharePoint user or group into a dynamic value, based on the principal name.

Messaging Activities

These activities provide the means for a workflow to make web service calls.

- **GetS2SSecurityToken**—Gets an OAuth server-to-server token for web service calls back to the SharePoint web site.

- **HttpSend**—Performs an HTTP call to a web site or service. A Server-to-Server (S2S) security token can be included to enable an OAuth connection to the service.

Miscellaneous SharePoint Activities

These activities perform various functions for SharePoint workflows.

- **AppOnlySequence**—Executes a sequence of activities in the security context of the workflow, rather than the user who initiated the workflow.

- **DelayUntil**—Pauses execution until a certain date and time.

- **Email**—Sends an e-mail message to one or more users of the SharePoint site.

- **WaitForCustomEvent**—Waits for a custom event to be published for the workflow.

- **WriteToHistory**—Writes an entry to the history list associated with the workflow.

Miscellaneous Non-SharePoint Activities

These activities are WF4 activities that are often useful in SharePoint workflows.

- **Assign**—Evaluates an expression and stores the result in a workflow variable.

- **Delay**—Pauses execution for a given period of time. Note: this activity takes a duration, not a specific date and time. See DelayUntil in preceding list.

- **TerminateWorkflow**—Cancels the current workflow instance.

The Workflow Services Manager

In most cases, it is not necessary to manage workflows programmatically. SharePoint associations can launch workflows and the activities available are sufficient to provide the control needed in most apps. In those cases where it is necessary to manage workflows using custom logic, Microsoft has provided the Workflow Services Manager (WSM) object. Since custom logic cannot be coded on the server side, SharePoint apps can access this object using the client-side object model libraries.

The WSM object resides in the Microsoft.SharePoint.Client.WorkflowServices namespace. The constructor takes a CSOM client context and a reference to the web whose workflows are to be managed. This is demonstrated in Listing 9-1.

Listing 9-1. Constructing the Workflow Services Manager Object (C#)

```
using (ClientContext context = TokenHelper.CreateRemoteEventReceiverClientContext(properties)) {
    Web web = context.Web;

    WorkflowServicesManager wsm = new WorkflowServicesManager(context, web);
    context.Load(wsm);
    context.ExecuteQuery();

    WorkflowInstanceService instServ = wsm.GetWorkflowInstanceService();
    context.Load(instServ);
    context.ExecuteQuery();

    // manage workflow instances using the service interface object
}
```

■ **Note**   The WSM object is most often used from a remote web site, so we will use the CSOM for .NET Framework libraries for our examples. The other CSOM libraries will work as well.

The workflow services manager object provides access to four service interfaces through its properties. These each handle a certain set of operations within the workflow service.

The first property is GetWorkflowDeploymentService, which returns a WorkflowDeploymentService object. This object manages workflow definitions within the site. It contains methods that can be used to publish and remove workflows and perform validations on workflow activities.

The next WSM property is GetWorkflowInstanceService, which returns a WorkflowInstanceService object. This service manages the running workflow instances in a site. Most of the methods on this object allow you to retrieve lists of the instances that are running on the site or a list item. The object can also be used to retrieve debug information from an instance, temporarily stop (suspend), resume, or terminate the instance. This object is also responsible for starting new workflow instances and sending custom event notifications to an instance.

The GetWorkflowInteropService property, and the InteropService object it returns, provide and interface to the SharePoint 2010 workflow host that is built into SharePoint 2013. Recall that SharePoint 2010 workflows are supported using the same architecture used in SharePoint 2010 Server. This interface allows custom logic to start, cancel, and manage the events of 2010-style workflows.

The last service available through the WSM object is the WorkflowSubscriptionService which is retrieved through the GetWorkflowSubscriptionService property. This interface is used to manage the subscriptions associated with a site. Like the instance service, most of the methods in this service allow you to query for existing subscriptions by workflow definition, list, or custom event source. There are methods for creating and deleting subscriptions as well.

The Workflow Services Manager object is designed to provide app developers with a single entry point to manage the workflow system. It does not matter if the workflow engine is running locally or in the cloud. This single object is used to access the Workflow Manager Client layer, which forwards commands to the correct service for your SharePoint environment.

EXERCISE 9-2

In this exercise, we will create a workflow to manage the grading of assignments that have been turned in by students. A student will turn in an assignment by adding it to a homework library. This will trigger a workflow that will record the date and time of the submission and notify the instructor. Once grading is complete, the grade will be recorded in the Grades list. If there is a problem with the submission, the teacher can reject the submission and the student will be notified.

First we will create a Homework library in the app web. We will also need to create a workflow that is triggered when an assignment is received. We will assign a grading task to the teacher, record the grade in the Grades list, and finally notify the student if the assignment is rejected.

We will start by creating a library for submitting homework. This will be a standard SharePoint document library.

1. Open Visual Studio 2012 and the Classroom Online solution, if they are not already open.

2. Add a new list item to the ClassroomOnline project named Homework.

3. From the Create a customizable list… drop-down box, select Document Library.

4. Click Finish.

5. In the Homework designer window, change the Title field's display name to Assignment Title and make the field required (see Figure 9-8).

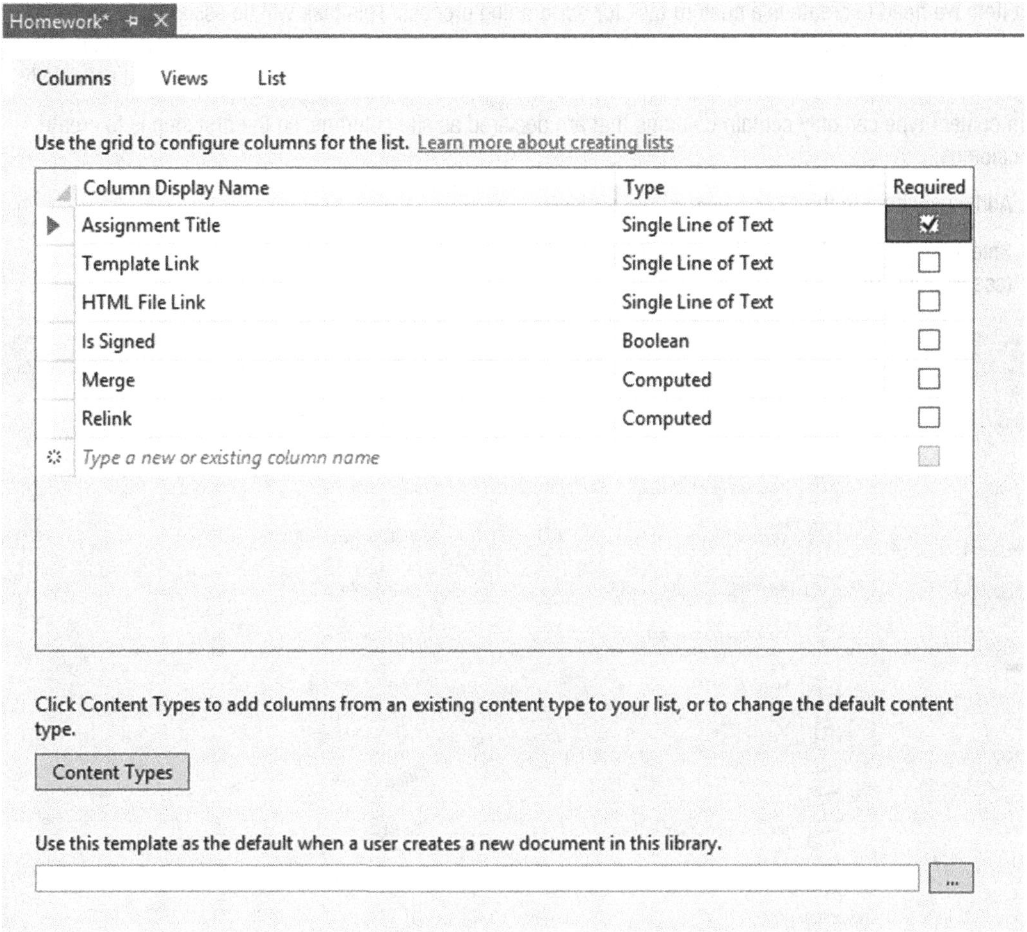

Figure 9-8. *Homework document library designer*

6. Save and close the designer window.

7. Open the `Schema.xml` file associated with the `Homework` list.

8. Find the string "`ListFieldsContentType`" in the `Schema.xml` file and change it to "`Homework`".

9. Find the following tag and delete it:

```
<ContentTypeRef ID="0x0101">
  <Folder TargetName="Forms/Document" />
</ContentTypeRef>
```

10. Save and close the `Schema.xml` file.

The last steps just shown adjusted the content types that are available in the `Homework` library so that there won't be any confusion when homework is submitted.

The next item we need to create is a custom task for our grading process. This task will be assigned to a user to inform them to grade an assignment. When they are done grading it, they will enter the grade information in the task. The workflow will then transfer that information into a new entry in the Grades list we have used previously.

A custom content type can only contain columns that are declared as site columns, so the first step is to create the site columns.

11. Add a new item to the ClassroomOnline project.

12. Select Site Column from the template list and set the name to PercentOfCourseGrade (see Figure 9-9).

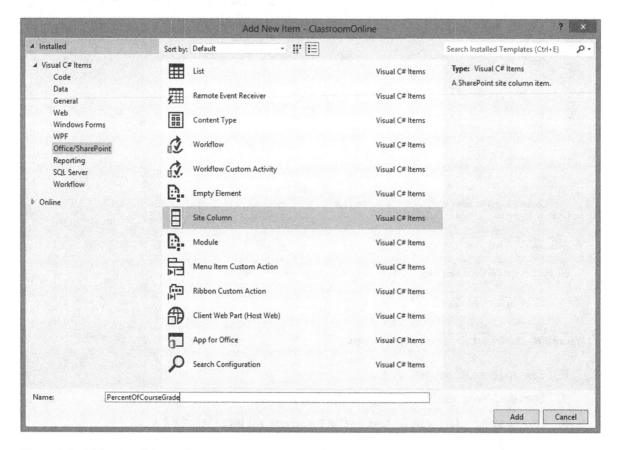

Figure 9-9. *Add a site column to the app*

13. Click Add.

14. In the Elements.xml file that is displayed for the site column, change the Type property to Number.

15. Create another Number site column called PointsPossible.

16. Create another Number site column called PointsAchieved.

17. Add a new item to the ClassroomOnline project.

18. Select Content Type from the template list and name the item GradingTask.

19. Click Add.

20. For the base type, select Workflow Task (SharePoint 2013). Be careful not to choose Task or Workflow Task as the base type.

21. Click Finish.

22. In the designer, add the three site columns you just created.

23. Mark each of the fields as required (see Figure 9-10).

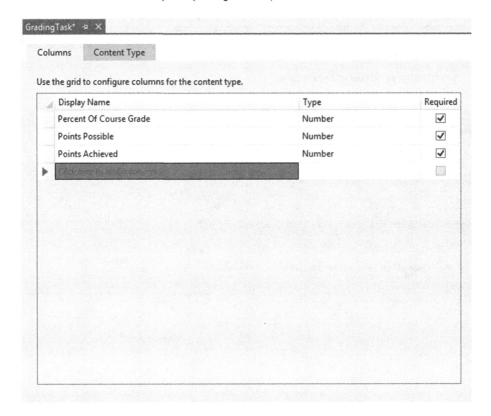

Figure 9-10. *GradingTask content type designer*

24. Save and close the GradingTask window.

The content type we just created will display a default input form that will accept values for the new fields, ensure that they are numbers, and verify that they are not left blank. If we needed any additional logic to be added to this form, we could create a custom ASP.NET form for editing this task. This form would become the task form for this type of task.

Now that we have the components assembled, we can move on to the workflow definition.

25. Add a new item to the ClassroomOnline project.

26. Select Workflow from the template list. Do not pick Workflow Custom Activity by mistake.

27. Set the name to GradingWorkflow and click Add.

■ **Tip** You might want to add a space in the workflow name to make it more readable. It will not affect the functionality of the workflow.

---

28. This will be a list workflow, so click Next.

29. Leave the check box checked and select the Homework library in the first drop-down.

30. Select <Create New> in both of the other drop-downs. This will cause a task and a workflow history list to be created for the workflow (see Figure 9-11).

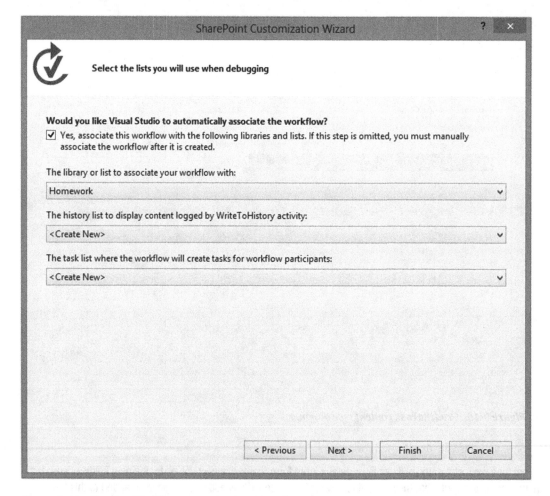

Figure 9-11. Grading Workflow customization wizard

31. Click Next.

32. Leave the default initiation conditions. A user will manually start the workflow.

33. Click Finish.

At this point, the workflow is opened in the designer window. The only shape on the screen is a single `Sequence` shape. All of the steps in our workflow will be placed into this container.

Before moving on, we need to add our custom task type to the `WorkflowTaskList` list definition that was just created.

34. Double-click on the `Elements.xml` file under the `WorkflowTaskList` node in the solution explorer.

35. Add this markup at the end of the definition, just before the `</Elements>` tag:

```
<ContentTypeBinding
    ListUrl="Lists/WorkflowTaskList"
    RootWebOnly="FALSE"
ContentTypeId="0x0108003365C4474CAE8C42BCE396314E88E51F00058195FAC66845428C7D0BB4B639773C" />
```

36. Open the `Elements.xml` file under the grading task content type.

37. Copy the `ContentTypeID` from the task type. (It will be different than the one shown in step 35.)

38. Close the task content type's `Elements.xml` file.

39. Replace the content type ID in the `WorkflowTaskList` `Elements.xml` file with the `ContentTypeID` from the grading task content type.

40. Save and close the `Elements.xml` file for the `WorkflowTaskList`.

41. Reopen the `GradingWorkflow` designer if it is not still open.

42. From the Toolbox, drag a `LookupSPListItem` shape from the Toolbox onto the designer and drop it on the `Sequence` shape.

43. On the title bar for the new shape, remove the current contents and type "Lookup Current SPListItem."

44. Press F4 to display the property panel.

45. Set the `ItemId` property to (current item). This is an option in the drop-down list for the property.

46. Set the `ListId` property to (current list).

47. Click on the Get Properties link. This adds a dynamic value builder to the workflow and attaches it to the lookup step.

48. Change the title of the new shape to `Get HW Item Properties`.

49. In the Variables panel at the bottom of the workflow, change the name of the new variable from `dv_0` to `hwProps`. This will hold the properties for the homework assignment.

50. Update the variable name in the `Source` field on the shape to `hwProps` as well.

51. On the lookup shape, set the result property to `hwProps`. The workflow design and the properties for the lookup shape should now look like Figure 9-12.

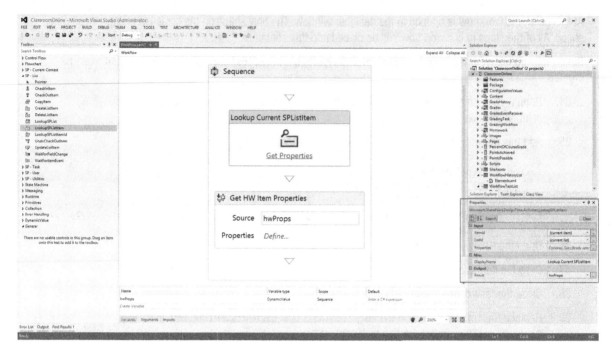

Figure 9-12. *Grading workflow (current state)*

52. On the Get HW Item Properties shape, click Define.... This will open a dialog box.

53. For Entity Type, select List Item of Homework. This is the type of item we are querying.

54. Under Path, select Modified By on the first line.

55. Select Assignment Title on the second line.

56. Click the Populate Variables link. This will create variables with appropriate names for each property being returned (see Figure 9-13).

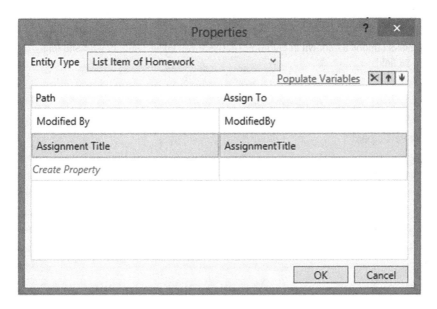

Figure 9-13. *Dynamic values property dialog*

57.   Click OK. Note that the new variables have been created.

So far, all the workflow has done is to retrieve two properties from the current list item, our homework assignment. Next, we will retrieve properties for the student using a similar combination of activities.

58.   Add a `LookupSPUser` shape from the Toolbox and name it `Lookup Student SPUser`.

59.   Set the `PrincipalId` property to `ModifiedBy`. This will use the full account name to lookup the user.

60.   Click Get Properties.

61.   Rename the dynamic value variable to `studentProps`.

62.   Click Define… on the student properties shape.

63.   Select the `Title` property and set the variable name to `Student Name`. (The title property in the user list contains the user's full name.)

64.   Click OK.

Now we will log the fact that the homework was submitted and assign the grading task.

65.   Drag a `WriteToHistory` shape from the Toolbox and place it at the end of the workflow.

66.   In the properties panel, set the expression for the `Message` property as follows:

```
StudentName + " has submitted '" + AssignmentTitle + "' for grading."
```

67.   Create Int32 variables named `GradingTaskOutcome` and `GradingTaskID`.

68.   Drag a `SingleTask` shape from the Toolbox and place it at the end of the workflow.

69. Click on the shape's Configure link.

70. Configure the tasks options as shown in Figure 9-14. Use a valid user name in your site for the `Assigned To` field.

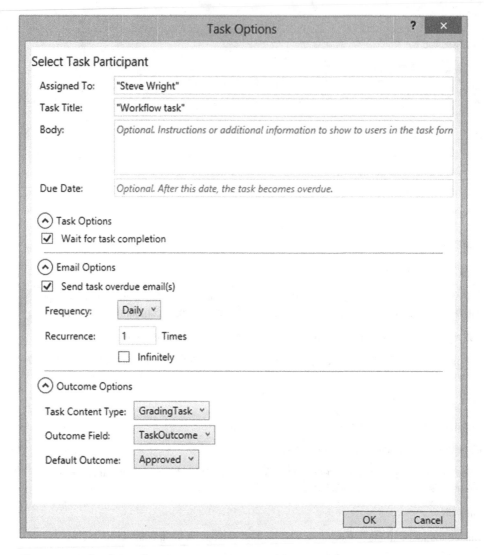

Figure 9-14. *Grading task options*

At this point in the workflow, we have assigned a grading task to a user. The workflow will pause here until the user takes some action on the task. The rest of the workflow will depend on that action.

71. Drag an `If` shape from the Toolbox and place it at the end of the workflow.

72. Set the condition field to `GradingTaskOutcome == 0`. The left side of the `If` will execute if the outcome is 0 (Approved). The right will execute if the value is 1 (Rejected).

73. Drop a `Sequence` shape into the left side of the `If`. This will allow us to configure multiple activities.

74. Drop a `LookupSPListItem` shape into the sequence container. Name it `Lookup Grading Task`.

75. Set the `ListId` property to `WorkflowTaskList`.

76. Set the `ItemId` property to `GradingTaskID`.

77. Click the Get Properties link to create a dynamic value builder.

78. Rename the variable to `taskProps`.

79. Click the Define... link.

80. Configure the properties as shown in Figure 9-15.

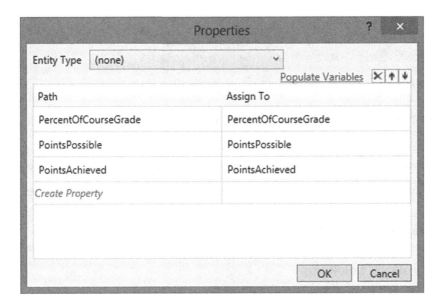

Figure 9-15. *Grading task properties to retrieve*

Now we will construct a new dynamic value variable that will route property values into a new entry in the Grade list.

81. Create a new variable named `gradeProps`.

82. Set the variables data type to `Microsoft.Activities.DynamicValue`.

83. From the Toolbox, add a `BuildDynamicValue` shape into the sequence on the left side of the `If` shape.

84. Rename the shape `Build Grade Item Properties`.

85. Set the `result` property to `gradeProps`.

86. Click the Define... link and configure the dynamic value as shown in Figure 9-16.

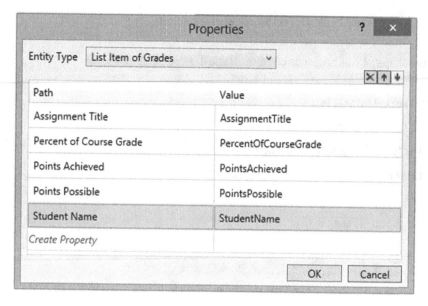

Figure 9-16. *Grade list item properties*

87. Add a `CreateListItem` shape to the end of this sequence and name it `Create Grade Item`.

88. Set the `ListId` property to `Grades`.

89. Set the `ListItemPropertiesDynamicValue` property to `gradeProps`.

This concludes our logic for approved assignments. Now we need to send an e-mail to the student if the assignment is rejected.

90. Drop an `Email` activity into the right side of the `If` shape and name it `Send Rejection E-Mail`.

91. Set the `Body` property to the following:

```
"Your submission for '" + AssignmentTitle + "' has been rejected. Please contact your
instructor."
```

92. Set the `Subject` property as follows:

```
"Assignment Rejected"
```

93. Set the `To` property to the following:

```
new System.Collections.ObjectModel.Collection<string>() { StudentName }
```

Note that this last property takes a string collection value. Even though we are only sending the e-mail a single address, we must still wrap that string in a collection.

The workflow design should now look like Figure 9-17.

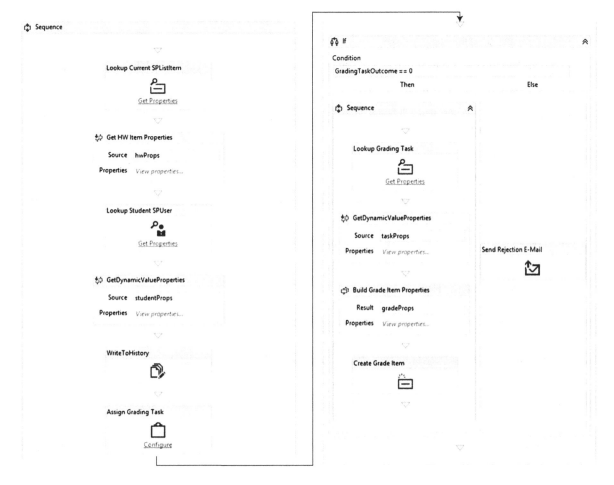

Figure 9-17. *Grading workflow (final)*

Now we will add a page that will provide links to make the workflow easier to test and debug.

94. Add a new page item to the ClassroomOnline project named Homework.aspx.

95. Replace the contents of the PlaceHolderMain content control with the following markup:

```
<p>
    <a href="../lists/Homework">Homework Library</a><br />
    <a href="../lists/WorkflowHistoryList">Workflow History List</a><br />
    <a href="../lists/WorkflowTaskList">Workflow Task List</a><br />
    <a href="../lists/Grades">Grades</a><br />
</p>
```

96. Save and close the page.

97. Open the AppManifest.xml file.

98. Select `ClassroomOnline/Pages/Homework.aspx` as the app's start page.

99. Save and close the app manifest.

We are done building the workflow and the site components that go into it. Now we will test the completed app.

100. Press F5 to deploy and launch the app.

101. After trusting the app, you will be taken to the default page we created. Click on the Homework Library link.

102. Click +new item.

103. Upload a file and click OK.

104. Now the app will ask for an Assignment Title for the file. Type a descriptive name and click Save.

105. Click the ellipsis (…) icon for the item you uploaded.

106. Click the ellipsis (…) icon on the pop-up menu that appears.

107. Click Workflows (see Figure 9-18).

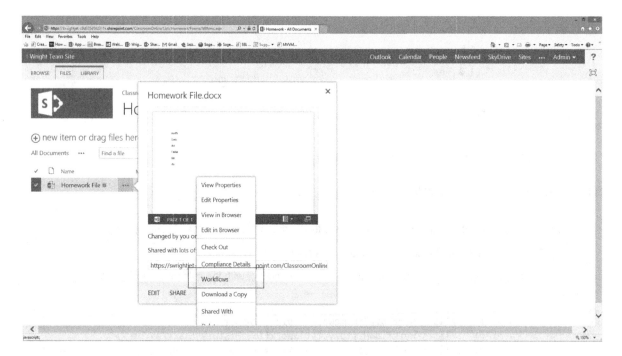

Figure 9-18. *Launch the item's Workflows page*

108. On the workflows page for the homework file, click the GradingWorkflow - WorkflowStart link.

109. Click the Classroom Online link in the header to return the default page.

110. Click the Workflow History List and verify that the submission has been logged.

> ■ **Tip** Hey, it didn't get logged! What happened?

Be patient. The workflow engine is processing your workflow's activities in the background. Depending on network delays, server load, and probably the phases of the moon, it may take a moment or two to traverse the activities. If the workflow is correct, the history and the grading task will appear in time.

111. Return to the default page and click the Workflow Task List link.

112. Click on the Workflow task item that has appeared in the list.

113. Click Edit Item in the ribbon menu.

114. Enter a grade for the homework (see Figure 9-19).

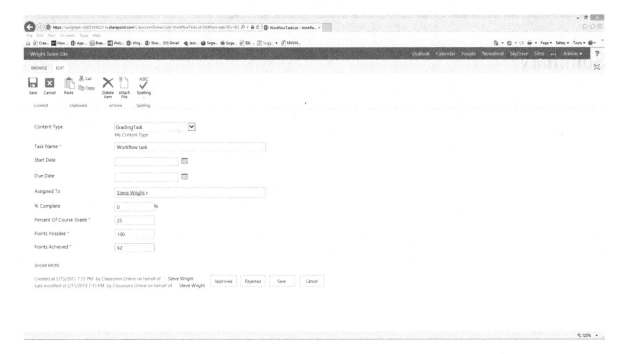

Figure 9-19. *Complete the grading task*

115. Click the Approved button.

116. Return to the default page and click on the Grades link. The grade you entered should be listed.

There are a number of improvements that could be made to this simple grading workflow. Some of these are listed here.

- The workflow could be modified to update the permissions on the assignment to prevent students from seeing one another's work. (That's probably a good idea.)

- The workflow could move the assignment to an entirely different library for grading.

- The user to whom the grading task is assigned could be added to the site's configuration and read by the workflow, instead of being hard-coded.

- The grading task could be sent to the entire group of faculty members allowing any of them to grade the assignment.

- The student could be provided a more convenient means of submitting homework than manually starting the workflow on the workflow page.

All of these features are well within the abilities of SharePoint workflows to implement.

Summary

In this chapter, we have detailed how a developer can leverage events and workflows in a SharePoint app. Remote event receivers allow us to capture and act on events that occur within SharePoint that may or may not be the direct result of a user's action. This creates logic that is independent of the user, but tied instead to the app's data and the SharePoint environment in which the app is running. SharePoint 2013 workflows provide a powerful platform for modeling business processes using standard communication protocols such as HTTP, OAuth, and REST. Unlike in previous versions of SharePoint, these workflows execute entirely outside of SharePoint, allowing them to fit naturally into the Cloud App Model.

In Chapter 10, we will continue moving up the application stack. We explore the tools and techniques available to SharePoint app developers for creating rich Internet applications that run within SharePoint. We will see how to create apps that blend seamlessly into the style and layout of the sites in which they are deployed. To accomplish this, we will leverage the client-side technologies we have already examined (JQuery, Knockout, the client-side object model, REST, etc.) in conjunction with new tools that integrate directly with the SharePoint Server.

CHAPTER 10

Developing the User Experience

In this chapter, we will continue moving up the levels of our architecture by looking at the user interface. We will discuss the various types of user interfaces that can be presented by apps in SharePoint and the tools that make them possible. In this chapter, we will go over the following points:

- We will examine the different types of user interface components that are available to apps for SharePoint, including client web parts, custom actions, and immersive pages.

- We will describe the components and configurations used when developing client web parts.

- The different types of custom actions will be explored through examples.

- We will discuss the tools made available by SharePoint 2013 to allow an app to adapt to the host site's brand.

- We will briefly discuss techniques for adapting to variations in the browser environment, such as language localization and different browser profiles.

User Experience Options for Apps

Apps for SharePoint present unique challenges for web designers. In a stand-alone web site, or even a SharePoint site, the process of designing and implementing the user experience begins by designing the site's brand. This includes the page layouts, fonts, colors, and any other visual components that are needed for the presentation of the site. These components are then implemented using a combination of HTML markup, Cascading Style Sheets (CSS), JavaScript, and other technologies such as Flash or Silverlight.

In a SharePoint app, we only control the visual components that we create. The rest of the host web remains largely beyond our control. The branding of the host web may be extensively modified relative to the default appearance of SharePoint. Our apps need to adapt to the brand of the host web in any way that is practical. Failure to do so can create a situation where our app's components create a jarring, obtrusive appearance in an otherwise well-designed site. In this chapter, we will explore how to create the components of our app so that they can be integrated seamlessly into the brand of the host site.

Note   In this chapter, we will deal with conforming the user experience of our apps to the branding that is already in place on the host site. Creating that brand in the first place is a very broad topic, and is beyond the scope of this book. For more information on branding SharePoint 2013 sites, take a look at *Pro SharePoint 2013 Branding and Responsive Web Development* (Apress, 2013), available at http://www.amazon.com/SharePoint-2013-Branding-Responsive-Development /dp/1430250283/ref=sr_1_1?ie=UTF8&qid=1374257033&sr=8-1&keywords=2013+branding+overfield).

The user interface components exposed by an app for SharePoint fall into three categories: immersive web pages, app parts, and custom actions.

We have already seen examples of *immersive web pages* in the exercises we have done in previous chapters. Immersive pages are application pages, served from either the app web or a remote web, that completely replace the host web page previously displayed in the web browser. An immersive page does not provide components to a host web page, but replaces it altogether. Because these are complete ASP.NET pages, they have the ability to use all of the usual tools available to ASP.NET sites. This includes user web controls, client-side scripting, custom CSS styles, and so on. For pages that are served from a remote site, not the app web, immersive pages can leverage server-side technologies such as server controls and server-side code. SharePoint 2013 provides tools that allow immersive pages to conform to the branding of the host site so that the user need not be aware that they have moved into a new area of the site. This includes automatically redirecting the browser when needed and adopting the host web's styles and menus.

Client web parts, also known as *app parts*, are similar to traditional SharePoint web parts. They can be added to pages in the host or app webs and configured just as server web parts are. The difference is that, with app parts, there is no need to configure assemblies in the SharePoint server farm or execute server-side code. We will create a client web part for our Classroom Online app that will allow the host site's owner to place a listing of the student's grades on a web part page.

Custom actions in SharePoint allow developers to configure custom buttons and menu options on a SharePoint site. In SharePoint apps, custom actions can be used to add ribbon menu items and Edit Control Block options to the host web site. These actions, when selected by a user, trigger logic in the app by navigating to a page or displaying a dialog. We can use custom actions to create a richer user interface that presents pages or dialogs that integrate well with the rest of the host site.

Client Web Parts

The word "client" in client web parts refers to the location where the logic of the web part resides. In a traditional "server" web part, a class executes on the server to generate the HTML to be rendered as part of a web part page. In a client web part, the UI is rendered by a separate web page that uses either JavaScript or server-side code in a remote web site to control the interface. Because client web parts are intended for use in apps for SharePoint, they are also called app parts. The two terms refer to the same concept.

In order to implement a similar concept using only client-side techniques, Microsoft chose to leverage a component that is standard in any modern web browser: the inline frame. An inline frame is created by embedding an IFRAME HTML tag in the page. The frame is then loaded with the contents of another web page. In the case of an app part, the app part declares the URL to be used on the IFRAME. This page is called the *client web part page*. SharePoint reads app part's configuration and places an appropriately configured IFRAME on the web page (see Figure 10-1).

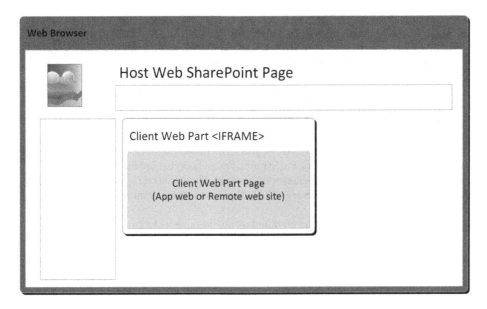

Figure 10-1. *A client web part*

On the URL's query string, SharePoint can pass parameters to the client web part page. These parameters include the standard tokens that apps normally receive, such as the host site's URL and the context token. The developer also has the option to declare custom configuration properties on the app part. These parameters are configured as part of the web part in SharePoint and are passed to the app part when it is rendered.

Creating App Parts

The process to create a basic web part is as easy as selecting the Client Web Part option when adding an item to the app project. The result is that multiple files are added to the solution.

The first file added is the Elements.xml file that contains the configuration of the app part. This file defines the name and title of the web part. It contains a default height and width for displaying the web part and the URL of the client web part page to be displayed. See Listing 10-1. Note that in this case, the client web part page is in the app web (~appWebUrl), not a remote web (~remoteWebUrl). The {StandardTokens} parameter is used to specify where the standard SharePoint app tokens should be added to the IFRAME's URL.

Listing 10-1. Elements.xml for a Client Web Part

```xml
<?xml version="1.0" encoding="utf-8"?>
<Elements xmlns="http://schemas.microsoft.com/sharepoint/">
  <ClientWebPart
      Name="MyGrades" Title="My Grades"
      Description="Lists My Grades" DefaultHeight="300" DefaultWidth="700">
    <Content Type="html" Src="~appWebUrl/Pages/MyGrades.aspx?{StandardTokens}" />
    <Properties>    </Properties>
  </ClientWebPart>
</Elements>
```

The other component added to the solution is the client web part page itself. When a new client web part is added to a SharePoint app project, it will be added to the remote web site by default if one is present. If there is no remote web, the page will be placed in the Pages folder in the app web. The template used for this page varies slightly depending on whether the page will reside in the app's app web or a remote web site.

On a remote web, the default client web part page is created as an empty ASP.NET page. This page contains an empty server-side form control, logic for conforming to the host site's styles, and an empty code-behind class to which server-side code can be added. The page does not include script links for JQuery or the SharePoint JavaScript CSOM. If you will be using these, they will need to be added manually. The page does not use any master page, since it is intended to be embedded within another page.

When the page is created in the app web, it is tailored to run using JavaScript instead of server-side code. The JQuery and CSOM libraries are included by default. The page does not, and cannot, have a code-behind file. Again, the page has no master page, but it does include a special tag that is needed by SharePoint. The `<WebPartPages:AllowFraming>` tag is a server-side control that informs SharePoint that this page will be displayed inside a frame. Without this tag, the client web part page cannot be shown on the host web.

Once the client web part page has been created, it can be modified using the same techniques we have used throughout our examples.

Setting Parameters

Many web parts allow configurations to customize their appearance or functionality. App parts can do this by declaring parameters in their `Elements.xml` file. When the user places the web part on a page and edits it, these parameters are exposed in the web part editor. The values entered are then passed to the web part in the query string of the client web part page.

The default XML in `Elements.xml` contains an empty `<Parameters>` tag. To declare a parameter, a `<Property>` tag is added to this collection. Multiple properties can be declared on a client web part. Table 10-1 includes the attributes that can be added to the property tag to customize the appearance of a parameter.

Table 10-1. *Property options on client web parts*

Attribute Name	Description
Name	This is the name of the parameter to be added to the web part. This name will be used to store and retrieve the value of the parameter.
Type	This is the data type of the parameter. Valid values are string, Boolean, int, and enum.
WebBrowsable	This indicates whether or not this parameter can be edited in the web part editor.
WebDisplayName	This is the display name of the property that will be seen by the user during web part editing.
WebDescription	This is a user-friendly description of the purpose of the parameter.
WebCategory	This is the name of the section in the web part editor where the parameter should appear.
DefaultValue	This attribute can contain a default value to be assigned to the web part when it is created.
RequiresDesignerPermission	This attribute is true or false, indicating whether the user must have Design permissions on the page in order to update the parameter's value.

Listing 10-2 declares two parameters. The first is a string parameter that can take any value. Parameters that take int or Boolean values are declared in the same manner. The second declaration is for an enumeration. In this case, a list of possible values is included in a `<EnumItems>` collection, as shown.

Listing 10-2. App Part Property Declarations

```
<Property
    Name="StringParam"
    Type="string"
    WebBrowsable="true"
    WebDisplayName="Test String Parameter"
    WebDescription="Enter any string in this value."
    WebCategory="Configuration"
    DefaultValue="No string configured"
    RequiresDesignerPermission="true" />

<Property
    Name="EnumParam"
    Type="enum"
    WebBrowsable="true"
    WebDisplayName="Test Enumeration Parameter"
    WebDescription="Select one of the values from the list."
    WebCategory="Configuration"
    DefaultValue="1"
    RequiresDesignerPermission="true" />
  <EnumItems>
    <EnumItem WebDisplayName="Option 1" Value="1"/>
    <EnumItem WebDisplayName="Option 2" Value="2"/>
    <EnumItem WebDisplayName="Option 3" Value="3"/>
  </EnumItems>
</Property>
```

The properties declared for a client web part are passed in the query string portion of the incoming URL for the client web part page. These are passed using the name of the properties. In order to add the properties into the URL correctly, the URL in the `<Content>` tag needs to be updated to include the configured values. For our properties just demonstrated, the content tag would be modified like this:

```
<Content Type="html" Src="~appWebUrl/Pages/MyGrades.aspx
?StringParam=_StringParam_&amp;EnumParam=_EnumParam_&amp;{StandardTokens}" />
```

Note that the parameter names are included surrounded by underscores where the value should be placed. This string requires encoding in XML, so the ampersand symbol is represented as &. The actual URL generated would look like this:

```
<appWebUrl>/Pages/MyGrades.aspx?StringParam=No+string+configured&EnumParam=1&<StandardTokens>
```

The values of the parameters can be retrieved by parsing the query string, just as we have done for other tokens using JavaScript or server-side code, as needed.

EXERCISE 10-1

In this exercise, we will add a client web part to the Classroom Online app. This web part will render a list of grades for the currently signed in user. The app part can be placed on any web part page in the host web site to include the student's grades.

Although we already have a remote web site in our solution, we will host the client web part page in the app web instead. This will allow us to reuse the model and view-model objects we have created previously. The app part we will create will simply be a new view in the MVVM model.

We will create a new client web part called MyGrades. We will then move the client web part page to the app web. Finally, we will add markup to the page, allowing our existing grade model and view-model objects to manage this view.

We will begin with the Classroom Online solution as it stood at the end of Chapter 9. If these files are not available, they can be downloaded from the Source Code/Download area of the Apress web site (www.apress.com).

1.   Open Visual Studio 2012.

2.   Open the Classroom Online solution.

3.   Add a new item to the ClassroomOnline app project.

4.   Select the Client Web Part (Host Web) item template.

5.   Set the name to MyGrades.

6.   Click Add.

7.   Leave default Create a new client web part page selected and click Finish.

At this point, two changes have been made. A new folder called MyGrades has been added to the app project. Also, an ASP.NET page called MyGrades.aspx has been added to the remote web site project. Because we want to host the client web part page in our app site instead of the remote web, we will remove the remote page and create a new page in the app web.

8.   Right-click on the MyGrades.aspx file in the remote web site project (ClassroomOnlineWeb) and select Delete.

9.   Right-click on the Pages folder in the ClassroomOnline project and add a page called MyGrades.aspx.

10.   Delete the contents of the MyGrades.aspx file and replace them with the following markup:

```
<%@ Page language="C#" Inherits="Microsoft.SharePoint.WebPartPages.WebPartPage,
Microsoft.SharePoint, Version=15.0.0.0, Culture=neutral,
PublicKeyToken=71e9bce111e9429c" %>
<%@ Register Tagprefix="SharePoint" Namespace="Microsoft.SharePoint.WebControls"
Assembly="Microsoft.SharePoint, Version=15.0.0.0, Culture=neutral,
PublicKeyToken=71e9bce111e9429c" %>
<%@ Register Tagprefix="Utilities" Namespace="Microsoft.SharePoint.Utilities"
Assembly="Microsoft.SharePoint, Version=15.0.0.0, Culture=neutral,
PublicKeyToken=71e9bce111e9429c" %>
```

```
<%@ Register Tagprefix="WebPartPages" Namespace="Microsoft.SharePoint.WebPartPages"
Assembly="Microsoft.SharePoint, Version=15.0.0.0, Culture=neutral,
PublicKeyToken=71e9bce111e9429c" %>

<WebPartPages:AllowFraming ID="AllowFraming" runat="server" />

<html>
<head>
    <title></title>

    <script type="text/javascript" src="../Scripts/jquery-1.7.1.min.js"></script>
    <script type="text/javascript" src="../Scripts/knockout-2.2.1.js"></script>
    <script type="text/javascript" src="/_layouts/15/MicrosoftAjax.js"></script>
    <script type="text/javascript" src="/_layouts/15/sp.runtime.js"></script>
    <script type="text/javascript" src="/_layouts/15/sp.js"></script>

    <script type="text/javascript" src="../Scripts/Models/siteconfigs.js"></script>
    <script type="text/javascript" src="../Scripts/Models/grades.js"></script>
    <script type="text/javascript" src="../Scripts/ViewModels/gradebook.js"></script>

    <script type="text/javascript">
        'use strict';

        // Set the style of the client web part page to be consistent with the host web.
        (function () {
            var hostUrl = '';
            if (document.URL.indexOf('?') != -1) {
                var params = document.URL.split('?')[1].split('&');
                for (var i = 0; i < params.length; i++) {
                    var p = decodeURIComponent(params[i]);
                    if (/^SPHostUrl=/i.test(p)) {
                        hostUrl = p.split('=')[1];
                        document.write('<link rel="stylesheet" href="'
                                    + hostUrl + '/_layouts/15/defaultcss.ashx" />');
                        break;
                    }
                }
            }
            if (hostUrl == '') {
                document.write('<link rel="stylesheet"
                        href="/_layouts/15/1033/styles/themable/corev15.css" />');
            }
        })();
    </script>
</head>
<body>
    <form id="form1" runat="server">
    <div style="height:300px;width:700px;overflow-y:scroll">
        <table border="1" cellspacing="0" cellpadding="5" width="95%">
            <thead style='background-color:gray;color:white'>
                <th>Student</th>
```

```
            <th>Assignment</th>
            <th>Points Possible</th>
            <th>Course Weight (%)</th>
            <th>Points Acheived</th>
        </thead>
        <tbody data-bind="foreach: gradebookEntries()">
            <tr>
                <td data-bind="text: studentName"></td>
                <td data-bind="text: assignmentTitle"></td>
                <td data-bind="text: pointsPossible"></td>
                <td data-bind="text: percentOfGrade"></td>
                <td data-bind="text: pointsAchieved"></td>
            </tr>
        </tbody>
    </table>
  </div>
  </form>
</body>
</html>
```

This page is different from the default app web page and the default client web part page that was created (and then deleted) in the remote web.

```
<%@ Page language="C#" Inherits="Microsoft.SharePoint.WebPartPages.WebPartPage,
Microsoft.SharePoint, Version=15.0.0.0, Culture=neutral,
PublicKeyToken=71e9bce111e9429c" %>
```

First, notice the ASP directives at the top of the file. The page directive does not reference a master page. As a result, the ASPX file will contain all of the markup for the page, including the `<html>` tag. There will be no content controls in this page.

```
<WebPartPages:AllowFraming ID="AllowFraming" runat="server" />
```

The `<AllowFraming>` tag is included because this page will be embedded in an IFRAME on the host page. By default, app web pages do not support frames. This tag indicates that framing is allowed for this page.

```
<script type="text/javascript" src="../Scripts/Models/siteconfigs.js"></script>
<script type="text/javascript" src="../Scripts/Models/grades.js"></script>
<script type="text/javascript" src="../Scripts/ViewModels/gradebook.js"></script>
```

In addition to the JQuery and SharePoint CSOM libraries, we are including the model and view-model JavaScript files for the gradebook page we created in previous chapters. These will be used to populate the data in this page.

```
<form id="form1" runat="server">
    <div style="height:300px;width:700px;overflow-y:scroll">
        <table border="1" cellspacing="0" cellpadding="5" width="95%">
```

The ASPX file contains a server form control that will contain all of the elements of the page. The `<DIV>` tag creates a fixed size container for the web part. The `<TABLE>` will display as many rows as needed. If they go beyond the size of the `<DIV>`, the content will scroll.

The rest of the HTML markup has been taken directly from the gradebook.aspx page. We have removed the elements that allow the data to be edited, since this is a read-only web part.

11. Save and close the MyGrades.aspx file.

The behavior of this view will differ from the gradebook page in one respect. It will always be in read-only mode. To accommodate this, we will add a check into the view-model to determine if the view contains the editing controls. If not, the view will contain read-only grades for the current student only.

12. Open the gradebook.js file in the Scripts/ViewModels folder.

13. Replace the line in gradebookViewModel() that sets the self.viewAsStudent value with this line:

```
self.viewAsStudent = viewAsStudent || ($(".buttonColumn").length == 0);
```

This line will look for the elements that contain the editing buttons. If they are not found, then this is a read-only view.

14. Save and close the gradebook.js file.

15. Open the Elements.xml file in the MyGrades folder.

16. Delete the contents of this file and replace them with the following:

```
<?xml version="1.0" encoding="utf-8"?>
<Elements xmlns="http://schemas.microsoft.com/sharepoint/">
  <ClientWebPart
    Name="MyGrades"
    Title="My Grades"
    Description="Lists the grades for the currently signed in user."
    DefaultHeight="300"
    DefaultWidth="700">

    <Content
      Type="html"
      Src="~appWebUrl/Pages/MyGrades.aspx?{StandardTokens}" />

    <Properties> </Properties>
  </ClientWebPart>
</Elements>
```

The only significant changes we have made to this file are to set the default height and width of the web part and to change the URL pattern for the client web part page. We have changed the URL to point to a page in the app web (~appWebUrl) instead of the remote web (~remoteAppUrl).

17. Save and close the Elements.xml file.

18. Press F5 to run the app.

19. On the gradebook page (the default app page), click on the host site link in the upper-left corner of the page.

20. On the host site's default page, click Page on the ribbon menu.

21. Click the Edit button in the Edit group on the Page tab. This puts the web part page into edit mode (see Figure 10-2).

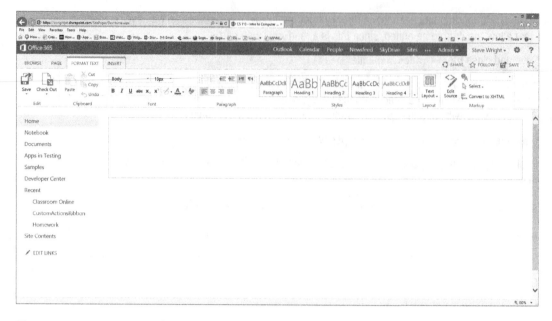

Figure 10-2. Home page in edit mode

22. Click the Insert tab on the ribbon.

23. Click the App Part button in the Parts group.

24. Select the My Grades app part (see Figure 10-3).

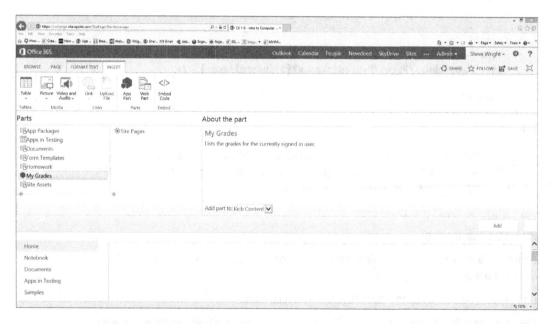

Figure 10-3. Add the My Grades client web part

25. Click Add.

26. Click Save in the Edit group on the ribbon menu to save the page changes.

As shown in Figure 10-4, the app part displays the grades table in read-only mode within the home page. If you examine the page using the web browser's debugger, you will see that the contents of the web part are displayed in an IFRAME tag that points to the client web part page for its contents.

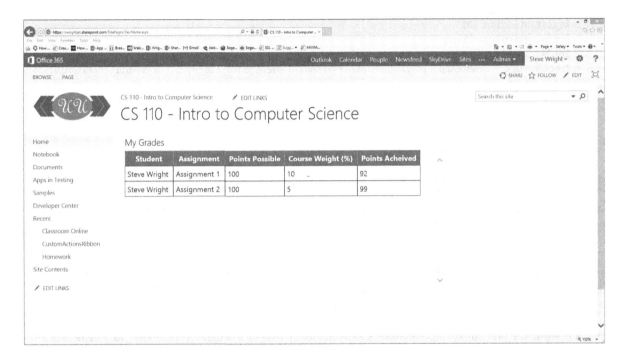

Figure 10-4. *The My Grades app part on the home page*

Custom Actions

Custom actions are commands that can be injected into the menu system of the app's host site. When a user selects one of these items, the custom action triggers a web page or dialog provided by the app. The app is provided with any context that is available to the command, including the current list and any selected list item or document. Using SharePoint's client APIs, the app can then retrieve and update information in SharePoint to implement the corresponding action. Custom actions are used to add application-specific menu actions to the host web's user interface. These actions can be anything that the user may wish to do in a certain situation, such as make a purchase, request assistance, provide feedback, or trigger a custom business process workflow.

A custom action is created by adding an item to the app's project. Visual Studio provides a wizard for creating basic custom actions that can handle most scenarios. The result is to add a new `Elements.xml` file to the project that contains one or more `CustomAction` tags.

```xml
<?xml version="1.0" encoding="UTF-8"?>
<Elements xmlns="http://schemas.microsoft.com/sharepoint/">
<CustomAction>
  <CustomAction
      Title="My Custom Action"
      ImageUrl="_layouts/15/images/placeholder16x16.png"
      Sequence="1"
      Location="EditControlBlock"
      RegistrationId="101"
      RegistrationType="List"
      Id="Action1">
    <UrlAction Url="~remoteAppUrl/MyAction.html?{StandardTokens}&amp;list={ListId}&amp;item={ItemId}"/>
  </CustomAction>
</Elements>
```

These tags define how and where the menu item should be displayed and what action will be taken in response to its selection.

Types of Custom Actions

When a custom menu item is activated, SharePoint will execute one of two types of supported actions: a navigation or a dialog.

■ **Note**　SharePoint supports custom actions that execute JavaScript instead of navigating to a page or showing a dialog. Custom actions that use scripts are not allowed in apps for SharePoint. The app will not be allowed to install.

A navigation action simply causes the user's web browser to navigate to a new location. The URL can include a number of parameters. For example:

```xml
<UrlAction Url=
"~remoteAppUrl/CustomActionTarget.aspx?{StandardTokens}&amp;Source={Source}&amp;
ListURLDir={ListUrlDir}&amp;ListID={ListId}&amp;ItemURL={ItemUrl}&amp;ItemID={ItemId}" />
```

- **~remoteAppUrl**—Indicates that the page that implements the custom action is hosted in the remote web site.

- **CustomActionTarget.aspx**—The name of the target ASPX page that implements the action.

- **StandardTokens**—Provides the standard app tokens to the page, including the host web URL and a context token.

- **Source**—Provides the URL of the page where the action was activated. This is usually used to return the user to that page after the action is completed.

- **ListUrlDir/ListId**—Provides the URL and ID of the list that was in context when the command was activated.

- **ItemUrl/ItemId**—Provides the URL and ID of the list item that was selected when the command was activated.

In some cases, it is better to open a dialog on the current page than to navigate to an entirely new page. To use a dialog instead of navigation, the HostWebDialog attribute is set on the CustomAction tag, like this:

```
<CustomAction
    Id="Action1"
    RegistrationId="101"
    RegistrationType="List"
    Location="CommandUI.Ribbon"
    Title="My Custom Action"
    HostWebDialog="true"
    HostWebDialogHeight="100"
    HostWebDialogWidth="300">
```

This will cause the target page to be opened in a modal dialog with the given height and width. All of the same parameters can be sent to this page as well. The dialog is created using the SharePoint client dialog system introduced in SharePoint 2010. The JavaScript interface for this system is in ~/_layouts/SP.UI.Dialog.js.

Custom Edit Control Block Actions

The Edit Control Block (ECB) is the pop-up menu that appears when the user clicks the ellipsis button on a list item, as shown in Figure 10-5.

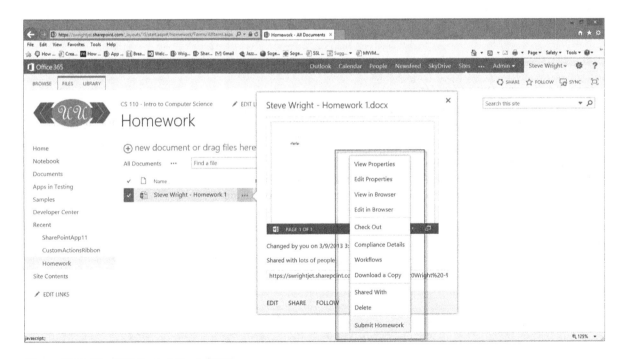

Figure 10-5. *The Edit Control Block (ECB)*

For example, we could include a menu option on any document to "Submit Homework," as shown here. When this item is triggered, the custom action would perform the action based on the list ID and item ID provided by SharePoint.

To add an ECB action, right-click the app project node in Visual Studio and add a new item. The item template is called Menu Item Custom Action. This will launch a wizard that will help configure the custom action (see Figure 10-6).

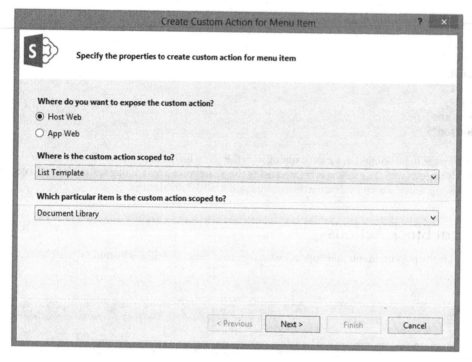

Figure 10-6. *Custom action wizard (screen 1)*

Figure 10-6 shows the first page of the wizard. An action can be installed in either the host or app web. The action is then associated with a list template, list instance, content type, or file name extension. In this case, we have chosen to associate it with all document libraries in the host web site.

On the second page of the wizard (see Figure 10-7), the menu item label and target page URL are specified. The page can be any page in the host or app webs. Note that there is no mention of creating dialogs on this screen. The attributes for creating dialogs must be added to the Elements.xml file by hand.

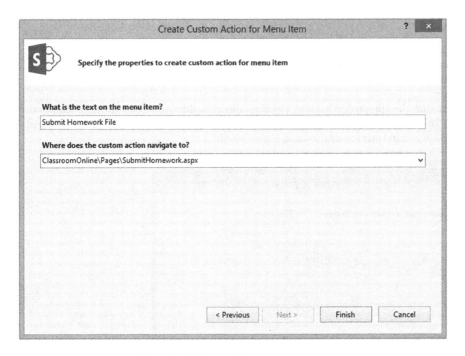

Figure 10-7. Custom action wizard (screen 2)

Clicking the Finish button on this screen will create and display the `Elements.xml` file in the Visual Studio editor window (see Figure 10-8). Notice that a default set of parameters has been added to the target URL, as follows:
`?{StandardTokens}&amp;SPListItemId={ItemId}&amp;SPListId={ListId}`

Figure 10-8. `Elements.xml` for an ECB action

Custom Ribbon Actions

Custom ribbon actions appear on the ribbon menu at the top of each SharePoint page. Unlike ECB actions, ribbon menu items can affect more than one item in a list. They can also be used to trigger global events that are not associated with a particular list item. For example, we could include a ribbon command to send an e-mail to another user such as the course instructor.

To add a ribbon action, right-click the app project node in Visual Studio and add a new item. The item template is called Ribbon Custom Action. This will launch a wizard that will help configure the custom action. The first page of this wizard is the same as for an ECB action (previously shown in Figure 10-6).

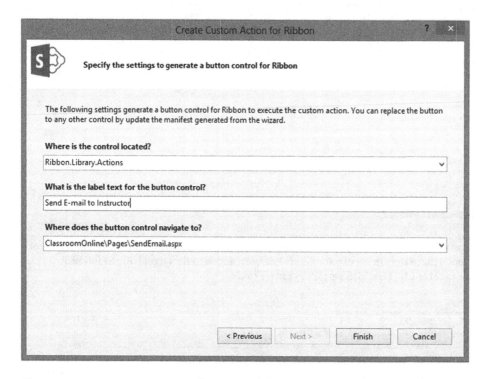

Figure 10-9. *Custom action wizard (ribbon action)*

The second page of the wizard (see Figure 10-9) takes the target URL and item label in same manner as for an ECB action. The difference for a ribbon is that you can specify the location of the menu item.

The ribbon menu is structured in a hierarchy of items. At the top level are the various tabs that appear at the top of the ribbon (see Figure 10-10). Within each tab are a series of option groups. Individual menu items belong to these groups. The location for a ribbon menu item is specified using a string in the form of `"Ribbon.<TabName>.<GroupName>"`.

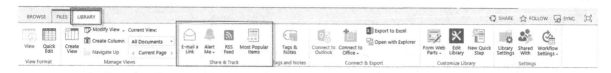

Figure 10-10. *The ribbon menu*

The wizard in Visual Studio provides a list of the most common locations where custom actions should be placed. A more complete list can be found at `http://msdn.microsoft.com/en-us/library/ee537543(v=office.14).aspx`. This list is for SharePoint 2010, but it still seems to be accurate for 2013.

Another way to find the location for your action is to use your browser's debugger. Open a SharePoint page that contains the menu you wish to target. In the debugger, select an item in the group where your item will be placed (see Figure 10-11). In this example, the location string is `"Ribbon.Library.CustomViews"`. Note that the names in the location string do not always match the label displayed in the SharePoint UI.

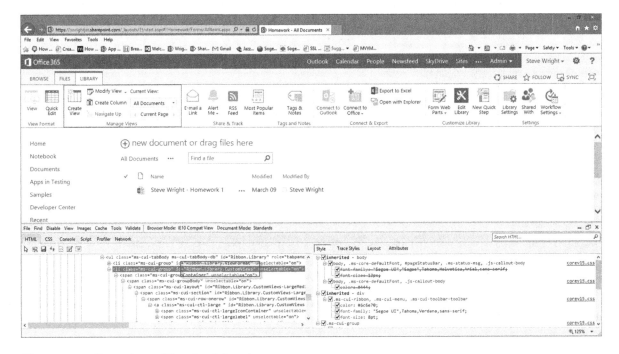

Figure 10-11. *Extracting a ribbon item's location*

The XML produced for a ribbon action (see Figure 10-12) is different from that for an ECB action in several ways.

- The location attribute of the `CustomAction` tag is `"CommandUI.Ribbon"` instead of `"EditControlBlock"`.

- Instead of a simple `UrlAction` to specify a target URL, this markup includes a `CommandUIExtension`. This allows the declaration of the command action, which provides for more customization of the UI.

- The `CommandUIDefinition` tag defines the location in the ribbon where the new command will appear.

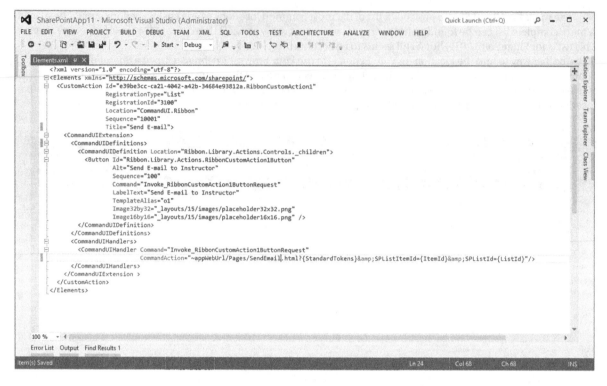

Figure 10-12. Elements.xml (ribbon custom action)

There are two different options for menu icons: 16 × 16 and 32 × 32. SharePoint will use them automatically in different situations.

Conforming to a Brand

One of the big challenges when designing an app is to create a user experience that does not clash or conflict with the host site. For an internal app that is deployed within an organization's intranet, this problem is limited to the brand used in the site. For an app that is to be widely distributed, the problem becomes more acute. How do we make our apps blend in with the host site's branding when we know nothing about that brand?

In SharePoint 2010, site branding was accomplished through a combination of master pages, page layouts, Office themes, and cascading style sheets. When a full-trust or sandboxed solution was installed, any web parts or UI components it provided ran on the SharePoint server farm within a SharePoint page. This made it possible to directly query SharePoint about the site's branding and adjust the UI as necessary. Using the Cloud App Model, this is no longer the case.

In SharePoint apps, we may know very little about the site that will be hosting the app. It could be using highly customized master pages, style sheets, and menus. SharePoint 2013 provides a set of tools to help apps conform to whatever branding is in place on the host site.

The App Master Page

Master pages are a fundamental part of ASP.NET web sites. They define the layout and content areas that a page contains. Each SharePoint site can use a different default master page. Individual pages can override this selection and use their own page, though this is not often done in most sites.

When a SharePoint app exposes a client web part to the host site, that web part becomes part of the host page. The host page's master page determines where the IFRAME that exposes the client web part will be located. As a result, client web parts do not typically use master pages. They contain a single set of content with a well-defined structure that fits into the IFRAME and does not affect the rest of the page's layout.

Immersive app pages replace the entire host site page with a new page. In this case, the app controls the layout of the page. The host site's master page is not used. When a page is served from the app web, it is still a SharePoint page even though it is hosted in a separate site from the host content.

SharePoint 2013 contains a new master page to help these pages adapt to the host site. The app.master page is the default master page used for any app web created when an app is installed (see Figure 10-13).

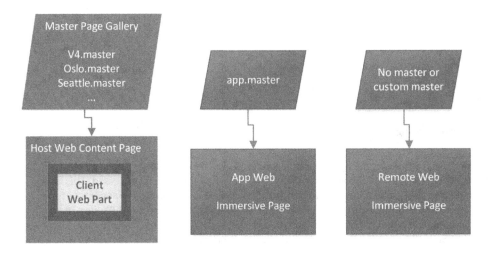

Figure 10-13. *Master pages for app pages*

The default app master page contains the standard SharePoint menus, site and page titles, and a main content area, as shown in Figure 10-14.

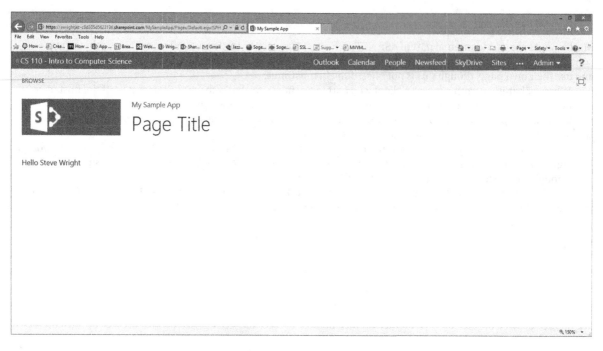

Figure 10-14. *Default app web page using the app.master page*

The ASPX files created by Visual Studio for the app web project refer to `~masterurl/default.master` as the master page. This string is replaced with the site's master page (`app.master`) when the page is processed. This is the same way that any other SharePoint page's master pages are handled. If you need to customize the `app.master` for your app, you can copy the file into your project and change the master page declaration in your ASPX files. In an on-premise installation of SharePoint 2013 server, this file can be found in `C:\Program Files\Common Files\Microsoft Shared\Web Server Extensions\15\TEMPLATE\GLOBAL\app.master`.

■ **Note** It is also possible to replace the default app web's site template by customizing the `ONET.xml` file that comes with SharePoint. This file is in `C:\Program Files\Common Files\Microsoft Shared\Web Server Extensions\15 \TEMPLATE\SiteTemplates\App\Xml\Onet.xml` by default.

The `app.master` master page only applies to immersive pages hosted in the app web. If an immersive page is hosted in a remote web site (auto- or provider-hosted), then the master page used is not one of SharePoint's master pages. Instead, it resides in the remote ASP.NET site. Creating remote pages that conform to the brand of the host site requires additional tools. These tools are described next.

Host Site Styles

In most cases, an app for SharePoint should try to look like a native part of the host site. The first step is to adopt the same cascading style sheet used by the host site. The app.master page performs this adaptation automatically for app web pages. For remote web pages and client web part pages, the host's style sheet is not linked by default.

SharePoint 2013 contains a special HTTP request handler to allow remote pages to retrieve the style sheet of the host site. In the /_layouts/15 folder of every SharePoint site, is a file called defaultcss.ashx. When a request is made against this URL, the site's default CSS file is returned. Therefore, if a remote web site knows the URL of the host site, it can link to its style sheet using a URL like this:

```
<HostWebUrl>/_layouts/15/defaultcss.ashx
```

The link for this style sheet can be added in either client- or server-side code. For client web part pages, the Visual Studio template contains the following client-side JavaScript:

```
<script type="text/javascript">
    (function () {
        var hostUrl = '';
        if (document.URL.indexOf('?') != -1) {
            var params = document.URL.split('?')[1].split('&');
            for (var i = 0; i < params.length; i++) {
                var p = decodeURIComponent(params[i]);
                if (/^SPHostUrl=/i.test(p)) {
                    hostUrl = p.split('=')[1];
                    document.write('<link rel="stylesheet" href="'
                                        + hostUrl + '/_layouts/15/defaultcss.ashx" />');
                    break;
                }
            }
        }
        if (hostUrl == '') {
            document.write('<link rel="stylesheet"
                                href="/_layouts/15/1033/styles/themable/corev15.css" />');
        }
    })();
</script>
```

This script parses the query string to find the SPHostUrl value. It then writes a link for the style sheet to the current document. If the host URL is not found, the SharePoint server's default style sheet is used instead.

The Chrome Control

Including the host web's style sheet will help the app's pages conform to the fonts and colors of the host web, but there is often a need to create a standard page header as well. SharePoint 2013 includes the *chrome control* for this purpose.

The chrome control is a client-side component that presents a page header that inherits much of its appearance from the host web and can be customized to fit the needs of the app. Figure 10-15 depicts the chrome control using the default SharePoint style sheet. There are several standard components on the header.

- **Breadcrumbs**—In the upper-left corner of the page is a breadcrumb control that allows the user to go back to the host site.

- **Settings Menu**—The Settings menu (the gear icon) contains a list of custom menu items for the app.

- **Help Page**—The app can specify a help page for the chrome control to present to the user.

- **App Icon**—The app's icon is displayed.

- **App Title**—The app's title is displayed.

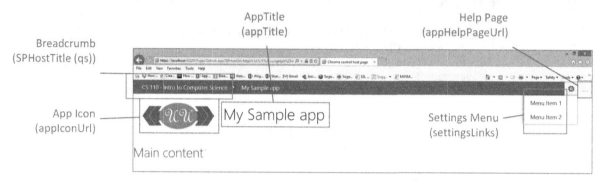

Figure 10-15. The chrome control

The chrome control obtains its appearance from multiple sources. Some of these are set automatically by SharePoint, and others require the developer's attention.

The control automatically includes the host web's style sheet, as described in the previous section. This style sheet is applied to the entire page, so when the chrome control is present on an app page, there is no need to link it separately as described before.

The next set of automatic configurations come from the browser's query string. There are four values that the chrome control will pick up automatically. The SPHostUrl and SPAppWebUrl provide the URLs for the host and app webs, respectively. Since these are included in the {StandardTokens} provided to most apps in the app manifest, there is no need to do anything special. The SPHostTitle value can be included in the URL using the {HostTitle} substitution in the app's manifest. The SPLanguage should be included in localized apps to provide the current language.

Most of the customization of the chrome control typically comes from the options provided to the control by the developer. Here is a list of the most common options:

- **appHelpPageUrl**—Sets the URL for the help page. A JavaScript callback can be specified by using appHelpPageOnClick instead.

- **appIconUrl**—Sets the URL to use for the app's icon.

■ **Hint**   If you wish to use the host site's icon, add SPHostLogoUrl={HostLogoUrl} to the URL in the app's manifest. This will include the icon's URL in the query string. It can then be easily retrieved and used to set this option.

- **appStartPage**—Sets the app's start page link in the breadcrumb.

- **appTitle**—Sets the app's title.

- **appWebUrl**—Overrides the default app web URL.

- **onCssLoaded**—Provides a JavaScript callback that is called once the control has been loaded. This is often used to make the control (or page) visible only after the CSS styles have been applied.

- **settingsLinks**—Creates links in the settings menu.

The options are set by creating a JavaScript variable containing them as properties. The overall process for displaying the chrome control happens in this sequence. Remember that the chrome control is a client-side component, so all of these steps occur within the web browser.

1. A <DIV> tag is declared somewhere on the page where the chrome is to appear. This tag must have an id attribute that will be used later.

2. The web page loads the JavaScript library containing the chrome control from SharePoint.

```
$.getScript(hosturl + "/_layouts/15/SP.UI.Controls.debug.js", onScriptLoaded)
```

3. When the script finishes loading, an option variable is created that sets the desired options for the control.

```
var queryString = document.URL.split("?")[1];

var options = {
    "appIconUrl": decodeURIComponent(getQueryStringParameter("SPHostLogoUrl")),
    "appTitle": "My Sample app",
    "appHelpPageUrl": "Help.html?" + queryString,
    "settingsLinks": [
        {
            "linkUrl": "MenuItem1.html?" + queryString,
            "displayName": "Menu Item 1"
        },
        {
            "linkUrl": "MenuItem2.html?" + queryString,
            "displayName": "Menu Item 2"
        }
    ],
    "onCssLoaded": "chromeLoaded()"
};
```

4. Finally, the control is created passing in the ID of the <DIV> tag and the options variable.

```
var nav = new SP.UI.Controls.Navigation("chrome_ctrl_id", options);
nav.setVisible(true);
```

The chrome control also supports a way to create the control declaratively. Instead of creating a JavaScript variable containing the control's options, the options are declared directly on the <DIV> tag. The SharePoint library is designed to recognize the data-ms-control attribute on the tag. When the attribute is seen, the library will automatically create the control using the options from the data-ms-options attribute.

```
<div
    id="chrome_ctrl_id"
    data-ms-control="SP.UI.Controls.Navigation"
    data-ms-options=
        '{
            "appHelpPageUrl" : "Help.html",
            "appIconUrl" : "MyIcon.png",
            "appTitle" : "My Sample App",
            "settingsLinks" : [
                {
                    "linkUrl" : "menu1.html",
                    "displayName" : "Menu Item 1"
                },
                {
                    "linkUrl" : "menu2.html",
                    "displayName" : "Menu Item 2"
                }
            ]
        }'>
</div>
```

The advantage of using the declarative method is that there is no need for custom JavaScript coding. The drawback is that without JavaScript running in the browser, there is no way to dynamically configure any of the options. While the values from the query string will still be processed by the control, none of the option values can be changed at runtime. For example, the URLs for the settingsLinks in this example will not contain the tokens that were passed to this page.

Adapting to the Browser

The final aspect of the user experience that we will examine involves adapting to the way the web browser interacts with the SharePoint site and the apps that are exposed through it. Specifically, we will look at maintaining the context of our app and localizing the user interface for different languages.

The Redirect Page

When a user first navigates to a SharePoint app, the normal sequence involves a hidden step. When the user clicks on the app's tile or link, the URL used does not go directly to the app's default page. If you hover over such a link, you will see that the URL provided looks like this:

```
<HostUrl>/_layouts/15/appredirect.aspx?instance_id=<GUID>
```

The appredirect.aspx page referenced here is SharePoint's standard redirect page.

The *redirect page* is provided by SharePoint to act as a traffic director for the apps installed in SharePoint. The GUID provided is that of the installed instance of the app. This ID allows SharePoint to generate the correct standard tokens and context token for the app. The redirect page then forwards the user to the app's default page. The redirect page can also be used by the app itself to retrieve its context information as needed. In this case, the redirect page sends the user's web browser to whatever URL was specified by the app.

In the examples in this book, we have been careful to include the {StandardTokens} on all of our pages. This ensures that a current context token is always provided when the app is launched. However, there are situations where this may not be sufficient. For example, a user could store a reference to a page within your app in their browser's favorites or bookmarks. They might alter or remove the query string parameters or leave them intact. Either way, the context token that was posted to the page will be lost. We need a graceful way to reestablish a proper context when this happens.

A common technique is to store the context token in a browser cookie for client-side use or a session state manager on the ASP.NET web server. This allows the app to function without reposting the context token or passing around a long query string. The only problem is that all tokens have a defined lifetime and will expire eventually. The app needs to be ready to respond when this happens. This is where the redirect page comes in.

When an app determines that it needs a new context token, it can request one using the redirect page. On a remote web site page using server-side code, the TokenHelper utility is provided to help format the required URL.

```
string redirectPageUrl =
    TokenHelper.GetAppContextTokenRequestUrl(
            appWebUrl, Server.UrlEncode(Request.Url.ToString()))
Response.Redirect(redirectPageUrl);
```

This code supplies the URL of the context site in SharePoint and the URL to which the context token should be returned. This is normally the current page, but it does not have to be. The URL used to retrieve the context token is somewhat different (see Figure 10-16) from the one used to launch the app.

```
<SharePointSite>/_layouts/15/appredirect.aspx?client_id=<GUID>&redirect_uri=<EncodedURL>
```

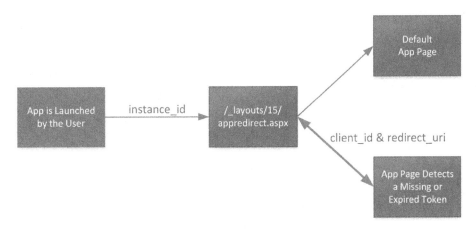

Figure 10-16. *The redirect page*

The client_id parameter contains the client ID from the remote web site that was registered with SharePoint. This can be found in the web.config file for the site. The redirect_uri is a URL-encoded string containing the address of the page to which the context token should be returned.

Because the logic for detecting an expired or missing token and retrieving a new one will be needed on any page that wants to use the context token, it is a good idea to create a utility for this. The utility can encapsulate the storage of the token and simplify refreshing it. This allows a simple procedure call to check that the current token is valid and perform the redirection if necessary.

Language Support

If your app is going to be distributed through the Office Store, it may be used on sites that use various languages. A high-quality app will contain localized text for many of these languages. SharePoint apps support the use of resource (RESX) files to provide multi-language support.

An app for SharePoint project contains two different types of resource files. One set is for localizing components in the host site (app properties, client web parts, custom actions, etc.) and the other is for items that appear on the app web (lists, content types, etc.).

Localizing Host Web Artifacts

To localize items that appear on the host web, we need to add support for our selected locales to the app manifest file, as shown in Figure 10-17. For the first locale added, two files will be added. The first is called `Resources.resx`. This is the "invariant" resource file that contains all of the default, non-localized strings for the app. The second is called `Resources.LL-CC.resx` where `LL` is the language and `CC` is the culture for the file. In our example, we have added support for generic English along with US English, Canadian English, and the Canadian dialect of French. You can see each of these files in the solution explorer to the left.

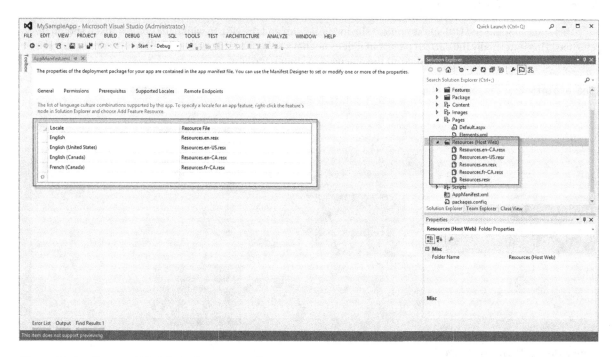

Figure 10-17. *Supported locales in the app manifest*

These resource files are no different from those used anywhere on the Microsoft platform. The most common approach is to create all of the required entries in the invariable file (`Resources.resx`) and then copy the contents into the other files. Then, someone with an appropriate command of the language can update the strings as needed for that language and culture.

These resources are used by referencing them in the XML files that define components in the host web. This includes the app manifest, client web parts, and custom actions. As shown in Figure 10-18, the resource is referred to using the `$Resources:<name>` notation used for the app's title. This value will be substituted with the correct version of the string at runtime.

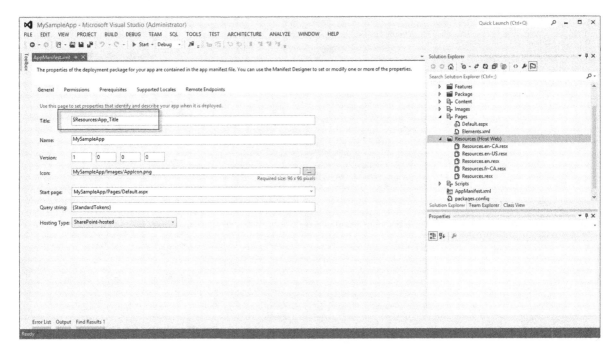

Figure 10-18. *Setting the app title with a resource*

■ **Warning**   Unfortunately, Visual Studio's support of these resource files is incomplete. While the tools in VS will help you declare and create these resource files, they do not connect them properly to the feature in the app package. The MSDN article at `http://msdn.microsoft.com/en-us/library/fp179919.aspx` describes how to work around this and even provides a tool to automate the work-around. Hopefully, Microsoft will fix this in an early service pack.

Localizing App Web Artifacts

To localize items that appear on the app web, the process is somewhat different. Resource files are still used, but they are created differently in the project.

Instead of opening the app manifest file, we need to file the feature in the app project. The default name for this feature is `Feature1`. To add a locale to the app web, we right-click on the feature node and select the Add feature resource… option.

Again, we have added an invariant resource file along with files for generic English, English-US, English-Canada, and French-Canada (see Figure 10-19). These resources can now be used to localize labels in the app's lists, fields, content types, and so on.

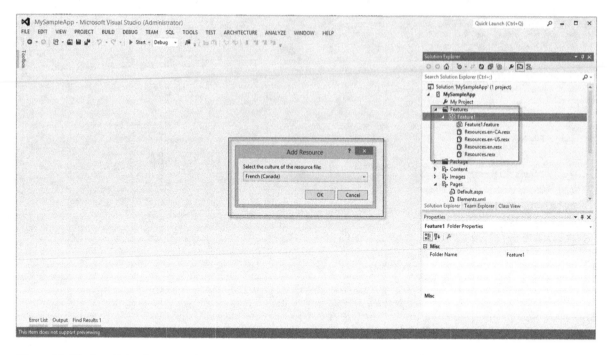

Figure 10-19. *Localizing the app web*

Localizing the Rest of the App

So far, we have discussed localizing the strings associated with the host web and app web components. There are two more important areas of the app that have yet to be addressed. These are the client-side JavaScripts and any web pages hosted in a remote web site. These components lay outside of SharePoint's control and, therefore, cannot be localized by SharePoint using resource files.

There are good resources online detailing techniques for localizing JavaScript and ASP.NET web applications. The same techniques apply to these types of components when they are associated with a SharePoint app. The following links provide guidance for localizing these elements.

- ASP.NET Web Sites

    - http://msdn.microsoft.com/en-us/library/fw69ke6f(v=vs.90).aspx

    - http://www.codeproject.com/Articles/15313/Globalization-and-localization-demystified-in-ASP

- JavaScript

    - http://jqfaq.com/how-to-internationalize-your-pages-using-jquery/

    - https://github.com/jquery/globalize

Summary

In this chapter, we explored the options we have available for creating a rich user experience in our SharePoint apps. Client web parts (a.k.a. app parts) were described and explored through our Classroom Online app. We implemented custom actions that add commands to the host web's menus. We examined the tools available for controlling the presentation of our app's components using master pages, the chrome control, and the host web site's style settings. Finally, we discussed the ways in which a SharePoint app can adapt to the environment it runs in including multi-language and multi-browser support.

In Chapter 11, we will begin exploring some of the other services provided by SharePoint and how we can leverage them in our apps. Specifically, the next chapter will deal with accessing SharePoint's search service and using that information in our apps.

CHAPTER 11

■ ■ ■

Accessing SharePoint Search

In this chapter, we will begin looking at the information available from other services within SharePoint. The first of these services is SharePoint Search. We will explore the ways in which apps for SharePoint can leverage the search infrastructure in SharePoint. In this chapter, we will go over the following points:

- We will review the new search architecture and related features in SharePoint 2013 Server and SharePoint Online.

- We will discuss how the search service organizes and sorts search results to provide the most relevant results to the user.

- We will describe how results from various search services can be combined in our apps.

- We will look at the different types of suggestions a search service can provide to improve the user's search experience.

- We will walk through examples of using the APIs available in SharePoint 2013 to access the search service.

Understanding SharePoint 2013 Search

SharePoint's search capabilities have been evolving rapidly over the last few releases of the product. In SharePoint 2013, Microsoft has simplified the choices and enabled a more unified approach to search.

As a developer of apps for SharePoint, the configuration of the SharePoint Search service in the host site is not under your control. An app makes a call into the SharePoint Search service and performs some action with the results. However, it is still important to understand how the search engine works in order to get the most out of it. In this section, we will discuss the concepts and architecture of SharePoint 2013 Search, but we will not discuss administration of the service since this is outside of our purview.

In SharePoint 2010, there were three distinct search engines available for use with SharePoint. The SharePoint 2010 Foundation Search provided a bare-bones ability to catalog and search the contents of the web sites in SharePoint Foundation. This search engine was easy to configure and use. Its abilities were very limited in terms of scale, performance, and flexibility. Foundation Search was only appropriate for small, department-level deployments.

SharePoint 2010 Server included an improved version of the SharePoint 2007 (MOSS) search engine called Enterprise Search. Enterprise Search was designed to manage medium to large search applications. It had the ability to index many different types of data sources beyond SharePoint sites including Exchange, file shares, Lotus Notes, and more. The strength of Enterprise Search centered on its deep integration with the SharePoint Server platform. It was relatively easy to administer and it provided sufficient performance and flexibility for most organizations.

The third search option for SharePoint 2010 was based on the FAST Search engine acquired by Microsoft when it purchased Fast Search & Transfer ASA in April of 2008. The FAST Search engine was packaged as an upgrade to SharePoint 2010 Server. FAST was designed to support massive scale search applications. It provided excellent performance and flexibility to organizations, whether they were using SharePoint Server or another platform. This additional capability came at a relatively high price compared to Enterprise Search, which was part of the standard SharePoint 2010 Server. It was also more difficult to administer and integrate with SharePoint.

In SharePoint 2013, Microsoft combined Enterprise Search and FAST Search into one search engine. This search engine improves on the best features of both products.

- SharePoint 2013 search is deeply integrated with SharePoint.

- The scalability of FAST has been retained.

- The sophisticated content-ranking models of both products are included.

- The search engine has a greater ability to discover the structure of unstructured data from many content sources.

- The user interface components used to retrieve search results are more modular and configurable.

- The crawling components have been improved to provide more efficient and customizable data collection.

- The search service now has the ability to proactively monitor and report on its own health.

The architecture of SharePoint 2013 Search is broken down into a set of independent components, as shown in Figure 11-1. Each of these components performs a specific task and can be configured and deployed to provide maximum scale and deployment.

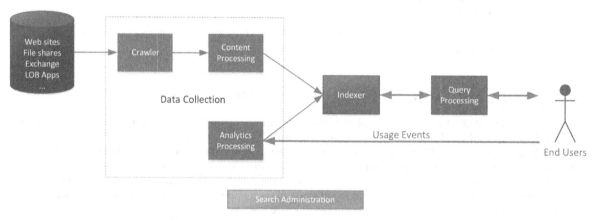

Figure 11-1. *SharePoint 2013 Search architecture*

- *Crawler*—These components scan various data sources across the network. The crawler is responsible for reading the content and extracting important metadata to enable the content to be searched.

- *Content Processing*—This service receives the source data retrieved by the crawler and maps it to metadata and properties within the SharePoint Server platform. This data is combined and passed to the indexer.

- *Analytics Processing*—This component tracks how users interact with the contents displayed in search results and combines this with the incoming data collected by the crawlers and content processing. This allows the SharePoint Search service to provide more targeted results based on how the endusers actually use search. This component constantly reconfigures the search engine to better match the needs of the organization.

- *Indexer*—The indexer service receives all of the data collected by the content and analytical processing components. It creates a set of databases and index files that are used to process end-user queries. These indexes are copied and updated automatically as needed throughout the server farm. This component is also responsible for performing data lookups for the query processing component.

- *Query Processing*—This is the component that interacts with the enduser. When a user submits a search request, the query processor analyzes the query to determine the optimal way to satisfy the request. The query processor then requests search results from the indexer or external result sources, as necessary.

- *Search Administration*—Administering search can be very complex. There are numerous content sources, query rules, and other settings to be configured. This component is responsible for managing all of this information and deploying the other service components that make up the search infrastructure.

Controlling Rank and Relevance

The key to making search results useful is being able to provide the most relevant results first. Any search may result in hundreds or thousands of possible matches. It is the search engine's job to promote the items that the user is most interested in to the top of the page. Most users will not go past the first page of a search result list because if what they are looking for is not present on the first page, it probably is not on the others either.

SharePoint 2013 normally sorts search results by relevance or rank scores. A rank score is a number calculated by the search engine. These scores are produced by a set of ranking models in SharePoint. SharePoint 2013 contains new and improved models from the original FAST and Enterprise Search engines. These models can be applied to web site content, intranets, people searches, or any other type of search supported by SharePoint.

A ranking model is made up of a series of rank stages. Each stage evaluates a set of rank features. Rank features correspond to attributes of the source content that are evaluated in various ways. The result is to increase or decrease the relevance score for the source item. Here are some common rank features used in SharePoint's search models:

- Do the query terms match the indexed data retrieved form the source, including the item's title and content?

- Does the query match the item's metadata, including properties such as author, date modified, file type, etc.

- Is the item linked from other content that is also relevant to the query?

- Are the query terms present in prominent locations such as titles and headers?

- Does this item tend to be clicked by endusers when it appears in search results?

A key new feature in SharePoint 2013 for improving search result relevance is the analytical processing component. This component receives event data from the user interface that provides valuable feedback to the SharePointSearch service. The content is analyzed for patterns, such as how data is connected using links and metadata and which items are clicked most often in search results. This data is fed back into the indexer to provide input to the ranking models. It can be used to generate search recommendations and deep links into content areas that are accessed frequently. This data is also used to compile search usage reports that administrators can use to improve search effectiveness as well.

Another relevance feature is the ability to create query rules. These rules define a condition and an action that are evaluated by the search engine while processing queries. A condition might include the inclusion of certain keywords or file type filters. When a rule's condition is met, the corresponding action is triggered. The action might promote the item to the promoted results block at the top of the results page, add an entirely new result block, or simply adjust the item's rank score within the current result set.

Federating Search Results

When performing a search in SharePoint, we are typically retrieving results only from the local SharePoint server farm. Much of this content may reside outside of the farm but the crawling, indexing, and analyzing of this content is still performed within SharePoint. There are times, however, when it is preferable to access search results that originate from outside of SharePoint altogether.

In SharePoint 2010 Enterprise Search, this type of search was performed using a federated location. The FAST engine also had the ability to bring in results from outside its own index. Search federation is enabled by configuring the SharePoint Search engine with the location of another search engine from which to retrieve results. Reasons for federating search instead of controlling the search index locally include the content's size or complexity, or simply the desire to offload the storage and processing of search queries to another service.

SharePoint 2010 also contained the concept of search scopes. Scopes were used to limit the results retrieved from a search. For example, a scope called "Company Intranet" might limit its results to items that originated on the local SharePoint farm.

SharePoint 2013 Search replaces the concepts of federated locations and scopes with the higher-level concept of result sources. A result source defines two primary properties for the search.

- *Query Transform*—This defines the conditions to be met in order for a result item to be returned from the query. The transform serves the same purpose as a search scope in SharePoint 2010.

- *Source Location*—This is the location or service from which the query processor will retrieve the search results. SharePoint 2013 result sources can retrieve results from the local SharePoint index, a SharePoint index on another server farm, Microsoft Exchange server, or an OpenSearch server.

OPENSEARCH

OpenSearch is an open specification (`http://www.opensearch.org`) that allows a client application to retrieve search results from various search engines in a standard format.

This is the same technology that enables web browsers such as Internet Explorer to connect to different search engines.SharePoint uses this interface to connect to external search providers.

OpenSearch is supported by all of the major search engines including Google, Bing, and Yahoo. OpenSearch also provides access to custom application platforms such as Wikipedia, Twitter, eBay, and IMDb.

Each result source included in a search produces a result block in the result page, as shown in Figure 11-2. These are subsets of items returned from each result source. A SharePoint app can receive these blocks and render them using whatever presentation is desired.

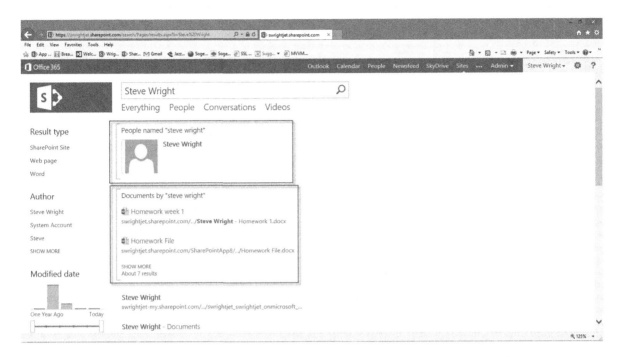

Figure 11-2. *Search result blocks*

Refining a Search

A common problem in all search engines is the tendency to find large numbers of marginally relevant results. In some cases, this is due to ambiguous or poorly constructed queries. It may also be the case that the user simply doesn't know what they are looking for. A good way to help users navigate the results of a search is to allow them to *refine* their search.

Search refinement refers to allowing a user to "search within a search." Once a user has completed a search and the first page of results has been displayed, the user may find that there are additional search terms that they might have added to focus the results. To help the user make these connections, SharePoint 2013 Search provides for the creation of *search refiners*.

When a search query is submitted to the SharePoint 2013 Search engine, a set of refiners can be specified as part of the request. These might include commonly searched metadata fields, such as author, editor, or company division. When the search results are returned, each of the refiners that was included will be provided with a list of likely refinements based on the data in the index. These search terms are typically presented alongside the search results, as shown in Figure 11-3. This tells the user what types of information are available in which they might be interested. Clicking one of the refinement links resubmits the search query with the additional refinement.

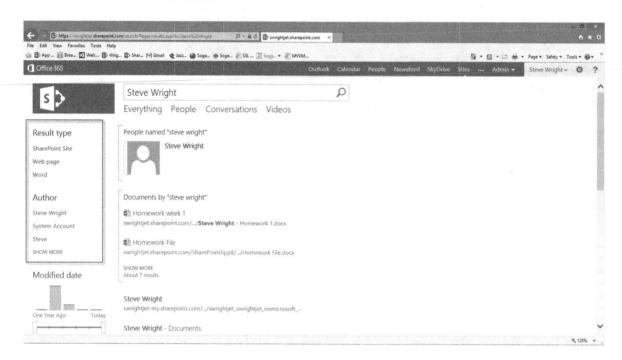

Figure 11-3. *Search refiners list*

The most useful refiners are those that users are most likely to select. Initially, a set of default refiners is used. Once the system has been in use for a period of time, the search usage reports provided by SharePoint 2013 can be used to provide more customized refiners based on how the users are using search.

Managing Query Suggestions

The last major feature area we will examine is using *query suggestions*. Also known as *search suggestions*, query suggestions provide the user with feedback on how to submit searches more effectively. These suggestions are based on the searches and behaviors of other users as well as the current user. There are different types of search suggestions of which to be aware.

- **Pre-Query Suggestions**—These suggestions appear before a query is submitted. As the user types, they appear in a drop-down list below the search box. The user can scroll down to or click on one of the suggested searches to immediately perform that search.

- **Post-Query Suggestions**—As the name implies, these suggestions are received after a search has been performed. They are presented as a suggested alternative to the search just performed. They usually appear just beneath the search box and start with a phrase such as "Did you mean ..." or "Try searching for ..."

- **Query Suggestions**—In this context, a query suggestion is a pre- or post-query suggestion that is based on the successful searches performed by all of the users of the system.

- **Personal Suggestions**—These are similar to query suggestions except that they are based on the searches performed specifically by the current user. If a user frequently uses the same search terms, the system will begin suggesting those terms to speed up the search process. For example, after writing 11 chapters of a book on apps for SharePoint, I find that when I type "sh" into a search box, it immediately suggests "SharePoint 2013 apps" as a search term.

Query suggestions are generated by SharePoint on a daily basis for each content area and result source. Each of these may produce very different suggestions, depending on the behavior of the users when they are visiting that content.

A successful search is one that has returned a result link that the user has then clicked on. By default, SharePoint will not begin suggesting a query until after it has been successful at least six times. On a large SharePoint farm with hundreds or thousands of users, it may take a great deal more successful searches to generate a suggestion for a query. A search that the user performs and then does not select a result is considered a failed search and does not trigger suggestions.

Configuring SharePoint 2013 to provide search suggestions is beyond the scope of this discussion. Here are some of the options available:

- Search suggestions must be *enabled* on the site before they will appear. An app that requests suggestions on a site where they are disabled will not receive them.

- Administrators can manually *add phrases* that always apply to all of the content areas for the server farm.

- Administrators can manually *exclude phrases* from ever being suggested.

Using Search APIs

In this section, we will explore how to access the search service from our SharePoint apps. As in any other area of the platform, our apps are restricted to using client-side APIs. The search service interface has a small number of objects with a large number of parameters and options.

The REST Search API

The first API we will look at is the REST/OData interface. This interface is called using the same techniques we saw in Chapter 7. The SharePoint 2013 Search service uses the following three primary REST access points:

- **/_api/search/query**—The query access point is used to retrieve search results from SharePoint using an HTTP GET request. The search terms and parameters (see Table 11-1) are included in the query string.

Table 11-1. *query and postquery REST Parameters*

Parameter Name	Description	Example
querytext	This contains the query terms for which the search will be performed. This string uses Keyword Query Language (KQL) format, which supports complex Boolean conditions.	?querytext=SharePoint
startrow	This tells the search service where in the results to begin returning records. This is generally used for paging.	?querytext=SharePoint&startrow=21
rowlimit	This limits the number of results to return. Used in conjunction with startrow for paging.	?querytext=SharePoint&startrow=41 &rowlimit=20
selectproperties	This specifies which managed properties should be included in the results. This saves network traffic by limiting the number of fields returned.	?querytext=SharePoint &selectproperties='Title, Path,Author'

(continued)

Table 11-1. (*continued*)

Parameter Name	Description	Example
refiners	This specifies which managed properties should be returned as potential refiners.	?querytext=SharePoint &refiners='Author,fileExtension'
refinementfilters	This is used when a request is using a refiner to filter inside a query. This value uses the Filter Query Language (FQL) for its format.	?querytext=SharePoint &refinementfilters= 'fileExtension:equals("docx")'

- **/_api/search/postquery**—The postquery access point is used to retrieve search results from SharePoint using an HTTP POST request. The search terms and parameters (see Table 11-1) are included in the body of the request. This interface is generally used when the number of parameters or characters to be passed to the search service is very large. This can make use of query string parameters impractical or impossible.

- **/_api/search/suggestion**—The suggestion access point is used to retrieve query suggestions from the search service. This interface handles both pre- and post-query suggestions. This interface uses an HTTP GET and passes its parameters (see Table 11-2) on the query string.

Table 11-2. *suggestion REST Parameters*

Parameter Name	Description	Example
querytext	This contains the query terms for which the search will be performed. This string uses Keyword Query Language (KQL) format, which supports complex Boolean conditions.	?querytext=SharePoint
iNumberOfQuerySuggestions	This controls the number of query suggestions returned by the search service.	?querytext=SharePoint &iNumberOfQuerySuggestions=8
iNumberOfResultSuggestions	This controls the number of personal suggestions returned by the search service.	?querytext=SharePoint &iNumberOfResultSuggestions=8
fPreQuerySuggestions	This controls whether the search service returns pre- or post-query suggestions. True requests pre-query suggestions. Use false for post-query.	?querytext=SharePoint &fPreQuerySuggestions=true

The following tables detail some of the most commonly used parameters on each of these REST interfaces. Note that these lists are far from complete and more documentation is available on MSDN.

Now we will walk through an exercise that uses the SharePoint Search REST API to query for content on our site.

EXERCISE 11-1

In this exercise, we will build a sample app that displays a simple search box, performs a search, and displays the results. Our sample will be a SharePoint-hosted app that displays the search interface and results on its default page.

1. Open Visual Studio 2012.

2. Create a new SharePoint app project using the C# project template.

3. Name the project ClientSearchSample and set it to use SharePoint-hosting.

4. Open the AppManifest.xml file in the editor.

5. Click on the Permissions tab.

6. Add a request for the QueryAsUserIgnoreAppPrincipal permission at the Search scope, as shown in Figure 11-4.

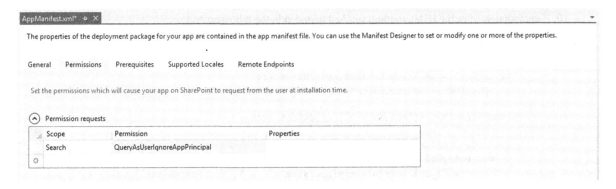

Figure 11-4. Request search permission in the AppManifest.xml file

7. Save and close AppManifest.xml.

■ **Caution** It is easy to forget to add this permission to the app manifest. If you do, the search API will still function, but there will be no results returned. If you ever find that your search seems to be working but it does not return any results, this may be your problem.

---

8. Open the Default.aspx page in the editor.

9. Replace the contents of the PlaceHolderMain content control with the following markup:

```
<div>
    Search:
    <input id="txtSearchText" type="text" size="40" />
    <input id="cmdSearch" type="button" value="Start Search" />
</div>
```

```
<p>
    <table border="1" cellpadding="5" cellspacing="0">
        <thead>
            <tr>
                <th>Title</th>
                <th>Author</th>
                <th>Last Update</th>
                <th>URL</th>
            </tr>
        </thead>
        <tbody id="results">
        </tbody>
    </table>
</p>
```

This is the HTML user interface for the page. It includes a text box for entering search terms, a button to execute the search, and a table for displaying the results. Now we will add the client-side script to make the search request and display the results.

10. Immediately after the HTML markup you just added, add the following code:

```
<script type="text/javascript">
    var results;
    var context = SP.ClientContext.get_current();
    var appWebURL = decodeURIComponent(getQueryStringParameter('SPAppWebUrl'));

    $(function () { $("#cmdSearch").click(onSearch); });

    function onSearch() {
        var queryUrl = appWebURL
            + "/_api/search/query?querytext='" + $("#txtSearchText").val() + "'";

        // No tokens or digests required since we are in the app web.
        $.ajax(
            {
                url: queryUrl,
                method: "GET",
                headers: { "Accept": "application/json; odata=verbose" },
                success: onQuerySuccess,
                error: onQueryFail
            }
        );
    }
```

This code attaches an event handler to the HTML button. When the button is clicked, a REST call is made to the app web's query access point. The only parameter being passed is the querytext.

11. Continue by adding the following code:

```
function onQuerySuccess(data) {
    $("#results").empty();

    if (data.d.query.PrimaryQueryResult != null)
        $.each(data.d.query.PrimaryQueryResult.RelevantResults.Table.Rows.results
            , function () {
                $("#results").append('<tr>');
                $("#results").append('<td>' + getValue(this, 'Title') + '</td>');
                $("#results").append('<td>' + getValue(this, 'Author') + '</td>');
                $("#results").append('<td>' + getValue(this, 'Write') + '</td>');
                $("#results").append('<td>' + getValue(this, 'Path') + '</td>');
                $("#results").append('</tr>');
            });
}

function getValue(row, fldName) {
    var ret = null;
    $.each(row.Cells.results, function () {
        if (this.Key == fldName) {
            ret = this.Value;
        }
    });
    return ret;
}
```

This code receives the results of the search in the data returned to the callback routine. The structure returned is fairly complex because this same object is designed to return any kind of results that may be requested. In our case, we are interested in the PrimaryQueryResults. In REST, the properties of the item found are returned as a series of name-value pairs called Cells.

12. Complete the code block by including these additional routines:

```
function onQueryFail(sender, args) {
    $("#results").append('Query failed. Error:' + args.get_message());
}

function getQueryStringParameter(urlParameterKey) {
    var params = document.URL.split('?')[1].split('&');
    var strParams = '';
    for (var i = 0; i < params.length; i = i + 1) {
        var singleParam = params[i].split('=');
        if (singleParam[0] == urlParameterKey)
            return decodeURIComponent(singleParam[1]);
    }
}
</script>
```

13. Press F5 to run the app.

14. Type a search term that will produce results in your environment.

15. Click the Start Search button and the results will be displayed (see Figure 11-5).

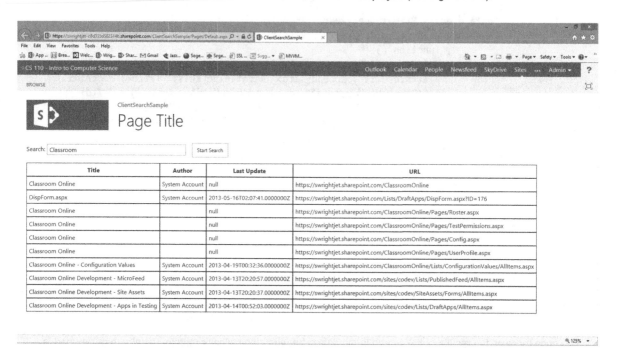

Figure 11-5. *Sample search results page*

Our sample app is complete. For additional practice, try implementing paging of results or creating refiners.

The JavaScript CSOM Search API

Instead of using the REST interface, we can also use the client-side object model for JavaScript. The CSOM for search resides in a separate script file from the sp.js and sp.core.js files we have used before. This file is called sp.search.js and should be included on any page that will call search from the CSOM.

The CSOM search interface is centered on two primary objects: KeywordQuery and SearchExecutor.

The KeywordQuery object provides a structure in which to define the parameters and options of the search to be performed. Some of the most commonlyused parameters are as follows:

- **QueryText**—This is the search term in Keyword Query Language (KQL) syntax.

- **StartRow** *and* **RowLimit**—These control paging and the size of the result set.

- **Refiners** *and* **RefinementFilters**—Used to retrieve and use refiners in queries.

- **SelectProperties**—A list of managed properties to retrieve from SharePoint.

If these parameters seem familiar it is because they are the same ones passed to the REST API. The two interfaces are virtually identical aside from being encapsulated in endpoints or objects, respectively.

The SearchExecutor object wraps the query in a request that is submitted to SharePoint. To submit a KeywordQuery object to SharePoint, it is passed into the executeQuery method on a SearchExecutor object. Remember that all calls in JavaScript CSOM are asynchronous. Therefore, after calling executeQuery, it is still necessary to send the request batch to SharePoint by calling executeQueryAsync on the client context object.

EXERCISE 11-2

In this exercise, we modify our sample app to perform the same search using the JavaScript CSOM instead of REST.

1. Open Visual Studio 2012.

2. Open the ClientSearchSample app created in the previous exercise.

3. Open the Default.aspx page in the editor.

4. Add the following markup at the end of the PlaceHolderAdditionalPageHead content control to include the CSOM script objects in the page:

```
<script type="text/javascript" src="/_layouts/15/sp.search.js"></script>
```

5. Replace the contents of the JavaScript code block with the following:

```
var results;
var context = SP.ClientContext.get_current();

$(function () { $("#cmdSearch").click(onSearch); });

function onSearch() {
    var query = new Microsoft.SharePoint.Client.Search.Query.KeywordQuery(context);
    query.set_queryText($("#txtSearchText").val());

    var exec = new Microsoft.SharePoint.Client.Search.Query.SearchExecutor(context);
    results = exec.executeQuery(query);

    context.executeQueryAsync(onQuerySuccess, onQueryFail)
}

function onQuerySuccess() {
    $("#results").empty();

    $.each(results.m_value.ResultTables[0].ResultRows, function () {
        $("#results").append('<tr>');
        $("#results").append('<td>' + this.Title + '</td>');
        $("#results").append('<td>' + this.Author + '</td>');
        $("#results").append('<td>' + this.Write + '</td>');
        $("#results").append('<td>' + this.Path + '</td>');
        $("#results").append('</tr>');
    });
}
```

```
function onQueryFail(sender, args) {
    $("#results").append('Query failed. Error:' + args.get_message());
}
```

This code has the same structure as the REST-based solution. However, instead of calling a REST endpoint, we are creating KeywordQuery and SearchExecutor script objects. When these are processed by calling executeQueryAsync, the request is sent to the search service.

Note that the data returned is much simpler that in the REST scenario. The properties are returned as JavaScript expando properties instead of as name-value pairs.

6. Press F5 to run the app.

7. Type a search term that will produce results in your environment.

8. Click the Start Search button and the results will be displayed, just as they were in the previous exercise.

Search queries in JavaScript CSOM involve less complex structures that the REST API, but there is no real difference in the functionality available.

The Managed .NET Search API

When performing searches from server-side code, such as in a remote web, we will need to use the .NET Search CSOM objects. This can be accessed by adding a reference to the Microsoft.SharePoint.Client.Search assembly. By default, you can find this assembly in the following location:

C:\Program Files\Common Files\Microsoft Shared\Web Server Extensions\15\ISAPI\Microsoft.SharePoint. Client.Search.dll

The .NET-managed CSOM objects are structured almost identically to the JavaScript CSOM objects. The KeywordQuery and SearchExecutor objects are used to process search requests. The only important difference is that it is possible to execute queries synchronously in server-side code using executeQuery instead of executeQueryAsync.

EXERCISE 11-3

In this exercise, we modify our sample app to perform the search using server-side code in a remote web site. Since our app is currently SharePoint-hosted, we will first need to convert it to an auto-hosted app.

1. Open Visual Studio 2012.

2. Open the ClientSearchSample app created in the previous exercise.

3. Create a new project, in the same solution, named ClientSearchSampleWeb.

4. Select the Visual C# ASP.NET Empty Web Application template, as shown in Figure 11-6.

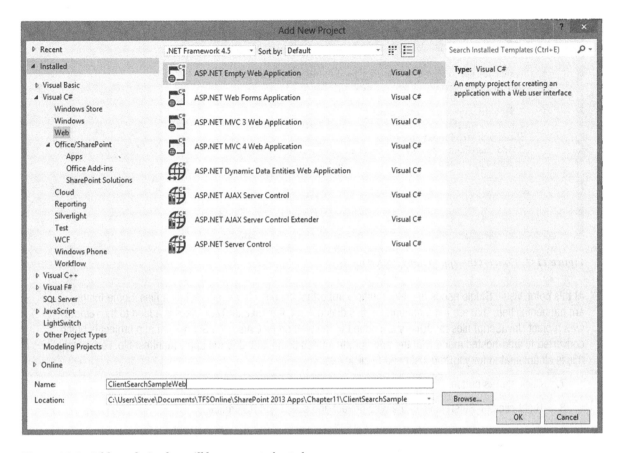

Figure 11-6. Add a web site that will become auto-hosted

■ **Caution**   Be sure to select Add ➤ New Project…, not Add ➤ New Web Site…. These use different project templates. We want an ASP.NET site designed to be packaged and deployed, not one to run directly on our server.

---

5.   Open the Properties panel (F4) for the ClientSearchSample project.

6.   For the Web Project property, select ClientSearchSampleWeb. The dialog shown in Figure 11-7 will appear.

Figure 11-7. *Convert the app to auto-hosted mode*

At this point, Visual Studio needs to make multiple important changes to the app solution files. Some things are happening here that are not mentioned in this dialog. First, the TokenHelper class is added to the remote web project. JavaScript files for JQuery are added to the web project. Also, the SharePoint app project is being converted to auto-hosted mode with the appropriate entries being added to the app's manifest file. Fortunately, this is all automated for you. You just need to click Yes.

7. Click the Yes button.

8. Right-click on References in the web project and select Add Reference....

9. The assembly needed is not listed in the standard listing. Use the Browse option to select C:\Program Files\Common Files\Microsoft Shared\Web Server Extensions\15\ ISAPI\Microsoft. SharePoint.Client.Search.dll and add it as a reference.

10. Add a page to the web project using the Add ➤ Web Form option.

11. Name the page Default and click OK. The Default.aspx file opens automatically.

12. Replace the contents of the <form> tag with the following markup:

```
<div>
    Search:
    <asp:TextBox ID="txtSearchText" runat="server" Width="200px"></asp:TextBox>
    <asp:Button ID="cmdSearch" runat="server"
                Text="Start Search" OnClick="cmdSearch_Click" />
</div>
<p>
    <asp:GridView ID="grd" runat="server" CellPadding="4"
                ForeColor="#333333" GridLines="None"
                AutoGenerateColumns="True" Width="100%">
        <AlternatingRowStyle BackColor="White" />
        <EditRowStyle BackColor="#2461BF" />
        <FooterStyle BackColor="#507CD1" Font-Bold="True" ForeColor="White" />
        <HeaderStyle BackColor="#507CD1" Font-Bold="True" ForeColor="White" />
        <PagerStyle BackColor="#2461BF" ForeColor="White" HorizontalAlign="Center" />
```

```
            <RowStyle BackColor="#EFF3FB" />
            <SelectedRowStyle BackColor="#D1DDF1" Font-Bold="True" ForeColor="#333333" />
            <SortedAscendingCellStyle BackColor="#F5F7FB" />
            <SortedAscendingHeaderStyle BackColor="#6D95E1" />
            <SortedDescendingCellStyle BackColor="#E9EBEF" />
            <SortedDescendingHeaderStyle BackColor="#4870BE" />
        </asp:GridView>
    </p>
    <asp:HiddenField ID="SPAppToken" runat="server" />
```

This markup provides the same user interface we saw before, except that it is now using server controls.

The hidden field, SPAppToken, is important whenever we wish to do CSOM or REST calls when the page is posted back instead of on the initial post. This field will contain the context token that we were passed in the initial request, allowing the TokenHelper to find it during a postback.

13. Save and close the Default.aspx file.

14. Open the Default.aspx.cs code-behind file.

15. Add these using statements to the top of the file:

```
using System.Data;
using Microsoft.SharePoint.Client;
using Microsoft.SharePoint.Client.Search;
using Microsoft.SharePoint.Client.Search.Query;
```

16. Add the following code to the Page_Load routine. This copies the context token to the hidden field when the page is initially posted.

```
if (!this.IsPostBack)
SPAppToken.Value = TokenHelper.GetContextTokenFromRequest(Page.Request);
```

17. Add this code beneath the Page_Load routine:

```
protected void cmdSearch_Click(object sender, EventArgs e)
{
    string contextToken = SPAppToken.Value;
    string hostWeb = Page.Request["SPHostUrl"];

    ClientContext ctx =
            TokenHelper.GetClientContextWithContextToken(
                        hostWeb, contextToken, Request.Url.Authority);

    KeywordQuery keywordQuery = new KeywordQuery(ctx);
    keywordQuery.QueryText = txtSearchText.Text;

    SearchExecutor searchExecutor = new SearchExecutor(ctx);
    ClientResult<ResultTableCollection> results =
                                searchExecutor.ExecuteQuery(keywordQuery);
    ctx.ExecuteQuery();
```

This code begins by creating a client context using the context token stored in the SPAppToken hidden field on the page. The search executor will return a collection of result tables.

18. Add the following code next:

```
DataTable dt = new DataTable();
dt.Columns.Add("Title");
dt.Columns.Add("Author");
dt.Columns.Add("Last Update");
dt.Columns.Add("URL");

if (results.Value.Count > 0)
    foreach (Dictionary<String, Object> resultRow in results.Value[0].ResultRows)
        dt.Rows.Add(resultRow["Title"], resultRow["Author"],
resultRow["Write"], resultRow["Path"]);

    grd.DataSource = dt;
    grd.DataBind();
}
```

The result item properties are returned as a dictionary of name-value pairs. The code builds a DataTable object containing the fields to be displayed and binds this to the data grid control.

19. Save and close the Default.aspx.cs file.

20. Open the AppManifest.xml file in the app project.

21. Select ClientSearchSampleWeb/Default.aspx as the app's Start Page.

22. Save and close the AppManifest.xml file.

23. Press F5 to run the app.

24. Type a search term that will produce results in your environment.

25. Click the Start Search button and the results will be displayed, just as they were in the previous exercise.

In this case, the page will not have the site's headers because we did not include the chrome control on our page.

Summary

In this chapter, we began exploring some of the services provided by SharePoint beyond storing and retrieving web content and documents. Specifically, in this chapter, we accessed the SharePoint Search service and used search results in our apps. We reviewed the relevant APIs in SharePoint 2013 and built sample apps that accessed the search service.

In the next chapter, we will move on to another major service provided by SharePoint: social computing. Social computing refers to all of the features in SharePoint 2013 that provide support for social features like MySites, likes, follows, and tagging. We will look at how we can leverage these services to create social-aware apps for SharePoint.

CHAPTER 12

■ ■ ■

Using SharePoint's Social Features

Social computing has become a cornerstone of modern collaboration solutions. SharePoint has always focused on collaboration using team sites. In SharePoint 2010, Microsoft introduced the ability to use social tagging with content. SharePoint 2013 adds whole new layers to the social experience. This chapter will describe the social features of the SharePoint 2013 platform and how these features can be leveraged by app developers. In this chapter, we will go over the following points:

- We will explore the relationships between social computing data elements, including posts, activities, feeds, likes, mentions, and tags.

- We will create the foundation for our organization's online community by deploying community sites and portals.

- We will describe the concepts of membership and reputation.

- We will look at SharePoint's My Site feature and its role in social computing.

- We will share documents and sites with other users in the organization.

- We will examine the APIs provided by SharePoint for querying and updating social information in the enterprise.

SharePoint 2013's social computing platform exists in two different dimensions of functionality. Vertically, there are new types of content areas, such as communities and extended My Sites that can be deployed specifically to support social collaboration. Horizontally, social computing concepts such as likes, follows, sharing, and feeds have been woven into almost every area of the product. This makes social computing ubiquitous throughout the platform.

Social Computing Basics

Social computing is one of those terms for which everyone has a slightly different definition. We know it when we see it, but we cannot always define it. When asked to explain social computing, many people start by naming web sites such as Facebook, Twitter, or eBay. Others describe the types of things you do on those sites. This is where the parts of English grammar begin to break down. Verbs such as "like," "follow," or "mention" tend to be used as nouns, as in "I gave him a like for that post." Nouns such as "friend" often end up being used as verbs, as in "I friended him on Facebook." Then, of course, there are the terms that get created from nowhere such as "unfriend" and "unlike."

SharePoint 2013 uses most of the same social computing terms used elsewhere on the Internet. In this section, we will describe these terms as they are used and organized within SharePoint.

The basic unit of social data in SharePoint is the *activity*. Activities are user-generated or system-generated data items that SharePoint stores, organizes, and presents. Collectively, this type of data is referred to as a *microblog* and the act of creating this content is `microblogging`. Activities are usually created by an action taken by a user. The system, and apps for SharePoint, can also create activities. There are several categories of activities that SharePoint can track.

- **Document Activities**—These activities occur when a document is created or modified in some way.

- **Microblogging**—These activities are created for posts/replies, likes, mentions, and hashtags.

- **Following**—These activities are created when a user chooses to follow a particular person or content item. This is similar to "friending" someone on other platforms.

- **User Activities**—These are generated for user actions such as updating a user profile or creating a posting.

When a user creates a new activity in SharePoint, it is usually in the form of a post. A *post* is a single message created and submitted to the system by a user. Posts can be *replied* to by other users. The content of a post can contain text, links, videos, and pictures. Posts are intended to be relatively short, so they can only be up to 512 characters long.

The relationship between posts, replies, and activities can be confusing. All activities are either a post or a reply. User-created posts create normal threads. Replies to a post are associated with the thread for that post. There are other types of threads called *reference threads*. Reference threads are created when users add social context without intentionally creating a new thread. The posts in these threads reference other posts and replies based on a like, mention, or tag created by a user.

The combination of an initial post, or *root post*, and all of the replies that arise from that post are referred to as a *thread*. Threads are also sometimes referred to as *conversations*. A single thread can contain up to 100 posts and replies. Threads are then grouped together into *feeds*. There are various types of feeds that contain different sets of threads depending on where the threads came from and what the user has asked to see. Users normally view their own feeds on their My Site. Other sites, such as community sites, can also contain feeds.

- **Newsfeed**—This type of feed contains a combination of threads from all of the areas of the system in which the user has indicated an interest. The most recent activity is typically presented first.

- **Personal**—This feed includes the posts and activities created by the current user.

- **Timeline**—This type of feed is similar to the newsfeed except that it is designed to display the content that is most relevant based on the user's social network.

- **Likes**—This feeds includes activities associated with the items that the current user has indicated that they like within the system.

Once a user has created a post, other users can *like* that post. Liking something adds it to a list of *liked* items and adds the current user as a *liker* of the item. If the user later decides they do not want to like the item anymore, they can *unlike* it. SharePoint provides feedback throughout its user interface about likes. Have I liked this item already? How many people have liked it?

Hashtags have become very common on sites like Facebook and Twitter. A hashtag (#tag) is a short word or phrase that is added to a post to indicate that the item is relevant to a certain topic. Other users can then view all of the activity related to that tag. For example, in November 2012, Microsoft held the SharePoint Conference 2012. As a way to generate buzz and help attendees find content, the conference organizers requested that when blogging or tweeting about the conference, attendees should include the hashtag #SPC2012. There are any number of other uses for hashtags, including political campaigns, marketing, and any other topic. Hashtags are very convenient because there is no overhead in creating one. You simply add a hash symbol (or pound sign) in front of the relevant word in the post and the system takes care of the rest.

In a similar vein to hashtags are mentions. *Mentions* are added to a post by placing a @ (at) symbol in front of a person's name. If the system recognizes the user specified, the post is automatically associated with that person. This allows a user to find all of the posts in which they, or someone they know, have been mentioned. Remember, hashtags are for topics. Mentions are for people.

For example, Figure 12-1 contains a post that has both a mention and a hashtag.

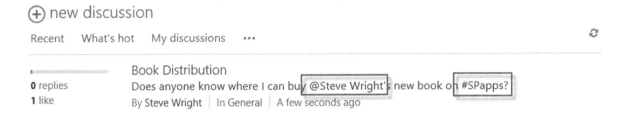

Figure 12-1. *A post with a hashtag and a mention*

When a user finds a person, site, document, or hashtag that they want to monitor on an ongoing basis, they can *follow* it. Doing so makes the user a *follower* of a *followed* item. Following people and content is the primary way to customize the social features of SharePoint to deliver the information in which you are most interested. The news and timeline feeds look for activities by people or about content that the current user has followed. Following is a passive way of gathering information automatically as it is added to the system. It is also possible for users to see who is following them or some piece of content they are working on.

When a user follows a site, they subscribe to a special type of feed called a *site feed*. A site feed is the series of activities generated by the users of a site. This feed is then made available to the user through their own newsfeed. Site feeds are automatically security trimmed. This means that users who subscribe to a site feed, but do not have access to a certain piece of content, will not see the activities associated with that item. The site feed feature can be enabled or disabled on a team site. It is enabled by default.

To understand how activities are published, it is helpful to consider where they are stored and how they are accessed. When a user performs an activity, it is stored in the content database containing that user's My Site. As a result, any user that doesn't have a My Site cannot use SharePoint's social features. When an activity is generated against an item in a site with a site feed, either by a user action or the system, that activity is saved in the site's content database. This means that an activity that a user performs against a site may be written to both locations. Finally, all activities are written to the *Distributed Cache*. The distributed cache is a service application in SharePoint 2013 that manages the storage and distribution of social computing activities within the server farm.

In summary, the social computing features of SharePoint 2013 provide users with the ability to stay up-to-date on the topics and events that are the most interest to them. Through likes and follows, users provide the system with information about those interests. Posts and replies allow users to create quick, lightweight discussions about specific content items, people, or other topics. Feeds organize all of this information and provide access to it without losing the context in which it was created. Later in this chapter, we will see how our apps for SharePoint can use client APIs to create and query this information and integrate it into the user experience for our application.

Building Communities in SharePoint

SharePoint 2013 introduces two new site templates designed from the ground up for social-style collaboration. These are the Community Site and the Community Portal. In the following sections, we will describe the contents and uses of these sites.

Using Community Sites

SharePoint has always provided collaboration site templates. These include team sites, document collaboration sites, and meeting workspaces. More recently, SharePoint has begun including more social-oriented templates for blogs and wikis. In 2013, SharePoint includes a new type of team site called the *Community Site* template (see Figure 12-2).

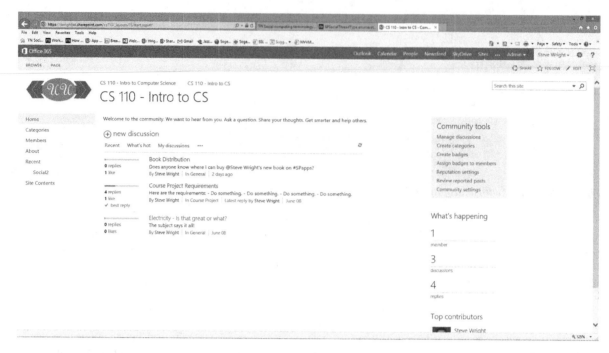

Figure 12-2. *The Community Site template*

A community site is designed as an online forum for social computing. It has many of the features present in both discussion lists and blogs in SharePoint 2010. The primary features of the community site template are as follows:

- A community site provides a single feed, or set of discussions, around a particular topic with built-in moderation functionality.

- A community site provides a membership system for tracking users that are interested in the topic of the community.

- Users can categorize discussions for quick reference.

- Users that join a community after it has existed for some time will immediately gain access to the community's history of discussions.

- Members can build their reputation within the community, based on their posts and replies, receiving likes from other members and being awarded recognition from the moderator in the form of *best answers* or *badges*.

- Members can report inappropriate posts to the moderator who can then review the post and take the appropriate action.

The Community Site template contains several pages that provide the forum user experience. The pages included are as follows:

- **Home**—The home page for the site contains web parts for the main discussion feed, What's Happening, Top Contributors, and management tools for authorized users.

- **Categories**—This page allows the site owner to create categories that members can use to organize content.

- **Members**—This page provides a listing of the community's members along with their reputation information and badges.

- **About**—The site owner or moderator can use this page to describe the purpose of the community.

The site template also includes lists for storing discussions, categories, badges, and member reputation information.

Community sites depend on various SharePoint services in order to function effectively. The User Profile service is used to manage profiles for the members of the site and provide integration with the users' personal feeds. This service also allows users that are following members of the community to discover the community through their own feeds. The Managed Metadata service is used to integrate with hashtags across the feeds in the farm. Community sites also leverage the Search service to help drive users to the community.

Community sites support a custom set of user roles that are implemented using SharePoint's normal permission system. Each type of user is allowed to perform certain actions within the site depending on the configuration of the site.

Like all SharePoint sites, community sites have one or more *site owners*. The owners of the site are specified when the site is created. These users are responsible for configuring the site, adding members to the site, and assigning roles to those members. Site owners have Full Control permissions in the site.

Moderators have rights very similar to site owners in that they can read and write any content in the site. They also have the right to moderate discussions by creating discussion categories and handling potentially inappropriate posts from members. Moderators can create and assign badges to users, mark featured discussions, and mark replies as Best Answers. Moderators set and enforce the rules of conduct for the community.

Members are registered users on the site. They can add, update, and delete content as well as acquire reputation through their contributions to the site. Members cannot make changes to site pages, discussion categories, or the membership list of the site. Members can be self-registered or registered by a moderator, depending on how the site is configured. Members have "contributor" rights on the site in addition to the ability to acquire reputation within the community.

Visitors are non-members of the community that can be given read-only access to the site. A visitor can also request to become a member. The site can be configured to accept new members automatically or only by acceptance by a moderator or site owner.

A community site can be created in one of two ways. The most straightforward means is to simply create a new site using the Community Site template. This template can be used at either the site collection or sub-web level. This procedure is most appropriate when you wish to create a new community that has no existing content. In cases where there already exists a community of users in a team site and a set of content relevant to the community, it may be preferable to add the features of a community site to the existing team site. In SharePoint 2013, we can do this using site features.

The social functionality of the community site template is enabled using a set of site-level features as described in the following list. These can be enabled individually using the Manage site features option on the Site Settings page.

- **Wiki Page Home Page**—This feature converts the site's home page into a SharePoint Wiki page.

- **Site Feed**—This feature adds a site feed to the site. The threads for this feed are housed in a new list called MicroFeed.

- **Following Content**—This feature enables the ability for authorized users to follow sites and documents.

- **Community Site Feature**—This feature adds the community site lists and pages to the site. This includes support for categories, reputation, discussions, and members.

Only the last of these features, the community site feature, is unique to community sites. The other three features are enabled for all team sites by default. This is why team sites always allow following and site feeds by default.

Using the Community Portal

Community sites provide a template for deploying social networking sites across the organization. Once deployed, users need a means of finding the communities that interest them or meet their information needs. This is the purpose for the other social computing site template introduced in SharePoint 2013, the Community Portal.

The Community Portal site collection template is a search-based user interface designed to help users discover new communities to join (see Figure 12-3). Because this page uses SharePoint's Search service, it is automatically security trimmed to show only those communities to which the current user is a member or has the permissions to access as a visitor.

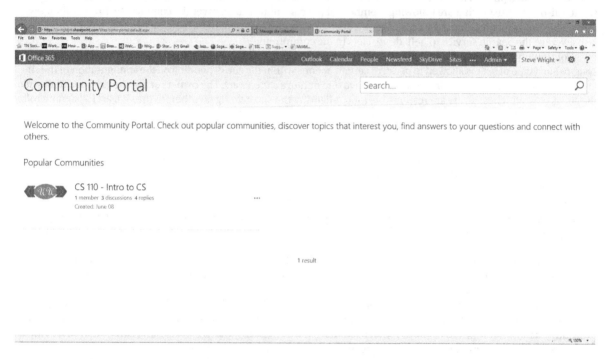

Figure 12-3. *The Community Portal template*

Each SharePoint tenant can have only one Community Portal. This site acts as a social collaboration hub for the organization. The portal can be modified and expanded to include any guidance or additional features the organization needs to drive social collaboration throughout the enterprise.

By default, this site contains one search page that returns a list of the most popular community sites. A community's popularity is based on the number of posts, replies, and members the site has. Posts are weighted more heavily than members or replies. This causes more active sites to be listed higher in the results.

Sharing Content

In previous versions of SharePoint, if one user wanted to grant access for an item to another user, they had to open the permissions page for the item, break the permission inheritance for the item, if necessary, and then assign the desired permissions to the desired user. This required that the user understand how SharePoint's permission hierarchy works to some extent and how to access the various administrative pages necessary to assign permissions. It also required the user granting permissions to notify the user receiving permissions that they now have access to the content.

SharePoint 2013 introduces a new way to assign permissions. *Sharing* allows users to explicitly invite individuals or groups to access content. A user with the necessary permissions can share a document or a site with another user or group of users simply by clicking on the Share link (see Figure 12-4).

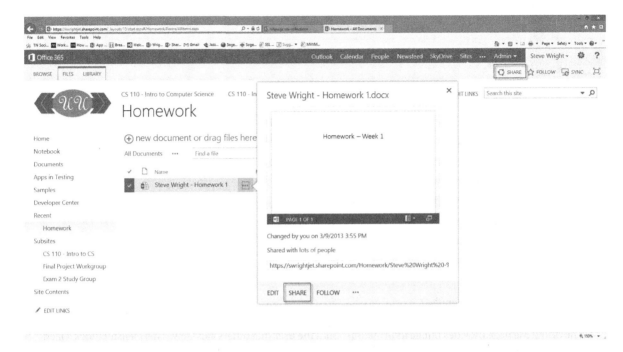

Figure 12-4. *Sharing a document or a site*

When the item is shared, an e-mail notifying the recipient of the sharing can be sent automatically. The share request indicates whether the user should be given read-only or read-write access, and the SharePoint permissions required are also set. The document or site that has been shared retains a list of shares that can be revoked later if needed.

Sharing is similar to following in that it associates users with content items. The difference is that sharing is about assigning permissions to the content. Following is only allowed for content that the user is already able to access.

Understanding My Sites

My Sites in SharePoint are personal workspaces for each user. A user's My Site is generated automatically when the user first attempts to access their profile or About Me page. My Sites are an optional feature that can be turned off on a server farm.

My Sites have been a part of the SharePoint platform for several releases. In each release, they are enhanced to encompass a more complete user work area. In SharePoint 2010, My Sites served as a central repository for shared and private documents owned by an individual user. A user's My Site allowed them to promote their activities and interests to the rest of the organization through the People Search feature. My Sites were extended to include a basic content tagging and note board functionality.

In SharePoint 2013, the basic purpose of My Sites has been preserved but the user experience is now very different (see Figure 12-5). Like the rest of SharePoint's 2013 user interface, this site is designed to have a very clean, uncluttered appearance. The primary pages are the Newsfeed page, containing the user's personal feeds, and the About Me page.

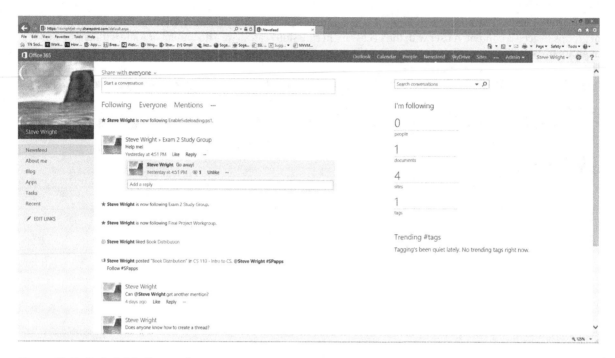

Figure 12-5. *Default My Site template*

The About Me page provides public information about the user that others can view. This page includes a feed of the user's activities, followed interests, and contact information. This page, like all pages in the My Site, can be customized to share as much or as little information as desired.

As in previous versions, My Sites in 2013 can store both private and shared documents. This feature is referred to as *SkyDrive Pro* after Microsoft's cloud-based file storage service known as SkyDrive. Unlike in SharePoint 2010, there are not separate document libraries for private and shared documents. Instead, users share documents in their SkyDrive using document sharing as described in the previous section. A document is always kept private until explicitly shared by the user. The SkyDrive also provides a centralized list of the documents that the current user is following.

■ **Caution** Be careful not confuse SkyDrive Pro with Microsoft's SkyDrive service. As Microsoft tends to do, they have gone a little overboard with the marketing hype in this case. Microsoft SkyDrive (http://skydrive.live.com) is a cloud-based file storage service provided by Microsoft. SkyDrive files are uploaded to Microsoft-hosted servers and can be retrieved, updated, or shared by authorized users anywhere on the Internet. SkyDrive Pro is just a marketing moniker for the document library that resides in each user's My Site by default. SkyDrive Pro files are stored in your own SharePoint farm, not Microsoft SkyDrive.

My Sites are organized somewhat differently from other types of sites. While a My Site appears to the user to be a single web site devoted only to the user, there are parts of the site that are actually shared between users. When My Sites are deployed in the server farm or tenant, a single root My Site is created that contains certain common pages, such as the Newsfeed and About Me. This is called the *My Site Host* site collection and must reside at the root of a SharePoint web application. Each user is then given an individual site collection under the host in which to store their documents, sub-sites, and other personal content.

There are some specific URLs that are useful to be aware of when navigating a user's My Site programmatically. In the following list `<MySiteHost>` refers to the URL of the My Site Host collection. This often takes the form of `http://my.domain.com`.

- My Site Host Collection
    - Newsfeed—`<MySiteHost>/default.aspx`
    - About Me (Current User)—`<MySiteHost>/person.aspx`
    - About Me (Other User)—`<MySiteHost>/person.aspx?accountname=useraccount`
- Personal Site Collection
    - URL—`<MySiteHost>/personal/useraccount`
    - My Documents—`<MySiteHost>/personal/useraccount/documents`
    - Followed Content—`<MySiteHost>/personal/useraccount/social`
    - Microfeed—`<MySiteHost>/personal/useraccount/microfeed`

The personal site collection sometimes uses my instead of `personal`. This is configurable. The `useraccount` in the site's path includes the full account and domain name encoded as a valid URL string. For example, `MyAccount@MyDomain.com` would appear as `myaccount_mydomain_com`.

The SharePoint 2013 Social API

The APIs for accessing social computing information in SharePoint 2013 are generally divided into three parts: feeds, follows, and sharing. Each of these areas has a manager object that is used to access the rest of the interface in that area. The three social APIs we will describe briefly in this section are the .NET Framework CSOM, JavaScript CSOM, and the REST API.

The managed .NET client-side object model libraries provide social data interfaces through the following assemblies. They can be found in the 15-hive directory with the default path of `C:\Program Files\Common Files\Microsoft Shared\Web Server Extensions\15\ISAPI`. These assemblies should be added as references in Visual Studio.

- *Assembly*—`Microsoft.SharePoint.Client.UserProfiles.dll`
    - *Namespace*—`Microsoft.SharePoint.Client.Social`
    - **SocialFeedManager**—Reads and writes to social feeds.
    - **SocialFollowingManager**—Manages following and followers.
- *Assembly*—`Microsoft.SharePoint.Client.dll`
    - *Namespace*—`Microsoft.SharePoint.Client.Sharing`
    - **DocumentSharingManager**—Shares documents with other users.

For JavaScript client code, social functionality is accessed using these JSOM libraries:

- *Script File*—`sp.userprofiles.js`
    - *Namespace*—`SP.Social`
    - **SocialFeedManager**—Reads and writes to social feeds.
    - **SocialFollowingManager**—Manages following and followers.

- *Script File*—sp.js

  - *Namespace*—SP.Sharing

    - **DocumentSharingManager**—Shares documents with other users.

The SharePoint 2013 REST contains access points for accessing social data. These are /_api/social.feed and /_api/social.following for feeds and follows, respectively.

In order to use any of these APIs, the app must request and be granted the required app permissions. There are three app permissions (see Table 12-1) for social computing of which to be aware.

Table 12-1. *Social App Permissions*

Permission	URI	Description
Social Core	`http://sharepoint/social/core`	Requests permission to access the current user's following information and basic metadata. This permission can only be granted on a My Site.
Social Microfeed	`http://sharepoint/social/microfeed`	Requests permission to access the content of a site's microblog. This permission can be granted on a user's My Site or a team site with a site feed.
Social Tenant (a.k.a. User Profiles)	`http://sharepoint/social/tenant`	This permission grants access to user profile information for all users.

In addition to the social permissions described in Table 12-1, the app must request content permissions to the content area affected by the use of these permissions. For example, if an app needs to access a site feed, it will need both the Social Microfeed permission and content permissions for that site. An app that requests permissions for all content within a tenant never needs to request the Social Core or Social Microfeed permissions, as they are granted automatically as part of the tenancy.

DEBUGGING MY SITE APPS

Working with apps that access social data in the current user's My Site is a little different than the other types of apps we have looked at before.

In order to access the user's social feed data, the app needs to have access to their microblog and their following information. To do this, the app must have the Social Core and Social Microfeed app permissions. The Social Core permission can only be granted on a user's My Site. The Social Microfeed permission can apply to a My Site or a team site with a site feed. As a result, running this type of app in Visual Studio against a developer site will always fail with a SocialListNotFound exception.

Of course, the app could request tenant-wide access but that may not be needed or desired. In order to test this type of app, the developer has the following options:

- Deploy the app to the App Catalog and test it using the developer's My Site. This option does not allow for interactive debugging with Visual Studio.

- During testing, replace the Social Core and Social Microfeed permissions with the Social Tenant and Content Tenant permissions. This will allow Visual Studio to debug the app from within a developer site.

- Configure Visual Studio to deploy the app directly to the developer's My Site for debugging. By default, this will fail because the My Site site template does not permit side-loading of apps as a developer site does. In order to make this option work, side-loading must be enabled.

For more information on enabling side-loading in a SharePoint site, see `http://social.msdn.microsoft.com/Forums/en-US/appsforsharepoint/thread/f30dcfa5-5047-4bd5-9f02-9feb7e935eec`. The process involves turning on a hidden site feature in the site against which you wish to test.

Managing Feeds

In this section, we will begin looking in some detail at the objects in the social API that allow apps to access social data. First, we will examine feeds.

There are a series of objects that expose feed data in SharePoint. The entry point for these objects is the `SocialFeedManager` (see Figure 12-6).

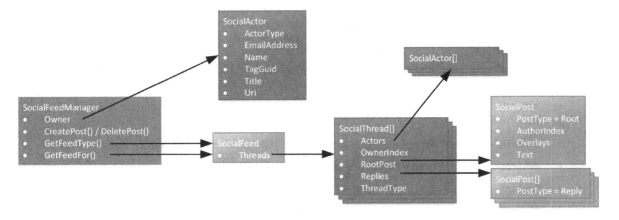

Figure 12-6. *Social feed object model*

■ **Note**   In discussing the social API object model, we will use the .NET Framework CSOM object names for simplicity. The JavaScript and REST interfaces also contain similar objects.

The `SocialFeedManager` object provides access to the feed-handling functionality in SharePoint. This includes querying feeds and managing posts. Here are some of the more important members of this class:

- **Owner**—This property is a `SocialActor` object representing the current user.

- **CreatePost/DeletePost**—These methods are used to create or remove posts. The post can create new threads on the user's microfeed or a site feed. It can also be a reply to an existing thread.

- **GetAllLikers**—Retrieves a list of `SocialActors` that have liked a particular post or reply.

- **GetFeed(type,options)**—Gets a feed based on the currently logged in user.

- **GetFeedFor(actorID,options)**—Gets the feed for a specified user or site.

- **GetMentions(clearUnreadMentions,options)**—Gets a feed containing threads that contain a mention for the current user.

- **LikePost/UnlikePost**—Adds or removes a like for the current user from a specified post.

When working with feeds in SharePoint, it is important to remember the difference between a social feed and a microfeed. A *microfeed* is a set of threads associated with a particular actor and stored in a particular location. For example, a user's My Site contains the user's microfeed. A team site may, or may not, contain a microfeed that is called a site feed.

A *social feed* object is more like the result from a database query. It may contain threads from a single source, such as a site feed, or it may contain threads from many sources. The GetFeed() method's first parameter is a type parameter that specifies which type of SocialFeed object to retrieve for the current user. These object types are as follows:

- *Personal Feed*—Based on the posts in the current user's microblog.

- *News & Timeline Feeds*—Contain threads from the current user and from people, documents, and sites that the user is following.

- *Likes*—Based on posts that the user has liked, where ever they may reside.

- *Everyone*—Based on posts throughout the organization.

The SocialFeed object has a Threads property that returns an array of SocialThread objects. This array contains the threads that meet the query criteria used to create the feed. The SocialThread object has these primary properties:

- **Actors**—This is an array of SocialActor objects. Other objects in the thread will refer to this list by index to indicate actions by a particular actor.

- **OwnerIndex**—This is the index in the Actors property that contains the owner of the thread.

- **RootPost**—This is the initial post that created the thread.

- **Replies**—This is an array of posting that are replies to the RootPost.

- **ThreadType**—This indicates the nature of the thread.

The ThreadType property describes the thread in terms of what the thread is used to represent. A thread that contains a post and replies intentionally created by users will have a type of Normal. The other types are called reference threads. A reference thread is generated by the system when a user creates a like, mention, reply, or tag in a post. This type of thread links the current thread to the post that contains the reference. The SocialThread object's PostReference property contains a pointer to the referenced post. In most cases, when reading threads from SharePoint, we will want to limit our results to normal threads only.

The RootPost and Replies properties of the SocialThread return the posts associated with the thread. These are represented by the SocialPost object which has the following properties:

- **AuthorIndex**—This is the index in the thread's Actors list that contains the actor that created the post.

- **PostType**—This indicates whether the post is a root post or a reply.

- **Text**—This contains the text of the post.

- *Overlays*—This is an array of social data items that are embedded in the post. These can be links, mentions, or tags. This data allows the post to be rendered with social-aware links to the appropriate content or feeds. See the last section in this chapter, "Creating Posts, Mentions, Tags, and Links," for more information about social data items.

The last social feed object is the `SocialActor` class. This is a structure that references a user, document, site, or tag within SharePoint. These items are referenced by the other objects in the model to identify items that are owners, authors, subjects, or containers of content.

- **ActorType**—User, Document, Site, or Tag.

- **Name**—Display name of the actor.

- **AccountName**—Fully qualified account name when ActorType=User.

- **Email**—User e-mail address when ActorType=User.

- **TagGuid**—Unique identifier for the tag when ActorType=Tag.

- **Title**—Document or site title when ActorType=Document or ActorType=Site.

- **Uri**—URL of the site or document when ActorType=Document or ActorType=Site.

■ **Note** The GUID for a tag must be retrieved from the SharePoint Managed Metadata service before it can be used in a `SocialActor`. The MSDN article at `http://msdn.microsoft.com/en-us/library/jj163217.aspx#bk_getTagGuid` describes how to query this information. We will cover the taxonomy interface briefly in Chapter 13.

EXERCISE 12-1

In this exercise, we will create a simple ASP.NET page that will dump the contents of various types of feeds in our environment. Specifically, we will dump the current user's personal feed, a site feed, and the personal feed of another user. We will use the .NET Framework CSOM in server-side code in an auto-hosted web site.

1. Open Visual Studio 2012.

2. Create a new auto-hosted SharePoint App, called `SocialDump`, using the C# project template.

3. Open the `AppManifest.xml` file in the editor.

4. Click on the Permissions tab.

5. Add the Full Control permission for the Tenant scope, labeled "Content Tenant."

6. Add the Full Control permission for the User Profiles (Social) scope, labeled "Social Tenant."

Note that we are only giving such broad permissions to our app so that we can avoid enabling side-loading while maintaining the ability to debug the app.

7. Save and close the `AppManifest.xml` file.

8. Add a reference to the `Microsoft.SharePoint.Client.UserProfiles` assembly in the `SocialDumpWeb` project.

9. Open the `Default.apx.cs` code-behind file in the editor.

10. Add these using statements to the top of the file:

```
using Microsoft.SharePoint.Client;
using Microsoft.SharePoint.Client.Social;
```

11. Replace the template code in Page_Load() with this C# code:

```
protected void Page_Load(object sender, EventArgs e)
{
    var contextToken = TokenHelper.GetContextTokenFromRequest(Page.Request);
    var hostWeb = Page.Request["SPHostUrl"];

    using (var clientContext =
                TokenHelper.GetClientContextWithContextToken(
                            hostWeb, contextToken, Request.Url.Authority))
    {
        SocialFeedManager feedManager = new SocialFeedManager(clientContext);
        clientContext.Load(feedManager);

        SocialFeedOptions feedOptions = new SocialFeedOptions();
        ClientResult<SocialFeed> personalFeed =
            feedManager.GetFeed(SocialFeedType.Personal, feedOptions);
        ClientResult<SocialFeed> siteFeed =
            feedManager.GetFeedFor("https://asite.mydomain.com/apath", feedOptions);
        ClientResult<SocialFeed> userFeed =
            feedManager.GetFeedFor("auser@mydomain.com", feedOptions);
        clientContext.ExecuteQuery();

        DumpFeed("Personal Feed", personalFeed.Value);
        DumpFeed("Site Feed", siteFeed.Value);
        DumpFeed("User Feed", userFeed.Value);
    }
}
```

This code creates a SocialFeedManager object using the current context and then uses it to retrieve three different feeds.

12. Update the site URL with the URL of a site in your environment that has an active site feed.

13. Update the user e-mail address in this code with the address of a valid user with a My Site in your tenancy.

14. Add the following C# code to the page class:

```
private void DumpFeed(string hdr, SocialFeed feed)
{
    Response.Write("<h2>" + hdr+ "</h2>");
    foreach (SocialThread thread in feed.Threads)
    {
        Response.Write(
            string.Format("{0} (Owner = {1})<ul>",
                        thread.ThreadType,
                        FormatActor(thread.Actors[thread.OwnerIndex])));
```

```
Response.Write(
    string.Format("<li>{0}: {1} (Author = {2})</li><ul>",
                    thread.RootPost.PostType,
                    thread.RootPost.Text,
                    FormatActor(thread.Actors[thread.RootPost.AuthorIndex])));

    foreach (SocialPost reply in thread.Replies)
        Response.Write(
            string.Format("<li>{0}: {1} (Author = {2})</li>",
                            reply.PostType,
                            reply.Text,
                            FormatActor(thread.Actors[reply.AuthorIndex])));
    Response.Write("</ul></ul>");
        }
    }
    private string FormatActor(SocialActor actor)
    {
        return string.Format("{0}: {1}", actor.ActorType, actor.Name);
    }
```

This code simply writes out the contents of the feeds to the web page.

15.   Press F5 to debug the app.

16.   Trust the app in the web browser.

The resulting page should look something like Figure 12-7.

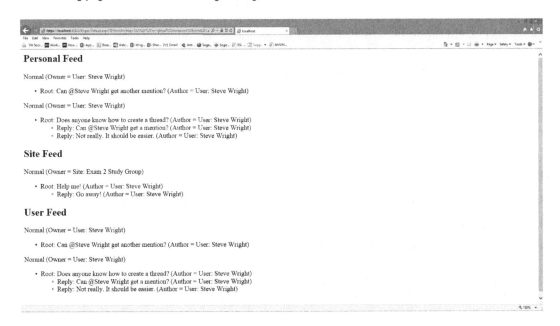

Figure 12-7. *SocialDump app output*

In the next section, we will add following information to this app.

Working with Follows

The next area of the social API we will look at enables an app to work with following information. A follow exists when a user follows another social actor of any type. This can be another user, a document, a site, or a hashtag.

Just as in working with feeds, we will access follows using a manager object: SocialFollowingManager. This object contains methods for adding and removing follows for the current user, retrieving a list of the items the user is following, or a list of the users that are following the current user. SharePoint also has the ability to recommend people that the user may wish to follow based on their common interests. Here are the key elements in this interface:

- **FollowedDocumentsUri/FollowedSitesUri**—These properties provide URLs to pages in the user's My Site that display the user's followed documents and sites, respectively.

- **Follow/StopFollowing**—These methods are used to add and remove follows for the current user. Note that removing a follow is done using StopFollowing, not UnFollow.

- **IsFollowing**—This function returns a Boolean value that indicates whether the current user is following a given actor in the system. This is useful for showing a "follow" or "stop following" link in the user interface.

- **GetFollowed**—This function returns an array of SocialActor objects representing the people and content being followed by the current user. The returned list can be limited to include only certain types of actors.

- **GetFollowers**—This function returns an array of SocialActor objects representing the people who are following the current user.

- **GetSuggestions**—This function returns an array of SocialActor objects representing users that may be of interest to the current user and who are not currently being followed.

There are two ways to construct the SocialFollowingManager object. The first way is to use an ordinary class constructor and passing in a client context object. A following manager object can also be retrieved using the FollowingManager property of a SocialFeedManager.

EXERCISE 12-2

In this exercise, we will add a page to our SocialDump app that will list out the follows, followers, and suggested follows for the current user.

1. Open Visual Studio 2012.

2. Open the SocialDump app solution from Exercise 12-1.

3. Add a new Web Form called Followers to the Pages folder in the SocialDumpWeb project.

4. Open the Followers.aspx.cs code-behind file in the editor.

5. Add these using statements to the top of the file:

```
using Microsoft.SharePoint.Client;
using Microsoft.SharePoint.Client.Social;
```

6. Replace the `Page_Load()` method with this C# code:

```csharp
protected void Page_Load(object sender, EventArgs e)
{
    var contextToken = TokenHelper.GetContextTokenFromRequest(Page.Request);
    var hostWeb = Page.Request["SPHostUrl"];

    using (var clientContext =
            TokenHelper.GetClientContextWithContextToken(
                    hostWeb, contextToken, Request.Url.Authority))
    {
        SocialFollowingManager m = new SocialFollowingManager(clientContext);
        ClientResult<SocialActor[]> f1 = m.GetFollowed(SocialActorTypes.All);
        ClientResult<SocialActor[]> f2 = m.GetFollowers();
        ClientResult<SocialActor[]> f3 = m.GetSuggestions();

        clientContext.ExecuteQuery();

        DumpList("Followed List", f1.Value);
        DumpList("Follower List", f2.Value);
        DumpList("Suggestion List", f3.Value);
    }
}

private void DumpList(string hdr, SocialActor[] lst)
{
    Response.Write("<h2>" + hdr + "</h2>");
    Response.Write("<ul>");
    foreach (SocialActor actor in lst)
        Response.Write(string.Format("<li>{0}</li>", FormatActor(actor)));
    Response.Write("</ul>");
}

private string FormatActor(SocialActor actor)
{
    return string.Format("{0}: {1}", actor.ActorType, actor.Name);
}
```

This code creates a `SocialFollowManager` object using the current context and then uses it to retrieve lists of actors for followed actors, followers, and suggestions.

7. Save and close the `Followers.aspx.cs` file.

8. Open the `AppManifest.xml` file in the `SocialDump` project in the editor.

9. Change the Start Page to `SocialDumpWeb/Pages/Followers.aspx`.

10. Save and close the `AppManifest.xml` file.

11. Press F5 to debug the app.

12. Trust the app in the web browser, if necessary.

The resulting page should look something like Figure 12-8.

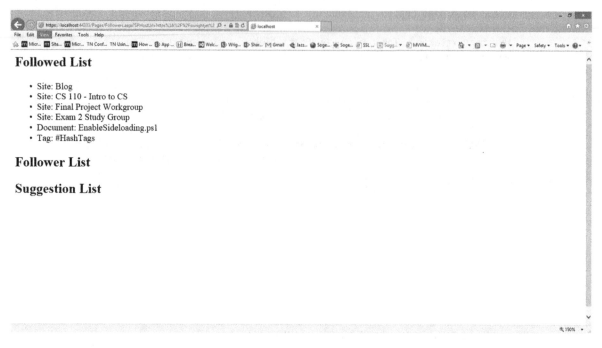

Figure 12-8. *SocialDump Follower page*

Creating Posts, Mentions, Tags, and Links

Creating a new post in a microfeed using client-side code is relatively simple, but embedding social networking information such as tags and mentions adds another dimension to the task.

To create a post, the app first creates a SocialPostCreationData object. This object contains the properties for the new post. For a simple post, with no embedded links, the only property required is the ContentText. The creation data object is then passed into the CreatePost method of the SocialFeedManager object.

```
SocialPostCreationData newPost = new SocialPostCreationData();
newPost.ContentText = "This is the text of the post.";
feedManager.CreatePost(null, newPost);
```

This code adds the post to the current user's personal feed because the first parameter to CreatePost, targetId, is null. To post to a site feed, this parameter should be set to the fully qualified URL for the site's newsfeed page; for example, https://www.mydomain.com/sites/myteamsite/newsfeed.aspx. To post a reply, the target ID should be set to the Id property of the existing SocialThread object.

Adding embedded links to a post is done by providing an overlay of social data items for the post. This overlay defines the overall content of the post with placeholders for the items to be inserted. For example, for a post with a link and a mention, the ContentText property would be set to Check out {0} by {1}. The numbered braces denote where the overlay text will be placed. This is similar to the .NET Framework's String.Format() function.

Each placeholder will be filled in by a `SocialDataItem` object. These objects represent both the text for the item to be placed into the post and the information necessary for SharePoint to connect the item to other social content. Here are the primary properties for the `SocialDataItem` object:

- **Text**—This is the text that replaces the numbered braces in the `ContentText` string.

- **ItemType**—This indicates what type of reference is being made by the post. The other fields in the object are used, or not used, based on the item's type.

  - **User**—Set `AccountName` to the user to be mentioned.

  - **Document**—Set `Uri` to the document's location.

  - **Site**—Set `Uri` to the site's location.

  - **Tag**—Set `TagGuid` to the GUID assigned to the tag. If `TagGuid` is blank, the `#tag` in the `Text` property will be used.

  - **Link**—Set `Uri` to the page's URL.

One or more `SocialDataItem` objects for a post can be added to the `ContentItems` array in the `SocialPostCreationData` object used to create the post. The text for these items is substituted for the numbered braces in the `ContentText` field when the post is rendered. The number inside the braces indicates the position in the array of the corresponding item.

```
SocialDataItem item0 = new SocialDataItem();
item0.ItemType = SocialDataItemType.Link;
item0.Text = "this great article";
item0.Uri = "http://mydomain.com/article.html";

SocialDataItem item1 = new SocialDataItem();
item1.ItemType = SocialDataItemType.User;
item1.Text = "Harold Pinkney";
item1.AccountName = haroldsAccountName;

SocialPostCreationData newPost = new SocialPostCreationData();
newPost.ContentText = "Check out {0} by {1}";
newPost.ContentItems = new SocialDataItem[2] { item0, item1 };
feedManager.CreatePost(null, newPost););
```

Summary

In this chapter, we explored SharePoint 2013's social computing features. These features include community sites and portals, My Sites, and feeds. By leveraging personal and site feeds, along with social tagging and mentions, we allow users to add context and meaning to otherwise static content. This encourages active conversations about people and processes that can improve the enterprise by leveraging the best ideas of everyone in the organization.

In the next chapter, we look at some of the other services provided by SharePoint 2013 and how we can use these in our SharePoint apps.

CHAPTER 13

∎ ∎ ∎

Enhancing Apps with SharePoint Services

SharePoint 2013 provides services that apps can use to better integrate with the rest of the platform. In this chapter we will explore three of these services and how we can leverage them in our apps. In this chapter, we will go over the following points:

- We will describe the managed metadata service and the client-side APIs available for querying and updating a site's taxonomy structure.

- We will look at how to record error information to SharePoint in such a way that administrators can use it to diagnose problems with an app.

- We will examine how to add licensing capabilities to our apps so that we can enforce user limits and ensure payment when we sell our apps through the Office Store.

Accessing Managed Metadata

SharePoint 2013's managed metadata service stores common taxonomy information for a SharePoint tenancy. *Taxonomy* refers to the terms used to describe a set of concepts, usually in a hierarchical form. For example, in biology class, everyone learns about the taxonomy of living things. This taxonomy contains several levels such as *kingdom*, *phylum*, *class*, *genus*, and *species*. SharePoint's managed metadata is structured the same way with different levels, as shown in Figure 13-1.

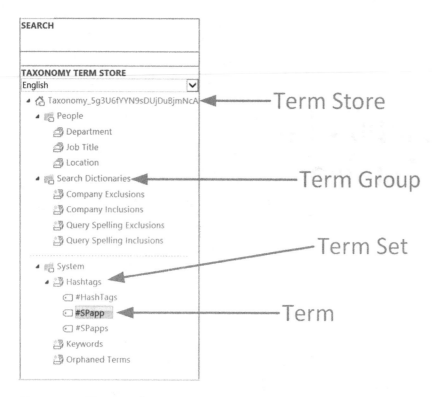

Figure 13-1. *SharePoint's taxonomic structure*

For those familiar with relational database management systems, or other types of IT systems, the term *metadata* is probably familiar as well. Metadata literally means *data about data*. In the case of an RDBMS system, metadata consists of lists of databases, tables, columns, and so forth. This type of metadata is not appropriate for storage in SharePoint's metadata service because the structure is very different. Instead, SharePoint metadata consists of a hierarchy of terms and concepts used to classify data within SharePoint.

A *term* is a single word or concept that can be related to other terms in a tree structure. A term can have different display labels for different languages, allowing users of different languages to use the same terminology. A typical use for metadata in SharePoint includes populating drop-down lists for selecting values in the SharePoint user interface. This data can also be used for sorting, searching, and navigating the data in a SharePoint site. In Chapter 12, we described hashtags (#tags) which are used to mark topics in social computing posts and replies. SharePoint 2013 manages these tags in a special area in the metadata service and new tags used by endusers are added to this area automatically.

Terms are grouped into sets of related terms. *Term sets* can be used to populate drop-downs or limit values for a certain type of field. For example, terms commonly put into sets include lists of a company's divisions and departments. There are also special-purpose term sets for terms like hashtags and enterprise keywords. The terms in a term set are often retrieved and updated together.

Term sets are collected into term groups. *Term groups* contain a collection of related term sets. The term sets in a group usually serve a similar purpose or relate to a specific topic. Term groups are primarily an organizational structure more than a functional one. Aside from categorizing term sets, term groups are most often used as a unit of replication from one system to another. For example, if an app has a need to store a copy of taxonomy data for some reason, it is often easiest to do this at the term group level. Term groups also provide a level of administrative delegation. Each term group can be assigned one or more group managers that can manage the sets and terms in the group.

The highest level grouping of managed metadata is the term store. A *term store* contains all of the term groups needed by a set of site collections. A term store is usually maintained for each tenant in a SharePoint farm or SharePoint Online. Term store administrators can be assigned by a farm administrator to manage the store. The term store administrator can create new term groups and assign term group managers to them.

SharePoint 2013 contains APIs for reading and writing the term store from within an app. In the .NET Framework CSOM, the `Microsoft.SharePoint.Client.Taxonomy` namespace contains these objects. These are available by referencing the `Microsoft.SharePoint.Client.Taxonomy.dll` assembly. In JavaScript, the `SP.Taxonomy` namespace exposes these objects in the `sp.taxonomy.js` file.

An app that wishes to use the taxonomy objects should first request the Taxonomy permission. The URI for this permission is `http://sharepoint/taxonomy`. This permission can be used to grant either read-only or read-write access to the managed metadata. There are very few types of apps that require write access to this information. In these cases, the user must also have administrator rights to the corresponding container (term store or group) in the taxonomy service in order for the app to function correctly.

The object model for accessing managed metadata is quite simple. The API consists of a set of objects that contain collections of lower-level objects. They also contain methods for querying the term store and managing its contents.

The first object is the TaxonomySession object. This is the manager object for the managed metadata service. It is constructed by calling a static factory method and passing in a `ClientContext` object.

```
ClientContext ctx = TokenHelper.GetClientContextWithContextToken(
hostWeb, contextToken, Request.Url.Authority);
TaxonomySession ts = TaxonomySession.GetTaxonomySession(ctx);
```

The TaxonomySession class contains methods for querying terms and term sets by language and other properties. It also contains a TermStores property that can be loaded to retrieve all term stores associated with the current tenant. There will usually be only one term store in the local tenancy.

```
ctx.Load(ts.TermStores);
ctx.ExecuteQuery();
TermStore tStore = ts.TermStores[0];
```

The TermStore object contains methods for querying and managing the term store. Some of these include the following:

- **DefaultLanguage**—This is the default language for the terms in the term store.

- **Groups**—This is a collection of the TermGroup objects in the store.

- **KeywordsTermSet**—This is the term set containing the enterprise keywords for the store.

- **HashTagsTermSet**—This is the term set to which hashtags are added automatically when they are used.

The term store can be used to traverse all of the groups in the store or to find specific terms, term sets or term groups within the store.

```
ctx.Load(tStore.Groups);
ctx.ExecuteQuery();
foreach (TermGroup tGroup in tStore.Groups){...}
```

The TermGroup object represents a term group in the current term store. It contains methods to manage term sets in the group.

- **TermSets**—This is a collection of TermSet objects.

- **CreateTermSet()**—This method creates a new term set using a given language.

- **GetChanges()**—This method returns a list of object IDs that have been changed in the term group in a given period. This list can be used to retrieve the current values of these objects for replication purposes.

```
ctx.Load(tGroup.TermSets);
ctx.ExecuteQuery();
foreach (TermSet tSet in tGroup.TermSets) {...}
```

The TermSet object represents a collection of related terms that can be retrieved together or separately. This class contains methods for updating the stakeholders list for the set and querying the terms in the set. There is also a GetChanges() method to allow for replicating terms at the term set level.

```
ctx.Load(tSet.Terms);
ctx.ExecuteQuery();
foreach (Term t in tSet.Terms) {...}
```

At the bottom of the taxonomy is the Term object. This represents a single term in the store. A term has several properties and methods that define the content of the term and its relationship to other terms and sets, including the following:

- **Labels**—This contains the display string for the term in different languages.

- **MergedTermIds**—Terms can be merged when they are redundant. This property maintains the integrity of any existing data that uses the individual terms.

- **LocalCustomProperties**—This is a dictionary of name-value pairs that defines custom attributes on the term. These attributes can be used to query for terms at higher levels in the hierarchy.

- **IsDeprecated**—A deprecated term no longer appears in the user interface and does not support new tagging operations. The previously recorded metadata associated with the term is still kept within the system. The term can be undeprecated (repreceated?) in the future, if needed. Doing so restores all previous tagging done with that term.

- **IsKeyword**—An enterprise keyword in SharePoint is a word or phrase that has been added to the keywords list in one or more documents by users. These reside in the keyword term set.

- **IsPinned**—A pinned term appears in more than one location in the term hierarchy. Only the original copy of the term can be modified. These changes are reflected in all occurrences of the term.

- **IsReused**—A reused term appears in more than one location in the term hierarchy. An update to any of these locations is reflected in all occurrences of the term.

- **IsRoot**—Terms can be nested in a hierarchy of their own, with the exception of keywords which cannot be nested. This flag indicates that this term is the root of such a tree.

The SharePoint metadata management service can be used to create complex hierarchies of terms by reusing, pinning, and nesting terms. Planning is essential to get the most out of your taxonomy. TechNet has several good articles about planning terms and term sets in SharePoint 2013. See http://technet.microsoft.com/en-us/library/ee519604.aspx.

Logging SharePoint App Errors

Up to this point, our apps have used very basic error handling to keep the examples simple. A professional app needs to consider how errors should be handled in the real world.

In a full-trust application, there are many logging options available both within SharePoint and outside the farm. We can write errors to log files, databases or SharePoint's Unified Logging Service (ULS). Apps for SharePoint generally do not have the permissions necessary to do logging using these interfaces. The app can request permissions to write to a centralized SQL database using BCS but this may not be appropriate in many cases. Apps need a simple way to record error information without requiring special permissions or data stores.

The SharePoint 2013 client-side object models contain a very simple interface for logging this type of information. App errors can be logged, throttled, or ignored based on the preferences of the tenant administrator. By default, app errors will be ignored unless the administrator chooses to "monitor" the app. At that point app usage and error logging can be enabled on an app-by-app basis.

The overall process for recording, collecting, and reporting on app errors is as follows:

1. An app is acquired either from the Office Store or an App Catalog in the SharePoint farm.

2. A tenant administrator enables app monitoring for the specific app.

3. The app records error information as it occurs.

4. An administrator reviews the errors logged.

Note that because the app must be configured for monitoring before errors will be logged, you will need to deploy the app to an App Catalog before it will record errors. Once the app is deployed and monitoring is enabled, the app can be debugged while recording errors.

The APIs for app error logging are very simple. The SharePoint 2013 core CSOM libraries contain a utility object that provides many methods to perform miscellaneous tasks. Two of these methods are used to record errors.

In JavaScript, code that runs within the app web in SharePoint-hosted pages can use the logCustomAppError method. This method takes a client context object and an error message string. It returns a value that indicates whether the logging was successful, throttled, or failed. App errors are said to be *throttled* when the administrator has configured SharePoint to limit the number of errors an app can record. This prevents a rouge app from filling up the server's logs with garbage.

```
    var r = SP.Utilities.Utility.
logCustomAppError(context, 'Grading workflow failed: Access Denied.');
    context.executeQueryAsync();
alert(r.get_value());
```

■ **Note**   The errors are initially written to an internal queue in the server. They are published to the administrator's error report asynchronously. It can sometimes take a few minutes for logged errors to appear in the administrator's error report.

The JavaScript and .NET Framework CSOM libraries also contain a separate method used to record app errors from remote web site code. The JavaScript library can be used for browser-based logging from pages served by a remote web site. The .NET Framework CSOM should be used for server-side code.

The remote logging method is part of the same utility object as the non-remote method. It is called LogCustomRemoteAppError and takes an additional parameter. This parameter provides the product ID of the app. The product ID for an app can be found in the app manifest file for the app. This GUID value will need to be copied to the location where the error logging code will be run. The following code demonstrates logging an error from remote server-side code:

```
public partial class Default : System.Web.UI.Page
  {
      private static Guid productId =
new Guid("{b7ca1c43-b258-4eb1-ba31-e31e13d87e6c}");

      protected void Page_Load(object sender, EventArgs e)
      {
          var contextToken = TokenHelper.GetContextTokenFromRequest(Page.Request);
          var hostWeb = Page.Request["SPHostUrl"];

          using (var ctx = TokenHelper.GetClientContextWithContextToken(
hostWeb, contextToken, Request.Url.Authority))
          {
              ClientResult<LogAppErrorResult> r =
Microsoft.SharePoint.Utilities.
Utility.LogCustomRemoteAppError(
ctx, productId, "MY ERROR MESSAGE HERE");
              ctx.ExecuteQuery();
              Response.Write(r.Value.ToString());
          }
      }
  }
}
```

Once the app has been updated to include error logging, it should be published to an App Catalog and installed on a site. Calling the logging methods when the app is not being monitored does not cause an error. The call is simply ignored. To enable monitoring, the tenant or farm administrator needs to access the app management service configuration. In SharePoint Online, a tenant administrator goes to the SharePoint admin center page and selects apps (see Figure 13-2).

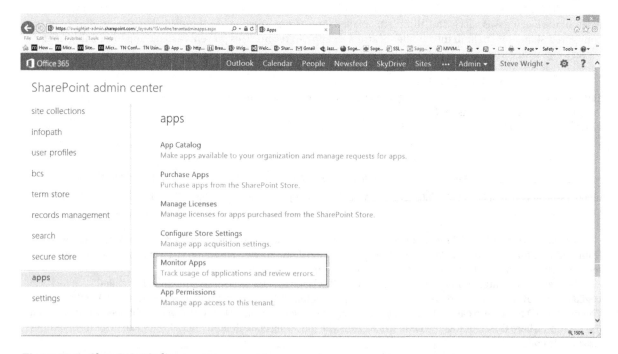

Figure 13-2. *SharePoint Online app management page*

Next, the admin selects Monitor Apps to see the list of apps being monitored in the tenancy. To begin monitoring the app, the user clicks on Add App in the central ribbon menu. A list of the apps available for monitoring is presented, as shown in Figure 13-3.

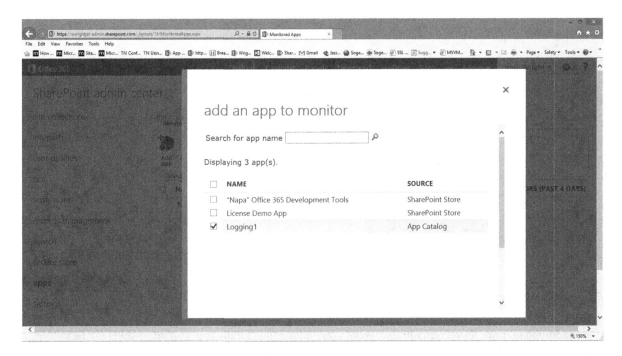

Figure 13-3. *Add an app to monitor*

After selecting the app and scrolling to the bottom of the window, the user will click Add to complete the process. At this point, that app's usage and error logging are being recorded by the SharePoint platform.

Once the app has logged its information, the administrator can return to the app monitoring page, check the app, and click on View Errors. The error log is shown in Figure 13-4.

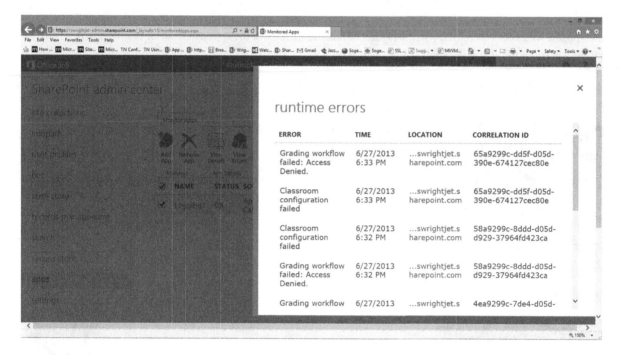

Figure 13-4. The app error log

In addition to errors, SharePoint will also record usage information for the app. This information can be viewed by clicking on View Details, instead of View Errors. The information presented includes licensing details and installation and upgrade counts. It also includes a graph of the app's usage as measured by the number of times the app was launched and by the number of unique users using the app. These counts are charted over time to show if an app's usage is increasing or decreasing.

Managing App Licenses

One of the most exciting aspects of apps for SharePoint is the ability to sell apps through the Office Store to a worldwide audience. These apps can be published by large commercial software firms and small, independent developers alike. In order to make this process practical, a common method of software licensing has to be implemented. The method used by the Office Store is called the *app license framework.*

The app license framework is a set of data formats, message exchanges, code libraries, and infrastructure that defines how licenses are acquired, maintained, and validated. An app license is a set of data elements that defines the rights of the user with regard to using and distributing an app purchased from the Office Store. The license is issued by the Office Store and stored within SharePoint. At runtime, the app can validate that the license is still valid using a web service call to the store's web site. SharePoint 2013 includes libraries that enable apps to access the licenses stored in SharePoint and validate them against the web service.

Since we have not used licensing prior to this point, it should be obvious that licensing is not a requirement when developing SharePoint apps. In fact, app licensing is only available for apps that are distributed through the Office Store. If your organization creates apps for its own internal use, these apps will not be able to use the app license framework. Apps obtained from third parties (for example, those downloaded directly from a vendor's web site), will not be able to leverage licensing either. This is why it is a good idea to distribute your public app, even free apps, through the Office Store. The licensing interface allows you to monitor the popularity of your apps.

License Types

SharePoint app licenses can be issued for a variety of purposes and with a variety of properties. The Office Store tracks these licenses as new purchases are made.

The first type of app license is the *free license*. Free apps are exactly what they sound like. They are provided free of charge. These apps can be downloaded from the Office Store without making any kind of payment. Once downloaded to a SharePoint farm, the app can be deployed to any number of sites and used by any number of users for an unlimited period of time.

A *trial license* is a restricted version of the free license. No payment is required to acquire a trial license, but it can be, and generally is, limited in the number of users supported and the time period for which it is valid. For example, a trial license might limit the number of users to five for a period of thirty days. After that period, the app is expired and will not function. Some trial apps may limit only the number of users or the time period, but not both. Another possibility is to allow unlimited users for an unlimited period of time while limiting the functionality of the product while under a trial license. Purchasing a full license would then unlock the additional functionality of the app. This is similar to the shareware concept.

The final license type is the *paid license*. Paid licenses do not expire, but they can limit the number of users allowed to use the app. When the license limits the number of users, it is referred to as a *per-user license*. Without this limit, it is called a *site license*. All users of the SharePoint deployment can use the app when a site license is in place.

The app license framework also supports test licenses for use during development. Test licenses are either free, trial, or paid licenses that are issued by the developer of an app and deployed directly to SharePoint. The Office Store license validation service is designed to recognize test licenses and respond with appropriate validation results. When an app is deployed to the Office Store, it should be modified to remove its ability to accept test licenses.

Acquiring Apps from the Office Store

When a user acquires an app from the Office Store (`http://office.microsoft.com`), they are referred to as the *purchaser*, even for free and trial app licenses. Figure 13-5 illustrates the process of acquiring an app from the Office Store.

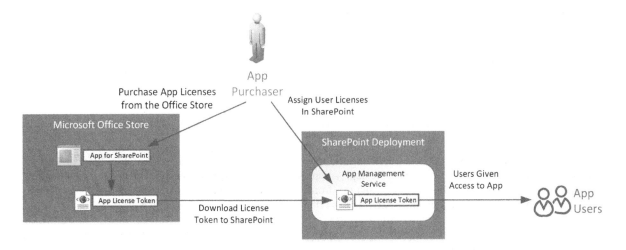

Figure 13-5. *Acquiring apps from the Office Store*

The first step in acquiring an app is to find the app within the Office Store and purchase it. The user must have permission within the current SharePoint deployment before being allowed to acquire an app. Users without this permission can be given the option to request that an app be acquired on their behalf.

The Office Store will record the purchase transaction and issue an app license token that is stored in the SharePoint server farm. This token contains information about the type of license issued, any user or duration limitations, and who acquired the license.

Once the license has been acquired and stored in the local SharePoint deployment, the purchaser, or a designated license manager, can assign licenses to users within the deployment. This assignment only applies to licenses, trial or paid, that specify a limited number of users for the app. Site licenses do not require that users be assigned.

For security reasons, assigning apps to users can only be accomplished through the SharePoint user interface. The client-side object models do not include the ability to assign user licenses programmatically.

Users that are assigned licenses for the app can install the app in a SharePoint site for which they have the necessary site ownership rights. Any authorized user can use the app within a site into which it has been installed.

Some app license tokens are designed to expire after a certain period of time. For example, trial licenses with a limited duration expire at the end of that period. This is a security feature that ensures that the license is still valid in the Office Store. SharePoint 2013 will periodically renew these licenses with the Office Store, based on a timer job. Licenses can also be renewed manually, but this is usually only necessary when a SharePoint server farm is being recovered from a failure.

App Licensing Scope

When an app license is acquired from the Office Store it only applies to a single SharePoint deployment. A *deployment* is defined by the presence of a unique instance of the App Management Service application. The App Management Service is the component within SharePoint that stores, renews, and manages app licenses. Each deployment is assigned a unique deployment ID, which is a GUID generated by SharePoint.

- In SharePoint Online, each tenant has a separate deployment ID.

- In SharePoint 2013 Server, there are the following options:

  ○ A farm will usually have a single App Management Service instance with a single deployment ID.

  ○ A farm running in multi-tenant mode will typically have a separate deployment ID for each tenant.

  ○ A single-tenant farm can be configured to use multiple App Management Service instances. In this case, each service will have a separate deployment ID. This is not common.

When the Office Store issues a license, it is for one app in one SharePoint deployment. The Office Store license contains both the product ID of the app and the deployment ID of the deployment. A license will not work within any SharePoint deployment with a different deployment ID from the one for which the license was issued. If a user needs to use an app in more than one deployment, they will need to acquire separate licenses to do so.

■ **Note** While the deployment ID is generated automatically by SharePoint, it is possible to set the ID to a specific value using Windows PowerShell. This can only be done within an on-site deployment of SharePoint 2013 Server, not in SharePoint Online. This is typically done in test environments or when performing disaster recovery or migration.

Validating License Information

Licenses are most often checked when the app is initially launched by the user. License checks can also be performed at other points in the execution of the app if needed. As shown in Figure 13-6, license validation is a two-step process.

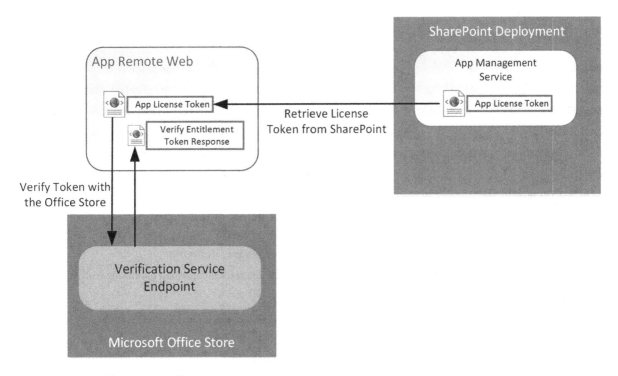

Figure 13-6. *Validating an app license at runtime*

The first step is for the app to retrieve the license token from SharePoint's App Management Service database. There may be more than one applicable license in the database. For example, if a trial license is upgraded to a paid license, both licenses may be present in the license database. Also, if additional user licenses are purchased for a per-user licensed app, the additional increment of user licenses is stored as a separate license token. When the app requests the license from SharePoint, it receives a list of the applicable licenses, in order of their relevancy. A license is more relevant depending on the type of license. Paid licenses are more relevant than free or trial licenses. Per-user licenses are only relevant to the users assigned to them. Table 13-1 describes the format and contents of the license token returned by SharePoint.

Table 13-1. *License Token XML Contents*

License Token XML	Description
`<r v="0">`	Required root node.
`<t aid="WA103524926"`	Asset ID assigned by the Office Store.
`did="{3F47392A-2308-4FC6-BF24-740626612B26}"`	SharePoint deployment ID supplied when the license is purchased.
`ad="2013-06-28T00:00:00Z"`	Acquisition date when the app was purchased.
`te="2023-06-28T00:00:00Z"`	Token expiration date when the token will no longer be valid.
`sd="2013-06-28T00:00:00Z"`	Date the token was last issued or recovered.
`test="true"`	Indicates that this is a test license.
`pid="{9447ab8b-ae57-471b-a158-34c334b283e5}"`	Product ID matching the app manifest file.
`et="Paid"`	License type is either `Free`, `Paid`, or `Trial`.
`cid="45C1423F59FDE73E"`	Identifies the purchaser of the app.
`ts="0"`	The licensed number of users for the app license. Use 0 for unlimited site licenses.
`sl="true" />`	Indicates that this is a site license.
`<d>449JFz+myOwNoCmO/h+Ci9DsF/ WOQ8rqEBqjpe44KkY=</d>`	An encrypted digest used to prevent tampering with the token.
`</r>`	

The second half of the validation process involves the Office Store validation web service. This web service is located at `https://verificationservice.officeapps.live.com/ova/verificationagent.svc`. The app will pass the license token XML string to the validation service which will look it up in its license database and return a response detailing the license's current status. The most important fields in this response are the following:

- **IsValid**—This indicates that this is a valid production, not test, license.

- **IsTest**—This indicates that this is a license used only for testing.

- **IsExpired**—This indicates that the time limit has expired for this license.

- **EntitlementType**—This indicates the type of license (`Free`, `Trial`, or `Paid`) that the user has for the app.

- **IsSiteLicense**—This indicates that the license is a site license.

The app can use these values to verify which features of the app, if any, to permit the user to access. For performance and security reasons, Microsoft recommends the following best practices for checking app licenses:

- ***Limit the number of times the license is checked.*** Retrieving the license from SharePoint and validating it through the validation service are non-trivial processes. Performing these checks too frequently (for example, with each page hit), can cause poor performance for the app. In most cases, it is only necessary to perform the check once per user session.

- ***Cache the results of the check.*** When a license check is performed, store the results in a location that is appropriate to the license type. For per-user licenses, check the license at least once per user session in case the user's license is revoked at some point. For site licenses, cache the results until the license either expires or is renewed.

- ***Prevent access to the license-checking code.*** The simplest way to get around a license check is to delete it from the app's code. Therefore, the check should not be done in browser-based code, which is vulnerable to this type of tampering.

The JavaScript and REST client interfaces do not include the interface for validating app licenses to discourage browser-based checks. It is still possible to perform these checks from the browser using the SharePoint web proxy, but this is strongly discouraged. There is very little point in checking a license in your code when it is so easy to circumvent the check. The .NET Framework CSOM library contains the methods necessary to perform these checks securely, as we will see in our next exercise.

EXERCISE 13-1

In this exercise, we return to our Classroom Online sample application. We will add logic to check the licensing of the app when the app is launched. In our case, we will be creating our app license as a site license. In a production app, we would store the license information in a server-side cache for later use.

In this exercise, we will create a test license and upload it to SharePoint for debugging purposes. We will add a new landing page to the Classroom Online remote web site to perform the license check. We will also add logic to retrieve the license token from SharePoint and pass it to the Office Store for validation. Finally, we will perform checks on the results of the check to ensure that the license is valid.

In order to create a test license, we need to execute some .NET Framework code in the context of a SharePoint app. The easiest way to do this is to create a temporary app to create the license and upload it to SharePoint for us. There is an excellent sample app on MSDN at `http://code.msdn.microsoft.com/SharePoint-2013-Import-f5f680a6` that can be used instead of creating a separate app. We will go ahead and walk through the process here for demonstration purposes.

1. Open Visual Studio 2012.

2. Create a new auto-hosted SharePoint app using the C# template and name it `CreateTestAppLicense`.

3. Open the `AppManifest.xml` file in the editor.

4. Select the Permissions tab.

5. Add the Site Collection permission with Full Control (see Figure 13-7).

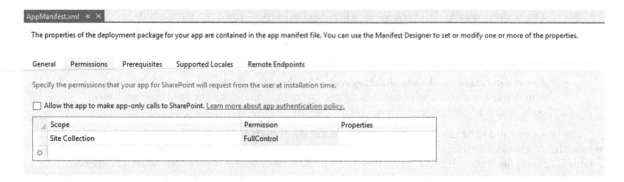

Figure 13-7. *App manifest permissions*

6. Save and close the app manifest file.

7. Open the `Default.aspx.cs` file for editing.

8. Replace the `Page_Load()` method with the following code:

```
protected void Page_Load(object sender, EventArgs e)
{
    var contextToken = TokenHelper.GetContextTokenFromRequest(Page.Request);
    var hostWeb = Page.Request["SPHostUrl"];

    using (var clientContext =
TokenHelper.GetClientContextWithContextToken(
hostWeb, contextToken, Request.Url.Authority))
    {
        string tokenXml =
            "<r v=\"0\">"
            + "<t aid=\"WA103524926\""
            + " did=\"{3F47392A-2308-4FC6-BF24-740626612B26}\""
            + " ad=\"2012-06-19T21:48:56Z\""
            + " te=\"2112-07-15T23:47:42Z\""
            + " sd=\"2012-02-01T23:47:42Z\""
            + " test=\"true\""
            + " pid=\"{9447ab8b-ae57-471b-a158-34c334b283e5}\""
            + " et=\"Paid\""
            + " cid=\"739835AE59FDE73E\""
            + " ts=\"0\""
            + " sl=\"true\" />"
            + "<d>449JFz+myOwNoCmO/h+Ci9DsF/WOQ8rqEBqjpe44KkY=</d>"
            + "</r>";

        Microsoft.SharePoint.Client.Utilities.Utility.ImportAppLicense(
            clientContext,
            tokenXml,
            "en-US",
            "US",
```

```
            "Classroom Online",
            Request.Url.AbsoluteUri.
Substring(0,Request.Url.AbsoluteUri.LastIndexOf("/"))
+ "/AppIcon.png",
"Pro SharePoint 2013 Apps",
            5); // SharePoint app with no Office integration

        clientContext.ExecuteQuery();

        Response.Write("License Import succeeded!");
    }
}
```

The most important element in the preceding code is the product ID. The ID used in the test license must match the ID in the Classroom Online app manifest in order for SharePoint to associate the license with the app properly.

The `ImportAppLicense` method passes its parameters to SharePoint, which records the data in its license database. The parameters are as follows:

- **context**—The client context to use for processing the request.

- **licenseTokenToImport**—The XML string representing the license token to import.

- **contentMarket**—Indicates the region and locale of the app.

- **billingMarket**—Indicates the region to use when charging for the app. It is used to control the billing process for an app.

- **appName**—The display name for the app.

- **iconUrl**—The URL to use for the app's icon on the Office Store web site.

- **providerName**—The name of the publisher of the app.

- **appSubtype**—A value that indicates the type of components in the app. The Office Store uses this value to categorize apps. Possible values include the following:

  - 1—Contains a single app for Office task pane.

  - 2—Contains a single content app for Office.

  - 4—Contains a single app for Office dictionary task pane.

  - 5—Contains a SharePoint app including multiple Office app components or SharePoint content other than Office apps.

Remember, creating and downloading the license token into SharePoint is normally performed by the Office Store. We are only doing this here because we need a test license. Because this is a test license, the Office Store will not verify much of the data in this license, such as the product and deployment IDs.

9. Save and close the `Default.aspx.cs` file.

10. Press F5 to run the app.

After trusting the app, you should see the "License Import succeeded!" message. To verify the existence of the license, you can either use SharePoint Central Administration or the SharePoint Online admin center, as shown in Figure 13-8. This page can be accessed through the apps link in the left-hand menu.

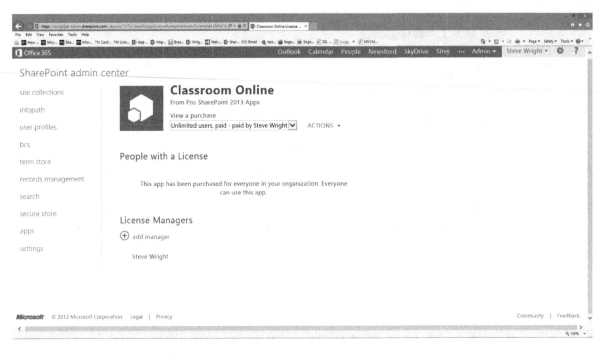

Figure 13-8. *Managing an app's license*

Now we will move on to adding the license-checking logic to Classroom Online.

11. Close the `CreateTestAppLicense` solution.

12. Open the Classroom Online solution as it existed at the end of Chapter 10. These files can be downloaded from the Source Code/Download area of the Apress web site (`www.apress.com`), if needed.

13. Add a new Web Form to the `Pages` folder in the `ClassroomOnlineWeb` project and name it `VerifyLicense.aspx`.

14. Open the `AppManifest.xml` file from the Classroom Online solution in the editor.

15. Set the app's start page to `ClassroomOnlineWeb/Pages/VerifyLicense.aspx`.

16. Select the Permissions tab.

17. Add a permission request with a scope of Web and permission of Read. This is the minimum permission required to retrieve the app's license token.

18. Save and Close the `AppManifest.xml` file.

19. Open the `VerifyLicense.aspx.cs` file in the editor.

20. Add the following line to the top of the file:

```
using Microsoft.SharePoint.Client;
```

21. Add the following line to the VerifyLicense class *outside* of the Page_Load() method. This is the product ID of the ClassroomOnline app:

```
private Guid _productID = Guid.Parse("{9447ab8b-ae57-471b-a158-34c334b283e5}");
```

22. Add the following code to the Page_Load() method. This code provides the skeleton of the method.

```
try
{
    var contextToken = TokenHelper.GetContextTokenFromRequest(Page.Request);
    var hostWeb = Page.Request["SPHostUrl"];
    var appWeb = Page.Request["SPAppWebUrl"];

    using (var clientContext =
TokenHelper.GetClientContextWithContextToken(
hostWeb, contextToken, Request.Url.Authority))
    {
    }
}
catch (Exception ex)
{
    Response.Write("Licensing failed: " + ex.Message);
}
```

23. Inside the using block, add the following code:

```
// Retrieve any app licenses stored within SharePoint, most RELEVANT first.
ClientResult<AppLicenseCollection> licenses =
    Microsoft.SharePoint.Client.Utilities.Utility.
GetAppLicenseInformation(clientContext, _productID);

clientContext.ExecuteQuery();

if (licenses.Value.Count == 0)
    throw new InvalidOperationException("No license");

string licenseString = licenses.Value[0].RawXMLLicenseToken;
```

The preceding code uses the .NET Framework CSOM utility class to retrieve the license token from SharePoint. The GetAppLicenseInformation() method is called with the product ID of the app. Note that this is CSOM code, so it is necessary to call ExecuteQuery(). The license information retrieved is in order of relevance, as described earlier. In most cases, we are only interested in the first license returned. The RawXMLLicenseToken property returns the same XML string we uploaded to SharePoint in the CreateTestAppLicense project.

Now we need to call the Office Store license validation web service. We start by adding a reference to the service in our web project.

24. Right-click on the `ClassroomOnli.neWeb` project web and select Add Service Reference….

25. In the address box, enter
     `https://verificationservice.officeapps.live.com/ova/verificationagent.svc`.

26. Click Go.

27. When the service finishes loading, select the `VerificationAgent` service.

28. In the Namespace box, enter `OfficeStoreVerificationService`(see Figure 13-9).

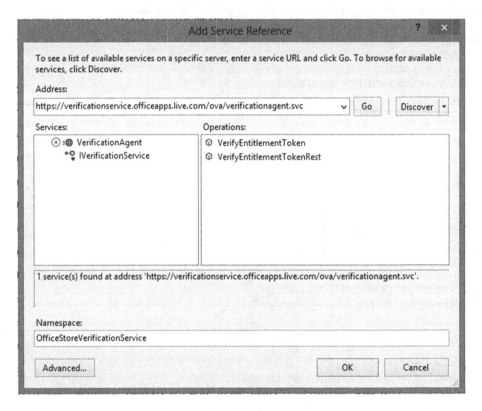

Figure 13-9. *Add a service reference to the Office Store*

29. Click the OK button.

30. Add this line to the top of the `VerifyLicense.aspx.cs`file:

     ```
     using ClassroomOnlineWeb.OfficeStoreVerificationService;
     ```

31. Add the following code after the declaration of `licenseString`:

     ```
     // Validate the license against the Office Store license service.
     VerificationServiceClient service = new VerificationServiceClient();
     ```

```
VerifyEntitlementTokenRequest request = new VerifyEntitlementTokenRequest();
request.EntitlementToken = licenseString;

VerifyEntitlementTokenResponse storeLicense = service.VerifyEntitlementToken(request);
```

The first line creates an instance of the web service proxy object. Then, a request is formatted for the validation service. Note that the "license token" is sometimes referred to as an "entitlement token" in SharePoint. Finally, the request is sent to the verification service and the response is received.

32. Add the following code after the previous code:

```
// Perform licensing checks.
//
// Use this version of the check in production:
//      if (!storeLicense.IsValid || storeLicense.IsExpired)
//
// Use this version of the check in test/debugging:
if ((!storeLicense.IsValid && !storeLicense.IsTest) || storeLicense.IsExpired)
        throw new InvalidOperationException("Invalid license");

// At this point, we have a valid license. We can retrieve the details
// of the license (type of license, acquisition date, etc.) from the
// license provided by the Office Store and take appropriate actions.

// <--TBD-->

Response.Write("Licensing Succeeded: " + storeLicense.EntitlementType.ToString());
```

The preceding code checks to see if the license is valid for production or if it is a test license. Before publishing the app to the Office Store, the check for a test license should be removed. Leaving this check in the code would allow anyone to issue their own licenses for the app. The license is also checked to see if it is expired.

33. Press F5 to execute the app. The app should display a message stating that the license is good and is a "Paid" license.

The data returned from the validation service provides details as to what type of licensing is in effect for *this app*, in *this deployment*, for the *current user*. If these checks succeed, the app can then cache the results and continue normally. If they fail, the app should provide a meaningful error message to the user to let them know that they have a licensing problem.

Summary

In this chapter, we have explored some of SharePoint 2013's service applications and how we can use them in our apps. We looked at accessing terms stored in the managed metadata service. We learned the simple APIs used to record error information from our apps. We discussed how to add licensing logic to our apps to ensure that an app is valid and paid for when it is used. These services allow us to create complete, professional applications that can be deployed and supported in various environments.

In our final chapter, we will go beyond the SharePoint platform and look at creating apps that leverage SharePoint data from other platforms. We will learn to create applications that integrate SharePoint information with the Windows Runtime (WinRT), Windows Phone, and apps for Office.

CHAPTER 14

■ ■ ■

Using Other App Environments

Throughout this book, we have explored the various ways an app for SharePoint can leverage the resources of the SharePoint farm. The components that make up our apps have been hosted locally or in remote web sites outside of SharePoint to enable us to use server-side ASP.NET logic. In all cases, the custom logic for our apps has executed outside of the SharePoint server farm in a web server, a web service, or a web browser. In spite of this separation, we have always had a connection back to the SharePoint farm, in the form of context or access tokens. We have had these because our apps were always launched from inside SharePoint.

In this chapter, we will step outside of SharePoint and look at how to access SharePoint resources without using apps for SharePoint. In doing so, we will go over the following points:

- We will describe how an application running outside of SharePoint can perform authentication and access resources within the farm.

- We will integrate the Microsoft Office client applications, such as Word and Excel, with our SharePoint app solutions.

- We will create applications that access SharePoint while running as a Windows .NET application or in the Windows Runtime (WinRT).

- We will extend the reach of our SharePoint data to include native Windows Phone apps.

Unlike in previous chapters, we will not be focusing on building SharePoint apps here. The applications in this chapter will access SharePoint from an untrusted connection, requiring the application to log on to SharePoint in order to ensure privacy and data integrity.

Authenticating with SharePoint

When a user launches an app for SharePoint, the server records the current user, the app, and other information making up the context of the app. SharePoint uses this information to create a context token, which is provided to the app as part of the page request that launches the app. The context token is then used to make requests back into the SharePoint server in a secure fashion.

When an app outside of SharePoint wishes to make a request into SharePoint, there is no pre-existing context with which to work. This means that the application is responsible for authenticating with SharePoint before any other requests can be processed. This process is sometimes referred to as *active authentication*. It is active in the sense that the application must actively perform the authentication process in its code. The authentication performed by SharePoint when launching app could be called *passive authentication*. The only difference is whether the authentication process is initiated by SharePoint or the application.

In order to access SharePoint through one of the client-side object model libraries, the REST interface or one of SharePoint's native web services, the results of either active or passive authentication must be provided in the client request. Later in this chapter, we will describe some of the techniques for performing active authentication and passing the results to SharePoint. In this section, we will disassemble the authentication process to understand what is happening under the covers.

Figure 14-1 illustrates the sequence of messages that must be passed between the application, the Security Token Service (STS), and the SharePoint farm. These messages occur in three request/response pairs. The first pair establishes the user's identity with the STS. The second "logs in" to SharePoint by supplying this identity to SharePoint. The third pair represents one or more client requests from the application to SharePoint.

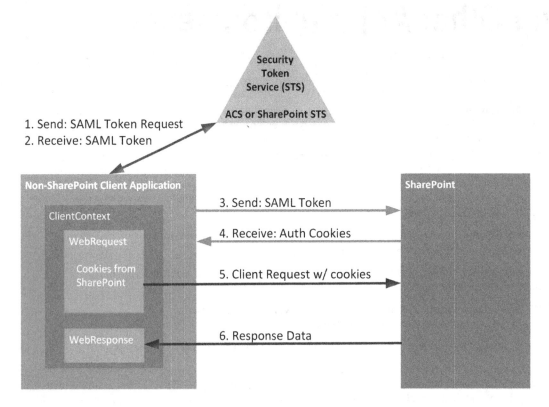

Figure 14-1. *Active authentication message sequence*

Step 1 in the figure involves formatting a request for the Security Token Service. When using SharePoint Online, the STS role is assumed by the Windows Azure Access Control Services (ACS). When running SharePoint in a local server farm, SharePoint's own STS is used. The request is formatted as a Security Assertion Markup Language (SAML) request. The SAML request is an XML document that contains the URL of the target SharePoint site, user name, and password, as shown in Listing 14-1.

Listing 14-1. Sample SAML Login Request

```
<s:Envelope
xmlns:s="http://www.w3.org/2003/05/soap-envelope"
  xmlns:a="http://www.w3.org/2005/08/addressing"
xmlns:u="http://docs.oasis-open.org/wss/2004/01/oasis-200401-wss-wssecurity-utility-1.0.xsd">
<s:Header>
<a:Action
 s:mustUnderstand="1">http://schemas.xmlsoap.org/ws/2005/02/trust/RST/Issue</a:Action>
<a:ReplyTo>
```

```
<a:Address>http://www.w3.org/2005/08/addressing/anonymous</a:Address>
</a:ReplyTo>
<a:To s:mustUnderstand="1">https://login.microsoftonline.com/extSTS.srf</a:To>
<o:Security s:mustUnderstand="1"
        xmlns:o="http://docs.oasis-open.org/wss/2004/01/oasis-200401-wss-wssecurity-secext-1.0.xsd">
<o:UsernameToken>
<o:Username>MyUserName</o:Username>
<o:Password>Pass@word1</o:Password>
</o:UsernameToken>
</o:Security>
</s:Header>
<s:Body>
<t:RequestSecurityToken xmlns:t="http://schemas.xmlsoap.org/ws/2005/02/trust">
<wsp:AppliesTo xmlns:wsp="http://schemas.xmlsoap.org/ws/2004/09/policy">
<a:EndpointReference>
<a:Address>https://swrightjet.sharepoint.com</a:Address>
</a:EndpointReference>
</wsp:AppliesTo>
<t:KeyType>http://schemas.xmlsoap.org/ws/2005/05/identity/NoProofKey</t:KeyType>
<t:RequestType>http://schemas.xmlsoap.org/ws/2005/02/trust/Issue</t:RequestType>
<t:TokenType>urn:oasis:names:tc:SAML:1.0:assertion</t:TokenType>
</t:RequestSecurityToken>
</s:Body>
</s:Envelope>
```

When the STS receives the SAML request, it verifies that the format of the request is correct, that the request is from a known source, and that the request is for a known target site. If the request is valid, the STS attempts to verify the login information. This may involve accessing the Microsoft Online Directory Service (MS-ODS) or passing the request to a federated identity service for validation. In **step 2**, the result of this validation is sent to the requesting application. If the request was successful, the STS returns a security token that has been generated for this session.

The application passes the supplied SAML security token to the SharePoint server as proof of the user's credentials in **step 3**. Note that the user's password is not included in this token. Only the STS ever sees the user's password. SharePoint validates that the security token is from a trusted STS and for a valid resource in SharePoint.

In **step 4**, SharePoint formats two cookies that are returned to the calling application. These are called FedAuth and rtFa. These cookies are represented by the context token in an app for SharePoint. In the remote application, these cookies are saved to allow for future client requests into the SharePoint site.

The application will format a request for SharePoint using one of the client APIs for SharePoint. The request can be a CSOM batch, or a WebRequest containing a REST interface call or web service call. In order to be processed by SharePoint, the authentication cookies provided by SharePoint must be included in the request. This is **step 5**.

Only requests that contain the correct authentication cookies will be acted upon by SharePoint. The CSOM libraries' client content object adds these cookies automatically when using passive authentication with a context token. When using active authentication, these cookies must be injected into the request by the application. In CSOM code, this can be accomplished by handling the context object's ExecutingWebRequest event. This event fires just before the request is sent to SharePoint, giving the application the opportunity to modify the request.

The final step, **step 6**, is a normal response message from SharePoint with the results of the request. This response is no different when using active or passive authentication. The type of response is determined by the type of request that was made (CSOM, REST, etc.).

Active authentication, also known as remote authentication, is a complex subject. There are several good articles on TechNet, MSDN, and elsewhere, as well as available sample code. Detailing all of these options is beyond the scope of this discussion. The best strategy is to pick a solution, wrap it into a set of common classes or scripts, and reuse that solution throughout your codebase. For more on active authentication, visit the following web sites:

- "Remote Authentication in SharePoint Online Using Claims-Based Authentication,"
  `http://msdn.microsoft.com/en-us/library/hh147177.aspx`

- "SharePointWinRTClient" sample project on CodePlex,
  `http://sharepointwinrt.codeplex.com/`

- "How to do active authentication to Office 365 and SharePoint Online,"
  `http://www.wictorwilen.se/Post/How-to-do-active-authentication-to-Office-365-and-SharePoint-Online.aspx`

- "Remote authentication in SharePoint Online,"
  `http://allthatjs.com/2012/03/28/remote-authentication-in-sharepoint-online/`

Creating Office Apps

The Cloud App Model described in Chapter 1 applies to more than just apps for SharePoint. Microsoft's Office productivity suite also supports the use of apps. An app for Office is basically an add-in that appears in the office client application. There are different types of apps for Office that can be surfaced in different members of the Office family of products. Apps for Office can also be used in the web-based versions of the Office Web Apps.

An app for Office is a web application that is designed to run in a small web browser window hosted within the Office application. As web pages, apps for Office can use technologies such as web services, REST, HTML, and JavaScript to provide a rich user experience. Office apps also have the ability, with proper permissions, to read and write data in Office documents and affect the state of the Office application.

In the following sections, we will describe the different types of Office apps, how they are hosted within an Office application, and how they are published to consumers. We will also see how these apps can be integrated into apps for SharePoint to create deep integration between apps for SharePoint and the documents with which they interact.

Anatomy of an App for Office

An app for Office is constructed by creating two components. Like an app for SharePoint, an app for Office uses a standardized XML manifest to describe its contents and properties. The rest of the app is defined by the contents of the web application that implements the logic of the app.

The manifest file for an app for Office is an XML file containing a description of the app and how it interacts with the Office client applications, as shown in Figure 14-2 and Figure 14-3. The General tab is used to set the name and version information. It also defines the permissions required by the app and the types of Office clients in which it can be used. Most important, Source Location contains the URL of the start page for the app. This is the web page that will be loaded into the app's window within the Office client when the app is launched.

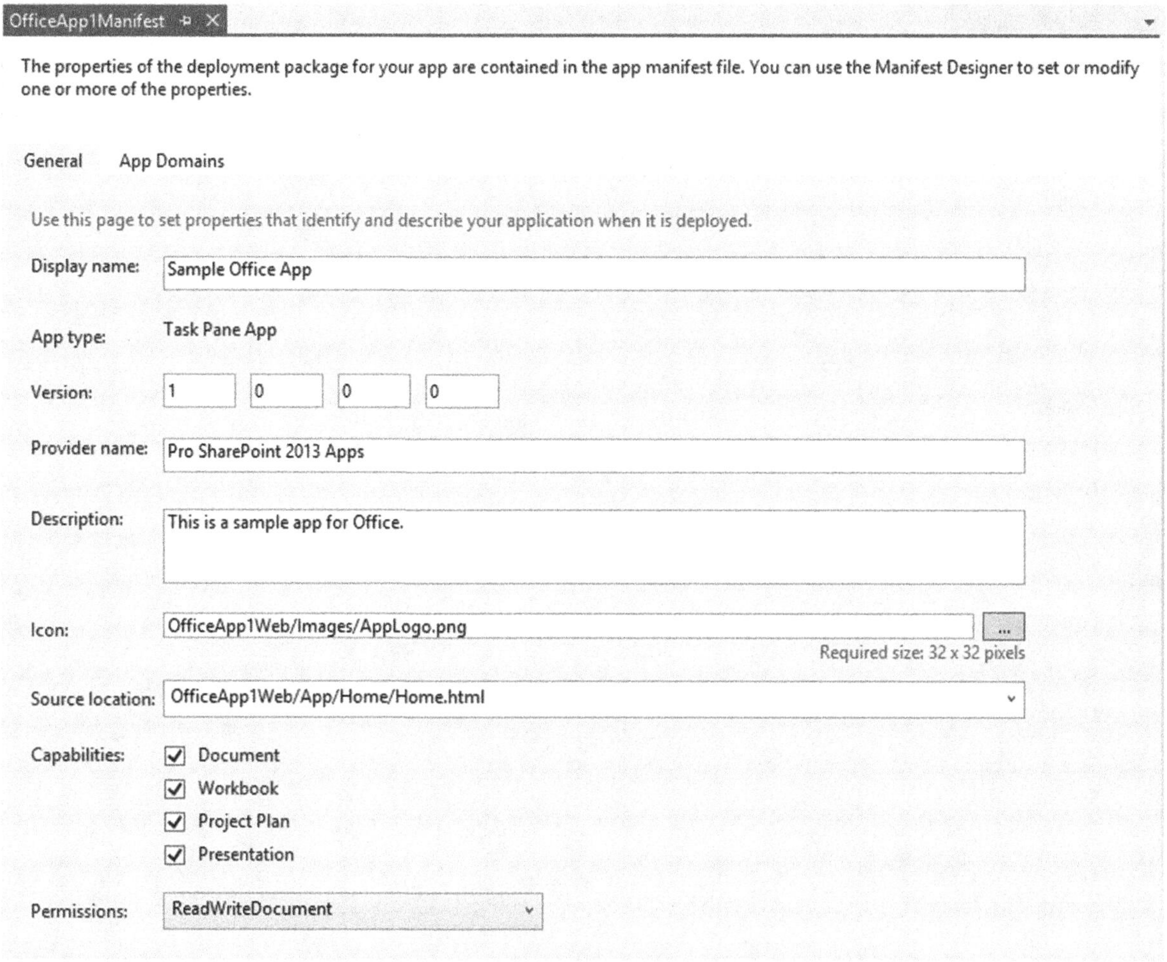

OfficeApp1Manifest ⊶ ✕

The properties of the deployment package for your app are contained in the app manifest file. You can use the Manifest Designer to set or modify one or more of the properties.

General   App Domains

Use this page to set properties that identify and describe your application when it is deployed.

Display name: Sample Office App

App type: Task Pane App

Version: 1   0   0   0

Provider name: Pro SharePoint 2013 Apps

Description: This is a sample app for Office.

Icon: OfficeApp1Web/Images/AppLogo.png   ...
Required size: 32 x 32 pixels

Source location: OfficeApp1Web/App/Home/Home.html   ⌄

Capabilities: ☑ Document
☑ Workbook
☑ Project Plan
☑ Presentation

Permissions: ReadWriteDocument   ⌄

Figure 14-2. *App manifest designer for Office apps (General tab)*

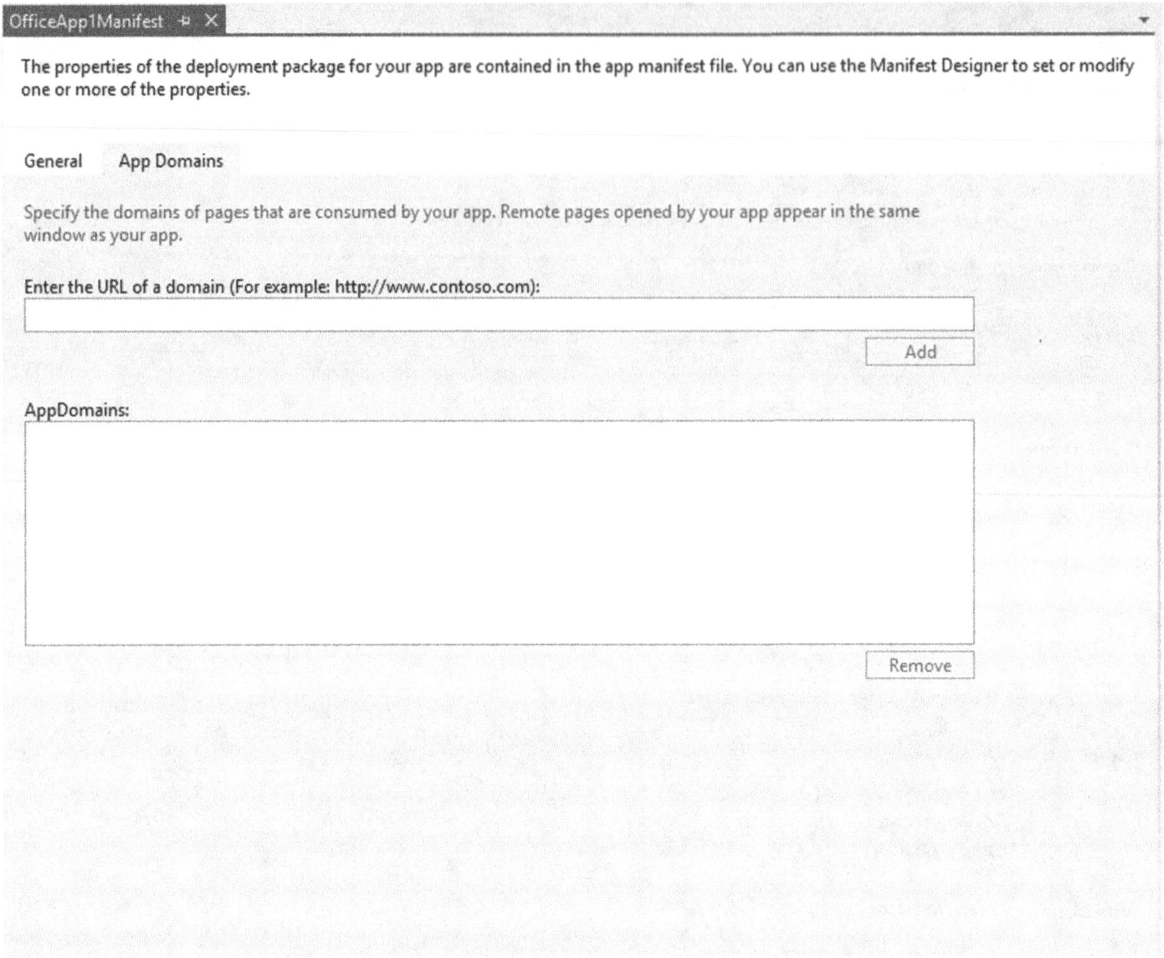

Figure 14-3. App manifest designer for Office apps (App Domains tab)

The App Domains tab defines any web domains that may be referenced by the app. If the app attempts to access any domains that are not listed, the app will fail.

The other component of an app for Office is the web content that is displayed in the app's window. Unlike SharePoint apps, there is only one hosting option for Office apps. Office app web pages must be hosted in a separate web server somewhere on the network. This is similar to a provider-hosted app for SharePoint. The content cannot be hosted within the Office application, analogous to a SharePoint-hosted app for SharePoint, because the Office applications do not contain web servers. Auto-hosting these pages in Azure is not an option because there is no host web with which to associate an auto-hosted site. When an app for Office is launched, it is associated with an Office document and an instance of the Office application, not a SharePoint site. A new Azure site would have to be provisioned every time the app was launched. This would make the provisioning and removal of auto-hosted sites prohibitively expensive.

The requirement for provider-hosted web sites means that most Office apps will require a company's infrastructure for support. For commercially distributed apps, these servers need to be available on the Internet 24/7. For internally developed apps, web servers for this content will need to be deployed on the organization's network.

SharePoint 2013 provides a partial answer to this hosting limitation based on the fact that, unlike a client application, SharePoint is a web server. We will explore this type of hosting later in this chapter.

Types of Office Apps

Apps for Office provide an enhanced user experience within one of the Office desktop or web-based applications. There are multiple types of apps that can be created, based on which application(s) will host the app and what type of functionality will be provided.

The first, and most flexible, type of Office app is a *task pane* app. A task pane appears beside the office document and provides additional options for the user, as shown in Figure 14-4. A task pane can read and write data in the document and access information over the network. Task panes are flexible because they can be used with any of the document-oriented Office applications that support apps. Note that the task pane is an add-in to the Office application and not a part of the content of the document. It is not saved with the document.

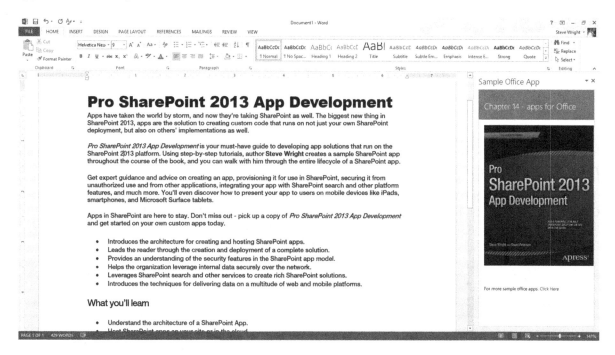

Figure 14-4. *App for Office task pane app*

The next type of Office app is a *content pane app* (or *content app*). Content panes are specific to Excel (see Figure 14-5). They provide additional visualization or reference information about the data in the spreadsheet. A content app can be used to embed graphics, text, video, or any other type of web content in the spreadsheet. Instead of appearing to the side of the document, as a task pane does, a content pane is part of the underlying document. When the document is saved, a reference to the app is saved as well. Excel must be able to access the app's online content when the document is reopened or the content pane will not function. This is important to remember when creating documents using apps in development. Once the Visual Studio debugger is shutdown, the app content is no longer available.

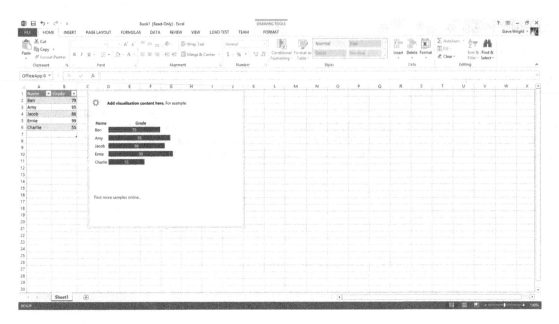

Figure 14-5. App for Office contentpane app

The last type of app for Office is a *mail app*. Mail apps appear next to e-mail messages or calendar items in Outlook, just as task panes do in document-based Office applications(see Figure 14-6). A mail app can access the fields in the current mail or calendar item as well as access information through the network. Because mail apps only work with e-mail and calendar objects, they are only relevant to Outlook 2013 and Outlook Web App.

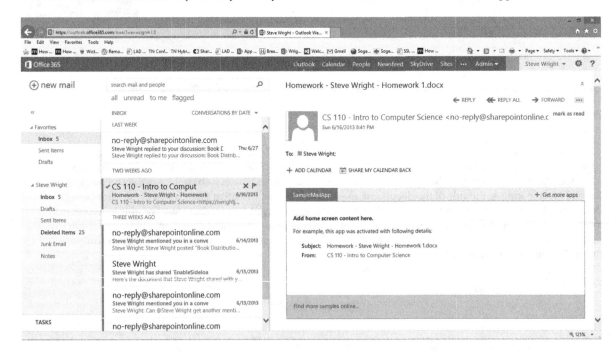

Figure 14-6. App for Office mailapp

■ **Note**   In order to use mail apps for Office, your organization must be using either Exchange 2013 or Office 365 for e-mail. While the Outlook 2013 desktop application can connect to other types of mail services, only Exchange supports apps for Office.

It is important to note which types of apps are supported in which client- or web-based Office applications. Table 14-1 provides a quick reference for which types of apps are supported in which applications.

Table 14-1. *Supported Applications for Office Apps*

Office Client	Task Pane Apps	Content Apps	Mail Apps
Excel 2013 andWeb App	X	X	
Word 2013	X		
PowerPoint 2013	X		
Project Professional 2013	X		
Outlook 2013 andWeb App			X

Office App Runtime Environment

Because apps for Office run as web applications, they have the same strengths and limitations as web applications running in an IFrame element on a web page. The Office application that hosts the app also imposes limitations that prevent badly behaved apps from impacting the host application.

- An app can render a rich UI via HTML and JavaScript, but only within the window set aside for it.

- An app can call web services and REST endpoints.

- Apps that need to use server-side code can be hosted on a web server supporting it.

- An app's web pages are subject to all of the same limitations as ordinary web pages, including security zones and cross-site scripting.

- Apps for Officeare isolated within a separate runtime environment that enforces read-only or read-write permissions and throttles the resources that can be consumed by an app.

In addition to rendering HTML and calling web services, apps for Office can also access the associated host application through the JavaScript API for Office (`http://msdn.microsoft.com/en-us/library/fp142185.aspx`). This is a JavaScript library that can be used by the app's web page to interact with whichever application is hosting it. This library contains members for managing document content, e-mails, contacts, and other application-specific objects. The entry point for these APIs is the `Office`object. This object'sproperties provide access to all of the other objects in the API.

Publishing Office Apps

Publishing apps for Office is very similar to publishing apps for SharePoint. In fact, they use the same storefront: the Office Store.

When a developer or organization offers an app for Office for sale (or for free) on the Office Store web site, the app is validated and signed by Microsoft to ensure its authenticity. The Office Store provides the checkout and download infrastructure for the all of the apps in its library. There is one important difference between apps for Office and apps for SharePoint in the store. An app for Office contains no content, only an app manifest file. Remember, all apps for Office are provider-hosted, so there is no means, or need, to deploy the app's web content files.

Like SharePoint apps, Office apps can also be deployed within an organization without using the Office Store.

For task pane and content apps, there are two ways to deploy within the organization. The first is to use the same App Catalog that is used for SharePoint apps. You will notice that the standard App Catalog site template contains one library for SharePoint apps and one for Officeapps. Users can acquire apps from either library using the same process we have described before.

Another option is to deploy the XML manifest files for the organization's apps to a network file share accessible by all relevant users. This rather low-tech option only requires that the file share be designated as a trusted App Catalog in the Office client application. This can be done by the enduser or a centralized IT department.

Mail apps are distributed differently because they only apply to Outlook and Exchange. Exchange 2013 contains its own App Catalog into which these apps can be published. Again, it is only the app's manifest file that is published. The web content is served from another location on the network.

The last, and most interesting(to us), means of distributing apps for Office is to embed them as part of an app for SharePoint. Content and task pane apps can be created within an app for SharePoint project and invoked automatically. Typically, a document template, such as a Word or Excel file, is included in the app and associated with a document library or custom action in the app's user interface. The advantage in deploying an app for Office in this way is that it can benefit from SharePoint's web server infrastructure to deliver the app's web content. The pages, scripts, and style sheets associated with the app can be included in the app for SharePoint, which will then host them in its app web or remote web as required. There is no need to deploy a separate provider-hosted web server for the app. We will see how to embed an Office app into a SharePoint app in the next exercise.

EXERCISE 14-1

In this exercise, we will demonstrate how to include a simple app for Office into an app for SharePoint. First, we will create an empty SharePoint-hosted app. Then, we will add an Office app and document template to the app. The app web, once deployed, will contain a document library that uses the template to create an Office document that embeds the app for Office.

1. Open Visual Studio 2012.

2. Create a new SharePoint-hosted app for SharePoint using the C# template. Name the project `SampleSPOfficeApp`.

3. Right-click on the `SampleSPOfficeApp` project and add a new item.

4. Select the App for Office item template, as shown in Figure 14-7, and name the item `SampleTaskPaneApp`.

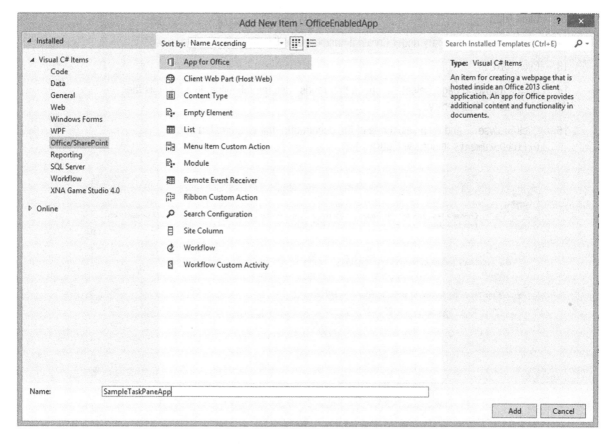

Figure 14-7. *New item dialog for App for Office*

5. Click Add.

6. The next page asks what type of app to create. Note that the Mail app option is grayed out because mail apps cannot be hosted in SharePoint. Make no changes to the dialog and click Next.

7. The final page offers the option to create a new document template or use an existing one. Leave the create option selected and click Finish.

At this point, the wizard will add several files to the SharePoint app project. The app is added as its own folder containing a default web page, style sheet, and script file. The app's manifest file is added to the project as well as an OfficeDocuments folder containing a document of each supported type. In our case, this includes a Word document, an Excel spreadsheet, and a PowerPoint presentation.

Now we will add a document library to use these templates.

8. Right-click on the project and add a new item.

9. Select List from the item types listed.

10. Name the list DocsWithApps.

11. Click Add.

12. Select Document Library under Create a customizable list template.

13. Click Next.

14. On the following page, select the option that reads "Use the following document as the template for this library."

15. Click Browse… and then select one of the documents that was created in the OfficeDocuments folder(see Figure 14-8).

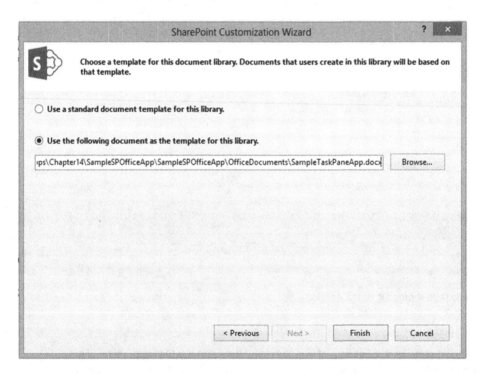

Figure 14-8. Add a document library document template

16. Click Finish.

17. Open the Default.aspx file in the editor.

18. Replace the contents of the div with the following markup:

```
<p>
To view the custom document library <a href="../lists/DocsWithApps">click here</a>.
</p>
```

19. Save and close the Default.aspx file.

20. Press F5 to start the app.

21. On the app's home page, click on the document library link.

22. Click on the Files tab in the ribbon menu.

23. Click on the New Document icon to launch a new document, including a task pane app.

At this point, we could add code to the content pages for the app for Office to include additional functionality in the task pane. We could, for example, use the task pane to collect custom metadata about the document that could then be stored in SharePoint.

Creating Windows and WinRT Apps

Windows desktop applications run directly on the Windows operating system without using SharePoint or another application as a host.When accessing SharePoint data, these applications can leverage the same CSOM libraries for the .NET Framework that we have used throughout this book for remote ASP.NET web sites that use server-side code. The difference when creating this type of application is that they do not get the benefit of passive authentication. In order to access SharePoint, they must implement the active authentication protocol described earlier in this chapter.

There are other types of Windows-based applications including Windows services, WCF services, and ASP.NET web sites (not associated with an app for SharePoint). In each of these cases, the same restriction holds true. These types of applications can use the CSOM or REST APIs for SharePoint, but they are responsible for performing their own authentication. As noted earlier, there are sample code libraries on MSDN and CodePlex that provide examples of these techniques.

A new type of Windows application was introduced with Windows 8. These applications run in a new subsystem called the Windows Runtime (WinRT). WinRT was designed to be a stripped-down version of the Windows operating system that could be hosted as part of Windows 8 on a desktop or laptop computer, or on a small tablet device such as the Microsoft Surface RT. The name used to describe these apps has changed over time. Originally introduced as "Metro" applications, they were later renamed to "Windows Store Apps." As this later name suggests, these apps can be purchased from the Windows Store in the same way that apps for SharePoint and Office can be purchased from the Office Store. We will refer to them as WinRT apps since that is the environment they run in.

WinRT apps are built using a subset of the full .NET Framework called .NET for Windows Store Apps (http://msdn.microsoft.com/en-us/library/windows/apps/br230232.aspx). These apps are typically built in Visual Studio using the MVVM pattern. The classes in the WinRT version of .NET are similar to those associated with the Silverlight subset of .NET. Unfortunately, there is no CSOM library specifically designed for use with WinRT apps (yet). Therefore, WinRT apps that need to access SharePoint will have to use the REST API or SharePoint's custom web services.

To explore the building of WinRT apps for SharePoint, we are going to use an excellent sample application that is available on CodePlex. The code for this project can be downloaded from http://sharepointwinrt.codeplex.com. When run, this app presents a login screen where the user puts in their SharePoint site URL, user name, and password. It then connects to SharePoint and reads the lists and items available and displays them, as shown in Figure 14-9.

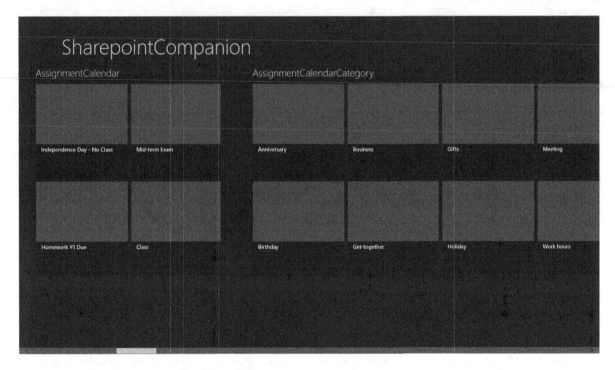

Figure 14-9. Sample WinRT application for SharePoint

Obviously, there are many ways to improve this user experience, but the point is that the contents of the SharePoint lists and libraries are available to the app. The project files for this sample app provide a good model implementation of the active authentication process(see Figure 14-10).

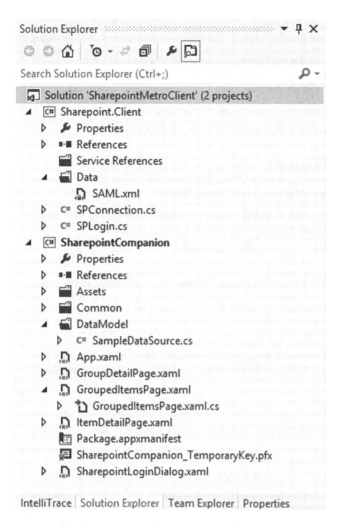

Figure 14-10. Sample WinRT application project files

The sample solution contains two projects. The first project is a class library called SharePoint.Client, which handles the SAML exchange and SharePoint login messages and cookies. Here are some of the key files in this project:

- **Data/SAML.xml**—This XML file is a formatted SAML token request. It contains three locations where substitutions will be made by the app. These are marked with "{n}" in place of the user name, password, and target SharePoint URL.

- **SPLogin.cs**—This class manages the SAML login sequence with the Security Token Service and the target SharePoint farm. This class retrieves and stores the authentication cookies from SharePoint.

- **SPConnection.cs**—This class is a wrapper for SharePoint's ListData.svc web service. The requestStreamAsync() method in this class applies the authentication cookies to the HTTP request sent to SharePoint.

The other project in the sample solution is `Sharepoint.Companion`. This project contains the WinRT app. It is built using the MVVM pattern for its user interface and the `SharePoint.Client` project for access to SharePoint.

- **App.xaml**—This XAML file defines the app's global user interface properties. Its code-behind file defines event handlers that handle the launch and suspend events. The launch event displays the login page and loads the main page for the app.

- **SampleDataSource.cs**—This source file contains multiple classes that implement both the model and view-model objects for the app. The data modeled is the list data from the SharePoint `ListData` service.

- **SharePointLoginDialog.xaml**—This XAML page and its code-behind implement the app's login form. This form acceptsthe user's name, password, andSharePoint siteURL. When the user clicks Connect, this page uses the `SPLogin` class to connect to the SharePoint site.

- **Package.appxmanifest**—Like all other types of apps, WinRT apps must have a manifest file. The app manifest defines the app's name, default language, supported layouts, and icons. It also defines the device capabilities that may be used by the app. This is similar to requesting app permissions.

The remaining files in this project are XAML and code-behind files for the various views displayed in the app.

Creating Windows Phone Apps

Another new platform for apps is the Windows Phone. Windows Phone apps use libraries from the Windows Phone Software Development Kit (SDK). The SDK enables Visual Studio to create and debug Windows Phone apps using a phone simulator instead of a physical Windows Phone.

■ **Note**   Windows Phone apps are specific to Windows Phone. They will not run on iOS or Android-based smartphones.

SharePoint 2013 contains new features that are intended to enrich mobile applications. SharePoint now has built-in field types for storing geographic location information that apps can use to integrate with mapping systems. For example, a retailer could build an app to quickly lookup the closest store to a mobile user by looking up available locations in a list. SharePoint can also generate push notifications to mobile users when data changes or events occur. A user might want to get notifications on their phone when new tasks appear for them in a task list on SharePoint.

To create Windows Phone apps that leverage SharePoint, there is an additional SDK called the Microsoft SharePoint SDK for Windows Phone. This SDK includes new classes to simplify authenticating with SharePoint and building SharePoint-related apps. The SDK also supplies a version of the client-side object model (CSOM) libraries for the Windows Phone platform.

Setting Up the Development Environment

Before creating Windows Phone apps for SharePoint, there is a certain amount of setup required in the developer's environment.

First, of course, Visual Studio 2012 must be installed. Then, we need to load the correct SDKs. SharePoint 2013 supports the two most recent versions of the Windows Phone platform: version 7.1 and version 8. Table 14-2 provides the URLs for downloading the necessary SDKs for each version. The Windows Phone SDK should be installed first, followed by the SharePoint SDK.

Table 14-2. *Windows Phone SDKs for Developing Apps with SharePoint*

SDK	Windows Phone 7.1	Windows Phone 8
Windows Phone SDK	http://www.microsoft.com/en-us/download/details.aspx?id=27570	http://www.microsoft.com/en-us/download/details.aspx?id=35471
Microsoft SharePoint SDK for Windows Phone	http://www.microsoft.com/en-us/download/details.aspx?id=35475	http://www.microsoft.com/en-us/download/details.aspx?id=36818

The Windows Phone SharePoint 2013 SDK installs four important assemblies for developing Windows Phone apps for SharePoint.

- **Microsoft.SharePoint.Client.Phone** *and* **Microsoft.SharePoint.Client.Phone. Runtime**—These libraries contain the client-side object model (CSOM) classes for the Windows Phone platform.

- **Microsoft.SharePoint.Phone.Application**—This assembly contains base types for SharePoint fields and lists including model and view-model base classes for these objects.

- **Microsoft.SharePoint.Client.Phone.Auth.UI**—This library contains classes that simplify creating the Windows Phone user experience when using SharePoint. It includes the following classes:

  ○ `BrowserLogin`—This class is the code-behind for an automated browser login page (`BrowserLogin.xaml`). This page is shown when login credentials are required.

  ○ `Authenticator`—This class greatly simplifies active authentication because it implements the exchange of SAML messages and tokens to authenticate to SharePoint. The result is a client context object that is ready to use.

  ○ `ODataAuthenticator`—This version of the authenticator class is designed to work with OData connections that may involve indirect connections to the data service.

The SharePoint SDK for Windows Phone also includes two Visual Studio project templates. These templates provide a starting point for developing apps. These templates will be described in the next sections.

■ **Note**   The Windows Phone project templates for SharePoint are only available in the C# language. No Visual Basic template is included at this time.

Windows Phone Empty SharePoint Application Template

The first template included in the Microsoft SharePoint SDK for Windows Phone is the empty application template. As the name implies, this template contains only the minimal set of files needed to create an app.

This template is basically the same as the empty app template that is included in the Windows Phone SDK. The difference is that this template includes references to the SharePoint SDK assemblies. This template includes a blank main page and an `App.xaml` file to define the app.

Windows Phone SharePoint List Application Template

The other template included in the SharePoint SDK generates a fully functional application that can read and write SharePoint data.

A common use of mobile apps is to review and update lists of data. Since SharePoint is very good at maintaining lists, it is not surprising that this is a common use for SharePoint apps on mobile platforms. The List Application template was created to provide a quick start to creating this type of app.

The List Application template uses a wizard to connect to an existing SharePoint site, read the views and fields for a list, and generate an app that can perform CRUD operations on the list's data. The template can read any list to create the app, including document libraries and custom lists. Apps based on lists that include custom field types or complex lookups may need to be modified before being ready for production use.

A list app contains a single project for the Windows Phone app. This project includes several files. The most important of these are the following:

- **App.xaml**—This file represents the overall Windows Phone application. The code-behind file associated with App.xaml contains event handlers for app lifecycle events such as launching, activating, deactivating, and closing of the application.

- **ListDataProvider.cs**—This class loads list items from the associated SharePoint list and views.

- **Views** *Folder*

  ○ List.xaml—This view presents the list items in each of the views selected in the wizard.

  ○ DisplayForm.xaml—This view presents a read-only form, containing all of the data fields selected in the wizard.

  ○ EditForm.xaml—This is a data entry form used to update an existing entry in the list.

  ○ NewForm.xaml—This is a data entry form used to create a new entry in the list.

- **ViewModels** *Folder*

  ○ ListViewModel.cs—This is the view-model object for the List view.

  ○ DisplayItemViewModel.cs—This is the view-model object for the DisplayForm view.

  ○ EditItemViewModel.cs—This is the view-model object for the EditForm view.

  ○ NewItemViewModel.cs—This is the view-model object for the NewForm view.

In our final exercise, we will use the wizard to create an app that reads and writes data in a SharePoint calendar list.

EXERCISE 14-2

In this exercise, we will walkthrough creating a SharePoint list app using the template included in the Microsoft SharePoint SDK for Windows Phone. This application will display a SharePoint list and allow a mobile user to view and edit its data.

■ **Note** The assumption is being made here that the developer's environment has already been updated to include the Windows Phone SDK and Microsoft SharePoint SDK for Windows Phone. The version of the SDKs selected should match the version of the target phone platform.

1. Log on to the target SharePoint site using an account that has site owner rights.

2. Create a new list using the Calendar list template. Name the list `Assignment Calendar`.

3. Add a handful of events to the calendar to occur over the next few weeks and months.

4. Open Visual Studio 2012.

5. Create a new project called `SampleSPWinPhoneApp` using the Windows Phone SharePoint List Application template (see Figure 14-11).

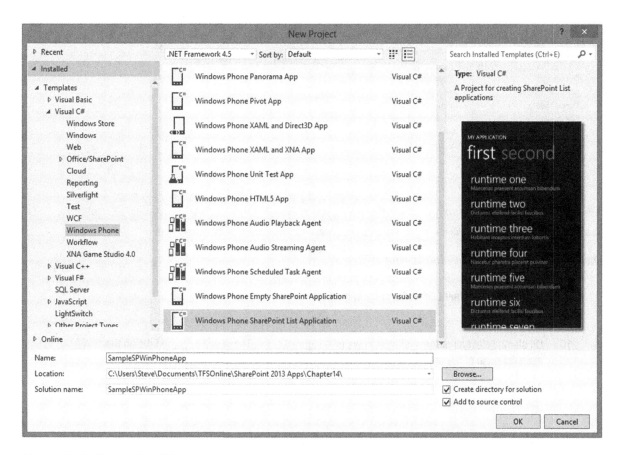

Figure 14-11. New project dialog

6. Click OK.

7. On step 1 of the wizard, enter the URL for the target SharePoint site and click Find Lists (see Figure 14-12).

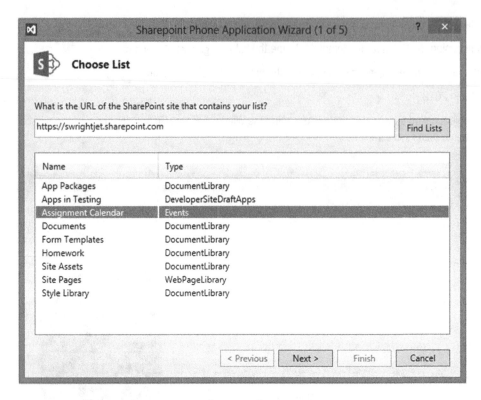

Figure 14-12. *List application wizard (step 1 of 5)*

8. Select the Assignment Calendar entry in the list.

9. Click Next.

10. On step2, select all of the available views (see Figure 14-13). These will become tabs on the main list page of the app.

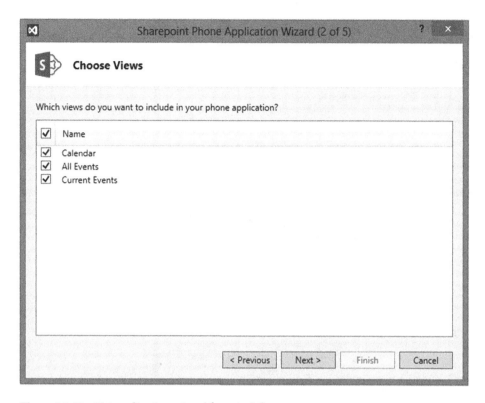

Figure 14-13. *List application wizard (step 2 of 5)*

11. Click Next.

12. On step 3, select all of the available forms. These will become views in the app (see Figure 14-14).

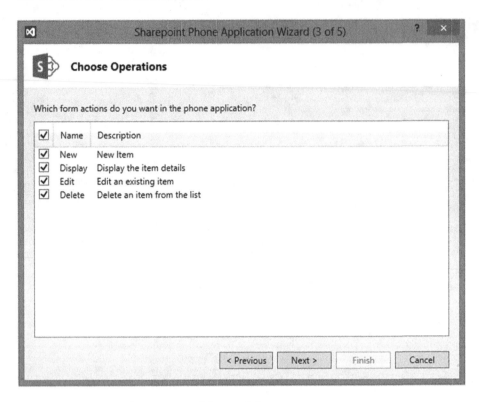

Figure 14-14. List application wizard (step 3 of 5)

13. Click Next.

14. On step 4, select all of the available fields. Note that any required fields are already selected and cannot be unselected (see Figure 14-15).

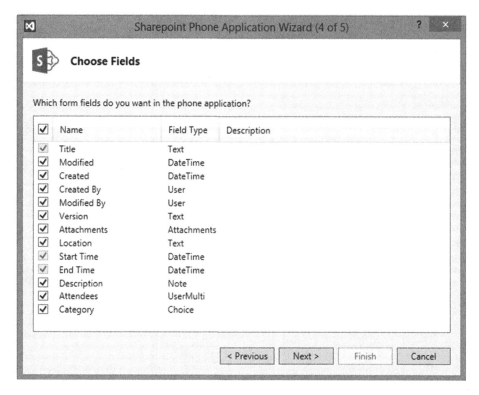

Figure 14-15. *List application wizard (step 4 of 5)*

15. Click Next.

16. On step 5, reorder the selected list as desired using the up and down arrows to the right of the list (see Figure 14-16).

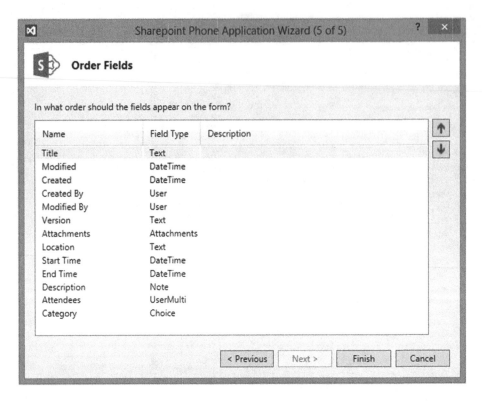

Figure 14-16. *List application wizard (step 5 of 5)*

17. Click Finish.

The wizard will now generate the app in a new project. This app uses the MVVM pattern to create the selected views using the data selected in the wizard.

18. Press F5 to debug the app using the Windows Phone emulator.

19. Once the operating systems and app have been loaded into the emulator, you will see a login screen. Enter the user name and password to be used on the site.

20. Click Sign in.

Once the app successfully signs in to SharePoint, it reads the list's data and displays the list view, as shown in Figure 14-17.

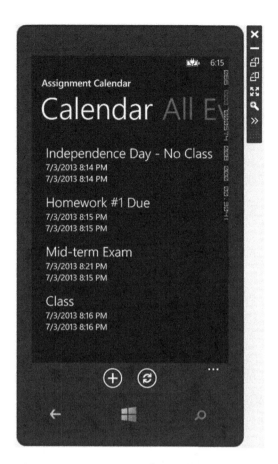

Figure 14-17. *List view in the Windows Phone emulator*

The emulator appears on the developer's desktop in a borderless window. The toolbar to the right of the emulator allows the developer to test different orientations and zoom in on the phone's display. The ➤ button on the menu opens an additional set of tools that can capture screenshots and test geo-location and accelerometer inputs.

21.   Click on one of the calendar items displayed.

22.   On the display view, click the Edit button on the menu. (Hint: The edit button has a pencil icon.) See Figure 14-18.

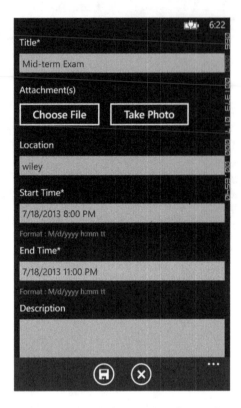

Figure 14-18. Edit form view in the Windows Phone emulator

23. Change the title or location for the item.

24. Click the Save button (diskette icon) on the menu bar.

25. Close the emulator by clicking the X on the emulator's toolbar.

26. Open the target SharePoint list in a web browser.

27. Open the same calendar item and verify that the changes were saved in SharePoint.

The app generated by the list application wizard is complete in most cases. Additional options and changes to the user interface can be implemented by updating the generated classes. These classes are only generated when the project is created, so any changes made later will not be overwritten. Conversely, any changes made to the underlying SharePoint list will need to be reflected in the app's source code manually.

Summary

In this chapter, we have moved beyond building apps for SharePoint to building distributed enterprise-class solutions on various platforms. While we have focused using Microsoft's tools and platforms, these techniques are equally applicable to any web-based application stack. The key is the authentication sequence. The exchange of tokens and cookies is what allows an external application to use SharePoint resources. That protocol can be implemented on any platform that supports HTTP.

We hope that you have enjoyed learning about building apps for SharePoint using the Cloud App Model. There are many opportunities for companies and individuals to use these techniques to create robust, highlyfunctional solutions. We wish you good luck in finding ways to extend the SharePoint platform both within your organization and in the cloud.

Index

■ K

■ L

■ M

■ X, Y, Z